KELLY MILLER, A. M., LL. D.
Dean of the College of Arts and Sciences, Howard University, Washington D. C.

KELLY MILLER'S HISTORY

OF

The World War

FOR

HUMAN RIGHTS

BEING

An Intensely Human and Brilliant Account of the World
War and Why and For What Purpose America and
the Allies Are Fighting and the Important
Part Taken by the Negro

INCLUDING

The Horrors and Wonders of Modern Warfare,
The New and Strange Devices, etc.

"Fighting for the Rights of Mankind
and for the
Future Peace and Security of the World"

By
KELLY MILLER, A. M., LL. D.

NEGRO UNIVERSITIES PRESS
NEW YORK

Originally published in 1919
by Austin Jenkins Co., Washington, D.C.

Reprinted 1969 by
Negro Universities Press
A DIVISION OF GREENWOOD PUBLISHING CORP.
NEW YORK

SBN 8371-1290-7

THE NEGRO'S PART IN THE WAR

By Professor Kelly Miller, the Well-Known Thinker and Writer.

This treatise will set forth the black man's part in the world's war with the logical sequence of facts and the brilliant power of statement for which the author is famous. The mere announcement that the author of "Race Adjustment," "Out of the House of Bondage," and "The Disgrace of Democracy" is to present a history of the Negro in the great world conflict, is sufficient to arouse expectancy among the wide circle of readers who eagerly await anything that flows from his pen.

In this treatise, Professor Miller will trace briefly, but with consuming interest, the relation of the Negro to the great wars of the past. He will point out the never-failing fount of loyalty and patriotism which characterizes the black man's nature, and will show that the Negro has never been a hireling, but has always been characterized by that moral energy which actuates all true heroism.

The conduct of the Negro in the present struggle will be set forth with a brilliant and pointed pen. The idea of three hundred thousand American Negroes crossing three thousand miles of sea to fight against autocracy of the German crown constitutes the most interesting chapter in the history of this modern crusade against an unholy cause. The valor and heroism of the Afro-American contingent were second to none according to the unanimous testimony of those who were in command of this high enterprise.

The story of Negro officers in command of troops of their own color will prove the wisdom of a policy entered upon with much mistrust and misgiving. It is just here that Professor Miller reaches the high-water mark. Here is a story never told before, because the world has never before witnessed Negro officers in large numbers participating in the directive side of war waged on the high level of modern science and system.

Professor Miller's treatise carries its own prophecy. He logically enough forecasts the future of the race in glowing colors as the result of his loyal and patriotic conduct in this great world epoch.

The author wisely queries: "When, hereafter, the Negro asks for his rights as an American citizen, where can the American be found with the heart or the hardihood to say him, Nay?"

The work will be profusely illustrated.

Washington, D. C., November 22, 1918.

INTRODUCTION.

While the underlying causes of the greatest war in all history must be traced far back into the centuries, the one great object of the conflict which was precipitated by the assassination of the Archduke Francis Ferdinand of Austria, in Bosnia, at the end of June, 1914, is the ultimate determination as to whether Imperialism as exemplified in the government of Germany shall rule the world, or whether Democracy shall reign.

Whenever men or nations disregard those principles which society has laid down for their conduct in modern civilized life, and obligation and duty are forgotten in the desire for self-advancement, conflict results.

Since the days of Athens and Sparta the world's greatest wars have in the large been conflicts of ideals—democracy being arrayed against oligarchy—men fighting for individual rights as against militarism and military domination.

In the present war, which has painted the green fields of France and Belgium red with blood and swept nations into the most significant and bitter struggle in all history, the fight is against the Imperial Government of Germany, by men and nations who concede that humanity the world over has rights that must be observed.

Germany has brought upon herself a threatened destruction by ruthlessly trampling upon her neighbors and assuming that "might is right."

The Imperial Government, led by the House of Hohenzollern is suffering from an exaggerated ego and is become paranoic. Her trouble is psychological. The men who study the strange workings and twists of the human mind which land some men in the institutions for the criminal insane, agree that when any man becomes obsessed with an idea and "rides a hobby" to the exclusion of all else, he loses his balance and develops an obliquity of view which makes him a dangerous creature.

Germany as a nation is obsessed with the spirit of militarism and almost everything else has been sacrificed to this idol. The very first appearance of Germans in history is as a warlike peoples. The earliest German literature is composed of folktales about war heroes. These stories tell of high ideals and manly virtues of the heroes.

It is true that there are many scientists, poets and musicians among the Germans, but their warlike side must never be forgotten. The entire race is imbued with the military spirit, the influence reaching to every phase of national life. All that is best in the nation has been raised to its highest efficiency through military training, but in the accomplishment of its purposes the House of Hohenzollern, which is responsible for the development of the national fighting arm, has neglected much and produced millions of creatures who are but human machines, taught to obey orders without consideration as to the effect their acts might produce, whether right or wrong.

In their criticisms of the Prussian militarism the world democracies define militarism as an arrogant, or exclusive, professional military spirit developed by training and environment until it becomes despotic, and assumes superiority over rational motives and deliberations.

This attitude is reflected in the conduct of the Kaiser, who, as illustrative of the point, is quoted, at the dedication of the monument to Prince Frederick Charles at Frankfurt-on-the-Oder in 1891, as having said "We would rather sacrifice our eighteen army corps and our 42,000,000 inhabitants on the field of battle than surrender a single stone of what my father and Prince Charles Frederick gained."

His speeches are filled with similar bombastic and extravagant expressions which have been the subject of international comment for many years. Other countries besides Germany have maintained great armies, but their maintenance has been but an incidental part of the general business of the nation and there was no submerging of the spirit which seeks and demands appropriate public ideals in government and action. So that while other elements have always tended to produce friction between neighboring countries, it was adamant, stubborn, military Prussianism which asserted itself in the middle of 1914 and set the world afire.

What the ultimate cost in lives, money, morals and weakening of humanity as a whole will sum up cannot be written for years to come. In our own great struggle, which had for its object the liberation of the negro, the scars which the South received have not yet been eliminated. Portions of the country devastated by the soldiers still bear the marks of the invasion, but what was lost in money and material things was made up by the welding together of the two sections of the country. The Union was made a concrete, humanitarian body of citizens. The battle was for the right and liberty triumphed.

Just as America fought for liberty in the stirring days of 1776, and her peoples fought one another in the trying days of 1861-65, so America has been drawn into the world's war that the principles of liberty for which she has ever stood may be perpetuated throughout the world and an international peace may be established, which will for all time end such convulsions as have shaken the world since August, 1914, when the first shots were fired in fair Belgium by German invaders.

CONTENTS.

CHAPTER VII.

WAR'S STRANGE DEVICES.

CHAPTER VIII.

WONDERFUL WAR WEAPONS.

CHAPTER IX.

THE WORLD'S ARMIES.

CHAPTER X

THE WORLD'S NAVIES.

CHAPTER XI.

THE NATIONS AT WAR.

CHAPTER XII.

MODERN WAR METHODS.

CONTENTS.

CHAPTER XXV.

AMERICAN FORCES BECOME FACTOR.

CHAPTER XXVI.

AMERICANS TURN WAR'S TIDE.

CHAPTER XXVII.

VICTORY—PEACE.

CHAPTER I.

THE FLASH THAT SET THE WORLD AFLAME.

TEUTONS FIND IN A MURDER THE EXCUSE FOR WAR—GERMANY INSPIRED BY AM-
BITIONS FOR WORLD CONTROL—THE STRUGGLE FOR COMMERCIAL SUPREMACY A
FACTOR—THE UNDERLYING MOTIVES.

THE assassination of the Archduke Francis Ferdinand, heir apparent to the throne of Austria, together with his wife, in Bosnia, during the last days of June, 1914, is commonly regarded as the blow which forged the chain that bound the European powers in bloody warfare. The tragedy was the signal for putting on the world stage the greatest war play of all times.

When Austria, regarding the murder of the Archduke as a National affront, precipitated the conflict which has convulsed the universe, she marked the way easy for Imperial Germany to put into effect a long-contemplated plan for territorial expansion, and to wage a warfare so insidious, so brutal and so ruthless in its character as to amaze the civilized world.

Word-pictures were drawn, so to speak, of a mighty nation striving to burst iron bands that were slowly strangling her, and her perfectly natural wish to find outlets for her rapidly growing population and commerce. Germany sought to obtain "a place in the sun," to use one of the Kaiser's most unfortunate expressions, and the world soon found that the "place" included the territory embracing a few ports on the English channel, with control of Holland and Belgium, Poland, the Balkan countries, a big slice of Asia Minor, Egypt, English and French colonies in Africa, not to mention remote possibilities.

Germany's ambitions may have been laudable, but her methods of trying to satisfy these ambitions were not such as

17

to either gain for her the "solar warmth" which she sought to win, or gain for her the friendship of the nations of the civilized world. The drama which Germany directed moved swiftly in this wise:

Austria claimed that Servia, as a Nation, was responsible for the assassination of the Archduke in Bosnia. She sent an ultimatum to Belgrade, making demands which the Servians could not admit. Thereupon Austria declared war and moved across the Danube with her army.

THE FOUR GROUPS.

Austria's attack threatened to disturb the balance of power, because at the time the continent was divided into four groups: The close alliance of the central powers—Germany, Austria and Italy—referred to as the Triple Alliance or Dreibund; the Triple Entente, or understanding between Great Britain, France and Russia; the smaller group whose neutrality and integrity had been guaranteed, or at least recognized— Belgium, Denmark, Holland and the Grand Duchy of Luxembourg, sandwiched in between Germany, France and Belgium, together with Switzerland. The fourth group included the Balkan nations: Bulgaria, Servia, Montenegro, Greece, Turkey and Roumania, all drawn close to Russia; Norway and Sweden, and the Iberian nations, Spain and Portugal. The increase in the power of one of these groups would at any time have been sufficient to precipitate a war, but in the movement of Austria against Servia there entered a racial element. There was a threatened drawing of another Slavonic peoples into the Teutonic system. Besides this, the action let loose the flood of militarism which civilization had been holding in check.

With this situation in mind, it is easy to understand how Germany could precipitate a world conflict by attempting to keep open the way to the near East, and controlling the markets as against Britain, France and Russia. Back of all this was the question of commercial supremacy, Germany showing her intention of keeping the way open to the near East and dominating the markets as against Britain, France and Russia.

Russia could not stand by and see one of her Slavonic wards crushed, and France, which held the Russian national debt, prepared to support her debtor, whereupon Germany, threatened on both sides, struck. In doing so the Kaiser ignored the rights of the small neutral states, invaded Belgium and brought his armies within threatening distance of England. France prepared to defend her country against Germany, and England, alarmed by the move of Germany and sympathizing with Belgium, struck back to avert the disaster which she felt must follow the German movement, which had been threatening for years.

REGARDED EACH OTHER WITH SUSPICION.

All attempts to maintain a balance of power between the European countries were from time to time jeopardized by various developments. The elements in the continental group struggled against each other, and the Nations, while seemingly at rest, regarded each other with suspicion. One of the underlying forces that the world knew must at some time be felt was of racial origin. The historical explanations of the war would involve the retelling of almost everything that has happened in Europe for more than a century.

But it is necessary to the long train of evil consequences which have followed the interference of other powers in the settlement of affairs between Russia and Turkey after the war of 1877, when Russia was victorious. Russia and Turkey had agreed upon a large Bulgaria and an enlarged and independent Servia, but at the Berlin Congress, which Austria had taken the initiative in calling, Austria showed that she wished to have as much as possible of this Christian territory of Southeastern Europe kept under the domination or nominal authority of Turkey. Austria feared Russia's influence with the new countries of Servia, Roumania, Bulgaria and Montenegro, and therefore she desired to have this territory remain Turkish by influence, to the end that she might some day acquire part or all of it for herself.

One of the articles of the agreement of Berlin turned Bosnia and Herzegovina over to Austria for temporary occupation and management. Austria was a trustee of the country which lies between Servia and the Adriatic sea, and while Austria's management was efficient, Servia looked forward to the time when a union could be effected with Bosnia, which would provide Servia with an outlet to the sea.

THE SERVIANS EMBITTERED.

But when Russia fell humiliated by the Japanese and the Young Turks reformed their government, and there was prospect that the Turks might demand the evacuation of Bosnia by Austria, the powers that had engaged in the Berlin treaty were informed that Austria had decided to make Bosnia and Herzegovina a part of the Austro-Hungarian Empire. The Servians were embittered, because this stood in the way of their attaining their ideals, and their country was landlocked.

With this bitterness rankling in her national breast, Servia joined forces with Bulgaria, Greece and Montenegro to drive the Turks out of Europe. The larger powers, including Austria, tried to prevent the action, but the heroic Balkan struggle is a matter of history. Servia was to have secured as a share of the conquered territory a portion of Albania, on the Adriatic. This would have compensated her for the loss of Bosnia, but the great powers, led by Austria, stepped in, and a plan was devised of making Albania an independent state or principality, with a German prince to rule over it.

The Servians were bitter, and both Servia and Greece demanded of Bulgaria portions of the territory acquired in the war and which had originally been assigned to Bulgaria as her share. Bulgaria stood upon her technical rights and precipitated the last Balkan war, which was really made possible, or probable, by the Austrian policy. When the war was concluded Servia had acquired more territory to the south, but she remained a landlocked country, with Bosnia, Montenegro and Albania stretching between her and the Adriatic sea.

This was the situation when the assassination of the Archduke Ferdinand and his wife occurred in Bosnia. The Archduke was, in effect, a joint ruler with the Emperor Franz Joseph, who was nearly 84 years of age, and the entire world realized that great events were likely to follow the killing of the heir apparent to the Austro-Hungarian throne. The murder was committed by a young Servian fanatic, and Austria determined to hold Servia responsible for the murder, and therefore presented her now-famous ultimatum.

NO CAUSE FOR WAR.

Students of history hold that if there had been a proper respect for the commendable desire of the Christian peoples in European Turkey to throw off the Turkish yoke and become self-governing states, there would have been no cause for war, so far as relates to Servia and the situation which precipitated the conflict. There would have been developed a series of peaceful and progressive countries of the non-military type of Denmark, Sweden and Holland.

A wiser treatment of the Balkan problem might have averted the war, but it could not have set aside racial differences, nor could it have ended the curse of militarism or set at rest the distrust and fear which it promotes.

The end of European militarism might have come about, however, through a better understanding between Germany and France. This might have been arrived at years ago if Germany had opened the Alsace-Lorraine question, and had rearranged the boundary line between the two countries so that the French-speaking communities lost in the Franco-Prussian war be ceded back to France. The cost of maintaining the feud over Alsace-Lorraine has been a burden to both France and Germany, and the progress which Germany has made in world affairs, despite the burden of militarism which she has carried, is one of the marvels of the century. And the situation compelled France to maintain a defensive military organization which was as great a burden to her and barrier to world peace as the military burden of Germany.

STRAIN BETWEEN GERMANY AND RUSSIA.

Whether Germany conspired to bring on the war so that she could wage a campaign of aggression has not yet been made clear, but the strain between Germany and Russia had been growing for some time, and the assassination of the Teutonic heir, Francis Ferdinand, by a ward of Russia, created an occasion which gave Germany an opportunity to fight, without being compelled to directly precipitate the conflict. Russia could do naught else but come to the aid of Servia, and Germany by reason of her alliance with Austria must aid the latter country.

Germany anticipated the entry of Italy into the conflict as the third member of the Triple Alliance, but Italy did not regard Germany's action as defensive and declined to aid Austria. Germany had made overtures to Great Britain, but England had an understanding with France, which was in the nature of a limited alliance, and Germany might have kept England out of the struggle; but Germany proceeded with a plan to invade France by way of Belgium, which was in violation of international agreement establishing Belgium's neutrality and independence. Germany had nothing to gain by choosing the Belgium route, for the fact is that even had the Belgian government approved the movement, there must have been a French counter-movement, which would have made Belgium the theatre of war just the same.

Pan-Germanism has been described as one of the underlying motives in the world war, and Pan-Slavism has always opposed Pan-Germanism. Pan-Germanism is described as a well-defined policy or movement which seeks the common welfare of the Germanic peoples of all Europe and the advance of Teutonic culture, while Pan-Slavism, represented by Russia, seeks in the main the uniting of all the Slavonic folk for common welfare. The contact between these two has always been seething, and the racial differences made burdensome the arbitrary alignment and political geography arranged by the Berlin Congress.

OUTLETS TO THE WORLD'S MARKET.

The commercial side, however, was a big factor, for Germany sought world markets for its products. In the near East are the grain fields of Mesopotamia, and in the far East are the vast markets of India and China. The great banking and financial interests of Europe have been seeking the conquest of Asia for nearly half a century. German capital built railroads through Asia Minor, but English capital controls the Suez Canal. Russia welded the Balkan states until the Slavonic wedge from the Black sea to the Adriatic barred Germany's way to the Orient. England threatened the Kaiser's expansion on the sea; while Russia, on one side, with France her strong ally, closed the Germans in on opposite sides. So Germany must have outlets to the world markets.

The religious element was also a factor in the affairs of Europe, for the territory has been divided into four large religious groups for centuries. Moslems counted several millions of Turks, Bosnians and Albanians in Europe, the Protestants among the Germans, English, Swiss and Hungarians number about 100,000,000, while the Roman Catholics in all the Latin countries, Southern Germany, Croatia, Albania, Bohemia, and in Russian Austria and Russian Poland are about 180,000,000. The Greek Catholics in Russia, the Balkan countries and a few provinces in the Austrian Empire number more than 110,000,000.

The differences in religion have precipitated many European struggles, but for more than a century the countries have been forced to assume an attitude of tolerance, so that churches other than those established by the State have thrived. But just what influence religions may have had in the various incidents of the war it is difficult to determine.

The outstanding fact is that but for the arrogant, militaristic policy of Imperial Germany, the differences between nations might have been settled, and almost indescribable horrors of the war would never have been experienced.

CHAPTER II.
WHY AMERICA ENTERED THE WAR.

THE IRON HAND OF PRUSSIANISM—THE ARROGANT HOHENZOLLERN ATTITUDE—
SECRETARY LANE TELLS WHY WE FIGHT—BROKEN PLEDGES—LAWS VIOLATED
—PRUSSIANISM THE CHILD OF BARBARITY—GERMANY'S PLANS FOR A WORLD
EMPIRE.

NOT merely to prevent Germany from opening avenues of commerce to the seas nor to throttle the ambitions of the Kaiser was America drawn into the vortex of war with France, England, Russia, Belgium, Italy and other nations; but that the iron hand of Prussianism, as exemplified in the conduct of the German Government, might be lifted from the shoulders of men, and the world given that measure of peace and security which modern civilization demands.

Germany by her ruthless submarine warfare brought desolation to many American homes. She sank without a pang of conscience the great transatlantic steamship Lusitania, and, while pretending friendship for the United States and pleading no intent to disregard American rights, broke her own pledges and repeated her overt acts, ignoring international law and the rights of all neutrals at sea.

She began her outlawry by the invasion of Belgium, which was followed by conduct on the part of the German forces which clearly marked them descendants of the "wolf tribes" of feudal days, fighting with the motto before them of, "To the victor belong the spoils."

But all of Germany's diabolical acts involving the peace and security of America and American citizens might have been the subject of international adjudication but for the arrogance of the ruling forces of the Teutons. In a broad sense, Prussianism is credited with responsibility for the devastating war and for the policy which drew America into the conflict.

The country, led by President Woodrow Wilson, who

temporized to an extent that for a time made him the subject of bitter criticism, found that war was being forced upon it by an autocratic and ambitious German Government—that of the Hohenzollern dynasty—which possessed an insane ambition to dominate the earth, leaving to America no alternative but to borrow the piratical terrorism of Imperialistic Germany, with temporary abandonment of its own constitutional free government, and join the Allies to defend it.

In the sense which Prussianism or militarism is here used it denotes a mental attitude or view. It is a condition of mind which is partisan, exaggerated and egotistical, and is developed by environment and training. Just as the professional spirit in any other occupation leads to an exhibition of exaggerated importance, the despotic doctrine of militarism assumes superiority over rational motives and deliberations. Everything must be sacrificed to perpetuate and maintain the honor and prestige of the military.

WHAT MILITARISM IS.

What that militarism is and what it has done to America, and to the whole world, is best summed up in the words of Secretary Lane, of the Department of the Interior, at Washington, who in an address before the Home Club of the Department on June 4, 1917, just when America was beginning to send forces to Europe, said:

"America is at war in self-defense and because she could not keep out; she is at war to save herself with the rest of the world from the nation that has linked itself with the Turk and adopted the methods of Mahomet, setting itself to make the world bow before policies backed by the organized and scientific military system.

"Why are we fighting Germany? The brief answer is that ours is a war of self-defense. We did not wish to fight Germany. She made the attack upon us; not on our shores, but on our ships, our lives, our rights, our future. For two years and more we held to a neutrality that made us apologists for things which outraged man's common sense of fair play and humanity.

"At each new offense—the invasion of Belgium, the killing of civilian Belgians, the attacks on Scarborough and other defenseless towns, the laying of mines in neutral waters, the fencing off of the seas—and on and on through the months, we said:

" 'This is war—archaic, uncivilized war, but war. All rules have been thrown away; all nobility; man has come down to the primitive brute. And while we cannot justify, we cannot intervene. It is not our war.'

IN WAR TO DEFEND RIGHTS.

"Then why are we in? Because we could not keep out. The invasion of Belgium, which opened the war, led to the invasion of the United States by slow, steady, logical steps. Our sympathies evolved into a conviction of self-interest. Our love of fair play ripened into alarm at our own peril.

"We talked in the language and in the spirit of good faith and sincerity, as honest men should talk, until we discovered that our talk was construed as cowardice. And Mexico was called upon to cow us.

"We talked as men would talk who cared alone for peace and the advancement of their own material interests, until we discovered that we were thought to be a nation of mere money-makers, devoid of all character—until, indeed, we were told that we could not walk the highways of the world without permission of a Prussian soldier, that our ships might not sail without wearing a striped uniform of humiliation upon a narrow path of national subservience.

"We talked as men talk who hope for honest agreement, not for war, until we found that the treaty torn to pieces at Liege was but the symbol of a policy that made agreements worthless against a purpose that knew no word but success.

"And so we came into this war for ourselves. It is a war to save America, to preserve self-respect; to justify our right to live as we have lived, not as some one else wishes us to live. In the name of freedom we challenge with ships and men, money and an undaunted spirit, that word 'verboten' which Germany has written upon the sea and upon the land.

"For America is not the name of so much territory. It is a living spirit, born in travail, grown in the rough school of bitter experiences, a living spirit which has purpose and pride and conscience, knows why it wishes to live and to what end, knows how it comes to be respected of the world, and hopes to retain that respect by living on with the light of Lincoln's love of man as its old and new testaments.

AMERICA MUST LIVE.

"It is more precious that this America should live than that we Americans should live. And this America as we now see has been challenged from the first of this war by the strong arm of a power that has no sympathy with our purpose, and will not hesitate to destroy us if the law that we respect, the rights that are to us sacred, or the spirit that we have, stand across her set will to make this world bow before her policies, backed by her organized and scientific military system. The world of Christ—a neglected but not a rejected Christ—has come again face to face with the world of Mahomet, who willed to win by force.

"With this background of history and in this sense, then, we fight Germany:

"Because of Belgium—invaded, outraged, enslaved, impoverished Belgium. We cannot forget Liege, Louvain and Cardinal Mercier. Translated into terms of American history these names stand for Bunker Hill, Lexington and Patrick Henry.

"Because of France—invaded, desecrated France, a million of whose heroic sons have died to save the land of Lafayette. Glorious, golden France, the preserver of the arts, the land of noble spirit. The first land to follow our lead into republican liberty.

"Because of England—from whom came the laws, traditions, standards of life and inherent love of liberty which we call Anglo-Saxon civilization. We defeated her once upon the land and once upon sea. But Australia, New Zealand, Africa and Canada are free because of what we did. And they are with us in the fight for the freedom of the seas.

"Because of Russia—new Russia. She must not be overwhelmed now. Not now, surely, when she is just born into freedom. Her peasants must have their chance; they must go to school to Washington, to Jefferson and to Lincoln, until they know their way about in this new, strange world, of government by the popular will; and

"Because of other peoples, with their rising hope that the world may be freed from government by the soldier.

GERMANY'S CRIMES AGAINST US.

"We are fighting Germany because she sought to terrorize us and then to fool us. We could not believe that Germany would do what she said she would do upon the seas.

"We still hear the piteous cries of children coming up out of the sea where the Lusitania went down. And Germany has never asked forgiveness of the world.

"We saw the Sussex sunk, crowded with the sons and daughters of neutral nations.

"We saw ship after ship sent to the bottom—ships of mercy bound out of America for the Belgian starving; ships carrying the Red Cross and laden with the wounded of all nations; ships carrying food and clothing to friendly, harmless, terrorized peoples; ships flying the Stars and Stripes—sent to the bottom hundreds of miles from shore, manned by American seamen, murdered against all law, without warning.

"We believed Germany's promise that she would respect

the neutral flag and the rights of neutrals, and we held our anger and outrage in check. But now we see that she was holding us off with fair promises until she could build her huge fleet of submarines. For when spring came she blew her promise into the air, just as at the beginning she had torn up that 'scrap of paper.' Then we saw clearly that there was but one law for Germany, her will to rule.

"We are fighting Germany because she violated our confidence. Paid German spies filled our cities. Officials of her Government, received as the guests of this nation, lived with us to bribe and terrorize, defying our law and the law of nations.

"We are fighting Germany because while we were yet her friends—the only great power that still held hands off—she sent the Zimmermann note calling to her aid Mexico, our southern neighbor, and hoping to lure Japan, our western neighbor, into war against this nation of peace.

GOVERNMENT THAT HAS NO CONSCIENCE.

"The nation that would do these things proclaims the gospel that government has no conscience. And this doctrine cannot live, or else democracy must die! For the nations of the world must keep faith. There can be no living for us in a world where the State has no conscience, no reverence for the things of the spirit, no respect for international law, no mercy for those who fall before its force. What an unordered world! Anarchy! The anarchy of the rival wolf packs!

"We are fighting Germany because in this war feudalism is making its last stand against oncoming democracy. We see it now. This is a war against an old spirit, an ancient, outworn spirit. It is a war against feudalism—the right of the castle on the hill to rule the village below. It is a war of democracy—the right of all to be their own masters. Let Germany be feudal if she will! But she must not spread her system over a world that has outgrown it. Feudalism plus science, thirteenth century plus twentieth; this is the religion of the mistaken Germany that has linked itself with the Turk; that has, too, adopted the method of Mahomet: 'The State has no conscience,' 'the State can do no wrong.' With the spirit of the fanatic, she believes this gospel and that it is her duty to spread it by force.

"With poison gas that makes living a hell, with submarines that sneak through the seas to slyly murder non-combatants, with dirigibles that bombard men and women while they sleep, with a perfected system of terrorization that the modern world first heard of when German troops entered China, German feudalism is making war upon mankind.

LIVE IN HAUNTED TERROR.

"Let this old spirit of evil have its way and no man will live in America without paying toll to it, in manhood and in money. This spirit might demand Canada from a defeated, navyless England, and then our dream of peace on the north would be at an end. We would live, as France has lived for forty years, in haunting terror.

"America speaks for the world in fighting Germany. Mark on a map those countries which are Germany's allies, and you will mark but four, running from the Baltic through Austria and Bulgaria to Turkey. All the other nations, the whole glove around, are in arms against her or are unable to move. There is deep meaning in this.

"We fight with the world for an honest world, in which nations keep their word; for a world in which nations do not live by swagger or by threat; for a world in which men think of the ways in which they can conquer the common cruelties of nature instead of inventing more horrible cruelties to inflict upon the spirit and body of man; for a world in which the ambition or the philosophy of a few shall not make miserable all mankind; for a world in which the man is held more precious than the machine, the system or the State."

In his denunciations of the Imperial German Government President Wilson and his advisers have indicted the House of Hohenzollern, of which Emperor Wilhelm is the head, and which has developed the unbending military spirit which has resulted in Germany being counted an outcast among the nations of the world.

America, it must be noted, has no antipathy for the Germans as a race, but modern civilization opposes that form of Government which has permitted the cruel characteristics of the "wolf tribes" of feudal times to be carried down through the generations, and capitalized by the Imperial powers to bring terror to the hearts of all who do not bow to the iron hand of the Kaiser and his ilk.

GERMANY A WARLIKE RACE.

The thing from which this Prussianism—this militarism—grew is easily traceable down the German ages. The very first appearance of the Germans in history is as a warlike race. The earliest German literature is composed of folk tales about war heroes—their ideals and manly virtues. And this ideal in one form or another, under varying circumstances and conditions, persisted throughout the centuries.

It is not merely that military service has been compulsory in Germany, but that almost everything else has been subjugated to the development of the army. While Germany has given to the world a generous quota of scientists, industrial geniuses, musicians and poets, the whole race is imbued with the warlike spirit and its influence is manifest in every phase of national life. Practically all that is best in the nation in the way of efficiency has been inspired or may be traced to the military discipline to which the people have been subjected for years. They have been created human machines, trained to obey orders and to perform the services to which they are assigned without protest and without question.

The history of Germany began with Henry, the Fowler,

about A. D. 929, who was essentially the first sovereign. He developed the system of margraves or wardens to guard the frontiers of the kingdom, fortified his towns and required every ninth man to take up arms for his country. Robbers were forced to become soldiers or be hanged, and as lawlessness was rampant there was no dearth of material to fill up the ranks of the army.

The margraves, or military leaders under them, grew in importance and influence until the offices tended to become hereditary. Gradually the country was divided into principalities, each of which maintained a force of arms. This limited form of military rule maintained for several centuries of troublesome times, or until about 1412, when Emperor Sigismund appointed Burgrave Frederick, of Nuremberg, "Stratthalter," or vice-regent.

BIRTH OF THE MILITARY SPIRIT.

This appointment marked the establishment of the Hohenzollerns in Brandenburg, and, in fine, fixes the birth of the military spirit in Germany.

Other princes of the German Reich maintained armies, but the Hohenzollerns were destined to imprint upon the nation the military ideal. In the beginning history says that Burgrave Frederick tried all the arts of peace, but it was only with the army of Franks and some artillery that he was able to batter down the castles of the robber lords and bring order into Brandenburg.

Thomas Carlyle gives a list of twelve electors who strove in turn to consolidate the power of Prussia, so that when Federick the Great became King of Prussia he found much of the work done. Among the rulers of these strenuous days to whom the Kaiser Wilhelm may point as having handed down to him the warlike spirit are Kurfuerst Joachim I, of Brandenburg (1529), who introduced Roman law and established a supreme court for all the provinces at Berlin; Kurfuerst Joachim II, of Brandenburg (1542), whom history describes as an unscrupulous despot, fond of luxury and display, and who changed his religion because it was an advantage politically for him to do so; Margrave Georg Frederick von Ansbach (1564), who caused the eyes of sixty peasants to be bored out upon winning the Peasants' war, and Kurfuerst Frederick William der Grosse, of Brandenburg (1652), known as the "Great Elector," a fighter, who had two clearly defined aims: to build up agriculture and maintain a big army.

For years the Hohenzollerns and their aids were fighting unfriendly neighbors and quarrelsome princes, and when after the lapse of time the Thirty Years' War finally turned Germany into a field of blood, the Great Elector emerged from the strife with the support of about 25,000 well drilled soldiers, and freed his country from foreign foes.

HELD EUROPE AT HIS MERCY.

The establishment of the power of the Junkers—the autocrats of Prussianism—is credited to Frederick the Great, who was the great drillmaster who organized the Prussian army on lines of efficiency and economy. It is related that Frederick, afterward "The Great," was taken from his women teachers at the age of seven years and subjected to rigid military discipline. He commanded a company of cadets, composed of the sons of nobles who were compelled to drill for him, and at the age of fourteen he was a captain in the Potsdam Guards, and when, in 1740, he became king, he took the army and held all Europe at his mercy. His successor, Frederick William II, was incapable, and the French revolution found Germany in a state of discord.

When Frederick William III acceded to the throne in 1797 he started to reorganize the army. Frederick William I had divided the country into districts, or cantons, and here began the system of compulsory military training. All males born were enrolled and liable to service when of age. The army was recruited by districts and every district had its regiment, though later exemptions were allowed. Under Frederick William III, Scharnhorst, a Hanoverian, was the military reorganizer, and he began the work with the slogan "All dwellers of the State are born defenders of the same."

Instead of depending for its development on king, the army was directed by genius of best men developed by the system. After the formation of the German Empire in 1871, which placed the king of Prussia at its head, the Constitution of the German Empire made every German a member of the active army for seven years. Service with colors three years and with the reserve four. In 1875 there were eighteen army corps, of which twelve were Prussian. The strength by law in 1874 was 400,000.

PEACE STRENGTH INCREASED.

In 1881 the established peace strength was increased by thirty-four battalions of infantry, forty batteries of field artillery and other forces, and in 1886 Bismarck, recognizing the power of Prussianism and its military influence, was compelled to dissolve the Reichstag, but after the election in 1887 thirty-one other battalions and twenty-four batteries were added. Two complete army corps were added in 1890, and in 1893 the color service, or length of time when reservists were subject to duty under colors only, was decreased by two years, bringing the peace strength up to more than half a million and the reservists up to 4,000,000. Step by step the strength of the military force was increased until after the adoption of the law of 1913, when provision was made for 699 battalions of infantry, 633 batteries of field artillery; 44 battalions of engineers; 55 battalions of garrison artillery; 31 battalions of communications and 26 battalions of train troops—a grand total of 870,000 actually in service in peace strength.

The German Empire is composed of twenty-six states—Prussia, Bavaria, Wurttemberg, Baden, Saxony, Hesse, Mecklenburg-Schwerin, Mecklenburg-Sterlitz, Oldenburg, Brunswick, Sax-Weimer-Eisnach, Sax-Coburg-Gotha, Saxe-Meiningen, Saxe-Altenburg, Waldeck, Lippe, Schaumburg-Lippe, Reuss (elder line), Reuss (younger line), Anhalt, Schwarz-Rudolsadt, Schwarzburg-Sonderhausen, Hamburg, Bremen, Lubeck and Reichsland—the Alsace-Lorraine. The area is less than that of the State of Texas while the population according to the most recent statistics is about 65,000,000.

Every male person between the ages of eighteen and forty-five is liable for military service. Reservists under the rules in force when the war started were subject to two musters annually and two periods of training not to exceed eight weeks in duration.

EGOTISTICAL AND EXAGGERATED UTTERANCES.

That the present Emperor is imbued with the harsh military spirit of his ancestors is illustrated by his many egotistical and exaggerated utterances. In dedicating the monument of Prince Frederick Charles at Frankfurt-on-the-Oder in 1891, he is quoted as having said:

"We would rather sacrifice our eighteen army corps and our 42,000,000 inhabitants on the field of battle than surrender a single stone of what my father and Prince Frederick gained." The thrills which such expressions arouse are born of an inveterate emotional habit, and are responsible for the obliquity of view and conduct which has made Germany an outcast among civilized nations.

But Germany was not satisfied with what she had obtained by her crusading. Developments of the war prove conclusively that the Kaiser has followed out the blood and iron politico-economic methods of Bismarck for the development of Prussian power and that while at times Germany has been reported to be maneuvering for peace, her peace moves have in reality been war moves, and that a truce would only give the Imperial Government time in which to further Prussianize and prepare for a greater world war the territory to the southeast which she has conquered under the guise of a friendly alliance.

It will be recalled that President Wilson declared that "America must fight until the world is made safe for democracy." This declaration refers immediately to the plans which it has developed Germany had for its conquest. Based upon reports received by agents of the United States, of England, of France and other countries, Germany aimed to form a consolidation of an impregnable military and economic unit stretching from the North Sea to the Mediterranean, cutting Europe permanently in half, controlling the Dardanelles, the Agean and the Baltic, and eventually forming the backbone of a Prussian world empire.

LEAGUE AT WORK SINCE 1911.

In her southeastern conquests, it is apparent, Germany followed almost in toto the long established plan of the Pan-German League, whose propaganda had been regarded outside of Germany as the harmless activity of extremists, too radical to be taken seriously. Coupled with this plan, as an instrument of economic consolidation, the German officials used with only slight modification the system of customs union expansion which aided Prussia in former years to extend her domination over the other German States now making up the empire.

As early as 1911 the Pan-German League is said to have circulated a definite propaganda of conquest, with printed appeals containing maps of a greater Germany, whose sway from Hamburg to Constantinople and then southeastward through Asiatic Turkey was marked out by boundaries very coincident with the military lines held today, under German officers, by the troops of Germany, Austria-Hungary, Bulgaria and Turkey. Adhesion of the German Government itself to such a plan was not suspected by the other Powers, although the propagandists were permitted to continue their activities unhindered and to spread their appeals in a country of strict press supervision. How closely the German Government did adhere to the plan in reality has been demonstrated clearly by the course of the war.

Following the footsteps of Bismarck, who used the Franco-Prussian war alliance to bring Baden, Bavaria and Wurttemburg into the German confederacy and then into the German Empire, Emperor William chose war as the means of establishing the broad pathway to the southeast which was essential for realization of the dream of a great Germany.

VERGE OF DISSOLUTION.

The subjugation of Austria-Hungary, which would have presented a different task under ordinary conditions, became in these circumstances comparatively very simple. A polyglot combination of States, having little in common and apparently held together only by the decaying genius of the aged Emperor Franz Joseph, the dual monarchy was regarded everywhere as on the verge of dissolution. Her helplessness before Russia's army became apparent early in the war, and the eagerness with which Germany seized the opportunity thus presented is pointed to as emphasizing the far-sightedness of the German plans.

Austria-Hungary's submission is declared to be complete, both in a military and economic sense. The German officers commanding her armies, abetted by industrial agents, scattered throughout the country by Germany, hold the Austrian and Hungarian population in a union which neither the hardships of war, the death of the Emperor nor the inspiration of the outside influences, such as the Russian revolution, can break.

Bulgaria's declaration of war on the side of Germany was actuated by a German diplomatic coup, which in itself is regarded now as further evidence that a clear road through to the Dardanelles was considered in Berlin as a primary and imperative purpose of the war.

In the case of Turkey, German domination is even more

complete than in Austria-Hungary and Bulgaria. Not only have German officers led in defending Turkish territory and in eradicating inharmonious elements, such as the Armenians and Syrians, but German industrial organizations have taken a firm grip on Turkish industry and a large delegation of German professors have been spreading German kultur among the population.

The developments threw a new light on many events before the war. Among them the long-unexplained declaration of Emperor William at Damascus in 1898 that all Mohammedans might confidently regard the German Emperor as "their friend forever." There also is a complete understanding now of Germany's eagerness to obtain, in 1899, a concession for the Bagdad railroad, an artery of communication now indispensable to the German operations.

These are the things and conditions to which the Allies referred when in replying to one of President Wilson's peace notes they declared that war must accomplish the "liberation of Italians, of Slavs, of Rumanians and of Tzecho-Slovacs from foreign domination; the enfranchisement of populations subject to the bloody tyranny of the Turk; the expulsion from Europe of the Ottoman Empire, and the restoration of Servia, Montenegro and Rumania."

America entered the war to fight for Democracy. On the surface the United States pledged itself to protect its ships and make secure the lives of its citizens on the highways of the world, but the principles for which the manhood of the country were called to fight have been summarized as follows:

That the nations of the world shall co-operate and not compete. The paradox of history is that every struggle leads to firmer unity. Wars cemented France, unified the British Empire, consolidated the American Union.

That national armaments be limited to purposes of internal police, no nation be allowed to have a force sufficient to be a menace to general peace, and a League of Peace be formed which shall have at its hand sufficient armed power to compel order among the States.

That nations be governed by the people that compose them, and for the benefit of those people, and not of a ruling class.

That every nation be governed with an eye to the welfare of the whole world as well as to its own prosperity or glory, and patriotism properly subjected to humanity.

That the power of government be dissociated from advancing the profits of capital, and made always to mean the welfare of labor.

That security of life, freedom of worship and opinion, and liberty of movement be assured to all men everywhere.

That no munitions or instruments of death be manufactured except under control of the International Council of the World.

That the seas be free to all.

That tariffs be adjusted with a view to the general welfare and not as measures of national rivalry.

That railways, telegraph, and telephone lines, and all other common and necessary means of intercommunication be eventually nationalized.

That every human being in a country be conscripted to devote a certain part of his or her life to national service.

That both labor unions and combinations of capital be under strict government control, so that no irresponsible group may conspire against the commonwealth.

That every child receive training to equip him or her for self-support and intelligent citizenship.

That woman shall enjoy every right of citizenship.

That the civil shall always have precedence over the military authority.

And that the right of free speech, of a free press, and of assembly shall remain inviolate.

CHAPTER III.

THE THINGS THAT MADE MEN MAD.

GERMANY'S BARBARITY—THE DEVASTATION OF BELGIUM—HUMAN FIENDS—FIRE-BRAND AND TORCH—RAPE AND PILLAGE—THE SACKING OF LOUVAIN—WANTON DESTRUCTION—OFFICIAL PROOF.

THE conduct of Germany in ignoring international treaties and invading Belgium first aroused the antagonism of the United States and the rest of the civilized world, and furnished the primary glimpse of how Imperialism made light of human rights. What the Kaiser and his arrogant followers did is fully set forth in the report which a special envoy, appointed by King Albert of Belgum, laid before President Wilson on September 16, 1914.

The mission consisted of Henry Carton de Wiart, Minister of Justice; Messrs. de Sadeleer, Hymans and Vandervelde, Ministers of State, and Count Louis de Lichtervelde, serving as secretary of the mission. On being received by President Wilson, Mr. de Wiart, for the mission, outlined for the world and for America, the situation in part as follows:

"His Majesty, the King of the Belgians, has charged us with a special mission to the President of the United States. Let me say how much we feel ourselves honored to have been called upon to express the sentiments of our King and of our whole nation to the illustrious statesman whom the American people have called to the highest dignity of the commonwealth.

"Ever since her independence was first established, Belgium has been declared neutral in perpetuity. This neutrality, guaranteed by the Powers, has recently been violated by one of them. Had we consented to abandon our neutrality for the benefit of one of the belligerents, we would have betrayed our obligations toward the others. And it was the sense of our international obligations as well as that of our dignity and honor that has driven us to resistance.

41

"The consequences suffered by the Belgian nation were not confined purely to the harm occasioned by the forced march of the invading army. This army not only seized a great portion of our territory, but it committed incredible acts of violence, the nature of which is contrary to the laws of nations.

"Peaceful inhabitants were massacred, defenseless women and children were outraged; open and undefended towns were destroyed; historical and religious monuments were reduced to dust and the famous library of the University of Louvain was given to the flames.

"Our government has appointed a Judicial Commission to make an official investigation, so as to thoroughly and impartially examine the facts and to determine the responsibility thereof, and I will have the honor, Exellency, to hand over to you the proceedings of the inquiry.

THE UNITED STATES' ATTITUDE.

"In this frightful holocaust which is sweeping over Europe, the United States has adopted a neutral attitude.

"And it is for this reason that your country, standing apart from either one of the belligerents, is in the best position to judge, without bias or partiality, the conditions under which the war is being waged.

"It is at the request, even at the initiative of the United States, that all civilized nations have formulated and adopted at the Hague a law regulating the laws and usages of war.

"We refuse to believe that war has abolished the family of civilized powers, or the regulation to which they have freely consented.

"The American people has always displayed its respect for justice, its search for progress and an instinctive attachment for the laws of humanity. Therefore, it has won a moral influence which is recognized by the entire world. It is for this reason that Belgium, bound as she is to you by ties of commerce and increasing friendship, turns to the American people at this time to let you know the real truth of the present situation. Resolved to continue unflinching defence of its sovereignty and independence, it deems it a duty to bring to the attention of the civilized world the innumerable grave breaches of rights of mankind, of which she has been a victim.

"At the very moment we were leaving Belgium, the King recalled to us his trip to the United States and the vivid and strong impression your powerful and virile civilization left upon his mind. Our faith in your fairness, our confidence in your justice, in your spirit of generosity and sympathy, all these have dictated our present mission."

THE INVESTIGATING COMMITTEE.

In the report handed to President Wilson, the preface sets forth that the committee appointed to investigate the conduct of the German invaders, and all of the surrounding circumstances, consisted of Messrs. Cattier, professor at the Brussels University; Nys, counselor of the Brussels Court of Appeals; Verhaegen, counselor of the Brussels Court of Appeals; Wodon, professor at the Brussels University; Secretary, Mr. Gillard, Director of the Department of Justice. Afterwards, when the invasion made it necessary to transfer the seat of the government from Brussels to Antwerp, a sub-committee was appointed there, consisting of Mr. Cooreman, Minister of State; Members, Count Goblet d'Aviella, Minister of State, Vice President of the Senate; Messrs. Ryckmans, Senator; Strauss, Alderman of the City of Antwerp; Van Cutsem, Honorary President of the Law Court of Antwerp. Secretaries, Chevalier Ernst de Bunswyck, Chief Secretary of the Belgian Minister of Justice; Mr. Orts, Counselor of the Legation.

In brief the report submits first, that in violation of the perpetual treaty of June 26, 1831, Germany notified Belgium that France was about to march upon Germany, and that Germany proposed to frustrate such a move by sending its soldiers through Belgium; that the German government had no intention of making war against Belgium, and that if Belgium made no opposition it would evacuate Belgium after hostilities ceased, and during the period the German forces were in the country, would buy everything needed for its army. Belgium replied that it had assurance from France that France had no intention of invading Belgium, and that if France attempted to pass through Belgium would oppose such an act with force. It informed the German Imperial Government that it would similarly oppose any move on the part of Germany to pass through.

Nevertheless Germany proceeded at once through Belgium. Quoting articles from the Hague treaty, the commission's report reads:

THE DAYS OF BABARISM.

"In the days of barbarism, the population of a territory occupied by the enemy was deprived of all judicial capacity. At that time," as Ghering writes ironically, " 'the enemy was absolutely deprived of rights; everything he owned belonged to the gallant warrior who had wrenched it away from him. One had merely to lose it.'

"In our days the rules of warfare clearly establish the difference between the property of the government of the territory occupied and the property of individuals. While the present doctrine allows the conqueror to seize, in a general way, everything in the way of movable property belonging to the State, it obliges him, on the other hand, to respect the property of individuals, corporations and public provincial administrations.

"The Hague Convention, signed October 18, 1897, by all the civilized States, among others by Germany, contains the following stipulations regarding laws and customs of warfare on land:

" 'Art. 46. The honor and right of the family, the life of the individual and private property, as well as religious convictions and the exercise of worship, must be respected. Private property cannot be confiscated.

" 'Art. 47. Pillaging is formally prohibited.

" 'Art. 53. When occupying territory, the army can only seize cash as well as funds and securities belonging entirely to the State; also depots of arms, ways and means of transportation, warehouses and provisions, and in a general way all movable property belonging to the State and liable to be used for warlike operations.

" 'Art. 56. Property of municipalities, property of establishments consecrated to worship, to charity and instruction; to art and science, even though belonging to the State, will be treated as private property.'

"In defiance of these conventional rules, voluntarily and solemnly accepted by Germany, she has committed, from the beginning of her invasion of Belgian soil, numerous attacks upon private property."

GERMAN CUPIDITY.

At Hasselt, the report shows that on August 12, 1914, the Germans confiscated the funds of the branch of the National Bank, which amounted to 2,075,000 francs. At Liege, on entering the city, they forcibly seized the funds of a branch of the same bank, amounting to 4,000,000 francs. Moreover, upon finding at that branch bundles of bank notes of 5-franc denomination, representing an amount of 400,000 francs, and which were not yet signed, they forced a printer to sign those bank notes by means of a rubber stamp, which they had also seized, and afterwards put the notes in circulation. The bank, it is explained, was a shareholders' corporation, the capital having been obtained by subscription from private parties and was in no wise an institution of the State.

The enormity of this offence is made apparent by the fact that in the war of 1870, when the Prussians entered Rhiems in the Franco-Prussian war, and they wanted to confiscate the funds of the branch of the National Bank of France, Crown Prince Frederick ordered that funds which were found at the bank could not be seized so long as they were not used for the maintenance of the French army, it having been contended by directors of the institution that the bank was not a State, but a private bank. But more than this Germany levied supplies from every Belgian city and tried to levy upon the city of Brussels the sum of 50,000,000 francs and the province of Brabant 450,000,000 francs.

TREATY OBLIGATIONS.

Categorically, the violation and disregard of every phase of the Hague treaty is described. In spite of the strict provision that undefended cities, villages and dwellings are not to be bombarded, and where bombardment is necessary the commanding officer of the attacking party must warn the authorities that such bombardment is to take place, German aeroplanes and dirigibles bombarded relentlessly from the beginning. In Antwerp a Zeppelin threw explosive bombs at the Royal Palace, but the missiles went astray, demolishing private residences, killing eight persons and injuring many. Servants were killed in their beds in one private house when the bombs tore away the top of the building.

"In the Place du Poids Public a bomb fell on the pavement. Fragments scattered all over the place. Not a house facing the square was untouched. A policeman was cut to pieces, all that was found of him being a leg covered with a few rags of his uniform. Five other persons who opened their windows were blown to atoms. The bed-rooms of two houses facing one another were visited. In the first there were three corpses. Blood was scattered all over the place. The floor was covered with fragments of windows and with blood-soaked underwear. On the ceiling and walls, parts of intestines and brains were visible. In the other house two old persons had been killed while looking down upon the street. Later Antwerp was bombarded, as was Heyst-op-den-Berg and the city of Malines, which was undefended, and where there was not a Belgian soldier. At Malines the batteries fired shell after shell in the direction of the Cathedral of Saint Rombault, a beautiful edifice, which was hit many times and badly damaged, though there was no military reason for the assault as the town was practically abandoned.

The commission turned over to President Wilson explosive bullets used by the Germans at Werchter, and submitted briefs from physicians who treated wounds made by the explosive bullets.

DETAILED ATROCITIES OUTLINED.

A few details of the atrocities are outlined as follows:

"German cavalry, occupying the village of Linsmeau, were attacked by some Belgian infantry and two Gendarmes. A German officer was killed by our troops during the fight, and subsequently buried at the request of the Belgian officer in command. None of the civilian population took part in the fight. Nevertheless, the village was invaded at dusk on August 10 by a strong force of German cavalry, artillery and machine guns. In spite of the assurance given by the Burgomaster that none of the peasants had taken part in the previous fighting two farms and six outlying houses were destroyed by gun-fire and burned. All the male population were compelled to come forward and hand over what they possessed. No recently discharged firearms were found, but the invaders divided the peasants into three groups. Those in one group were bound and eleven of them placed in a ditch, whither they were afterward found dead, their skulls fractured by the butts of German rifles.

"During the night of August 10, German cavalry entered Velm in great numbers; the inhabitants were asleep. The Germans, without provocation, fired upon Mr. Deglimme-Gever's house, broke into it, destroyed furniture, looted money, burned barns, hay, corn stacks, farm implements, six oxen, and the contents of the farmyard. They carried off Mme. Deglimme half-naked, to a place two miles away. She was then let go and was fired upon as she fled, without being hit. Her husband was carried away in another direction."

Farmer Jeff Dierckx, of Neerhespen, bears witness to the following acts of cruelty committed by German cavalry at Orsmael Neerhespen, on August 10, 11 and 12:

SHOCKING BARBARITIES.

"An old man of the latter village had his arm sliced in three longitudinal cuts; he was then hanged head downward and burned alive. Young girls have been raped and little children outraged at Orsmael, where several inhabitants suffered mutilations too horrible to describe. A Belgian soldier belonging to a battalion of cyclist carbineers who had been wounded and made prisoner was hanged, while another who was tending his comrade was bound to a telegraph pole and shot."

The sacking of Louvain, which was one of the vile acts of the Germans during the early days of the war, is described briefly in the report of the commission as follows:

"The Germans entered Louvain on Wednesday, August 19, after having set fire to the towns through which they passed.

"From the moment of their having entered the city of Louvain, the Germans requisitioned lodgings and victuals for their troops. They entered every private bank of the city and took over the bank funds. German soldiers broke the doors of houses abandoned by their inhabitants, pillaged them and indulged in orgies.

"The German authorities took hostages; the mayor of the city, Senator Vander Kelen, the Vice Rector of the Catholic University, the Dean of the City; magistrates and aldermen were also detained. All arms down to fencing foils had been handed over to the town administration and deposited by the said authorities in the Church of St. Peter.

"In the neighboring village, Corbeck-Loo, a young matron, 22 years old, whose husband was in the army, was surprised on Wednesday, August 19, with several of her relatives, by a band of German soldiers. The persons who accompanied her were locked in an abandoned house, while she was taken into another house, where she was successively violated by five soldiers.

LUSTFUL CRUELTY OF THE GERMANS.

"In the same village, on Thursday, August 20, German soldiers were searching a house where a young girl of 16 lived with her parents. They carried her into an abandoned house and, while some of them kept the father and mother off, others went into the house, the cellar of which was open, and forced the young woman to drink. Afterwards they carried her out on the lawn in front of the house and violated her successively. She continued to resist and they pierced her breast with bayonets. Having been abandoned by the soldiers after their abominable attacks, the girl was carried off by her parents, and the following day, owing to the gravity of her condition, she was administered the last rites of the church by the priest of the parish and carried to the hospital at Louvain."

Upon entering villages occupied by the Germans after they were driven back to Louvain, the report says the Belgian soldiers found that the German soldiers had sacked, ravaged and set fire to the villages everywhere, taking with them and driving before them all the male inhabitants. "Upon entering Hofstade, the Belgian soldiers found the corpse of an old woman who had been killed by bayonet thrusts; she still held in her hand the needle with which she was sewing when attacked; one mother and her son, aged about 15 years, lay there pierced with bayonet wounds; one man was found hung.

"In Sempst, a neighboring village, were found corpses

of two men partially burned. One of them was found with legs cut off to the knees; the other was minus his arms and legs. A workman had been pierced with bayonets, afterward while he was still living the Germans soaked him with petroleum and locked him in a house which they set on fire. An old man and his son had been killed by sabre cuts; a cyclist had been killed by bullets; a woman coming out of her house had been stricken down in the same manner."

A LAME EXCUSE OFFERED.

Concerning the sacking of Louvain itself, the report says that one detachment of the Germans met another detachment while in full flight from the Belgian soldiers, and attacked one another. This was the basis for the pretext that they had been attacked by the citizenry of Louvain and was responsible for the bombardment of the city. The bombarding lasted until 10 o'clock at night, and afterward the German soldiers set fire to the city.

"The houses which had not taken fire were entered by German soldiers, who were throwing fire grenades, some of which seem to have been provided for the occasion. The largest part of the city of Louvain, especially the quarters of 'Ville Haute,' comprising the modern houses, the Cathedral of St. Peter, the University Halls, with the whole library of the University with its manuscripts, its collections, the largest part of the scientific institutions and the town theatre were at the moment being consumed by flames.

"The commission deems it necessary, in the midst of these horrors, to insist on the crime of lese-humanity which the deliberate annihilation of an academic library—a library which was one of the treasures of our time—constitutes.

"Numerous corpses of civilians covered the streets and squares. On the routes from Louvain to Tirlemont alone one witness testifies to having seen more than fifty of them. On the threshold of houses were found burnt corpses of people, who, surprised in their cellars by the fire, had tried to escape and fell into the heap of live embers. The suburbs of Louvain were given up to the same fate. It can be said that the whole region between Malines and Louvain and most of the suburbs of Louvain have been devastated and destroyed.

BASE INDIGNITIES TO CLERGYMEN.

"A group of 75 persons, among whom were several notables of the city, such as Father Coloboet and a Spanish priest, and also an American priest, were conducted, during the morning of Wednesday, August 26, to the square in front of the station. The men were brutally separated from their wives and children, after having received the most abominable treatment after repeated threats of being shot, and were driven in front of the German troops as far as the village of Campenhout. They were locked, during the night, in the church. The following day, at 4 o'clock, a German officer came to tell them that they might all confess themselves and that they would be shot half an hour later. When, finally, they were released, the report continues, they were recaptured by another German brigade and compelled to march to Malines, where they were finally liberated.

"An eye witness testified that he met nothing except burned villages, crazed peasants, lifting to each comer their arms, as mark of submission. From each house was hanging a white flag, even from those that had been set on fire, and rags of them were found hanging from the ruins. The fire began a little above the American College, and the city is entirely destroyed, with the exception of the town hall and the depot. Today the fire continues and the Germans, instead of trying to stop it—seem rather to maintain it by throwing straw into the flames, as I have myself seen behind the Hotel de Ville. The Cathedral and the theatre have been destroyed and fallen in, and also the library. The town resembles an old city in ruins, in the midst of which drunken soldiers are circulating, carrying around bottles of wine and liquor; the officers themselves being installed in arm chairs, sitting around tables and drinking like their own men.

"In the streets dead horses are decaying, horses which are completely inflated, and the smell of the fire and the decaying animals is such that it has followed me for a long time."

And the policy which developed such outrageous conduct on the part of the Kaiser's soldiers in the early days of the war, against which Belgium protested to the world, inspired brutal acts, ruthlessness and cruelty at every stage and during every period of the war. Nowhere is there written a single line which tells of the humanitarian acts of the German soldiers. Those who fight against them acknowledge their stoical bravery, the efficiency of the army, the navy and the people as a whole, but there is no reflection of refined instincts in any of the acts of Germany or the Germans.

THE AMERICAN MINISTER'S REPORT.

Of ·those conditions which existed in Belgium when the German soldiers overran the country, America's own minister to the devastated country, Brand Whitlock, sent a report to the State Department in the beginning of 1917, when President Wilson was protesting against the treatment accorded the helpless people of Belgium by the Germans.

Mr. Whitlock tells how the Germans determined to put the Belgians thrown out of employment to work for them. "In August," says the report, dealing with the treatment of the helpless Belgians, "Von Hindenburg was appointed supreme commander. He is said to have criticised Von Bissing's policy as too mild, and there was a quarrel; Von Bissing went to Berlin to protest, threatened to resign, but did not. He returned, and a German official said that Belgium would now be subjected to a more terrible regime, would learn what war was. The prophecy has been vindicated.

"The deportations began in October in the Etape, at

Ghent and at Bruges. The policy spread; the rich industrial districts at Hainaut, the mines and steel works about Charleroi were next attacked, and they seized men in Brabant, even in Brussels, despite some indications and even predictions of the civil authorities that the policy was about to be abandoned.

"As by one of the ironies of life the winter has been more excessively cold than Belgium has ever known it and while many of those who presented themselves were adequately protected against the cold, many of them were without overcoats. The men, shivering from cold and fear, the parting from weeping wives and children, the barrels of brutal Uhlans, all this made the scene a pitiable and distressing one.

RAGE, TERROR AND DESPAIR.

"The rage, the terror and despair excited by this measure all over Belgium were beyond anything we had witnessed since the day the Germans poured into Brussels. The delegates of the commission for relief in Belgium, returning to Brussels, told the most distressing stories of the scenes of cruelty and sorrow attending the seizures. And daily, hourly almost, since that time, appalling stories have been related by Belgians coming to the legation. It is impossible for us to verify them, first because it is necessary for us to exercise all possible tact in dealing with the subject at all, and secondly because there is no means of communication between the Occupations Gebiet and the Etappey Gebiet.

"I am constantly in receipt of reports from all over Belgium that tend to bear the stories one constantly hears of brutality and cruelty. A number of men sent back to Mons are said to be in a dying condition, many of them tubercular. At Molines and at Antwerp returned men have died, their friends asserting that they have been victims of neglect and cruelty, of cold, of exposure, of hunger.

"I have had requests from the burgomasters of ten communes asking that permission be obtained to send to the deported men in Germany packages of food similar to those that are being sent to prisoners of war. Thus far the German authorities have refused to permit this except in special instances, and returning Belgians claim that even when such packages are received they are used by the camp authorities only as another means of coercing them to sign the agreements to work.

A MORTAL BLOW TO BELGIANS.

"By the deportation of Belgians to work in Germany," says Mr. Whitlock's report, "they have dealt a mortal blow to any prospect they may ever have had of being tolerated by the population of Flanders; in tearing away from nearly every humble home in the land a husband and a father or a son and brother; they have lighted a fire of hatred that will never go out; they have brought home to every heart in the land, in a way that will impress its horror indelibly on the memory of three generations, a realization of what German methods mean, not as with the early atrocities in the heat of passion and the first lust of war, but by one of those deeds that make one despair of the future of the human race, a deed coldly planned, studiously matured, and deliberately and systematically executed, a deed so cruel that German soldiers are said to have wept in its execution, and so monstrous that even German officers are now said to be ashamed."

And if these acts were not sufficient to convince the world that Germany "is without the pale" so far as civilized warfare is concerned her conduct in wantonly destroying property in Flanders while in retreat could permit of no other conclusion.

After the violation of Belgium and the destruction of the Lusitania and the adoption of the policy of sinking neutral ships on sight for military advantage, or "necessity," why shouldn't the soldiers pollute wells, kill trees, carry off the girls, smash the household furniture not worth taking away and smear the pictures on the wall, just for revenge or in the sheer lust of destruction?

It makes no difference, so far as the principles of humanity are concerned, whether the German army is in victory or suffering defeat, advancing or retreating. The treatment accorded the evacuated cities of the Somme district was foretold by the treatment of the cities occupied early in the war. Here is the wording of an order posted during the victorious invasion of Belgium:

"Order—To the people of Liege. The population of Andenne, after making a display of peaceful intentions toward our troops, attacked them in the most treacherous manner. With my authority the general commanding these troops has reduced the town to ashes and has had 110 persons shot. I bring this fact to the knowledge of the people of Liege in order that they may know what fate to expect should they adopt a similar attitude.

"GENERAL von BULOW.

"Liege, Aug. 22, 1914."

CRUEL EXTREME OF PUNISHMENT.

And yet this order showed only a cruel extreme of punishment where some punishment was to be expected. It was left for the retreating Germans of 1917 to destroy, without provocation and without purpose, motived by revenge and obsessed by the Nietschean doctrine of "spare not."

Before Baupaume was evacuated it was deliberately converted into a mass of muck. There is no Bapaume now. It is perfectly understandable that the retreating soldiers should destroy their trenches and put up the question, "Tommy, how do you like your new trenches?" But why smear filth over the photograph of three little girls, a family treasure? All around Bapaume the villages were looted and the night the deliverers entered the destroyers made the sky lurid with the fires of towns and hamlets. Some 300 in the evacuated region were burned.

At Nesle, Roye and Ham there was not time enough to

destroy everything. The house of a doctor at Nesle, a specially attractive home, was not blown down for strategic purposes, but some soldiers did find time to drive axes through the mahogany panels of the beds and smash the clocks and mirrors. They were angry at being compelled to leave the house.

Villages like Cressy, near Nesle, where a shell never fell in the course of the war, have been completely destroyed.

PERONNE A HOPELESS RUIN.

There is not a habitable house left in Peronne. The sixteenth century church of St. Jean is but a relic. W. Beach Thomas wrote after the retreat that nothing was left that was valuable enough to be worth collection by a penny tinker or a rag-and-bone merchant. Foul what you cannot have, was the motto.

The famous ruins of the Feudal Castle of Coucy, one of the finest relics of architecture of its period, was wantonly blown up by the Germans on retreat. It was built in the thirteenth century by Enguerrand III and passed to the French crown in 1498, and was one of the great historic landmarks of Northern France.

Coucy was one of the noblest relics of the Middle Ages, respected by the most barbarous wars of the past, whose donjon (greatest in all Europe) dates almost from Charlemagne, harmless, time-wrecked, illustrious Coucy!

To give an idea of Coucy's importance, the French, in their first astonishment and sorrow, proposed to make reprisals on Hindenburg, should it take ten years. Of course, they will not; it is not their way.

Coucy is a mountain of blasted stones. Shoun Kelly, American, owned one of the outer towers of the great castle and the story of its ownership is the American antithesis of German ravage. Americans were always faithful tourists to Coucy; but among them, one loved more than all the glorious old ruin and its story which began with Enguerrand, the Sire of Coucy, in the year 1210. This was the late Edmund Kelly, of New York and Paris, international lawyer and for many years counsel of the American Embassy in Paris. He meditated on the motto of old Enguerrand: "I am not king, nor prince, nor duke, nor even count: I am the Sire of Coucy!" In fact, the Sire made a record for standing off local kings.

"He was a good American ahead of his time," said Lawyer Kelly; and he took to reading up the ancient chronicles, how Enguerrand's descendants stood off royalty for some 200 years, until finally bought out by the wealthy Louis of Orleans, and all the later glories of the place. Mazarin dismantled Coucy, but left it standing in its beauty; and Lawyer Kelly discovered it to be a State museum, impossible to be purchased, in these latter days, even by a millionaire. Not being one, he preferred it so, loving Coucy more than ever, the cultured American did the next best thing.

A LITTLE TOWN REDUCED.

The little town, once so rich, had dwindled since Mazarin. On the castle side stood two massive towers of the inner defense, belonging to the town. Mr. Kelly asked Mayor and department legislature to make a price on the nearest. As soon as he had bought his tower, he used loving care restoring it. He pierced windows through walls 16 feet thick. He built rooms in three stories, furnishing them in massive antique style. The tower roof was his shady terrace, covered with a little grove of century-old trees! From it he dominated Coucy. All its soul of beauty lay beneath his view.

All was systematically blown up, the town, the towers, the castle, by retreating Germans in their rage. Just masses of crumbled stones. The German papers boast that it took 28 tons of high explosives, and any one can see, this hour, the plain of Coucy covered with a white layer of powdered limestone, for miles around.

What for? To clear a battlefield, they say. It is not true.

Nothing is cleared. The masses of crumbled stone remained, when they fled their "battlefield."

The donjon was very high. It stood on a kind of bluff or elevation, overlooking the country, and before the days of aeroplanes it might have been used for observation. The donjon walls were 16 yards thick, not feet, but yards! No other tower in Europe had those dimensions. They tell a story about Mazarin. He deemed so strong a place, so near to Paris, might be dangerous to the Crown; so he dismantled Coucy militarily, without destroying its architectural beauty. The donjon worried him in those days when artillery could make no impression on its massive thickness. So Mazarin put 16 barrels of powder inside the tower, and set them off. The tower just converted itself into gun barrel! The powder blew out all the stories and the roof—shot them up like a gun pointed at the sky! But the tower stood, exactly as before.

OF MASSIVE ARCHITECTURE.

The masonry was admittedly the heaviest achieved by the Middle Ages. From the donjon extended three great vaulted halls. Massive buildings continued. There was a Gothic chapel, a Tribunal Hall, the Hall of the Nine Peers (whose statues remained), the Hall of the Nine Countesses (whose medallion-portraits were carved on the monumental chimney). There was a Romanesque chapel (relic from Charlemagne, like the original donjon), the separate Fortified Chateau of the Chatelain (the Sire's First Officer), and so on, and so on.

The retreating Germans have not only blown up Coucy, but that other priceless relic, the Tower of the Grand Constable and the entire historic Chateau of Ham, and equally the Castle of Peronne, a jewel of beauty—all in one corner of the Vallois! On the smoking wreck of Peronne, they left a humorous placard:

"Nicht aergen! Tur wundern! Don't be angry, just wonder!" Noyon and Peronne are sacked and ruined. At

Chauny 1800 houses out of 2500 were deliberately burned, and at a distance they bombarded the remainder, full of old folks and children whom they had parked there. All the public buildings, churches, hospitals and poorhouse were blown up. Three hundred towns and villages were burning at one time in this small section of the Cradel of France. Hindenburg was at Roisel when they rounded up the populations, went through their pockets for their money (giving "receipts"), took their clothes off their backs (so that all the American relief agencies in Paris were overwhelmed with telegrams of appeal) and burgled all the safes in banks and business houses before setting fire to the town and blowing up the main street!

ACCORDING TO THE PRINCIPLE OF WAR.

The German official communique said that it was "all done uniquely according to the technical principles of modern war." At Berlin they caused an American correspondent to cable these words to his papers: "The enemy will find great difficulty to take shelter on a battlefield where everything has been completely razed. We regret the destruction of a beautiful region of France, but it was necessary to transform it into a clear field of battle before we quit it."

They blew up the precious Romanesque Church of Tracy-le-Val (which dates before the Gothic). The church was situated in the midst of the great forest of Laigue; they blew up the church—and left the forest standing! No battlefield was cleared, but they hacked the bark to kill great noble trees by thousands. They made no effort to clear the forest; but weeping old French peasants told how half a German regiment was occupied three days in barking trees to prevent the sap from mounting. The crushed pearl of architecture lies in a dying forest.

At Le Novion, torch in hand, they burned 223 houses; but all the gutted walls are standing.

What technical principles of war command the wholesale

destruction of young fruit trees? In 20 orchards, by count, in sweet Leury (hidden at the bottom of a valley) every peach, plum, apricot and pear tree has been assassinated—hacked and standing, when the trunks are thick, and sprawling, severed by one blow of a sharp hatchet, young trees from the thickness of your wrists to your thumb. The French, with loving care, trained peach and pear trees against sunny walls, as if they were grapevines. The slender trunks are cut—and the garden walls left standing.

DESECRATION OF TREES.

The soldiers spared neither the orchards nor the single trees that took a generation to grow, and would have borne fruit for generations to come. Reapers and binders and other farming machines were collected and broken to pieces. One might see a measure of advantage that the deliverers would gain from these things if not destroyed, but it is an awful war doctrine that refuses to discriminate between the immediate and the eventual, the direct and the indirect, the important and the negligible advantage that would impoverish posterity to get a dime in cash. No military advantage is sufficient motive for such wanton ravishment. It is military fanaticism.

Ambassador Sharp, after a 100-mile trip through the evacuated territory, declared that never before in the history of the world had there been such a thorough destruction by either a vanquished or victorious army.

One thing alone was left, after the red-brick villages had been turned into heaps and the murdered fruit trees into black fagots, on the hill outside of St. Quentin. This was the log hut and shooting box of the Kaiser's son, Eitel Friederick. Its white-barked beech was unburnt, its glass windows unbroken, its inside adornments unlooted, the tables and chairs of its terrace beer garden remained. All around the works of man and God were destroyed. The contrast made this destroyer's lodge a sort of boast of his destruction.

The shocking ruin to human life in the evacuated region is of even greater moment. The half-starved civilians of Bapaume were forced to make trenches there and later for the defense of Cambrai also. All men and boys strong enough to work were taken along with the retreating forces. Near Peronne some hundreds of old men, women and children were found locked in a barn. One woman pathetically asked of an English officer, "Are you many?" And he was able to answer, "We are two millions now," and see her anxiety turned to relief and joy. Children who had been slowly starving for a year wandered about the ruins of their homes, but soon found reasons for smiling at the soldiers who had rescued them.

NEITHER MEAT NOR MILK.

These children had had no meat for months and no milk for a year and had almost forgotten the taste of butter. They probably never received a quarter of the rations Americans sent. Girls were compelled to attend the market gardens, and then the Germans took all the produce. The region was desolated and left inhabited by women and children moribund with misery and starvation.

At Noyon, where the Germans had concentrated 10,000 Belgian refugees, they promised to leave the American Relief Committee with sufficient supplies to feed them. But the last patrols completely sacked the American relief storehouses of all eatables and then dynamited the building. And it was from this place that fifty young women, from 18 to 25 years of age, were taken by the officers. Their distracted mothers were told that they were to be used as "officers' servants."

At Ham, when a mother of six children, seeing her husband and two eldest daughters being carried away, remonstrated, she was told that as an alternative she might find their bodies in a canal in the rear of the house.

Nothing could be more significant of the Government's attitude than the incident told by James W. Gerard. The people of a town were imprisoned or fined for their conduct toward a delayed train of Canadian prisoners. When he heard it he thought that at last the Government was going to put a stop to the maltreatment of prisoners. But he learned on invesigation that the townsfolk had been punished for giving a little food and drink to the starving and fainting prisoners.

And yet the most singularly brutal phase of this destruction of nature and wealth and art and life is the German defense of it. War is always hell and most of the awful things in this war have had their counterparts in other conflicts, though the Teutonic element has brought some peculiar refinements of cussedness and has given a thoroughness and "pep" and "kick" to the war business.

BETTER PREPARED NEXT TIME.

German writers, instead of making excuses for turning the nation into a war machine for forty years, complain that Germany was not prepared as she should have been and would be better prepared next time. Her professors do not regret that the soldiers at the front are so unrestrained in cruelty, but urge that they are too soft and kind to make effective war. The German correspondents all write enthusiastically of the devastation of the country they are leaving and of the desert created by German genius. Editors speak of the mercy which tempered the necessary hardness towards this once beautiful stretch of country and its inhabitants. The destruction of property which can serve no military purpose is defended on the ground that it is legitimate from a strategic point of view.

This all amounts to saying everything must give way to the considerations of war. It is taking the argument in the fable of the wolf and the lamb as serious philosophy and accepting the position of the wolf. They fail entirely to see the humor of the fable, and hence the fallacy of the wolf's argument.

The greatest hope of civilization, which trembled for a time before the spectre of German barbarity, is that frightfulness cannot endure the long and full test. The great initial advantages are more than offset by new opponents. The gain of the invasion of Belgium was canceled by England coming into the war. The advantage against England of the U-boat campaign was more than canceled by the entrance of the United States in the war.

Irvin Cobb says that the trouble with the Germans is that they are not "good sports and lack a sense of humor. It is impossible to conceive of a group of German officers playing football or baseball or cricket and abiding by the rules of the game. If Barbara Frietchie had said to a Prussian Stonewall Jackson, 'Shoot, if you must, my gray old head,' he'd have done it as a matter of course."

ARTICLE IV.

THE SLINKING SUBMARINE.

A Voracious Sea Monster—The Ruthless Destructive Policy of Germany—Starvation of Nations the Goal—How the Submarines Operate—Some Personal Experiences.

ALMOST the entire story of the world war is written around the development of the submarine. One can scarcely think of the terrible conflict without bringing to mind the wonderful "underseas" boat which has made infamous Germany famous. The truth is that, in so far as America is concerned, the conflict was precipitated by the ruthless submarine warfare which Germany waged as part of her plan to starve out England, France, Belgium—and all nations which opposed her.

The slinking submarine proved an efficient instrument, whose activities clearly indicated the diabolical intent and purpose of Germany to make the whole world suffer, if necessary, to the end that she might gain her point and perpetuate the Hohenzollern dynasty. It was not so much that her submarines wrought havoc—for death and disaster stalk always with war—but the methods by which Germany waged their warfare and disregarded all the rules which had been laid down for the guidance of civilized countries at war proved conclusively that even the innocent could expect no quarter from her.

The story of the sinking of the brave ocean steamship Lusitania on May 7, 1915, contains in its brief recital a typical illustration of Germany's lack of humanitarian instincts. The vessel, torpedoed off the coast of Ireland, went to the bottom of the ocean, carrying to death more than 1150 persons, many of them prominent Americans. With an audaciousness which has no counterpart in the history of civilized warfare, German agents in the United States had caused advertisements to be printed in the public press, warning citizens against sailing on the vessel, and advised that she was in danger of being destroyed.

The world stood aghast and believed it impossible that Germany should carry out her threat, but they were soon to be disillusioned. Because the handsome vessel passed through a zone of the seas which the Teuton war lords declared blockaded, they sent a torpedo from an underseas boat into her bowels. The horrors of that event are still fresh in the minds of millions. No such ruthless and wanton destruction of innocent human beings had been accomplished by a so-called civilization at war.

THE DUTIES OF WAR CAST ASIDE.

Articles of The Hague agreement defining the rights and duties of nations at war, and which Germany had accepted, were thrust aside and disregarded by Imperial Germany. The Hohenzollern dynasty was above rules and regulations. International law and the rights of non-combatants at sea were as nothing. That all nations had agreed that the enemy ship must give the captain of the vessel attacked opportunity to land innocent passengers was forgotten. There had not been a word of warning.

And Germany, and the adherents of the Imperial Government, expressing regret that Americans should have been sacrificed, professed deep sorrow on one hand and on the other shouted with glee. America protested vigorously, quoting the laws and demanding that Germany recognize them—not merely that she leave American vessels alone—and give assurance that no such further acts would be committed.

Contending that the sinking of the ship was justifiable, in the exigencies of war, Germany ceased for a short time her wanton sinking of boats without warning. For almost a year her underseas crafts had been preying upon the small British coasting vessels, and sunk hundreds of fishing boats, trawlers and steamships. England's mercantile marine was the object of the Teuton's attacks, and no one had anticipated any danger to Americans or American interests.

Germany had no reasons for desiring to attack American boats and she promised to mend her ways. There followed a brief period in which no vessels were sunk on which were Americans, and then without warning the campaign against all vessels was renewed. A dozen were sunk on which were American seamen or non-combatant passengers, none of whom was given warning or time to land before a torpedo sent the boat to the bottom of the ocean. Threats on the part of President Wilson to take action against Germany finally brought another cessation.

GROWING DISTRESS AND AMAZEMENT.

"The sinking of the British passenger steamship Fabala and other German acts constitute a series of events which the Government of the United States has observed with growing concern, distress and amazement," said President Wilson in a note on the submarine warfare. "This Government cannot admit the adoption of such measures or such a warning of danger as in any degree an abbreviation of the rights of American shipmasters or American citizens, bound on lawful errands as passengers on merchant ships of belligerent nationality. It must hold the Imperial German Government to a strict accountability for any infringement of those rights, international or incidental.

"The objection to their present method of attack lies in the practical impossibility of employing submarines in the destruction of commerce without disregarding those rules of fairness, reason, justice and humanity which all modern opinions regard as imperative.

"American citizens act within their indisputable rights in taking their ships and traveling wherever their legitimate business calls them upon the high seas.

"No warning that an unlawful and an inhuman act will be committed can possibly be accepted as an excuse or palliation for that act, or as an abatement of the responsibility for its commission. * * *

"The Imperial German Government will not expect the Government of the United States to omit any word or any act necessary to the performance of its sacred duty or the inalienable rights of the United States and its citizens, and of safeguarding their free exercise and enjoyment."

WHOLESALE DESTRUCTION OF VESSELS.

Apparently Germany modified her submarine policy for a period of upward of a year, or until in February, 1917, when to the astonished world she threw aside all pretense and declared her intention of destroying any vessel which attempted to cross or sailed into a zone which she established along the English coast and around English and French ports. America's further protests availed not; her citizens, many of them, went to the bottom of the seas, and some of them suffered almost unbelievable cruelties or neglect, when the captain of a German sea raider with some humanitarian instincts permitted these innocent passengers or seamen to be rescued from the torpedoed vessels on which they were.

Even the Red Cross vessels and Belgian relief ships carrying supplies and food to the maimed or sick at war and the starving children of Belgium did not escape the torpedo from the submarine. English hospital ships were attacked, and men unable to protect themselves were subjected to danger because the Germans feared that something might be carried on the boat which would prove valuable to the Allied forces in making war.

Dozens—even hundreds of vessels of all sorts—were sunk from week to week. Food and supplies for the Allied forces were destroyed, until both England and France were threatened with starvation.

All this was the work of the submarine.

One smiled twenty-five years ago when he read that highly imaginative story of Jules Verne, "Twenty Thousand Leagues Under the Sea," and wondered if it would ever be possible for man to create such a marvelous underseas craft as that which the famous French writer described. Today the imaginative detail of the submarine which the novelist described has been crystallized, and the world has learned that dreams sometimes come true.

Marvelous things have been developed by the war which is involving the peace and security of the world, but no single device has had such an effect upon the warfare and upon the methods of waging it as the diabolical submarine, which, like an assassin in the night, sneaks upon the great ships along the water highways of the world and sends them with their human freight to the bottom of the ocean.

TORPEDO'S DEADLY WORK.

A giant cigar-shaped missile, whose nose is pointed with guncotton and filled with high explosives—and which the world knows as the torpedo—launches forth from the submarine, and speeding under the drive of a propeller at the stern steers its way into the side of the battleship or great steamship. The torpedo plunges into the bowels of the vessel. There is a tremendous explosion, and the watertight compartments of the vessel are torn open; the boat fills, and the pride of the seas is no more.

Had the vessel's master and her crew any warning? No; unless the vigilant officer on the bridge should note a thin pole with a hooked end projecting above the surface of the ocean some miles away, and turning his glasses upon it discover that it is the "eye" of a submarine—the periscope—which is protruding above the surface. Then he may turn his larger vessel and ram the submarine, or change the course of his craft so that the torpedo launched by the submarine will miss its mark, or perhaps expert gunners may turn the muzzles of their rapid-fire guns upon the underseas craft and riddle it before it can get far enough below the surface of the water to make the attack upon it futile.

EFFICIENCY OF THE SUBMARINE.

The enormous inroads on the world's shipping made by German submarines during the war shows the efficiency of this diabolical device. In the first two years and a half of the war statistics were compiled to show that more than 10 per cent of the world's merchant marine was destroyed by Germany's underseas craft of the U-boat type. Incidentally, the name U-boat as applied to submarines developed because Germany, instead of naming these slinking boats, as is the custom with surface-cruising vessels, painted upon the conning tower or nose of the craft the letter U, representing the word "underseas," coupled with the numeral denoting the number of the boat. Thus those who sail the ocean highways came to recognize the fact that a conning tower or low, sharp-nosed craft bearing the mystic characters U-9 was a German underseas boat No. 9.

The statistical records at the end of April, 1917, showed that nearly 3000 vessels of almost 5,000,000 gross tons were destroyed by the U-boats in the war. More than half of the vessels sunk belonged to England. Norway and France were the next greatest sufferers from the submarine warfare. In one week after Germany announced her intention to give no quarter, but to sink any vessel which came within the range of the U-boat torpedoes, the toll of ships lost was more than 400,000 tons.

At the beginning of the war the submarine was to all intents and purposes a novelty—a boat of recognized possibilities, but existing very largely in the experimental stage. Its use was very largely ignored by naval men, although it was conceded that when properly developed it would prove a wonderful agency of destruction. The proud commanders of the great battleships, with their 10, 12 and 14 inch guns, which sent great shells miles across the ocean, looked down upon the little underseas boat, and applied to it the sobriquet of "tin sardine."

But the "tin sardine" has grown up, and the commander of the monster war vessel is at the mercy of the little craft which he ridiculed. A short time ago Holland, the American inventor of the modern submarine, died of a broken heart. His type was necessarily an experimental one. He built five boats before he was able to sell one to the United States Government, and this latter one, after being bought by a junk dealer, who intended to break it up for its metals, was finally rescued from such an inglorious end by the city of New York, which has placed it in her municipal museum.

PRINCIPLE OF THE SUBMARINE.

Germany has developed the highest type of submarines, which she has used to the fullest advantage. The principle of the submarine is that of a floating bottle. An empty bottle, as every one knows, will float on the surface, but submerges as soon as it is filled with water. The submarine has, as part of its constructive features, a number of compartments which, as they are filled or emptied of water, enables the craft to submerge or rise.

At the bow and stern, respectively, there are two horizontal rudders, and as these are manipulated at various angles so the bow points either upward or downward, and with a steady gliding motion the submarine slides under or is brought to the surface.

This, in brief, is the story of the submarine. Its history is another matter; its radius of action and results achieved one of the marvels of the ages. A long-sheathed body, the shape of a cigar with the butt end to the fore, the inside filled with machinery and compactness the order of the day, might be regarded as a fair description from a physical standpoint. It has spread terror to all corners of the earth, and, taken in proportion to its size and steaming radius, may well be said to be the superior of the superdreadnought.

The manner in which the submarine is operated is difficult to describe. It leads a sort of dual existence. When cruising along the surface "awash," it is propelled like a motorboat, the power being provided by a gasoline engine; but when it dives or submerges it is operated underwater by electric motors, and the steering, pumping, handling, loading and firing of the torpedoes is done pneumatically and electrically. The interior of the submarine is a marvel of mechanical complexity and scientific detail. There are gauges to show the water pressure, to indicate the speed, to show the depth; sensitive devices by which the commander can tell of the approach of vessels; wheels, cranks, levers and instruments which are used in driving and controlling this almost human mechanical agency of the seafighter.

SUBMARINE AN ANOMALY IN WARFARE.

The submarine is the sudden and amazing problem of the naval world. While naval men assert with confidence that it can never win the mastery of the seas, in the same breath they will admit that it may easily prevent the older and better known types of ships from establishing the mastery that was once theirs. It is an anomaly in warfare.

Many are the tales of horror told by survivors of ships which have been torpedoed by the undersea boats of the Teutons. The lordly Lusitania, on board of which were some of the leading lights of literature and some of the world's wealthy men, was sent to the bottom without the least warning. Neutral shipping has been devastated, and men, women and children have been murdered by the hand of the Kaiser, as exemplified in the lurking submarine.

One of the dastardly tragedies of the war was the sinking of the Lars Kruse, a ship flying the Danish flag and which had been chartered by the Belgian Relief Commission. This was sunk in the early part of February, 1917, and the crew of nineteen men, together with the captain and other officers, with the exception of the first mate and Axel Moeller, the first engineer, perished in the bitter cold sea. No warning was given by the attacking submarine; indeed, no sight of it was had by the crew. Delivering its torpedo as it lay submerged, it silently stole away into the night after the murders had been done.

In the maritime court in Copenhagen Mr. Moeller tells of the sinking of the ship. Dressed as the regulations of the German autocrat demanded, with the balloon, flag and bunting displayed at each of the mastheads, together with other marks of identification, the ship was steaming along in the bright moonlight when she was struck, according to the testimony of the engineer.

SHIP NOT STRUCK BY A MINE.

The fact that the ship was hit near the fourth hatch alone combats the theory that she was struck by a mine. In this latter case the mine would have struck her nearer the bow. The ship was near the mouth of the English channel when hit. In an instant she started to settle, and the crew at once lowered away the single lifeboat.

The boat had hardly started over the side, however, before the ship lurched, and with a mighty heave went down stern first. She seemed to turn a back somersault, according to the engineer, and because of the fact that the lifeboat was not clear it was dragged under. The men succeeded in cutting the ropes, however, and the lifeboat came to the surface, although bottom side up. Engineer Moeller was struck on the head as the boat came to the surface, but, although he was momentarily stunned, the icy water quickly revived him.

Striking out for the lifeboat, the engineer soon had a tight grip on her side. A man struggling in the water grasped his wrist, but by a quick movement he wrenched himself free, and then, climbing upon the boat, reached out and caught the man by the hand. Then began a slow struggle to get him aboard, but the men were unequal to the task, and the man in the water sank. Part of the skin and flesh of his hand remained in the fingers of Moeller, showing the desperation with which he had clung to the man's hand.

Three other men, who were fast becoming exhausted, were assisted upon the boat, where they lay sprawled across its bottom. Four others were in the water, making a total of seven who were alive.

Water and air were freezing cold, and Moeller, who was in the water, together with three others, held to the gunwales with stiffened fingers. Within the hour one of the sailors gave up the struggle, and with a farewell to the others slid quietly into the depths.

PASSENGERS' AGONIZING SUFFERINGS.

Finally Moeller climbed upon the upturned boat, where he lay listening to the shrieks of his companions. He said that their cries were most pitiful. The cabin boy was the next victim. He cried pitifully for a time, but finally became silent and slid into the water. One after another, the men died of exposure and slipped into the peaceful sea.

After a time the only persons remaining, besides the third mate, were the two who had thrown themselves across the bottom of the boat. Finally one of them gave up the struggle, and the other, in an effort to combat the cold, pulled the clothes from his dead body and wrapped them about himself. The boat settled a little, and finally both were corpses, lying with feet and hands dipping into the sea. The engineer said that he did not have the heart to push their bodies into the water, although he knew they were dead.

Finally the third mate was the only other man alive. The clothes of the engineer were frozen fast to his body, and he felt that he was dying of cold. The third mate started to get a sort of bluish black from the cold, and with a gasping cry he attempted to sit up straight. Then reason left him, and for a couple of hours he shouted and shrieked, and, as the sun began to streak the sky and dawn brought slight comfort, the demented man raved and swore.

Then a flash of reason seemed to return to him and he spoke to Moeller.

"I'm going," he said. "Give my love to my wife."

The man had been married just before starting on this ill-fated voyage. With this farewell message on his lips he died. When Moeller returned to his home he found that it was impossible to deliver the message to the wife of the dead man, because of the fact that worry had driven her insane.

TROUSERS USED AS SIGNAL.

Shortly after the death of his companion Moeller saw the smoke of a steamer on the horizon. Summoning all his strength, he tore the trousers from the limbs of one of the dead men, and, using them as a means of signaling, swung them about his head to attract attention. As the engineer made every effort to attract the attention of those aboard the steamship, he saw a sneaking submarine slowly edging toward her. This made him shout all the louder, thinking thereby to warn the captain of the ship of his danger. His efforts were vain, however, and in a short time the ship had gone to the bottom and the crew was adrift in the lifeboats. The sunken ship proved to be a Russian steamer.

In his efforts to attract the attention of the intended victim of the U-boat, the drifting man had attracted the attention of the captain of the submarine, and it was this boat to which his cold-stiffened body was hauled a few minutes later. It was a time before his numb body could be thawed out.

Seeming to know from which ship he had been cast off, the engineer was closely questioned by the captain of the submarine. As the captain talked he made motions, as though to shut out from before his eyes a horrible sight. He told Moeller afterwards that the most horrible sight he had ever seen was the overturned boat with the two corpses laying on it, and the lone man signaling for help. The victim was black from cold, and his legs were rubbed by members of the crew. Port wine was given him, and later food and coffee.

Then the captain continued his questioning. He knew the name of the boat on which Moeller had been engineer, and from his intimate knowledge of the sinking of her, the engineer felt sure it was his submarine that had done the work.

SUBMARINE TOWS RUSSIAN SHIP.

Turning his attention to the lifeboats of the Russian ship which he had just torpedoed, the captain of the submarine promised to tow them to the French coast. He had been towing them but two hours, however, when he came below and told Moeller that he had sighted a French destroyer, and that he would have to make his escape. He gave the engineer his choice of staying on the submarine, in which case it would be fourteen days before he touched port, after which he was promised his freedom, or the privilege of getting aboard one of the lifeboats, and taking his chances of rescue by the destroyer.

Electing to take his chances in the lifeboat, Moeller was fitted out with new clothing, the outfit being topped off with a fur-lined overcoat. It turned out, however, that the captain had taken this clothing from the stores of the Russian steamer before sinking her, and the engineer learned when he got into the lifeboat that he was wearing the greatcoat of one of the shivering Russians.

Just before submerging the U-boat set off a couple of red-light bombs, for the purpose of attracting the attention of the crew of the destroyer, and submerged. The drifters were picked up by the destroyer, which steamed for France. The captain of the U-boat had promised Moeller that he would not attack the destroyer, although he had been trailing her for two weeks. The U-boat was sunk before she reached port, and all perished.

An American importer who, because of his German name and the intimate relations he enjoyed with certain important men in Berlin, had been taken to the hearts of some of the leaders, became a factor in pro-German activities in Cuba. He was taken into the confidences of many of the officials and learned the plans of the Tirpitz group.

Deciding that his allegiance was American, he returned to the United States. In his possession were many of the inner secrets of the German Government, and these were given to the officials in Washington. His information with reference to the submarine has been of great value to the government.

For the sake of convenience we will call the man Johann Schmidt. This is his story:

THE U-BOAT TYPE OF SUBMERSIBLE.

Germany's most successful and highly developed class of submarine has been, of course, the U-boat type of submersible. These are the terrors of the sea which have succeeded in crossing the Atlantic, and have been developed both as the fighting and as the commercial U-boat.

Herr Schmidt reported that Germany was constructing submarines 25 per cent larger than anything the United States had ever seen or heard of. His information was to the effect that Germany had a building capacity for ten submarines a week. The ability to produce these boats with such rapidity is due to the process of standardization—the practice of modern efficiency which has made it possible for American factories to turn out such big quantities of automobiles in a limited period.

All parts of the German U-boats are made in standard sizes and from the same original pattern. Consequently, these parts are turned out by machinery in replica, and the building of the finished boats is merely a matter of assembling them at points to which the various parts have been shipped. The

Diesel oil engine, which is regarded as the ideal power-producing engine for submarines, has been developed to its highest state of efficiency by Germany, and is made at the famous Krupp gun works, the great engine works in Augsburg, Emden and Nuremburg, and other less well-known places in Germany.

It has been estimated that Germany has anywhere from 250 to 500 submarines, and it is said that the aim is to produce 1000 of these craft, to absolutely destroy the commerce of the seas and starve into submission England and France.

HOW SUBMARINES WORK.

According to Herr Schmidt, the submarines work in groups of four. Because of the limited capacity of the boats for carrying provisions, supplies and fuel, it is necessary for them to have supply bases, to which they can return and secure torpedoes. In operation each group consists of four submarines, traveling along in a diamond-shaped formation, one in front, one on either flank and one in rear. Eight miles separate the boats. The leading submarine carries the extra gasoline and supplies and acts as a scoutship; she sights a vessel, reports its speed and direction and then submerges—her task is done.

The two torpedo carriers on either flank immediately change their courses so as to converge on the prey, and they arrive one on either side of her—they get her in between them. The boat in the rear keeps them informed as to the doomed ship's progress, and submerges at the last moment. She carries the extra crews for the fighting pair. The U-boats are fairly well protected against the onslaught of the light torpedo-boat destroyers and chasers, because the decks are protected by several feet of water at almost all times, while the commanding tower is covered with from two to three inches of the best steel armor plate.

It is related that at the outset of the U-boat menace, England ordered its commanding officers to ram the U-boats on sight. The length to which the Germans will go in an effort to win is illustrated by the fact that, in consequence of this order, a Von Tirpitz council presented this answer: Attacking submarines were equipped with explosive mines containing 300 to 400 pounds of nitroglycerin or guncotton. To the top of this mine was fastened a fake periscope. This devilish device was attached to the submarine by a light cable, and towed along the surface of the water 1000 feet or more behind the submarine. The result that would follow any attempt on the part of a commander to run down one of these decoys is readily imagined.

DESCRIPTION OF A PERISCOPE.

The periscope is distinctly a submarine device which is worthy of brief description. It is, in effect, a long tube, with an elbow joint at the top and a similar one at the bottom. At the elbow joints at both ends are arranged reflectors. The reflector in the upper end catches the object which comes within the range of vision, and reflects the image down the tube to the mirror at the lower elbow, where the pilot sees it. The principle of the periscope is the same as that of the "busybody," familiar to householders, and which is placed on the sill of an upper window, so that a person inside the house may see who is at the front door.

The Germans have recently devised a new form of periscope, designed to make the device invisible to the lookout of approaching boats. This device consists of two mirrors, put together like a "Y" lying on its side, the wide part in front. These skim through the waves and converge the image upon the low periscope's lens, which shoots the light down the tube to the receiving apparatus below. When looked at from a distance the mirrors reflect the surface of the sea, so that a lookout sees nothing but the waves as they are reflected in the mirror.

The Germans use the bottom of the sea as regular "land" for their supply bases, and when the submarines go to the surface it is precisely like an aeroplane mounting the air. The submarine fleet boasts also of "mother boats." They lie on the bottom of the ocean, in designated places, and rise at night to hand out their supplies. Crews are changed and tired men go back to the bottom to rest up, while fresher comrades take their places.

So, too, the submarine, with its ability to rest on the bottom of the sea, has become an efficient boat for mine laying. The mine layers work from the undersea boats without fear of disturbance, the divers walking out from the submarines to the floor of the sea without being seen or without ever coming to the surface.

TALES OF REMARKABLE EXPLOITS.

American citizens landed from vessels sunk by German submarines tell remarkable tales of the strenuous exploits of the U-boats. In one case three undersea boats appeared simultaneously alongside the ship, one being a submarine cruiser, 300 feet long, and the others old-fashioned submarines, with a length of about 120 feet.

In another case a German submarine wore an elaborate disguise of a fishing boat. This submarine carried a gun which had a range of nearly five miles.

In at least two cases the crews of vessels sunk by submarines were rescued from open boats by passing ships, only to suffer a repetition of disaster when the ship on which they had taken refuge fell prey to an underwater boat.

A seaman from Pensacola, who was a member of the crew of a Swedish sailing vessel, said:

"We were almost within sight of land late in the afternoon when we observed a Norwegian sailing vessel in an encounter with a submarine eight miles away. Apprehending that our turn would come next, we prepared a lifeboat. A

300-foot submarine came up to us in due course and fired three warning shots from its heavy gun.

"We pulled our boat over to the lifeboat from the Norwegian ship previously sunk, and a dozen hours later were picked up by a British steamer. We had only a brief stay on the British boat, as she was torpedoed the same morning. After a few hours in the boats we were found by a British patrol and landed."

A Baltimore seaman from a Danish sailing vessel said:

THE SHIP ABANDONED.

"We abandoned ship in response to three shots from a submarine. Thereupon the submarine fired twenty-two shots into the hull of the ship, sinking her. We tried to speak with the submarine commander, but he told us he was in a hurry, as he had to attend to a Norwegian bark which was waiting a short distance off.

"We pulled for the nearest land, and all our twenty-five men got ashore safe, although both lifeboats were badly smashed up in the surf as we were beaching them."

A Philadelphian described the manner in which his steamer escaped being sunk.

"We were attacked by a submarine disguised as a fishing vessel," he said. "She opened fire on us at five miles, sending fifteen shots at us, and smashing our wireless. She pursued us for an hour. We did not use our gun. Finally a British patrol boat appeared. The submarine submerged, disguise and all, presenting a ludicrous sight as the carefully prepared equipment simulating a fishing boat sank beneath the waves."

The captain of an American sailing ship which was sunk said:

"Submarines are lying along the sea lanes in regular nests. They keep well under the water most of the time, coming up now and then for periscopic observations, or on hearing the approach of merchant craft, which often can be identified readily by the sound of the engines. By thus conserving fuel the submarines are able to remain away from their base a long time, and also they find means of renewing their stores from ships which they sink.

"The U-boat which sank us had been out for six weeks. She had one British captain on board. She renewed all her supplies from our boat and took all the nautical instruments. The submarine gave us a sharp signal to halt, with a shell from a distance of two miles. It was good marksmanship. The shot hit the ship squarely, but caused no casualties. We stopped and took to the boats. The submarine came up in leisurely fashion, sank the ship with bombs and passed the time of day with our boats. She had a crew of thirty-seven, and was 250 feet long.

"We were picked up by a Norwegian sailing vessel, on which we spent six days. She was then attacked by a 120-foot submarine. We all took to the Norwegian's boats. The submarine commander declined to look at the Norwegian captain's papers. We had another twenty-four hours in open boats, and then were picked up by a British patrol and landed."

CHAPTER V.

THWARTING THE U-BOAT.

Nets to Entangle the Sea Sharks of War — "Chasers" or "Skimming-dish" Boats—"Blimps" and Seaplanes—Hunting the Submarine with "Lance," Bomb and Gun—A Sailor's Description.

THE advantage which Germany gained by the development of what has been termed the supersubmarine placed the other nations where it became absolutely necessary for them to concentrate their energies in an effort to counteract the devastation which the U-boats brought upon the seas. England tried first to protect the English channel and many of its ports with mines, floating bombs and submarine nets, and while the latter served as barriers which prevented the submarines penetrating into some of the important waters and harbors, they could act merely in a protective sense.

The submarine net is a specially devised net with heavy iron or wire meshes, similar to a fishing net. These nets—miles in length—were born of the nets originally devised to sweep harbors clear of mines. They are carried between two boats described as trawlers, which are a form of sea-going tug with powerful engines, that can draw a heavy load. A heavy cable runs from trawler to trawler, and from this the chain net is suspended in the water. It is heavily weighted at the bottom so as to hold it in a perpendicular position. The trawlers steaming along, side by side, sweep up with the net anything which may be placed in the water for the purpose of blowing up or injuring vessels.

The submarine nets in some places have been anchored to form a regular barrier against the passage of submarine boats, and in this way were effective, but their use could in no way restrict the underseas boats in their work upon the open seas.

The most effective plan of overcoming the dire consequences of the U-boat warfare was found, therefore, to lie in the use of submarine chasers and airships, the two operating together in conjunction with the battleships, cruisers and torpedo boat destroyers.

The submarine chaser is a light-draught, high-powered, skimming-dish type of husky motorboat, mounting rapid-fire, 3 or 4-inch guns. In order to prove effective against the submarine it is necessary to have many of these boats, and it is a matter of particular interest that the marvelous resources of the United States at the time of her entrance into the war enabled her to immediately begin a campaign for the construction of chasers, which would be able to guard the seas in the channels of traffic and along the ports into which the submarine might attempt to sneak.

NO EXPERT NAVAL KNOWLEDGE REQUIRED.

The operation of the chaser does not require the degree of technical skill and knowledge of naval strategy required in the handling of ships of the naval type. A fleet of chasers is manned largely by naval reserves, who have a certain amount of training, but who are neither navigators nor experts in naval affairs. The operations are, however, directed by the naval authorities.

The submarine chaser is effective because it draws very little water, has high speed, can be quickly turned and diverted from its course and does not present any great depth of hull at which the submarine can fire a torpedo. It would be possible for a torpedo to pass under a chaser without hitting it—if the submarine cared to waste such an expensive weapon on so small an adversary. When the submarine attempts to come to the surface and use the rapid-fire gun with which she is armed she is at a disadvantage, because it takes her several minutes to emerge. Additional time is required to swing the gun up through its automatic hatch while the men scramble to the deck to man it.

The chaser, with a speed of approximately 35 to 40 miles

an hour, will travel somewhere between a mile and a half to two miles in this period. Its gun has been ready from the start, and the chaser has had half a dozen shots or so with only a single hit needed to put the submarine out of commission. Even if the submarine is at the surface and has her gun mounted ready for action, she is at a disadvantage with the chaser. The chaser, taking advantage of her speed and small size, goes skimming across the water at the rate of 40 miles an hour, and it takes a mighty fine gunner to be able to hit a small craft, going in a zigzag course over the water at such speed.

The chaser may continue to circle the submarine awaiting her opportunity which will of necessity come when the U-boat attempts to submerge. The submarine must go through the regular form of running back her gun, and battening down the water-tight hatches, before she can submerge, and the latter process again takes several minutes. Therefore while the submarine is preparing to dip, the chaser can run upon her and let loose the fire from its rapid-fire gun.

A POOR SURFACE FIGHTER.

The submarine, by very virtue of the qualities which make it a good submarine, is a poor boat for surface fighting. It can carry no very heavy armament, and it is not heavily armored. The problem of stowing away all the heavy machinery, supplies, torpedoes and devices necessary for her operations and maneuvering has presented about all the difficulties the constructors have been able to handle. The highest speed of the submarine is not in execess of 20 miles an hour. The submarine must be light and easy to handle. It gains in steadiness and certainty of operation with increased size, but it loses in capacity for quick and delicate maneuvering.

In addition the submarine has what is termed a strategic vulnerability. A shot which might mean nothing more serious than a hole in the side to a surface boat would end the submarine's usefulness for underseas work and convert her into a helpless hulk of surface craft.

The submarine is an easy quarry for a chaser, for even when submerged and moving along, the U-boat creates a distinct wave on the surface of the water which can be followed by the chaser. The little boats are just what their name implies—chasers—and besides having the qualities already described they may conceal themselves behind large steamers, and when the submarine in preparing to launch a torpedo makes its presence known the chaser may speed from its hiding place and drive the underseas craft away, even if it does not succeed in injuring it.

OPERATING IN CONNECTION WITH AN AEROPLANE.

The chasers also have a special facility of operation in connection with the aeroplane or seaplane, principally because of their high speed; and next to the chaser the aeroplane is one of the submarine's worst enemies. Used in conjunction with the regular torpedo boat destroyers of the navy, the chaser and the aeroplane promise in future wars to minimize the effectiveness of the underseas craft. This is proven by the fact that immediately after the United States naval forces joined those of the Allies in European waters, the disasters resultant upon submarine attacks were greatly reduced. The speedy destroyers, while not actually sinking many submarines, by their vigilance prevented the submarine from operating.

Large types of the chasers ordered in this country by the Russian Government are 72 feet long by 11 feet 3 inches wide and draw 3 feet 3 inches of water. Each boat carries three of the 8-cylinder $6\frac{3}{4}$x$7\frac{3}{4}$ Duesenberg, 350 to 400 horsepower motors. The boats carry an 18-inch torpedo tube amidships and a 47-millimetre rapid-fire gun on the forward deck. They are controlled from the bridge deck with a sheltered cabin for the quartermaster, with controls from either the shelter or bridge deck. They have a guaranteed speed of twenty-eight knots.

Deck arrangements consist of the following: A hatch to the fo'castle, followed by the emplacement for the rapid-fire gun. Following this is the steering shelter containing duplicate controls, &c., for the engine room and for the steering. Immediately aft of the steering shelter is the bridge deck, located on top of the engine room trunk house. The entire after half of the vessel is a clear sweep of deck with the exception of a booby hatch to crews' quarters well aft.

The boats are arranged for wireless with foremast and jigger mast. Rail stanchions in the way of the torpedo tube are hinged down, giving clear sweep to the tube for firing purposes.

PROVISION FOR OFFICERS AND CREW.

Below decks ample space has been provided for the crew and officers. The forepeak is arranged for chain lockers and bosun's gear lockers, followed by ship's galley, which has two pipe berths. Next to the galley is located the officers' cabin and wireless room, which is entered by a hatch from the steering shelter. This cabin accommodates two officers and includes lavatory, officers' desks, wireless desk and folding mess table.

Next aft is the machinery space, in which are located the three eight cylinder Duesenberg motors, a three k. w. universal lighting set, the necessary oil tanks, batteries and a work bench. The next compartment contains fuel tanks, with 1300 gallons capacity. Aft of this compartment is located the crew's quarters, berthing eight men, with lavatory attached. The hull is divided into six watertight compartments by steel bulkheads.

The hull is of wooden construction, as developed for this service by the builders.

The 72-footers develop a speed of twenty-eight knots and have a cruising radius exceeding 1200 miles. The design of the hull is the concave bottom, square bilge type, developed for this particular service. It furnishes a steady gun platform, which, with the necessary speed, is the most vital feature of a submarine chaser.

The demand for speed and stability was borne out by the experience of the Russian and Italian navies in their active work and no consideration at all is given propositions from these two countries which do not range well about twenty-five knots.

Exceptional success was attained by the Russian Black Sea and by the Italian high speed fleets in actual use and their demand for exceptional speed was based on experience.

It is a well known fact that the Russian government was successful in patroling its shores and in protecting its harbors and shipping. The Italian government also was exceptionally successful in maintaining its mercantile fleet in comparative safety and in protecting its harbors against the offensive work of enemy submarines. The entire Italian fleet of submarine chasers consists of high speed, high powered motor patrol boats, most of which were equipped with American made motors.

CATALOGUED AS "PATROL BOATS."

In a general way the "chasers" are catalogued in naval circles as "patrol boats." England has thousands of them, ranging from motorboats to naval auxiliaries, raking the English Channel, the North Sea and the waters all about the British Isles. As a rule the boats work in groups of five or six, one boat serving as a flagship—and often there is a "blimp" attached to the fleet. The armament of these small vessels is distinctive. Each carries, besides a deck gun, a "depth charge," half a dozen lance bombs and arms for each member of the crew. The deck gun fires a shell that weighs about thirteen pounds.

The "depth charge" is a submarine bomb, so constructed that it is discharged at any determined depth of water when thrown overboard. If the water is 100 feet deep the bomb will explode at that depth. The bombs are used to drop in places where the submarine has been located or is expected of lurking in the bottom of the sea. While the exploding bomb may not strike the underseas boat it will create havoc on board the underwater craft if discharged in close proximity, the extra water pressure exerted causing disarrangement of the delicate mechanism, if not rendering the boat unfit for service.

Some of the patrol boats of the English have been armed with "lance bombs." These are bombs of highly explosive character which are fastened to the end of a long pole or staff. They are used just as a harpoon is used when by chance a submarine may emerge from the water in too close proximity to the chaser. It is not of record that any U-boats have been sunk with these strange javelins, but official reports show that the boats are armed with them for emergencies.

CHASER TROUBLES THE SUBMARINE.

What with dragging bombs through the water, and setting traps and nests for the submarines, the chasers make great trouble for the underseas craft, but the ingenious Germans are constantly on the alert, and it has been proved that in one or two instances at least the submarines cut their way through the heavy chain nets which were set to catch them near Havre. It was said that the submarine was provided with steel knives or wire cutters, and shears operated by electricity or pneumatic pressure, which enabled the boat to cut its way through the barrier of chains and wires.

As a means of visualizing the operations of the "chaser" and giving some idea of the excitement which attends the attempt to run down the under-seas craft, the following description by an English sailor is interesting. The chase occurred off the Isle of Wight:

"Offshore a short distance was a patrol boat lying very low and flying distress signals. We had run over to her and learned that about an hour before the periscope of a submarine had been stuck up not far from her, then the craft had submerged, appeared again about a mile away, and fired four shots, which let in enough water slowly to sink the patrol, which before the war had been nothing but a dirty little trawler.

"Finding the crew of the patrol could take care of themselves in their small boats and learning that the submarine had run over to the westward, where we knew chain net traps to be laid, we circled in that direction.

"Our powerful motors thrummed evenly. The water seemed to part ahead of us, and the gunners squinted along the surface, looking for the glimpse of a periscope or the first sign of the hull of the U-boat if she should be proceeding awash.

CREW THRILLED WITH JOY.

"Suddenly, off to the west, we made out her periscope. Intense joy thrilled our little crew. She was inshore from us. She was between our circular course and the chain nets—in the trap. The periscope we had seen might be a dummy, for a submarine frequently casts loose a phoney periscope to draw fire, but, at any rate, she must have been between us and the nets if she cut it loose.

"Presently, probably after a look around, the periscope suddenly disappeared, and we knew it was a real one with a German U-boat on the end of it. Like a flock of falcons we were swooping down on the prey.

"Abruptly the lead boat comes to a dead stop and lists heavily to starboard. Evidently something is wrong. We see men crawl out over the stern and fish around with boat hooks and poles. Cold as it is, one man goes overboard and remains under water so long we could not believe he would come up alive. The boat had fouled the chain nets.

"Circling round in an ever smaller radius, we search the water for a periscope, a shadow, or the conventional "streak of dirty grease' or 'line of bubbles.'

"All of us have towing torpodoes out. These are bombs on long cables which are towed astern and sink to a certain specified depth. If the cable fouls anything at all, as the boat goes ahead, the bomb pulls up to it, and, when it bumps, it explodes.

"We are in line. Suddenly there is a crash and a roar just ahead of us. I am thrown off my feet. Barrels of water splash down into our cockpit and roll off the decks. The bow lifts itself clean for a second. I think that the submarine has blown us up. Perhaps I am dead already.

"Then we settle down again, and except for a scared look on the faces of a couple of men and rather nervous, forced jests on the lips of others, we are plowing ahead just as before.

"Nothing has happened except the towing torpedo of the boat in front of us in the line fouled a submerged spar, or a bit of wreckage, and exploded right under our bow. 'If we had been a few yards closer we would never have been there any more.'

FOULS A SUBMERGED SPAR.

"As we realized what had happened, our tongues were loosened, and, if the crew of the boat ahead could have heard what we said about them, we would have lost their friendship most assuredly.

"Way inshore, after a circling chase of perhaps twenty minutes, the submarine came up. She was in such shallow water that she probably was having trouble in operating submerged. She was gone then.

"What followed was very business-like. It illustrates the attitude the British have come to take toward the submarines because of their flagrant violations of every form of international law and decency. It is the attitude which any country, obliged to fight against them, will assume. To the British mind, submarines must be exterminated, just as one would exterminate a nest of poisonous vipers, or a nest of hornets. People ask me how many submarines are being captured now. Very few! Many are destroyed, but few captured.

"No sooner did the hull of the submarine show itself than

we began to hammer her with our three-inch guns. She opened fire, but her shots went wild, and, in a few seconds, she disappeared.

"As fast as we could, we ran over to where she had gone down. If the principles which obtain on land, in the air or in the navy at large, existed in submarine warfare, we would have gone over to see if we could rescue any of the wounded, but it was a U-boat and we simply made sure that there was nothing left of the craft.

"About where she went down, a quantity of gas and air bubbles were rising, and the dirty patch of oil was once more in evidence. That was a pretty certain sign the career of one U-boat was at an end, for the sea must have been pouring into her, and even though all her crew did not drown, once the salt water reached the storage batteries, the chloride would do the work.

WERE TAKING NO CHANCES.

"But we are taking no chances. We circle round and round the spot and drop depth bombs—deadly machines. These are powerful explosives which are set so they will detonate at a certain depth. We first sounded the bottom and then set our bombs for ten fathoms. Suddenly I hear a cry from the boat behind us. One of the crew reaches out, grabs the collar of a man who has just dropped a depth bomb over the stern and yanks him unceremoniously into the cockpit. At a glance I see what has happened.

"The engineer has stalled his motor—just as the bomb was let go. It sinks slowly, and there is a slight momentum left in the submarine-chaser. We hold our breath and watch in suspense, expecting any second to see our comrades hurled into the air among a mushroom of water and splinters.

"There is no way to help them. Suddenly there is a muffled roar, a column of water rises to what seems a hundred feet, and falls back, drenching every one who is near it. But our comrades are unhurt. The momentum of their boat has carried them just far enough to save them from being blown to atoms. That is the second narrow escape for our little squadron in this chase after a single submarine.

"But our work is done. There is no doubt now about the fate of the U-boat. It is not necessary for one of the depth bombs actually to come in contact with the submerged craft to destroy it. When under water, a submarine's rigidity is multiplied. Its elasticity is next to nothing. An explosion as powerful as that of a depth bomb near it, is almost certain to cripple it if not destroy it. It is the same principle as that which kills fish in a pond when dynamite is exploded beneath the surface of the water. The shock is sufficient to kill the men in the U-boat, and so we glide along homeward, secure in the knowledge that even if our gunfire did not finish the enemy, the bombs have done the work. On the surface, we notice swarms of dead fish."

THE HAWK-EYED AEROPLANE.

The last wrinkle developed for submarine hunting was the aeroplane. Like a fish-hawk it can see its prey beneath the water by flying high in air. Another step just a bit in advance of aeroplane scouting for submarines is the use of a small dirigible for the same purpose. But the cleverest development of the aeroplane-submarine idea involved the use of seaplanes for the purpose of launching submarine torpedoes at enemy ships.

Here's how this is practiced. As most folks know, the seaplane differs from the land-flying craft in that it rides on floats instead of wheels. These floats permit the seaplane to come to rest on the waves, and to launch itself again. Between these floats, which resemble a pair of broad home-made sleds, may be slung a torpedo. The same type of missile, this, that is used by the submarine and the destroyer—a long, cigar-shaped cylinder, operated by compressed air driving a propeller, and equipped with a warhead filled with guncotton. The torpedo is held by slings, delicately adjusted so that they can be released in an instant.

The great seaplane, swinging the missile of death between, its giant floats, climbs the skies in search of an enemy ship. From a distance of miles, perhaps, the seaplane looks like a gull. To the observer in the plane, however, sweeping the horizon with his binoculars, a ship is plainly and easily seen.

NOT TO BE OUT-DISTANCED.

Off in the distance is spied a ship suspected of being an enemy transport. It isn't hard to determine—the ship cannot steam away from them, no matter how swift its engines. A seaplane can go so fast that it makes the fastest torpedo boat destroyer look as if it were standing still. The attacked transport may try to bring its anti-aircraft guns to bear, if luckily it is equipped with them. Failing this, the soldiers will man the decks with their rifles ready. Then there is a duel of skill and daring between the men on the cruiser and the lone fighters in the seaplane.

The seaplane must swoop sufficiently close to the water to release the torpedo and let it drop without damage. And this must be done from a sufficient distance to safeguard the seaplane from the vessel's guns. The superior speed and mobility of the seaplane gives it a great advantage over the ship attacked.

Another of the weapons or instruments of warfare devised largely for use in destroying the evil submarine is the "blimp." This is nothing more nor less than a small dirigible balloon, hundreds of which the United States government started to build when it entered the war.

The blimp is an aerial sea-scout. Its principal employment is for observation. It is a watcher of enemy movements on the water. But it is also serviceable for attack, and especially for assailing submarines.

The British used blimps for the latter purpose, and to great advantage. The dirigible sausage-balloon, when a submarine is descried, can hover over it (as an aeroplane cannot), remaining as nearly stationary as may be desired, and waiting for an opportunity to drop a bomb with accurate aim.

If the submarine be under water, and its presence betrayed by the peculiar surface-ripple that marks its wake, a bomb with a delay-action fuse can be dropped upon it, the projectile not exploding until it reaches a depth of fifty feet or so. In case the first bomb does not score a hit, there are others to follow, with better luck perhaps.

THE IMPORTANCE OF THE "BLIMP."

Thus, it will be seen that the blimp is an important auxiliary of the flying-machine in the pursuit of the submarines. Both together, in this exciting sport, supplement the swift power-boats called "submarine-chasers."

For some time the Navy Department has trained enlisted men and officers for this work, chiefly at a Gulf port, where a school—it is no war secret—of aviation and ballooning has been maintained. Six officers and 40 men are required for each coast station.

The Navy Department adopted for the blimp a standardized pattern, with definite published specifications, in accordance with which contractors turned them out in numbers. It is a sausage-shaped balloon 160 feet long, with a great diameter of $31\frac{1}{2}$ feet, and containing, when inflated, 77,000 cubic feet of hydrogen gas.

The fabric of the "envelope"—that is to say, of the gasbag—is coated both outside and inside with rubber. It is required that the balloon shall not lose more than 1 per cent of its gas-content in 24 hours. When inflated it must be able to carry (including its own weight) a total of 5275 pounds.

If the "Zeppelin" be excepted, the blimp is the most highly-developed and scientific heavier-than-air flying machine ever devised. It has a cruising speed of 35 miles an hour, but at a pinch can travel ten miles an hour faster. At the "cruising" rate, it carries enough gasoline to keep going for sixteen hours; at 45 miles, its load of "petrol" will suffice for ten hours.

Even the best war balloons of a few years ago were at the mercy of the winds. It is not so with the blimp. Barring storms, it is able to navigate the air as it wishes. It can rise safely to an altitude of a mile and a half. To furnish fuel for its engine of 100 horsepower it carries, in two tanks, 100 gallons of gasoline.

DESCRIPTION OF THE "BLIMP."

In effect, the blimp is a combination of balloon and aeroplane. Like the latter, it is provided with "skids" (resembling sled runners and made of ash wood), or sometimes with bicycle wheels, for safe landing on terra firma. When designed for sea scouting, floats—cylinders of waterproof fabric stuffed with vegetable fibre—are attached to the skids, or to the wheels, so that the airship, in calm weather, may be able to rest, like a sea bird, on the waves, if desired.

The blimp's balloon envelope must contain two smaller balloons, together holding 19,250 feet of hydrogen gas. The idea, of course, is that if anything happens to the major balloon—puncturing by gunfire or by other mishap—the "balloonets" inside of it will keep the machine afloat.

The wingless aeroplane is suspended from the balloon by cables of galvanized wire. There is a special arrangement by which the "pilot"—the man who steers and operates the airship—can at any time measure the pressure of hydrogen in the balloon, thus knowing what he has to count on in the way of carrying power.

The front part of the blimp's car is occupied by the engine and radiator, behind which is a bulkhead of sheet steel. In the rear of this bulkhead sits the pilot, and behind him the "observer," who makes sketches and takes notes of anything important that he sees. Behind the observer are the tanks for fuel oil and 300 gallons of water ballast. The body of the car is covered with aeroplane linen, save for the engine, which is sheathed with sheet aluminum.

In order to hold whatever position in the air may be desired, the blimp is equipped with two horizontal fins and three vertical fins. Not every blimp, that is to say, but the pattern approved and required of contractors by the Navy Department. These fins are made of wood and light steel tubing, reinforced with wire, covered with aeroplane linen rubber painted and finished with varnish.

THE "BLIMP" WELL EQUIPED.

There are also two horizontal rudders and two vertical rudders, for steering up and down or sidewise. They work on ball bearings. A blimp, one should understand, is a fish in the ocean of air, a swimmer—just as the aeroplane is a flyer, like the bird.

The blimp's "car" carries an electric storage battery to furnish lights. The same battery energizes a searchlight for night scouting. A wireless apparatus, for transmitting information to the shore station, is part of the equipment.

The blimp, as already stated, is a sea scout. It is meant to be operated from a base on shore—which base is in constant communication by telegraph and wireless with the great radio stations that are strung all along our coasts at intervals of 200 miles. These stations, in turn, are in communication with the huge wireless outfit at Arlington (across the Potomac from Washington), whose "antennae," uplifted on tall steel towers, receive instantaneous war news from half the world.

Thus if (just for illustration) a blimp spies a hostile submarine, the news is instantly transmitted to the Navy Department. The department orders its "chasers" and warplanes nearest to the scene to go after the undersea boat. Within a few minutes the pursuit has started, and the U-boat finds itself in much the same situation as a fox hunted by hounds. In this case, however, the hounds are in the air, as well as "quartering" the aqueous terrain.

The United States' blimps are modeled on European patterns. But they are to have special improvements of their own. To make sure of their efficiency and structural correctness, each contractor, in offering bids to furnish them, was required to exhibit a model, exactly like the sausage balloons he proposed to make, but of toy size—one-thirtieth the length of the full-sized, completely equipped aerial sea scout.

CHAPTER VI.

THE EYES OF BATTLE.

AEROPLANES AND AIRSHIPS—THEY SPY THE MOVEMENTS OF FORCES ON LAND OR SEA—LEAD DISASTROUS BOMB ATTACKS—VALUABLE IN "SPOTTING" SUBMARINES—THE BOMBARDMENT AT MESSINES RIDGE.

JUST as the submarine has revolutionized warfare on the seas and presented new problems for the naval experts to solve, so the aircraft of the last decade has had its effect upon the operation of land forces. Probably the aeroplane and the dirigible balloon have had a greater influence on the conduct of battles and military campaigns as a whole than any other device utilized in connection with the war.

It is significant, too, that just as America produced the first submarine, and then failed as a nation to develop it to its highest state of efficiency for military use, so American inventors were pioneers in the construction and successful operation of aeroplanes, or airplanes, which were first developed to their greatest efficiency and utility by the French and Germans.

Some of the most striking events of the war centre around the use of the airplanes or dirigibles, and aside from the picturesqueness and thrilling atmosphere that seem to surround their use, the operator of the aircraft has proved himself one of the most valuable servants in modern warfare. He has reduced the proudest cavalry to second place in the matter of reconnoissance, and has rendered services which have heretofore been impossible.

The air-man sails out over the lines of battle, so far above the earth when necessary as to be out of range of the most powerful guns, and with glasses looks down upon the whole country. His machine, whether it be a dirigible balloon or airplane, is equipped with a wireless telegraph instrument with which he is able to send brief messages back to his own line or military headquarters. He can and does mark the changed positions of the contending forces, note the entrenchments and reinforcements, follow movements, and last but not least, as was noticeable in one of the desperate attacks upon the German position in June, 1917, swoop down upon the enemy, attack the lines and forces with bombs, and rain bullets upon them from rapid-fire guns.

No longer can the enemy mask its heavy batteries or conceal them beneath earthen mounds, plant them in corners of the forests or in clumps of bushes without their being located. The "eyes of the sky," as the planes are now termed, can spy them out. And when the airman has communicated to his military commanders the positions of the opposing batteries, he acts as a director in instructing the friendly gunners in finding the range and cleaning out the enemy.

THE AIR SCOUT'S USEFULNESS.

The air scout can detect the enemy's lines of communication and raid it with bomb attacks. Even when the land forces cannot reach the enemy with gunfire he can rain missiles of all sorts upon them. Sometimes the airman flies over the enemy lines and drops glittering tinsel or bright metal devices, which falling to the ground serve as marks for the artillerymen in finding the range.

Where the cavalry scout or creeping scout of days gone by could never have proved successful, the airman has easily accomplished his purpose. He has carried messages from one frontier to another in hours, when it would have taken days for a scout on horseback or on foot to have rendered the service, if they could have accomplished it at all. He has eliminated distance.

Trench warfare developed in the world-war in a way that has never before been deemed necessary or possible, but the miles of trenches which conceal the men from the fire of the enemy are plainly visible to the airmen. And armed with cameras having powerful telescopic lenses they can photograph the entire scene and send to their own military headquarters not mere indicated plans of the battle lines, but exact photographs.

The war has shown conclusively that once the formation of the battle line has been decided upon it is, in a measure, a fixture. It may be subject to rearrangement, but this is when the force of battle demands, or for strategic purposes, but such an arrangement requires a great deal of time and much work. The battle fronts on the borders of France and Belgium have ranged from 100 to nearly 300 miles in length, with nearly 3,000,000 strung out in opposing lines along the entire distance.

LIKE AN IMMENSE GRIDIRON.

The ground has been dug up and trenched until the surface of the earth looks like an immense gridiron. The soldiers almost live within the trenches and dug-outs beneath the ground. Telephone and telegraph wires run through the trenches and even railroad tracks are laid so that small engines go whirring through the ditches like "dinky" locomotives in a coal mine.

And the "eyes in the skies" make it possible for the commanders to know each other's strength and the disposition of the forces at all times.

Particularly has the air scout proved valuable in enabling commanders to execute their final orders without grievous error. There is danger of possible misjudgment because of the great length of the firing lines. The airmen verify positions and make last minute reports, taking minutes to perform services that cavalry forces or other scouting parties would have taken hours or days to render.

Operated in conjunction with cavalry scouts, and motor and cycle squads, the airplane is a destruction-directing and defensive force. And it was the large fleet of aircraft that aided Germany in making such rapid advance in its drive toward Paris in the early days of the war. The scouts reconnoitering in the early dawn were able to report the situation and give the commanders time to move their forces before the Belgians and French were aware of what was being done.

Germany had probably the largest fleet of airplanes at the beginning of the conflict and is said to have possessed upward of 500, of various sorts, and this does not include the famous Zeppelins or dirigible balloons. She also had something like two dozen factories which could turn out flying machines, and had been at work on the development of her air craft long enough to have her patterns and methods of manufacture somewhat, if not entirely standardized. During the third year of the war it was estimated that she had more than quadrupled her force of flying machines.

GERMANY'S PREPAREDNESS.

Germany's preparedness in this as well as in other directions was what enabled her to obtain such a tremendous advantage in the beginning of the war. Later England and France concentrated on the development of aeroplane squads or corps, and when the United States entered the war one of the first detachments sent into France consisted of 100 aviators. How rapidly the aeroplane forces were developed is indicated by the statement made in the beginning of 1916 that the air forces of the Allies were represented by 3380 aeroplanes of various types and 64 dirigible balloons, while Austria and Germany had 2000 aeroplanes and 70 dirigibles.

The dirigibles—the type of airship commonly referred to as Zeppelins—have the advantage over the heavier-than-air machines of being almost silent in their operations, while at the same time they can remain for a longer time suspended in air over a camp or battleground without being detected. The Zeppelin is the development of the old balloon, made, however, in a conical shape with a long basket or car attached. They are driven by propellers similar to those used with aeroplanes, but as the power generated by the engines is merely used to drive the machines and has nothing to do with maintaining their position in the air, the motors do not have to be so powerful. They are steered by rudders.

Some of the largest Zeppelins which have been leading factors in night raids conducted by the Germans on London and English coast resorts are capable of maintaining a speed of 60 miles an hour. One of these immense Zeppelins was reported to have covered 1300 miles in less than forty hours, covering the German borders, and still keeping in touch with its base. The Zeppelins, because of their large size, can carry large quantities of bombs, wireless apparatus, signals and electric searchlights. They can rise to a height that places them fairly beyond the range of the aerial guns used for fighting the air forces of the army.

MANY KINDS OF BOMBS.

The bombs used are as diversified as the crafts on which they are carried. The French aviators at one time dropped long steel billets or arrows which had swedged heads and sharpened points. These missiles, dropped from the height of a thousand feet or more, attained a velocity and force which made them dangerous weapons of the minor sort.

The bombs, in the main, however, consist of jacketed shells containing high explosives, some of which are constructed on what is called the delayed-action principle. Such bombs explode after penetrating the fort or object which they strike, instead of going off by contact. Germany is said to have developed some of these that were of such size and power as to penetrate an armored ship. As much as 50 pounds of explosives or chemicals is declared to have been carried in some of the larger ones.

The big dirigibles mount machine guns of superior range.

Some of them have been armored to an extent, and to make them less easily detected they have been painted tints and colors to harmonize with the clouds and sky. Special kinds of gas have been used to fill the envelopes or bags, and instead of one large bag they consist of a series of bags enclosed in an envelope or casing, so that if a bullet would penetrate the envelope it would only destroy one of the gas bags, and not cause the whole thing to collapse.

Besides having proved of great value in the land campaigns, the aircraft has shown itself to be one of the most effective devices of warfare for use against the submarine, and all manner of naval craft. From the heavens they can see the submarine under the water, and as either the dirigible or the aeroplane can develop a speed greater than that of any battleship or cruiser, it is not difficult for it to soar over the vessel and drop bombs upon it. Even gas bombs have been used in the raids by the aircraft.

ACCURACY THE GREAT DIFFICULTY.

The difficulty in the use of bombs has been in accurately directing the death-dealing devices when the airship or aeroplane is in motion. To assist in this work aerial range finders have been devised. These are constructed on the principle of the finder on a camera, with graded scale markings to indicate the allowance that must be made for speed and motion. Complete apparatus has been built up for launching the projectiles from the large dirigibles, and to insure the missiles traveling properly vanes have been attached to some of them.

In a test made under the auspices of the French Government and the Aerial Club of France, a few years ago, one of the bomb-launching machines on an aeroplane scored eleven bull's-eye shots in a target ten yards in diameter, from an altitude of more than 2000 feet, while the aeroplane was going at a speed of more than 65 miles an hour.

Though there has not been any widespread use of the plan

the air has been "mined" in an experimental way to protect certain sections against night raids by the airmen. Mining the air consists of locating small balloons over an area, each balloon being attached to the other with wires. The small balloons have attached to them explosive bombs which would destroy the larger aircraft if it was to run into this nest of air vessels in the dark.

Reverting to the use of aircraft in naval warfare it may be said that to the aeroplane the relatively fast fleet is virtually stationary. About the only case parallel to the aeroplane looking over the hill and down on concealed enemy positions would be in rising above the smoke screen thrown out by destroyers.

THE SMOKE SCREEN.

The smoke screen, by the way, which has been used by the British with marked success in many instances, is an American invention. The low, swift craft are equipped with special oil burners which throw off dense volumes of heavy smoke, which float low over the surface of the water, concealing the maneuvers of the larger boats and protecting them from the skill of enemy gunners. Its effectiveness, of course, is influenced by the direction and strength of the wind. Used generously by small craft convoying a ship through a submarine area, it should be of great value.

A battleship can see about as far as it can shoot, anyhow. Except for smoke screen, or the famous "low visibility," which means foggy weather or darkness, no enemy within range can be concealed.

What the fleet commander wants to know is how those enemy vessels beyond the horizon, which may be within range of his guns tomorrow, the day after, or next week, may be distributed, and how many of them there are. This is where the speed of the airplane comes in.

A machine which can travel 100 miles an hour covers a thousand miles in 10 hours. Locating an approaching enemy fleet this distance away, it brings back the news of the approach in 10 hours. It takes the fleet, traveling at 15 miles an hour, two days and 18 hours to cover this distance. The aeroplane can beat it by two days and eight hours.

But the aeroplane flying high enough to give it the widest practical range of vision is able to see only over a path 75 miles wide under the most favorable weather conditions. Haze will cut this down considerably. This means that for anything like complete scouting work a fleet must be equipped with a large number of them.

PROPORTION OF FIGHTING PLANES.

Then, too, there must be a generous proportion of fighting planes to spread out in a very wide circle beyond the fleet. It will be appreciated that this circle must be a mighty wide one if the enemy planes be kept far enough away to prevent their counting the number and type of ships in the command. There is required also a large detail to guard against the submarines. While an aeroplane can see quite deep in the sea, this penetrating vision is limited to the water directly beneath it. It can see straight down in the water, but not off to the side at an angle.

If such a thing is possible, air control at sea is more important than over the land, and of first value is the fighting plane. In this connection there is an aeroplane gun which works well. It is a double-ender. That is, there is a breech in the middle, and the two ends are muzzles. In air fighting it is seconds and fractions of seconds that count, and the advantage of this gun lies in that it can be fired in opposite directions, thus cutting down the length of the arc through which it has to be swung to be brought to bear on the enemy.

Of exceptional value to the United States navy is the super-American type of planes which the Curtiss factories have developed and which have done such wonderful service for the British. In this type the fuselage is entirely enclosed, built with a hull much along the lines of the motorboat or hydroplane. The 'plane may thus come to rest safely in the open sea.

It weighs nearly 6000 pounds and can carry a useful load of more than 2000 pounds. The boat is slung well below the planes, eight feet below the lower one, which has a span of 66 feet. Eight feet above this is the upper plane, which overlaps the lower plane by 13 feet on each side. The complete span of the upper plane is 92 feet. It can carry six to eight men, if necessary, altogether a huge, sturdy, dependable machine with two powerful motors.

And what was done to give America the equipment of 'planes which we needed?

RESOURCES AT GOVERNMENT'S COMMAND.

Fifteen aeroplane manufacturers, with a combined capital of $30,000,000 and a total capacity of 175 machines a week, organized and placed all their resources at the command of the government. The organization provided for the interchange of ideas and plans and for the standardization of manufacture, which resulted in a material increase in output.

One hundred and seventy-five machines a week should give us, in a year, 9100. And there are other conditions which may modify the estimate both favorably and unfavorably. There is, for instance, a limit to the amount of seasoned lumber available in this country of the peculiar type and quality needed for airplane construction. Provision must be made for the future in this respect. All-steel machines have been made and used in Europe to some extent, but no metal alloy has been developed which is likely to take the place of wood in general construction. The manufacturers developed some interesting things along these lines which were not given to the public.

In the Spring of 1917 the fighting in the air took on an entirely new interest abroad, because of the German policy of painting their machines most grotesque patterns. They seemed to have taken this idea from the old American Indian custom of painting their faces to frighten their opponents, or else the fancies of the German airmen were allowed to run riot with vivid color effects.

British pilots daily brought home from over the lines new reports of fantastic creations encountered amid the clouds. The gayest feathered songsters that came north with the Spring did not rival the variegated hues of the harlequin birds that rose daily from the German airdromes. The coming of this fantastic order of things in the air was first heralded by a squadron of scarlet German planes. It then was noticed that some of the enemy machines were striped about the body like yellow-jackets.

GAUDY TASTES OF AIRMEN.

Nothing appeared too gaudy to meet the tastes of the enemy airmen, who seemed to have been given carte blanche with the paint brush. There were green planes with yellow noses, silver planes with gold noses, khaki-colored planes with greenish-gray wings, planes with red bodies, green wings and yellow stripes, planes with red bodies and wings of green on top of blue, planes with light blue bodies and red wings. Virtually all the gaudiest machines were in red body effects, with every possible combination of colors for their wings. Some had one green wing and one white; some had green wings tipped with various colors.

One of the most fantastic met had a scarlet body, brown tail and reddish-brown wings, with white maltese crosses against a bright green background. One machine looked like a pear flying through the air. It had a pear-shaped tail and was painted a ruddy brown, just like a large ripe fruit. One of the piebald squadrons encountered was made up of white, red and green machines. There still were others palpably painted for what became known as "camouflege" purposes, as guns, wagons and tents often are painted to blend with the landscape and thus avoid detection.

This lavish use of paint, however, did not reduce the heavy daily loss inflicted on the Germans by the British flyers. But it must not be imagined that the Germans did not put up a stalwart fight. Just as their resistance was strengthened on land, so it was increased in the air. Just as the Germans threw in new divisions of infantry and new batteries of artillery to check the Allies' offensive, so they sent aloft hundreds of new machines to contest for the mastery of the air, an important phase of modern war.

The manner in which the British flying corps dominated the air during the battle of Messines Ridge in June, 1917, and completely smothered the German aviation service for the time being is one of the most thrilling and remarkable stories of the entire war.

Hundreds of British planes were well behind the German lines when the battle broke into its fury at dawn. They had stolen over during the darker intervals of the brief night when the moon was hidden by storm clouds. Other hundreds went aloft with the first faint streaks of coming day and, guided by the flashes of the guns, flew into the thick of the fighting.

COMBED BY MACHINE GUNS.

During the night British machines combed enemy railway stations, trains, ammunition dumps and troops coming up on the march. Others hovered above German airdromes and circled low among airplane sheds and fired hundreds of rounds from machine guns into them and prevented the enemy machines from coming out. Later in the day, while the fighting was most intense, British airmen dropped about three tons of bombs on the German flying grounds as a further deterrent, which proved highly effective.

In addition to shutting the German airmen out of any early participation in the battle, the British airplanes were in a large degree responsible for the fact that the Germans could not launch a counter attack of appreciable strength until forty hours after the battle for the ridge began and every bit of ground desired by the British in this particular operation had been taken and secured.

Far back of the German lines the British planes seached out troops in every hamlet, town and village. In several places they saw them gathering or marching in the main streets, whereupon they flew down low at times and opened a fire which scattered the gray-clad soldiers in all directions. All pilots report that their accurate fire had a most demoralizing effect upon the hostile troops. Convoys and ammunition and supply columns were attacked while on the march and the disorganized men left their teams and automobiles on the roads while they sought shelter in nearby ditches.

AIRPLANES ATTACK TROOPS.

Airplanes attacked troops in the support trenches and sent them scurrying to the cover of their dugouts. One pilot made so many of these attacks that he finally ran out of ammunition, but he delivered his last stroke by letting go his signal rockets at a platoon of soldiers who, evidently mistaking this for some particularly horrible new style of war frightfulness, fled in all directions.

German troops were fired upon in the more distant back areas as they were entraining for the front. Many of the enemy retreating from the British attack and hiding in shell holes were seen by the low-flying airmen and pelted with bullets.

One British pilot patrolled a road for half an hour before he saw anything to shoot at. Then a German military automobile with three officers sitting in the back seat came along. The Britisher dived at them from a height of three hundred feet, firing at them as they came. He flew so low eventually that the wheels of his under carriage barely missed the automobile, which swerved into a ditch while going at about forty miles an hour and crashed into a tree.

This same pilot later came across an active field gun battery and charged it, scattering the gun crew and hitting a number of them. Still further along he attacked a column of Germans marching in fours. The column broke when he opened fire, scattering to both sides of the road. At no time during his stay inside the German lines was this pilot more than 500 feet from the ground.

ON CONTACT PATROL WORK.

Large numbers of British machines were on contact patrol work, flying low over the advancing lines of infantry, constantly watching their movements, their progress, any temporary reverse, any attempt to form counter-attacks and all the while sending detailed reports back to corps and army headquarters.

Of the fourteen planes lost during the day of the battle, a majority were those contact machines. They had to fly through a frightful storm of their own as well as the enemy's artillery fire, and they succumbed to chance blows from these exploding missiles.

Late on the day of the battle, when the enemy machines had finally arrived from more distant airdromes, there was some good fighting in the air, some of it at close quarters with collisions barely avoided. Twenty enemy machines were accounted for in the fighting, some flopping about until they broke up in the air and others being driven down on their noses in yellow buttercup fields so far back of the fighting line that no shell had ever marred the symmetry of the landscape.

Some of the most marvelous work was done by artillery airships. One squadron of these alone, acting with several batteries of British heavies, succeeded in silencing seventy-two German batteries before six o'clock on the morning of the attack which began at 3.10 o'clock in the morning. These planes also directed the firing on the enemy's guns en route to the front, some of the big weapons being drawn by caterpillar tractors. Wherever a thousand or more troops were observed forming for possible counter-attacks the artillery planes directed "shoots" upon them.

So complete was the British domination of the air along the front of attack that not a single one of the British artillery observing aeroplanes was lost during the week that the intense bombardment was going on. During the battle British aeroplanes also attacked and silenced a number of enemy machine-gun positions.

The growth of the aeroplane industry has developed as many makes of machines as there are makes of automobiles, but in a general way aeroplanes are divided into four classes— monoplanes, biplanes, triplanes and hydroplanes. About 90 per cent of all designs are monoplanes and biplanes, and the types are distinguished by their single set of wings or planes or the double planes or wings. Both types have their advantages in use, the biplane being regarded as more stable for certain scouting purposes than the monoplane. It can carry heavier weights—has greater lifting power—but is not capable of as great speed or as easily maneuvered.

MACHINE ON PRACTICAL BASIS.

The War has placed the machine on an intensely practical basis. The manufacturers have learned that machines constructed along certain lines will travel at such and such a speed and have a certain lifting capacity, will rise under a particular speed and may be expected to do certain things under certain circumstances, but with all the advance which has been made in the construction of the air machines, the designers do not yet understand all the "factors" that enter into the "why" of the case.

The makers have, however, succeeded in standardizing their machines to a degree. The story of how the aeroplane flies is a highly technical and scientific one, but the basic principle is the reaction of air and an inclined surface in motion.

It might be likened to a stone skipping across the surface of a pond, if the imagination can conceive of the water as being air. It is simplicity itself to drive an inclined plane against the air with such force that the impact will produce a lifting power. In raising an ordinary kite, for instance, the boy runs into the teeth of the wind. His kite is so attached to a string as to stand at an angle, and as he runs the pressure against the air drives the kite upward. In the aeroplane the propellers drive the machine into the air with such force that the planes, standing at an angle, guide the machine upward.

There are innumerable problems to be solved—those of buoyancy, delicacy of balance and many others—but the designers themselves have not been able to determine upon a precise formula for their solution. It is sufficient that the aeroplane has reached a degree of practicability in construction and use which insures its permanent existence, and has given the military and the naval forces one of the greatest agencies in the world for protecting themselves and watching their enemies.

CHAPTER VII.

WAR'S STRANGE DEVICES.

CHEMISTRY A DEMON OF DESTRUCTION—POISON GAS BOMBS—GAS MASKS—HAND GRENADES—MORTARS—"TANKS"—FEUDAL "BATTERING RAMS"—STEEL HELMETS—STRANGE BULLETS—MOTOR PLOWS—REAL DOGS OF WAR.

THINGS new and passing strange—thousands of them—have been brought into being by the great world war.

Human minds have developed things undreamed of by science or fiction—things that a few years ago would have been considered too strange and fantastic for even the professional romancer to weave into the tissues of his stories.

Every known science has been called upon to produce its quota of new things which might be used for the destruction or the protection of men at war. The wonders of chemistry have always lent descriptive inspiration to the pen of writers, but mankind to get a vivid conception of the horrors of chemistry has had to wait for the great world war.

The conflict which has involved the entire world might almost be termed a warfare of chemists. Without their diabolical products, ranging all the way from high explosives to poison gases, it would have few of the characteristics of ultra-frightfulness that render it unique in the history of international struggles.

But of all the instruments of destruction used in this war, there is none more horrifying than the so-called "incendiary bomb," which sets instant fire to whatever it touches and which spreads flame in a manner so terrific that three or four such gravity-projectiles dropped from an aeroplane burned up the whole of a peaceful Dutch village in a few minutes.

Now, what is the fearsome stuff with which such bombs are loaded? A new chemical compound? Not at all. What they contain is simply the mixture of two of the most harmless things in the world—oxide of iron (which is simply iron rust) and powdered aluminum.

When these two innocent substances are mixed together the result is a compound truly infernal in its potentialities for mischief. It is not an explosive but if set on fire it burns with an intensity that is positively appalling. Nothing will put it out; no quantity of water has any effect upon the raging flames it engenders.

This is the material used for loading incendiary bombs. It is ignited in such projectiles by a mercury-fulminate cap that sets off a fuse containing powdered magnesium—the stuff photographers employ for flashlights.

THIN SHELLS OF STEEL.

These bombs are thin shells of steel or iron—mere containers for the mixture before described. They are so contrived that the fuse is instantly ignited when they strike.

Whereupon the shell is melted by the heat generated within it and a flood of fiercely burning metal is scattered in all directions. All of this seems rather extraordinary, and it is worth explaining.

Oxygen has an affinity for iron, readily combining with the latter—which is the reason why iron is liable to rust. This rust is a chemical compound of iron and oxygen; in other words, oxide of iron. But oxygen has a much greater affinity for aluminum. And so, when the two metals are powdered and mixed together and heat is applied the oxygen flies out of the iron rust and combines with the aluminum.

The process is started in the bomb by the burning magnesium. And then the oxygen passes out of the iron and into the aluminum so rapidly that an enormously high temperature is developed. It runs up to 3500 or 4000 degrees Fahrenheit—which means, of course, a tremendous combustion. The mixture of aluminum and iron burns like so much tinder—though such a way of putting it is absurdly feeble.

The present war has been conspicuously marked by reversions to ancient methods of fighting. In this line the incendiary bomb offers an excellent illustration. It is in effect merely an adaptation of an idea utilized by the Saracens—we should call them Turks nowadays—in their warfare with the Crusaders of the Middle Ages.

DREAD INSTRUMENT OF WAR.

The instrument of war most dreaded by the Crusaders, as they found it in the hands of the Turks, was the incendiary bomb—a projectile that flew through the air "like a fiery dragon" as they described it, and set fire to whatever it touched. Sometimes it was provided with iron barbs, by which it clung to buildings.

This was one of the ways in which the Saracens employed the celebrated "Greek fire"—an inflammable compound that is understood to have been a mixture of petroleum, saltpeter and pitch. The chief horror of it, from the Crusaders' point of view, was that it was unquenchable. Mere water had no effect upon it. Hence they were sure that it must be of diabolical origin.

But the up-to-date incendiary bomb is a great improvement on its original of the Middle Ages. The modern contrivance is thoroughly scientific, and it does its destructive business with certainty and dispatch.

No less effective are the gas bombs which were introduced by the German soldiers at Rheims, and which when exploding near the trenches occupied by the French and English threw off vapors and poisonous gases which killed or overwhelmed thousands of brave men. These devices used in violation of all rules of civilized warfare sent hundreds to the hospitals. Seventy-five victims were taken at one time from the trenches to the hospital at Zuydcoote, north of Dunkirk, where it was found that some of those who had inhaled the fumes turned a violet tinge.

Altogether it was estimated that from 3000 to 5000 men were affected by the gas fumes in this first onslaught and at least 10 per cent of those who were overcome succumbed to the deadly fumes. Many of those who inhaled the poisons expectorated blood and for days afterward were racked by terrible coughing. In many cases fever developed in a few days ending with pneumonia. When the men were not sufficiently poisoned to cause death they were so affected that their usefulness as soldiers was ended for all time. The poison made them confirmed invalids.

INTRODUCTION OF GAS MASK.

Naturally human ingenuity was called into play to protect men against the poisons and the gas mask came into being. These were of many types. The early creations consisted primarily of a nose and mouth covering with a receptacle for inclosing a sponge or gauze soaked with a chemical which possessed the power to neutralize the gas fumes. Such devices have been used by fire fighters in large cities the world over where the men battling to save buildings have been compelled to enter smoke-filled rooms and cellars. Other types which have proven more effective are designed after the fashion of the diving apparatus, and having a small tank of compressed oxygen with feeding tubes running to the mask. The oxygen combines with the contaminated air breathed through absorbent cotton or sponge and provides the wearer with the proportion of oxygen necessary to existence. And even the horses have been provided with such masks.

But to go back to bombs. All through France and Belgium, and wherever the Prussian soldiers found their way, there was evidence of the use of hand grenades which were thrown against the sides of or into buildings to set them in flames. Some of these devices, made of sheet metal, were in their action similar to the "Fourth of July torpedoes" familiar to every American school boy. When thrown they exploded throwing oil and chemicals over walls and floors. Some of them seem to have been loaded with bullets and were in effect hand shrapnel.

Then there developed from the primary use of these nefarious weapons the recognized hand grenade, which is actually hand-shrapnel, plied by men at close quarters. Thousands of these have been thrown by the armies in their charges on the trenches. And then, to offset the use of these devices in the offensive, there came into being also the smoke bombs. These when exploding throw up great clouds of black smoke which hang over everything.

EFFECTIVE IN A HUNDRED WAYS.

The use of such bombs has proved effective in a hundred ways. They have been used to create a perfect shield of smoke to conceal the movements of troops, or prevent the enemy from finding the range with their long distance guns. Similarly bombs which contained burning chemicals have been used to hold in check the approaching enemy forces.

Half way between the great gun and the hand grenade stand among war weapons the trench mortars. The first of these were used by the Japanese in their war with Russia. The Japanese mortars were mere logs hollowed out and strengthened by wrappings of bamboo rope. The projectiles fired from these were empty provision tins filled with high explosives, scraps of metal, bits of stone or whatever, in the emergency, could be found to fill them.

The mortars are pitched at an angle and the projectiles are shot with a skyrocket effect, to land in the trenches or camp of the enemy. The Germans developed the idea and the perfected mortars are of steel, and capable of throwing bombs weighing several hundred pounds.

And then the great moving fort which has been called "the tank!" Those snorting, fire-spitting dragons which were depicted for us in childhood can scarcely bring to our mind a greater element of the fanciful, the horrible, and the powerful than the steel hulks which came into being in this war under the name of "tanks."

We see them in our mind's eye spitting fire as they crossed No Man's Land, amid the smoke and dust of bursting shells. Keeping steadily on their courses they dived into huge craters made by exploding shells; stretched themselves across trenches, brushed trees and boulders aside, and kept steadily on their courses. German wire entanglements were as so many pieces of string before their huge frames. Nothing deterred them. They moved forward into the face of the enemy, reaching the first line of German trenches. There the soulless devices sat complacently astride the trenches, and turning their guns along the ditches swept them in both directions.

THE TANK DEFIES ALL OBSTACLES.

The tanks which were introduced by the English, move along on revolving platforms, so to speak. These platforms enable the tank to overcome all obstacles as the caterpillar tread is curved up in the arc of a huge circle at the front which gives the vehicle its wonderful tractive powers. This large curvature acts as a huge wheel with a tremendously long leverage equal to the radius of the circlet or the spokes of the imaginary wheel of the same diameter. Only that portion of the assumed wheel which would come in contact with the ground acts as the lever, and it is just this portion that is reproduced in the front end of a caterpillar belt.

Although varying in size and details, all tanks have the common characteristic of being divided into three main compartments between the two side caterpillar frames. The first is the observation compartment in which the driver and his helper are perched high above the ground to direct the movements of the huge steel beast.

In the middle is the ammunition room from which the guns carried in the two side turrets are fed. At the rear is the

engine room. From two or four gasoline engines are used—
these driving the rear axle and its integral sprockets over which
the caterpillars run. The latter run an idler pulley or sprockets at the extreme front ends and are supported by means of
rollers attached to the upper portion of the frame on each side
when passing over the top. This movement of the caterpillar
belts is exactly analogous to that of the ordinary variety of
garden insect with the same name which similarly lays down
his own track by humping his back continuously and regardless of the land surface.

The tanks are steered by a pair of small ordinary wheels
at the rear. These are supported in a pivot on a frame extended from the rear. They are merely for steering, and support
none of the weight of the tank except when bridging wide
trenches or dips in the surface. Steering can be accomplished
by making one caterpillar go faster than the other by manipu-
lating clutches on the driving mechanism.

TANK'S "CATERPILLAR" FEATURE.

The "caterpillar" feature of the tank had its origin in the
caterpillar belts or shoes which were first used on the great
field guns and mortars—those tremendous weapons which
shoot bombs and shells weighing tons and containing 500 or
more pounds of gun-cotton or explosive which on contact is
discharged, rending everything for yards around.

These guns, as well as the smaller field guns, have had
attached to them great shields of steel behind which the gunners stand, so that they are protected against the old-fashioned
sharpshooters whose duty it was to pick off the gunners.

The caterpillar or wheel belts on the big guns consist of
flat blocks, or shoes, wider than the tires of the wheels. They
are hinged and fastened together so as to form a great chain,
and when placed on the wheels present broad surfaces to the
ground and keep the gun carriages from sinking into the soft
earth. With a set of these shoes a heavy gun can be drawn

over soft and irregular ground, which would be almost impass-able where the gun is mounted on wheels of ordinary width.

Before these belts were devised it was necessary for every gun crew to carry a supply of beams, jackscrews and devices to be used in extricating the heavy guns when they got fast in the mud. Now every gun has these belts which can be put on or detached in a few minutes.

Paradoxically, this is the day of the big gun's greatest effectiveness, and the day of its greatest limitations. The war has taught us more in two years about gunnery and the effect of various types of ordnance under varying conditions than could have been learned in twenty years of theoretical research —for actual experience proves where theoretical research merely gives ground on which to base an opinion.

NATIONAL RESOURCES TO DISLODGE A MAN.

One of the things that we have learned is that when man takes unto himself the humble pick and shovel and proceeds to dig a hole for himself in the ground, we can get him out of that hole only by drawing on the combined resources of a nation, by constructing one of the most complex and expensive instruments in the world, and with it hurling at man dug-in a projectile weighing a good part of a ton.

The blunder, perhaps unavoidable, which stands out with equal emphasis among the preliminary preparations of all the nations engaged in the struggle was the underestimation of the artillery power required for the conduct of a successful military campaign under modern conditions of warfare. It was an underestimation so great that in the light of developments it will some day prove ridiculous.

At the opening of the war two opposed theories of artillery effectiveness were held by the combatants. The French swore by the medium calibre, rapid-fire, low-trajectory field piece. The Teutons had devoted their best efforts to the development of guns so big that their opponents were tempted, before they learned better, to regard them as too unwieldy for effective field service. Both were right, the French in the full sense and intention of the term, the Teutons by pure accident.

It should be explained here that the word Teuton is used advisedly, for in reality it is to the Austrians before the Germans that the development of the 11-inch and bigger field gun, with its special carriage and caterpillar-tread wheels owes its existence. It was Austrian guns and Austrian gunners that first made the heavy artillery of the Teuton armies famous.

The French field piece performed all that was expected of it, but it was handicapped by unforeseen conditions of warfare. The heavy Teuton guns performed their mission in the very introductory stages of the war, then failed, and later, by the irony of fate, proved to be the very things required when the unforeseeen war conditions developed.

A WONDERFUL GUN.

The Germans and Austrians believed that they could develop a big gun which could be given sufficient mobility for use in the field, and with commendable and methodical application they proceeded to do so. The theory was, first, that it could batter down any permanent fortifications that man could build, and when it was pitted against the concrete ramparts of Liege and Namur it blew them out of existence in a few hours. The Teutons had scored, and scored so heavily that the Allies barely escaped the fate the Germans had prepared for them in an overwhelming sweep on Paris. That they did escape this fate is no doubt in a large measure due to the fact that the second effectiveness claimed by the Teutons for their heavy ordnance failed in its full accomplishment. Used in open fighting, the great explosive shells hurled by these guns did not do the damage expected to the wide, open firing lines of the Allies, nor did they produce the moral effect expected. The great shells tore tremendous craters in the ground, from which the force of the explosion was expended upward in a sort of cone-shape, shooting above the heads of any troops in the vicinity except those immediately adjacent to the explosion. In the meantime the field pieces of the French, with their extreme mobility and rapidity of fire, were scattering death and destruction with their straight shrapnel fire in the solid formations which were so popular with the Germans in the early stages of the war, and which today they do not seem to be able to drop entirely.

So far the French piece did all expected of it. The German piece had proved its ability only to blow up permanent fortifications, and this was nullified immediately by the action of the French in abandoning the concrete shelters and moving their own guns into newly and quickly-constructed trench forts.

A THING UNDREAMED OF.

But the thing that neither side had dreamed of was the settling down of the war on the west front into an eternal line of opposing trenches to face each other for years. That it did so was due to the monumental blunders on the part of the German staff in allowing itself to be outmaneuvered and beaten back from the gates of Paris by numerically inferior forces, and still further outmaneuvered in the extension of the lines northward in that famous series of flanking movements which finally reached the sea.

It was their success in driving the German army to earth when it was stronger than they were that saved the Allies and gave them the breathing time required in which to further their preparations and train new troops, and likewise it is this same mode of trench warfare which has made their task so difficult when they have taken the offensive.

Against ordinary trench lines, as known in the early stages of the war, the French field pieces were more effective than the heavy cannon of the Teutons, just as they had been in the open. Shooting in flat trajectory across the trench, and exploding just above it, the shrapnel scattered more death downward than the heavy projectile could scatter upward after it had buried itself in the soft earth.

But with the continuous line of trenches stretching from Switzerland to the sea, with consequent impossibility of out-flanking, demonstrated by the Germans to their sorrow in repeated repulses of their drives to cut through to Calais, each side felt justified in replying to the artillery of the other by digging deeper and more permanently, with many feet of shelter overhead. This ended the effectiveness of shrapnel except for the repulse of attacks, and again the heavy guns swung into the position of pre-eminence.

A SITUATION ALMOST BEYOND CONTROL.

It was at this stage, however, that both sides realized how totally inadequate the supply of these heavy guns and ammunition was to cope with the situation. While the heavy gun was more effective in blasting out the enemy from his dug-outs than the field piece, it required many times the artillery power which either side possessed to handle the job.

Then commenced the race of the ammunition and gun factories to turn out their products by the ton where they had been turned out by the pound before; a race in which the Allies took and held the lead.

With the greatly increased number of heavy guns it be-came possible to develop the famous curtain of barrage fire, also known as drum fire, with this type of ordnance, as well as with shrapnel.

It is with this form of attack that the Allies blasted their way slowly but steadily through the strongest networks of trenches which the Germans were able to build.

Along a given section of the front, or rather just behind it, the guns were placed singly or in pairs, widely scattered, some close to the line and some well back from it, all concealed as far as possible from enemy aviators. There were also many dummy batteries, so that if the enemy air scout saw a gun or group of guns, he had no way of telling whether they were real or imitation.

In such an instance before the actual advance of the troops the fire of all these guns is concentrated along parallel lines to the enemy trenches, first, second and sometimes third. Each gun has its work mapped out for it in advance on a map covered with tiny squares. The actual point may be well beyond view of the gunners. The shell is landed in its appointed square solely on mathematical calculation. The commander of each gun knows, for instance, that he must fire into this, that or the other square for so many minutes or hours, and exactly at a given minute change his fire to another source.

RAIN OF SHELLS LIKE STREAMS OF WATER.

In effect on the enemy a continuous rain of shells, comparable to streams of water from hundreds of hoses is poured in a line right down the trench. At the same time a parallel line of fire is concentrated at a given distance back of the enemy's first trench and in front of the second, or in it. This means that the troops in the first line must not only take their bombardment without hope of retreat or escape, but that it is impossible to get reinforcements to them through the second curtain.

When it is calculated that the first line has been destroyed or demoralized, the troops leap from their trenches and advance strictly according to schedule over the ground between the opposing trenches. Their arrival at the enemy's first trench is timed to the second, and just as they are on the verge of plunging into their own curtain of fire this latter is gradually thrown forward, forming a screen between the newly captured trench and the enemy's second line. This means two curtains of fire through which the enemy would have to advance to counter-attack.

Time is given to rout out what remains of the enemy from

the first line dug-outs, and then the troops advance again. In the meantime the curtain of fire has preceded them as before, moving up to the line of drum fire which has been playing on the second line of trenches or just in front of it. If any of the enemy have attempted to flee before the attack from the first line they are caught between these two barrages which are gradually brought together.

When the first and second lines of fire have been brought together they are poured with redoubled fury into the second line of the enemy trenches, and then moved forward again just as the advancing troops reach this line.

DEPENDING ON LOCAL CONDITIONS.

The performance is made continuous so far as possible under the conditions peculiar to the given section in which the attack is being made. Sometimes it is possible to advance over three, four or five trenches in a single attack. At others it is as much as can be accomplished to capture one, which must be consolidated before further advance is made. It depends on the strength of the trenches, the nature of the ground, the distance apart that they are, and, of course, the amount of artillery fire which the enemy is able to concentrate in return.

When a sufficient advance has been made, it also becomes necessary to suspend operations for a time while the guns behind the lines are moved forward to new positions.

This is always the period of the counter-attack in force by the enemy, who seizes the opportunity when a certain proportion of the artillery is unable to fire because it is being moved. And it is during this period that the infantry have to do their hardest fighting, which consists, not in making the advance over no-man's land to the enemy trench, but in holding that trench afterward when the bringing up of their own artillery behind them to more advanced positions robs them of some of the support of the drum fire.

Still another factor of delay at this period is the time

required by the air scouts to find the rearranged positions of the enemy guns after the advance, for these must be taken care of also before a new advance can be made.

An explanation of this form of attack shows why news dispatches have told first of an advance of the British, followed by a period of quiet, during which an attack by the French in some other section of the line was in progress. Then suddenly the scene of action switched back to the British lines again while the French were consolidating their new positions preparatory to pushing the general advance a step farther.

GERMAN EQUIVOCATION.

It also explains just what has happened when the Germans state that the "enemy penetrated our first trenches in a small sector, but his attack broke down before our second line." When the next attack is ready, of course, the former second German line is referred to as the "first," and so, on paper, as far as the uninitiated are concerned, the German publicity office is able to build up a continuous series of enemy attacks which "break down," and somehow never, never "penetrate our invincible line." Actually an advance of this nature is extremely slow, but it is sure, and it is made at the expense of tons upon tons of ammunition rather than at the expense of lives, for ammunition can be made faster than soldiers.

Even the old battering ram of feudal times with which the ancestors of Kaiser William used to knock down the castles of the baron robbers has been approximated by his warring tribes. With the retreat of the German troops from Flanders the Allied forces found crude battering rams such as have been shown in the stirring "movies" when the ancient warriors stormed the gates of the city.

One of such devices was in the form of an upright frame made of heavy timbers. An immense log was suspended from the cross-piece by a heavy chain. An iron band circled one end of the log which was used for battering purposes and at the opposite end were handles, used by the operators in their nefarious work. The ram was used to batter in the doors of houses which had been locked or barricaded against the German soldiers. In their most destructive moods, it is charged that they used these devices to destroy the standing walls of houses and cottages after they had been gutted by fire. The Germans would not permit even so much as a wall to stand which might be used by the poor peasant in rehabilitating himself and building a new home.

NEW METHOD OF WARFARE.

The new method of warfare, with men working in trenches and dug-outs and millions of shells breaking over head, while missiles rain all about, necessitated the development of some device to protect the heads of the fighters. Therefore the steel helmet.

It has been shown that, due to trench warfare, about seventy-five per cent of the wounded on the western front had been hit with shrapnel or pieces of shell traveling at a low velocity and therefore had torn wounds and in many cases smashed bones. About three per cent of the wounds were in the head and about fifteen per cent in the face or neck. This led to the adoption by the French of a steel helmet called after its inventor, Adrian. The helmets were first used in May, 1915. That their use is justified is shown by statistics. Among fifty-five cases of head wounds, forty-two happened to soldiers without helmets.

Twenty-three of these had fractured skulls, while the remaining nineteen had bad scalp wounds. Of the thirteen who wore helmets, not one had a skull fracture. Five had slight wounds only, while none of those who had worn a helmet died. Quite a number of those who had not did.

In the Academy of Medicine Dr. Roussey brought up the point that due to the helmet the number of cases of sudden death from wounds in the head had been so decreased that the number of wounded with head injuries treated in the hospitals had materially increased.

The French helmet proved such a success that Belgium, Serbia, Russia and Roumania equipped their troops with the same model. The French helmet has a bursting bomb as insignia on its front and is light blue or khaki color, depending on whether it is worn by the metropolitan, the French home army or the French colonial army.

THE BELGIAN HELMET.

The Belgian helmet is khaki-colored, with the Belgian lion on the front; the Italian, greenish blue, with no insignia; the Serbian, khaki-colored, with the Serbian coat of arms; the Russian, khaki-colored, with the Russian coat of arms, and the Roumanian, blue-gray, with the Roumanian coat of arms.

The French have made more than 12,000,000 helmets, using about 12,000 tons of steel. In other words, a ton of steel will make 1,000 helmets. The British also equipped their troops with a steel helmet, which has no ridge running from front to rear. as has the Adrian, no decorations, and a rather wide brim, which runs all the way round. It is of a khaki color.

The Germans issued to a certain number of their men, generally those most exposed in trench fighting, a steel helmet considerably heavier than any of the allied helmets. It has a much higher crown, and comes down more over the eyes and the sides and back of the head.

All these helmets are supported by means of a leather skull cap inside, which fitting closely to the head, distributes the weight over the whole of the skull, instead of simply around the edge of it, as is the case with ordinary headgear.

Of course, these helmets will not protect against high velocity projectiles. However, as they do protect the wearer from low velocity projectiles, and as these are, because of infection, often as fatal as severe wounds, it can easily be seen how much good has been accomplished.

A French writer in La Nature shows that 332 out of 479 abnormal wounds were caused by shrapnel and pieces of shell having a low velocity.

In 13 out of 15 cases of lung wounds, the projectiles did not have velocity enough to completely traverse the body and come out.

In 71 cases of joint wounds, 66 were due to low velocity shrapnel and only 5 to high velocity bullets. Practically every one of these wounds could have been prevented by breast and body pieces and knee and elbow caps of armor.

LOW VELOCITY MOST EFFECTIVE.

As for every man who afterward dies from a wound made by a high velocity bullet there are about ten who die from wounds made by the low velocity shrapnel and shell fragments, the importance is seen of protection against these low velocity wounds if it can be had.

The wearing of armor means the lessening of the mobility of the soldier. In the open field lessening of mobility means a decrease in efficiency, which cannot be tolerated. However, in trench warfare the mobility of the individual does not count for so much, as even during an attack he does not have to go far, and generally does it at a walk in the rear of the barrage fire of his own artillery.

Efficiency in warfare, as indicated by the keeping of such records, has set the brains of the world at work, and armor is used to a limited degree for the protection of men in greatly exposed fronts or open positions.

The Japanese in modern times were first to resort to the forerunner of armor. They used shields of steel and in the siege of Port Arthur such shields were strapped to the front of the body. The Germans in the charges have frequently used double shields, advancing in groups of four behind a steel protector carried by two men, leaving the other two free to fire at the enemy through port holes in the armor shields.

None of the armors has, however, proved its resistance to the high velocity bullets which the powerful field guns rain against it. Experiments are being made continuously along these lines, and Guy Otis Brewster, of New Jersey, has developed a bullet-proof jacket and headgear which it is said approximates perfection.

In the presence of ordinance officers from the Picatinny Arsenal he invited an expert military marksman to fire at him from a distance of 60 yards. A Springfield rifle was used, with regulation ammunition. The steel bullet had a velocity of 2740 feet a second. Only one shot was fired, but it failed to penetrate the armor.

COMPOSITION A SECRET.

The composition of the latter is a secret, beyond the fact that it consists in part of steel. Jacket and headgear weigh 30 pounds; but the material is so flexible that the soldier wearing such an outfit can kneel, lie down, rise and run, charge from the trenches, use the bayonet, or throw hand grenades, without impediment to his movements.

It has been denied that dum-dum bullets, placed under ban by all civilized nations, have been used by the Germans, but there is no doubt that explosive bullets have been used. The report of the Belgian Commission, which investigated the horrors when the Germans first invaded King Albert's country, contains testimony which proves conclusively that such missiles were used. These bullets were, in effect, small shells containing an explosive chemical which was set off by contact. Photographs taken of wounds show the effect which these bullets produced.

More than that, the Russians charged that along the northern frontier the Germans fired glass bullets, although there is nothing to sustain the belief that such missiles were generally used.   The dum-dum bullet is a soft-nosed missile which, when it strikes a bone, flattens out and splatters, creating a jagged wound which it is almost impossible to treat or heal.   The Germans, in ordinary, use a steel jacketed bullet which possesses high penetrative powers, while the French at the beginning of the war were using the ordinary lead bullet.

AN AMERICAN BULLET.

Among the recent developments is a bullet which had its origin in one of the United States arsenals for manufacturing ammunition. This is a steel bullet covered with lead. The effect of such a combination on the penetrating quality of the bullet may be readily understood by anyone who has ever tried the experiment of driving an ordinary needle into a board through a cork. If the cork is placed on the board and the needle pressed down through the cork until it touches the board, a powerful blow from a hammer will force the needle into the board without breaking. In the application of this principle to the manufacture of the bullet, experiments proved that the soft lead acted as a guide or sustainer which permitted the inner steel to penetrate without deviation.

And just as these oddities of warfare have been created to meet arising situations, others have been created to care for the sick and injured—those who have fallen victims of the agencies of destruction.   Who ever heard of a sand sled?

Such sleds have been used effectively on the Eastern fronts to carry wounded soldiers to the hospitals.   They are long, staunchly constructed sleds similar to those used on the farms in America for hauling plows, cultivators and other agricultural implements across the fields which have been furrowed.

The sleds have broad runners which do not sink into the sands and can be drawn easily. In winter these same sleds have served to haul the wounded and sick over miles of snow and ice on the Russian frontier.

Then, though it is not a weapon of offense, there is the

tractor plow which works at night. It is a war device to the
extent that as England's need for food has been great and constant the tractor plow has been used to solve the problem of
working the ground. On the estate of Sir Arthur Lee, the
director-general of food production in England, great agricultural motors equipped with acetylene searchlights were kept
at work in the fields day and night.

Dogs too have been ushered into the arena. No longer
may the old English expression, "Let Slip the Dogs of War,"
be regarded as a mere figure of speech. The war dogs, and particularly the animals used by the Red Cross on the battlefields,
have assumed a regular status in the armies of the world. In
the European armies are thousands of dogs which have been
trained to act as messengers or spies, or to seek out on the battlefields the wounded. The Germans use a canine commonly
known as "Boxers." These animals are a cross between the
German mastiff and the English bulldog, and on the fields of
Europe they have proved to be "kings" among the Red Cross
dogs. The animals are first taught to distinguish between the
uniforms of the soldiers of their own country and those of the
enemy. Then they learn that the principal business in life for
them is to find and aid wounded soldiers.

The animals are trained to search without barking and to
return to headquarters and urge their trainers to follow them
with stretcher bearers. Sometimes the dogs bring back such
an article as a cap, tobacco pouch or handkerchief. The dogs
of the Red Cross carry on their collars a pouch containing a
first aid kit, by means of which a wounded soldier may staunch
the flow of blood or help himself until assistance arrives.

It is reported that one of these dogs rescued fifty men on
the Somme battlefield in France. The animal known as Filax
of Lewanno, is a typical German sheepdog. Such dogs weigh
from 50 to 65 pounds and are very powerful, but the Irish ter-
riers and Airedales have also been trained to do effective work,
as have the Great Danes and St. Bernards.

CHAPTER VIII
WONDERFUL WAR WEAPONS.

IT is a long step from the old, smooth bore, flintlock rifle of the Revolutionary days to the modern magazine gun, with its long-pointed cartridges; and it is almost as great a step from the crude iron cannons and smooth bore mortars of the Civil War, with their canister and grape shot, down to the huge, 42 centimeter guns which have boomed their way through France and Belgium.

The patriotic citizen who is unfitted for military service no longer sits at home and aids the armed forces of his country by melting pewter spoons into bullets, or cutting patches of cloth to serve as wads to pack down into the muzzle of guns. The powder horn and the bullet mould are devices of the past. The whole world working in the old-fashioned way could not have in the course of the "war-of-nations" made sufficient bullets to supply the forces for a single week.

Those who must sacrifice in the stress of war now turn their silverware and precious metals into nuggets that may be sold to produce revenue, so that the armed forces may purchase the machine-made cartridges and weapons required to fight the enemy.

Modern warfare has developed the climax in armament and the world has learned more within the last few years about the devilish instruments of destruction which human ingenuity has devised than was known in all the ages before. Since Germany and Austria were the first into action—actually precipitated the great conflict—and as by their years of preparation they were ready for the emergency, it best serves the purposes of those who seek enlightenment on the subject of armaments

133

and weapons to deal with the equipment of the Teuton forces.

Other nations—England, France and the United States in particular—have, in some directions, surpassed the Germans in developing efficient weapons, but in the main, when Germany plunged into the war, she had all around what was conceded to be the best equipment that science and mechanics could supply.

INFANTRY AND FIELD ARTILLERY.

While stories told of the awful havoc wrought by the German siege guns in reducing the forts and fortifications in France and Belgium are true, it is also true that the bulwark of the military organization is the infantry and field artillery. The big guns may level the forts and reduce them to powder, driving off the opposing forces, but the infantry must advance and the small arms and rapid-fire guns must keep the opposing forces from resuming the position which they had abandoned.

The difficulty of handling the big guns has always been a problem, except in fortifications and at fixed points of defense, and it has only been within a few years that a solution of the trouble has been found. The solution lay in the use of tractors, or the tractor principle, which every person familiar with farming and the "traction engine" can recognize.

Germany and Austria, as in many other matters, solved the problem by building mortars for field service which outclassed the heaviest artillery of the old type, and mounting them on tractors. It would require a team of probably forty horses to pull one of the German 42-centimeter guns over the rough ground, and then a relay would be required every few hours. An immense number of horses would be required and the transportation would be slow, and not certain at best.

Early in the war Austria sent to the front a battery of 30-centimeter howitzers, and from the famous Krupp gun works there were 21 and 28-centimeter howitzers. Later came the 42-centimeter guns, which are classed as automobile field artillery. These are the weapons which leveled the forts at Liege and were used to bombard Fort Maubeuge.

The immense howitzers, with their caterpillar wheels, are taken apart and transported to the scene of action in sections, or units. An automobile tractor carries the artillery crew and tools and furnishes the motive power. The second car carries the platform and turntable on which the gun is mounted, and the third hauls the barrel, or gun proper.

THE MOVING OF HEAVY WEAPONS.

The weapons can be moved anywhere, though they weigh as much as forty tons in some cases. Sometimes it is necessary to build special roads where fields must be crossed, but on the highways there is little trouble. The big howitzers are built on the principle of the large caliber guns used on battleships—that is, there is a system of recoil springs and air cushions to take up the shock when the gun is fired, so that the terrific energy, when the charge is exploded, shall not be borne by the breech of the gun. The howitzers can be turned in any direction, and the gearing attached to the mounting is such that the barrels can be pitched at any angle.

Such guns fire an explosive shell weighing from 500 to 1000 pounds, and because of their form of construction—they have shorter barrels than the naval guns—which reduces the surface of the barrel subject to erosion, they are longer lived than the long guns. The endurance of the guns is a factor because it is difficult to get repairs for such great weapons on the field of battle.

At the outbreak the contending forces are said to have had 4,000 guns in the field artillery. Among the devices of interest identified with the artillery is the armored automobile, which has been described as the "cavalry" of motor driven artillery. The advent of the armored automobile in the war changed many features of campaigning and helped to revolutionize military methods. The armored automobile is an ordinary chassis with a body made of chilled steel.

Many types have been devised, including turreted automobile, mounting one or two rapid fire guns which can be turned in any direction. The armored motors have high-powered engines, and the chassis chosen for these new instruments of war are of the heaviest types. Some have been constructed especially for the purpose. One of these, used by the Germans, had a "barbette" top, which looked like the shell of a tortoise, fitted down over the chassis. Guns protruded from holes in the front, back and sides.

VALUE OF ARMORED CARS.

The armored cars have proved extremely valuable for scouting purposes. They can sneak through and complete scouting where mounted men would be detected, and besides, are better able to protect themselves against attack. The cars also possess the ability to speed away out of range of enemy detachments.

The army officer, too, has taken to the armored automobile, and put aside his horse. You cannot kill an automobile; and the armor laughs at the bullets from small caliber guns. The officers can, with the high-speed armored cars, travel from one end of a line to the other and in a few hours make surveys and complete observations which would take days were horses used.

Very few of the light-armored cars used by the officers are armed, the attache or aide of the officer carrying a rifle. Some of the armored cars used for scouting and by the officers have, in the case of Germany, been provided with sharp knives attached to the front of the machine. These are steel blades vertically attached to the frame and hood, and are designed to cut wires which the enemy may have stretched across highways or passages to hinder progress.

The armored covering on some of these cars is little more than a steel box, with "port" holes all around. There is no hood, dome or cupola, and the men are supposed to protect themselves by keeping their heads below the sides of the box. Besides the driver, some of the cars carry two or three men, who are further protected against the bullets of the enemy and the chance missile from the sharpshooter by steel headpieces or helmets.

The Belgians have a type of car of heavy design, equipped with huge headlights, as well as a searchlight to operate at night. The car has a rapid fire gun mounted in a cupola-formed revolving turret. In the matter of automobiles in the army, Italy outranked Germany at the beginning of the war. While Germany had Mercedes and Opel trucks, mounting five to seven rapid fire guns, which, with their steel armor and solid tire disc wheels, were actually miniature forts, the Italians had more formidable mounted creations of the same sort.

ITALY'S SINGULAR POSITION.

As a matter of fact, Italy's position in regard to motors is unique among the other countries in the war. Not only are the transportation conditions different, but the motorcar industry in the country is on a different basis. It is said to have been the only one of the countries which was able to meet the demand put upon it for motors without going into some other land to augment its supply. Italy did not buy a single American motor vehicle for war purposes. There are cars of foreign makes in the army and with the Red Cross, but these vehicles were in the country—purchased for private use—when the war broke out and were requisitioned.

The big guns of the army are handled by motor tractors, 95 per cent of the army mail service is motorcar service and 95 per cent of the drinking water for the fighting forces is delivered by motortruck. Profiting by the lessons of the other countries called to war, Italy had time in which to prepare for emergencies, and when the order for mobilizing forces was issued the motorcar factories were speeded up and the workers were permitted to stay on the job, instead of being called out to fill up the ranks of the army.

Compared with the resources of America, the Italian motor industry is not large; but the product is uniform and practically all of the factories are conveniently located for distributing the machines to the army on the frontier and readily providing repairs and parts. The physical conditions of the country necessitated the use of certain types of trucks and motors and the dropping of some of the practices of other countries in motor usage.

The rugged, irregular country, with its narrow roads, makes impracticable the use of trucks larger than three and one-half tons, and "trailers," largely employed by the French, German and Belgian armies, were found not satisfactory. What is described as the Isotta Fraschini heavy model armored artillery car of Italy is considered one of the most effective of the "motor forts" or "land cruisers" developed during the war.

THE WHEELED FORT.

The wheeled fort has a battery of four rapid fire guns and a revolving turret. Besides being full armored and turreted, the car has steel wheels of the disc type, and is as formidable in appearance as it has proven in practice. France has a type of the completely enclosed armored motorcar which affords its crew unobstructed view on all sides through lattice panels. Even the windshield is made on this plan. This car also has a revolving turret and carries a 5-centimeter rapid fire gun and possesses high speed.

All of the powers have armored automobiles, and in Germany, England and France the exigencies of conflict impelled the Governments to practically commandeer all of the automobiles in the countries for war purposes. Many of these cars were turned into armored cars of the lighter type, and the number of such automobiles in use runs far into the thousands. The

United States has not made much fuss about it, but has had
armored cars in the regular army for several years.

The experience gained in the campaign in Europe indi-
cates that the military authorities believe the high-powered,
speedy cars, clad with armor of medium weight and mounting
one or two machine guns, are the most valuable of all the
"sheathed" cars. They can appear suddenly, maintain a
withering fire for a short period and then disappear suddenly.

As an instance of what the armored car accomplishes, it is
recited that when the German troops sought to invade the Belgian town of Alost a detachment was sent through the streets
in armored cars. The houses were barricaded and the Germans
feared snipers. There were no snipers when the motorcars
returned. More than a thousand Belgians were mowed down
in the streets by the rapid fire guns of the armored cars.

IMPORTANCE OF THE AUTOMOBILE.

Evidence of how greatly the automobile is appreciated in
its relation to the modern army service is found in the fact that
when America entered the war and began the mobilization of
its forces and resources, the Quartermaster at Chicago was
ordered to obtain bids for the delivery of 35,000 motortrucks of
one and one-half tons capacity and 35,000 trucks of three tons
capacity. Bids were also asked on 1000 five-passenger automobiles, 1000 runabouts, 1000 automobiles, in price ranging
from $1500 to $2000, several hundred motortrucks of half,
three-quarter and one ton capacity and 5000 motorcycles, and
the same number of motorcycles with auxiliary passenger
capacity, or side cars.

The motortruck, too, in modern warfare is a shoeshop.
The care of the feet is an important matter in the army, and
the men, besides being provided with good footwear, must have
that footwear kept in serviceable and comfortable condition.
It is some job to keep the shoes of half a million or more men
in repair, and the United States Quartermaster Department,

in connection with their mobilization, included in its equipment portable motor-power machines to nail on half soles for troops in garrison and campaign. Such a machine will nail on a pair of soles in five minutes. It weighs but 27 pounds and can be transported with the troops on a motorcar, and may be used anywhere to keep the shoes in serviceable shape until the troops can reach permanent camps, where new footwear can be provided.

FRANCE'S TRANSPORTATION RESOURCES.

At the outset of the war France is said to have had 100,000 passenger cars, 25,000 motorbuses, taxicabs and motorcycles and 10,000 motortrucks available for military use, and was able to give the various departments of her military organization excellent transportation service. Besides this, she had squads of automobile aeroplane cannon, and about 84 12-centimeter and 15 5-centimeter Rimailho howitzers of the armored artillery type. Russia is said to have been weak in automobile equipment, having less than a thousand trucks in the Empire available for military use; but this number was rapidly increased, upward of half a thousand having been purchased within a short time.

Austria and Germany together are said to have had something like 1500 trucks and about 20,000 passenger cars available for army use. At the start Germany alone had 250 armored automobiles, several score of searchlight automobiles, or night scout cars, probably 8000 motorcycles and more than 500 motor-driven field guns, besides the big tractors used to draw the heavy howitzers. Aside from this, practically all the motor vehicles in the country were commandeered, numbering upward of 75,000.

While they are stationary devices, the forts which were stormed by the Germans at Liege and Antwerp are properly part of the military equipment used in the war. These forts, known as turret forts, are described on preliminary inspection as looking like a row of huge tortoise or turtle shells rising a few feet above the ground. The shell is, however, a shell of chilled steel. Through it the guns protrude and are operated very much like the guns on a battleship, the turret revolving. Under the dome are vaults and the compartments of concrete, containing the mechanism for moving the turrets, operating the guns, lifting the big shells and handling the ammunition generally.

The fortifications, which at Antwerp included nine intrenched sections, were regarded as almost impregnable; but when they were built there were no such field guns as the famous 42-centimeter guns which the Germans brought to the atack. The forts themselves had no guns larger than a 7-inch caliber.

FRANCE'S ARMORED FIGHTING MACHINES.

In the matter of movable guns, the French and Germans both had them mounted on armored trains. One such train used by the French included armored locomotive, flat cars on which were mounted the guns in "barbettes," or steel turrets, and completely protected armored cars, used to transport troops or detachments of men.

A feature of the train was the observation tower. It was mounted upon what would ordinarily be the cab of the locomotive. Such towers have in one form or another become very common in the war. One type resembles the motortruck ladder and platform devices used by the man who repairs electric lights and wires in our city streets. Another is patterned after the hook and ladder truck of the fire department. The tower, or ladder, is raised after the fashion of the ladders in fighting a fire. A couple of soldiers turn a crank, and the ladders are raised to a perpendicular position and extended high into the air on the sliding or telescope principle.

The German and Austrian engineers also utilize observation ladders of a less complicated mechanical nature. In use, and with a soldier perched on top of them, they remind one of the toy devices with which we played as children, using the slotted acrobats to do wonderful things atop the "ladders." The ladders are carried in short sections, which may be fastened together in a variety of ways, but a good idea of the manner in which the ladders are used may be obtained if you can imagine a letter Y made of ladders and turned upside down, with a soldier standing on top of it.

THE IMPORTANCE OF OBSERVATIONS.

And making observations is a highly important matter in modern warfare; more important than it was in the old days. The long-range guns are aimed and their fire directed by observation and calculation. The gunner cannot see the target he is required to hit. His job is a mechanical one—perhaps it would be better to say scientific—for he must read mathematical calculations and interpret them into accurate gun action. The guns may be on one side of a hill and the enemy on the other, and they may be miles apart, yet the gunner must be able to get the range. His efforts are directed by observers in aeroplanes or balloons, and the range is established by calculations, so that the gunner must be proficient in geometry, trigonometry and mathematics generally.

Not all the great guns in the war when it started were owned by the Germans, for England had 100-ton Armstrong pieces which were capable of hurling a 2,200-pound projectile; but it was the modification of the design of the large caliber guns and the method of mounting them, which permitted them to be drawn wherever needed, that gave Germany such an advantage.

Most of the big guns are in the navy—on the huge dreadnoughts and batleships—and therefore the fortifications at Helgoland, which are designed to resist the bombardment of the heaviest naval guns, must be regarded as equipment. Helgoland is the protecting fort of Germany's most vulnerable point. It is the Gibraltar of Germany, and protects the entrance to the Kiel Canal from the North Sea. If the British could get past the fortifications to the Kiel Canal, it could establish a close-in blockade which would render Germany helpless in a short time.

Helgoland is an island fortress in the North Sea, in the center of which is a mortar battery mounting 11-inch and 16-inch guns, capable of puncturing the decks of the battleship which comes within range; and these batteries have a range of from six to eight miles. The batteries are ranged in tiers, one above the other, to a height of almost 180 feet above the sea level, the heavy guns and pieces being placed below and the lighter ordnance in the upper tiers. The guns range from 17.7-inch caliber down to 8.2-inch. Germany calls Helgoland the "fortress impregnable," and the developments of the war seem to indicate that the description fits.

SMALL GUNS OF VARIED INTERESTS.

In the smaller guns used in warfare there are many varieties of interest. The United States prior to and with their entrance into war, particularly during the period of the trouble along the Mexican border, experimented with almost every known make of rapid fire machine and field gun, and there was for a time much criticism because the government did not adopt for army use the Lewis gun, which was adopted by some of the foreign countries.

The German army rifle carried by all the infantry is of the Mauser type, first introduced in 1888 and gradually improved until 1898. The weapon, because of the adoption of the improved model in 1898, has come to be known as the "ninety-eight gun." It is a quick-firing weapon, from which 20 to 30 shots a minute may be projected by the soldier. The gun is universally used and has a caliber of 7.9 millimeters, which provides for the use of the smallest bullet which will work sufficient injury on the enemy to make its use profitable.

Experience in the Russian-Japanese war proved to the military authorities that the use of a smaller caliber was not advisable. It was found that the smaller bullet could, and in many cases did, pass through a man's body without actually rendering him useless, and that in a large percentage of cases—more than one-third—the wounded were back with their troops within a few months.

In the United States all of the forces are now provided with standard arms or weapons. The army, the Marine Corps and the organized militia of the States, absorbed into the body proper of national troops, have the same firearms—the same service rifles, the same machine guns and field guns and the same automatic pistols. One kind of cartridge—containing a cylindro-conical bullet of copper-nickel, with a lead core—serves for all rifles and for the machine guns as well.

OLD FLINTLOCK IN WAR.

Many people, perhaps, will be surprised to learn that the Mexican war was fought mainly with the antiquated flintlock muskets. When the trigger was pulled the flint came down hard upon a piece of steel, and the resulting spark was thrown into the "pan," igniting a pinch of powder. The fire ran into the powder charge and the gun went off. Round balls were used, and the loading was done with the help of a ramrod.

There were already percussion rifles in those days, but General Winfield Scott, who bossed the Mexican war, declared that he would have nothing to do with those new-fangled weapons. The old smooth-bore flintlock was good enough for him. In truth, the percussion gun of that period was not as reliable as might have been wished. The cap was liable to get wet and to fail to go off, whereas a good flint could be counted upon to yield a spark every time.

It was not until 1858 that the percussion rifle, still a muzzle-loader, was generally used by the United States army. The Springfield, which was the first breech-loader (one cartridge

inserted at a time) came along in 1870. In 1892 it was replaced by the first of our magazine rifles, the Krag, and simultaneously we adopted smokeless powder, a European invention.

The regulation United States service rifle is a great improvement on the Krag. It is loaded with "clips," holding five
cartridges each. The velocity of the bullet is greater, and the
accuracy and rapidity of fire are superior.

FIGHTING RANGE 800 YARDS.

In the Mexican war the ordinary fighting range, with the
smooth-bore flintlock, was about 250 yards. In the Civil War,
with the percussion muzzle-loader, it was 350 to 400 yards.
With the new service rifle, the fighting range is 700 to 800
yards, and the infantryman is able to fire at least twenty times
as many shots in a given number of minutes as was possible
fifty years ago.

The field artilleryman carries no rifle, but is provided with
a 45-caliber automatic pistol and twenty-one cartridges. The
men who compose the machine-gun platoons have no rifles, but
each one of them is armed with the same sort of service pistol
and a bolo. The latter is a weapon new to our army, adopted
as a result of military experience in the Philppines. It is in
effect a machete (a sugar cane chopping knife), shortened and
made heavier. At close quarters it is a formidable weapon.

The bolo embodies the best principles of the various razor-
edged fighting blades of the Filipinos, and was first adopted as
a side arm of the Marine Corps officers. The bolo, which is
much heavier than an ordinary sword, measures 24 inches from
tip of handle to tip of blade. and is forged from a piece of file
steel.

For many years the Marine Corps, except upon dress
occasions, has had no cutting weapon. It is not strange, therefore, that many of the officers of the corps, while on duty in the
Philippines, adopted for use in the field that weapon of the
Moro tribesmen.

The introduction of the bolo as the field arm of the Marine Corps—the sword having given place to the pistol several years ago in this branch of the service—robs the time-tried and traditional Mameluke saber of the corps of the distinction of being the only cutting weapon in the equipment of this division of the Government's sea fighters.

The Mamelukes are inseparably associated with the military history of Egypt, the first country in which a regular military organization was established, and a country in which the fighting element was the most honored and powerful of all classes. This type of blade was adopted by our Marine Corps in 1825, and later by the officers of the Royal Horse Artillery of England.

Until recently the allowance of machine guns in our army has been two to a regiment, but aboard four to six are used.

AUTOMATIC MACHINE RIFLES.

These guns are automatic machine rifles, firing ordinary rifle cartridges, which (in the Benet-Mercie weapon, a French invention which we have adopted) are supplied in brass clips of thirty. A small part of the gas generated by the explosion of the individual cartridge operates the mechanism, discharging the bullet, throwing out the empty shell and making ready for the next shot.

A machine gun is designed to enable one man to fire the equivalent of a volley, or series of volleys, discharged by an entire platoon (one-third of a company) of infantrymen. As at present developed, it represents a step toward the evolution of a shoulder-rifle that will throw a continuous stream of bullets.

The latest government rifle—the weapons of the individual soldiers—are manufactured at the Springfield (Mass.) Armory, which is the government's great small-arms factory, and at the Rock Island (Ill.) Arsenal—the facilities of the latter having hitherto been held in reserve for emergency purposes. The rifle cartridges are turned out at the Frankford Arsenal, in Philadelphia, and at private plants in Lowell, New Haven, Bridgeport and Cincinnati. These concerns and another near St. Louis also make the cartridges for the automatic pistols.

At the outbreak of the world war we had 150 batteries of light field guns and 45 batteries of heavy artillery (four guns to each battery), including cannon provided for by Congress, and since then delivered. There was an inadequate supply of ammunition for the heavy guns.

MUNITION SUPPLY AUGMENTED.

The ammunition supply was immediately augmented and field guns of various calibers turned out as fast as possible, including 9-inch howitzers.

A 3-inch field gun fires projectiles weighing 15 pounds, with a muzzle velocity of 1700 feet per second.

A 4.7-inch field gun fires projectiles weighing 60 pounds, with the same velocity.

A 6-inch howitzer fires projectiles weighing 120 pounds, with a muzzle velocity of 900 feet per second.

The principal difference between the field gun and the howitzer is that the latter can be pointed at a high angle, to assail infantry protected by intrenchments, or for other purposes.

While reference has been made to siege guns, which were used by the Germans in their attacks on the Belgian and French forts, the fact is that the large caliber mortars and howitzers are what wrought the havoc.

The large caliber howitzers and mortars throw shells containing huge charges of explosives, and are more adaptable in their application than the ordinary siege guns or cannons.

One novelty which had not been used up to the entrance of the United States into the war is a device invented by a Los Angeles man, which makes a "periscope gun" of any ordinary service piece.

In trench warfare, as developed abroad, the periscope has been used by the men in the trenches to observe the movements of the opposing forces and watch for scouts without exposing themselves to the fire of "snipers" or sharpshooters, who are always looking for a head or mark to aim at.

The new device comprises two mirrors attached to the gun by a metal frame in such manner that one mirror is above the range of vision and reflects the image to be fired at upon the other mirror below the stock or butt of the gun. The attachment enables the soldier sitting in a trench or shelter to accurately aim his gun and conveniently shoot while his head is kept below the safety line, or top of the parapet, or properly built trench.

THE TRENCH PERISCOPE.

With this attachment, approved by the United States Ordnance Department, a rifleman, from his concealed point of vantage, can survey a 30-foot field at 200 yards. The attachment can be removed at will and the metal bars and parts can be easily carried. The device adds about one and one-half pounds to the weight of the gun.

In the same category with the aeroplane, the automobile, the submarine, the torpedo, in their effect upon the method of waging modern warfare are the telephone and the wireless telegraph. There were no telephones and no wireless instruments in the days of our own Civil War, and the stories related of the bravery and astuteness displayed by orderlies, messengers and scouts of those days will not be repeated.

Today the army carries a complete telephone system and wonderful wireless apparatus. The commander sits in his headquarters and communicates with his officers in all parts of the field, reaching points miles distant. Wires are strung through trenches, along fences and wherever needed, and telephone "booths" are set up wherever it is found necessary. Switchboards are mounted on motor cars and encased in armor plate. The "repair" wagons are motor vehicles, and lines cut or destroyed are quickly repaired or replaced.

Aerial stations for the wireless are carried, and are of many varieties. Some of them are similar to the observation towers and ladders. The French army regulations provide for wireless service between the general staff headquarters and the army corps, connecting these with the heavy cavalry divisions and lines of communication. The wireless companies in the French army are made up of 10 officers and 293 men.

Nearly all of the other nations have patterned their wireless companies after the French. The company carries 302 miles of wire and cable and about 96 sets of instruments. The rate of operation is more than 400 words a minute. The mast for the aerial station is made in sections, on the telescope plan, and can be erected by a trio of men in a few minutes. The whole outfit for a station weighs about 750 pounds and the range of service is about 200 miles.

"KNAPSACK" STATIONS.

There are, in addition to the field stations, "knapsack" stations, which are divided into sections so that four soldiers can carry an outfit. The sections weigh about 20 pounds each. The small station set up with this apparatus has a range of from 5 to 10 miles and in service replaces the orderlies and such visual signs and signalling, as was used before the wireless came into existence. Such an outfit can forward more information in a few minutes than a whole squadron of orderlies could riding at full speed.

The aeroplanes carrying a wireless outfit can communicate with the field stations, and have rendered wonderful service on the battlefields. The cavalry also carry wireless outfits, and in the Allied armies the second regiment of every cavalry brigade has a wireless detachment of 4 troopers, 1 cyclist and 3 horses, besides a wagon. There is also a division with tools and material for both destroying and repairing lines.

The French army also has automobile wireless stations. The automobile outfit is complete in every particular and is not augmented. It carries its own crew and has a traveling radius of several hundred miles. The car containing the station is completely enclosed and the walls are deadened so that the noise made by the apparatus may not betray the presence of the station to the enemy scouts.

The practical application of portable wireless outfits to military usage is probably less than four years old, but the portables can transmit messages over a radius of 200 to 250 miles. Expressed in technical terms, the portable stations have a capacity of about 200 mile wave-lengths.

The one weakness of the wireless is that the enemy can purloin secrets, though adroitness in manipulation can overcome some of this difficulty.

A WORD ABOUT "HEAVY ARTILLERY."

It would not do to mention armaments and weapons without a word about the "heavy artillery" of the commissary department, for this branch of the army service is represented by formidable field kitchens, which are again carried on trucks or motor cars. The officers' field kitchen follows the advance of the officers to the field of action. Some of these kitchens, particularly those of the Kaiser and the Crown Prince in the German army, are described as almost luxurious. They contain complete equipment—range, bake-oven, pantry, ice-box, china closet and every device needed for preparing a complete meal.

Supplies are hurried after the troops in motor trucks from stations where the supplies are delivered by rail and soups and sturdy meals are prepared which were lacking in the campaigns through which the soldiers of the Civil War passed. The pioneer mobile military field kitchen which has been the subject of widespread comment was developed by the German army.

It consists of a four-wheeled vehicle drawn by two horses,

though motors have supplanted the horses in some cases. The front carriage is detachable from the rear and is actually a separate contrivance. On the rear truck is a 200-quart copper, double, or jacketed vat. Also a 70-quart coffee tank. Both receptacles have separate fireboxes and ash pits. One section carries extra rations for the men, the daily quota of provisions, extra rations for horses, folding canvas water pails and utensils.

The actual food is cooked within the vat or caldron inside the water jacket, so that the heat does not come in contact with the food direct, thus preventing burning. The food will cook slowly for hours when once the water is heated, and will remain hot for a long time. The men can get water in an emergency and hot coffee is always ready for the sentries and men on guard duty to carry with them at night. Of course a bottle of the thermos type is used by these men so that they can have hot coffee when on the line of duty. The kitchen outfits are complete and so arranged that they can be rushed over rough ground without spilling their contents.

Electric flash lights, batteries for setting off dynamite and other explosives used for blowing out trenches and other fortifications, searchlights, mirror signaling devices, illuminating bombs, which are shot high in the air to explode and illuminate the field for hundreds of yards, signal bombs, and many ingenious contraptions never dreamed of are part of the army's equipment used on the battlefields of the greatest war that the world has ever known.

CHAPTER IX

THE WORLD'S ARMIES.

NO one scoffs at the military organization which Germany has developed through the years—yes, almost centuries —of moulding and training, for Germany has proved herself efficient, even if egotistical and domineering. She built up what at the beginning of the war was recognized as the most powerful, most efficient and well balanced military organization the world has ever known. And it was not an army in the sense that America has been taught to think of armies. It was a trained nation for war—a nation armed—rather than a small, compact fighting machine.

The strength of the German army on October 1, 1913, has been given in fairly authentic reports as 790,788 men and 157,916 horses. Of the men 30,253 were officers and 2,483 sanitary officers. There were 104,377 non-commissioned officers and 641,811 common soldiers. The general divisions were 515,216 infantry and 85,593 cavalry, 126,042 artillery, and the rest in the general service, including the commissary and quartermasters' departments, as these are known in America. The estimated army on a war footing is more than four times this number and approximates about 4,000,000, while the entire available force was given at probably 8,000,000.

The infantry is designated as the main body of the army. The infantrymen carry the "98" gun, already referred to, which is an improved Mauser, and the non-commissioned officers and ambulance drivers carry revolvers. There are several classes of infantrymen, a distinction being made between the

152

sharpshooters, and some of the others, variously known as grenadiers, musketeers and fusileers.

The cavalry is armed with lance, saber and carbine. There are distinctions in this branch of the service, too, among the cavalry units being cuirassiers, hussars, uhlans and dragoons. The field artillery carries batteries of cannon and light howitzer, and the drivers are armed with a sword and revolver. The cannoneers have a short knife or dagger as well as the revolver.

The communication troops are what parallel the engineers in the United States army. They build the roads, put up the telegraph lines and telephone service, construct bridges and make the travel possible.

STRENGTH OF GERMAN ARMY.

While the full strength of the German army is given at 4,000,000 on a war footing, the total availables from the nation's reserve is double that sum. These forces are gathered from three sources: the first line, with an estimated strength of 1,750,000; the Landwehr 1,800,000, and the Landsturm 4,500,000.

All who enter the service pass into the Landsturm after 19 years and remain until they are 45. The cavalry service is three years with the colors and four years in the army reserve. The horse artillery are subject to the same service, while those in other branches serve two years with the colors and five with the army reserve. The soldier passes from the army reserve into what is described as the Landwehr, where artillerymen and cavalrymen remain three years; those of other branches of the military five years. The soldier passes from the first division or class of Landwehr to the second, where he remains until his 39th birthday.

The Landsturm of the first class includes those between the ages of 17 and 39, who have not reached the age of service, and those who have not been called into active service because the ranks were full and there was no room for them in the regular army. The second class includes those who have passed through the other branches and whose ages are between 39 and 45.

There is a wide difference between the military organizations of the different countries. Whereas the United States army regiment approximates 1500 men, the German army regiment contains almost 3000. In the German army six battalions form an infantry regiment. Two regiments form a brigade, two brigades a division, and two divisions an army corps. There are 10 divisions composed of 3 brigades each, but of course the whole organization was augmented when war broke out. Adding the necessary auxiliary troops, viz: an artillery brigade of 12 batteries composed of 6 guns each—or 4 in the case of the horse batteries—a regiment of cavalry of 4 squadrons, an engineer battalion, sanitary troops, etc., a German 3-brigade division at war strength numbers about 21,000, and an army corps—to which are further attached 4 batteries of howitzers and a battalion of rifles—about 43,000 combatants. The cavalry division is composed of 3 brigades of 2 regiments each and 2 or 3 batteries of horse artillery, a total of 24 squadrons and 8 to 12 guns.

In a general way it may here be interpolated that the organization of an army is given in the military manuals as follows:

INFANTRY.

A squad is 8 men under the command of a corporal.

A section is 16 men under the command of a sergeant.

A platoon is from 50 to 75 men under a lieutenant.

A company is 3 platoons, 200 to 250 men, under a captain.

A battalion is 4 or more companies under a major.

A regiment is 3 or more battalions under a colonel, or a lieutenant-colonel.

A brigade is 2 or 3 regiments under a brigadier-general.

A division is 2 or more brigades under a major-general.

An army corps is 2 or more brigades, supplemented by cavalry, artillery, engineers, etc., under a major-general or lieutenant-general.

CAVALRY.

A section is 8 men under a corporal.

A platoon is 36 to 50 men under a lieutenant, or junior captain.

A troop is 3 to 4 platoons, 125 to 150 men, under a captain.

A squadron is 3 troops under a senior captain, or a major.

A regiment is 4 to 6 squadrons under a colonel.

A brigade is 3 regiments under a brigadier-general.

A division is 2 or 3 brigades under a major-general.

ARTILLERY.

A battery is 130 to 180 men, with 4 to 8 guns, under a captain.

A group or battalion is 3 or 4 batteries under a major.

A regiment is 3 or 4 groups (battalions) under a colonel.

When regiments are combined into brigades, brigades into divisions, and divisions into army corps, cavalry, artillery, and certain other auxiliary troops, such as engineers, signal corps, aeroplane corps, etc., are joined with them in such proportions as has been found necessary. Every unit, from the company up, has its own supply and ammunition wagons, field hospitals, etc.

THE UNITED STATES ARMY.

Prior to 1915 the regular United States army was a mere police body as compared with the armed forces of other countries. It was concededly highly efficient, but for the purpose of entering into conflict with such forces as those presented by Germany, France and some of the other European countries it was admittedly inadequate.

The entire force consisted of 5,004 officers and 92,658 men. The forces were divided into 15 regiments of cavalry and 765 officers and 14,148 men; 6 regiments of field artillery, with 252 officers and 5,513 men; the coast artillery with 715 officers and 19,019 men, and 30 regiments of infantry, with 1,530 officers and 35,008 men. The Philippine scouts had 182 officers and 5,733 men; the Military Academy 7 officers and 6,266 men and the Porto Rico regiment of infantry with 32 officers and 591 men.

The signal corps had 106 officers and 1,472 men, and the engineer corps 237 officers and 1,942 men. There were also about 6000 recruits in the various branches of the service under training.

The marine corps, under the direction of the Secretary of the Navy, had 346 officers and 9,921 enlisted men.

THE REGULAR ARMY.

The regular army was supplemented by the National Guards of the various States which had 7,578 regiments with 9,103 commissioned officers and 123,105 enlisted men, or a total organization of 132,208. The "reserve militia," which was in fact little more than a name, consisted of the availables for service between the ages of 18 and 45 years, and estimated on the basis of population, numbered about 20,000,000.

Before there was any real indication that the country would become actively involved in the world war steps were taken to reorganize and develop an efficient army, and under the Act which became effective on July 1, 1916, and which provides for the establishment of basic units for the army, the War Department orders and regulations fixed the basis of the organization as follows:

Sixty-four infantry regiments, 25 cavalry regiments, 21 regiments of artillery, a coast army corps, the brigade division, army corps, and army headquarters, with their detachments and troops. A general staff corps, adjutant general's department, inspector general department, judge advocate general department, quartermaster corps, medical department, corps of engineers, and ordnance department, signal corps, officers of the bureau of insular affairs, militia bureau and detached officers.

The law specifies that the total armed force shall include the regular army, volunteer army, officers' reserve corps, enlisted reserve corps, and the National Guard of the various States, subject to call for duty within the borders of the United States.

The reorganization of the army was being effected at the time Uncle Sam was called to fight for humanity, and only an approximation of the condition can be made, for about two-thirds of the National Guard had been taken into the regular service incident to the trouble with Mexico, when the Guardsmen were summoned to the border to protect the country, and recruiting was proceeding in all branches of the service to bring all the regiments up to a war footing.

UNITS ON WAR FOOTING.

The various units, on a war footing, are: Infantry regiment, 1,800 men; cavalry regiment, 1,250 men; field artillery, light regiment, 1,150; field artillery, horse regiment, 1,150; field artillery, heavy regiment, 1,240; field artillery, mountain regiment, 1,100; engineers, pioneer battalion, 490; engineers, pioneer battalion, mounted, 270; engineers, pontoon battalion, 500; signal troops, field battalion, 160; signal troops, field (cavalry) battalion, 170; signal troops, aero squadron, 90 men. Trains—infantry division: ammunition, 260; supply, 190; sanitary, 530; engineer, 10. Cavalry: ammunition, 60; supply, 220; sanitary, 300.

A division of infantry consists of 3 brigades of infantry, 1 cavalry regiment, 1 artillery brigade, 1 regiment of engineers, 1 field signal battalion, 1 aero squad, 1 ammunition train, 1 supply train, 1 engineer's train and 1 sanitary train, and comprises approximately 22,000 men and 7,500 horses and mules, and 900 vehicles, including guns. The latter figures are, however, changed by reason of the introduction of motor trucks, and automobiles, there being a consequent reduction in the number of horses and mules and a slight increase in the number of men.

A cavalry division consists of 3 cavalry brigades, 1 regiment of field artillery, 1 battalion of mounted engineers, 1 field signal battery, mounted; 1 aero squadron, 1 ammunition, 1 supply, 1 engineer and 1 sanitary train.

A brigade, in the main, consists of three regiments, the infantry having 5,500 men, cavalry brigade 2,500 and artillery brigade 2,500 men.

Under the reorganization plan the United States army would have about 293,000 in the service, but with the advent of the country's entrance into the conflict of world powers Congress passed the Conscription bill authorizing the drafting, for military purposes, all young men between the ages of 21 and 31 in the country.

MILLIONS NOT IN THE COUNTRY'S SERVICE.

The registration of those subject to call under this bill showed that there were about 11,000,000 men in the country, not in the army, navy or supporting branches, available. The bill designed to produce, within a year from the time of the signing of the law by President Wilson, of a national army of more than 1,000,000 trained and equipped men, backed by a reserve of men and supplies and by an additional 500,000 under training.

Meantime the State authorities were authorized to fill up the National Guard units and regiments to full war strength, so that with the regular army there would be a total of 622,954 —293,000 regular and 329,954 guardsmen, to be taken over by the War Department. This was the physical state of the army when the country found it necessary to ship men into France to assist the Allies in their fight against the German and Austrian forces, and General Pershing was sent to command the American troops.

The United States army and all of the military branches are armed with the Springfield magazine rifle, which holds five cartridges. It shoots a pointed bullet of tin and lead and is of .30 inch caliber. The Colt automatic pistol is used as the service weapon by officers and those requiring this sort of arm. It is a .45 caliber pistol with a magazine holding seven cartridges, which can be fired successively by simply holding the trigger back.

THE FRENCH ARMY.

Military spirit in France has had an almost incredible resurrection within the past few years. The increase in the standing army of Germany was watched closely, and as new units were added to the standing army of the latter country France retaliated by lengthening the term of military service from two to three years. This accomplished practically the same purpose without causing a ripple of excitement, and as France determined to recover her lost provinces of Alsace and Lorraine her fight is to the limit of her endurance.

There were, at the outbreak of war, 869,403 men in the National Army of France, which was composed of the Metropolitan army, having a total of 753,403 men, of the Colonial army, numbering 116,000 men. These figures do not include the personnel of the Gendarmerie, or military police, which numbered 25,000 men.

Military service is compulsory in France and all males between the ages of 20 and 48 years must serve three years in the army, the only cause for exemption being physical disability. Following the active service the soldier passes to the reserve for 11 years, after which he is seven years in the Territorial army and seven years in the Territorial reserve. The training in the active reserve consists of two periods of training and maneuvers which last for four weeks each, in the Territorial army one period of two weeks, and in the Territorial reserve, no fixed period. There are more than 2,000 reservists per battalion produced by the length of the reserve service, and when the troops are mobilized the active units can be easily maintained at full war strength. The number available in this way gives enough men for each battalion and regiment in the field with enough men left over for routine home guard work.

FRENCH MILITARY DIVISIONS.

There are two infantry regiments, composed of from six to eight battalions, to the brigade, in the French army, with two brigades to a division and two divisions to an army corps. A field artillery regiment, consisting of nine batteries of four guns each, is attached to each division. With nine field and three howitzer batteries and six reinforcing batteries added under mobilization, each corps on a war footing has 144 guns. There is also added to every army corps in the field one cavalry brigade of two regiments, one cavalry battalion, engineer companies and sanitary and service troops. The cavalry divisions are composed of three brigades of two regiments each—together with three batteries of horse artillery. There is in an army corps, when mobilized, approximately 33,000 combatants, and in a cavalry division 4,700 men. An aeronautical corps in the French army consists of 334 aeroplanes and 14 dirigibles.

In the Reserve army at the time of mobilization there were two divisions in each region, corresponding to those in the active army. When they were mobilized the 36 reserve divisions contained virtually the same organization and strength as the troops of the line. There were a large number of troops for garrisoning the various fortresses when the regional regiments, engineers and foot artillery were utilized for this work.

The Territorial army also consists of 36 divisions and garrison troops. When the remaining men of the Reserve and Territorial armies were summoned to the depots they were available to maintain the field army at full strength.

In the French field army there were 20 army corps, a brigade consisting of 14 battalions, and 10 divisions of cavalry; when war was declared. When this was raised to its full war strength the active army numbered 1,009,000 men, the reserves and depots 1,600,000, the Territorial army 818,000, and the Territorial Reserve 451,000, a grand total of 3,878,000 soldiers. At this critical time, therefore, France had at her command about 5,000,000 trained men.

Lebel magazine rifles of .315 inches caliber are used by the infantry, while the cavalry uses the Lebel carbine. The field piece is a rapid-fire gun of 7.5 centimeters, or 2.95 inches, of the model of 1907, and is provided with a shield for the protection of the gunners. A howitzer of 12 or 15.5 centimeters is the type used by the French army.

The French artillery is generally admitted to be in a class by itself, and the commissariat is excelled by none other. The infantry is most deceptive in appearance, but the ability of the French to march and attack has never been surpassed.

THE RUSSIAN ARMY.

There are 1,284,000 men in the Russian army in times of peace, while the war strength is 5,962,306. The young man of Russia is compelled to enter the army at the age of 20 years, the military service being compulsory and universal, terminating at the age of 43 years. The period of service in the active army is three years in the case of the infantry and artillery, and four years in other branches of the service. The soldier then passes to the reserve, where he serves for 14 or 15 years, during which period he receives two trainings of six weeks each. After 18 years in the active and reserve armies he is transferred to the Territorial army for five years. There also exists a modified system of volunteers for one year who supply the bulk of officers required for the reserve upon mobilization.

The Russian army is divided into three forces, the army

of the European Russia, the army of the Caucasus and the Asiatic army. There are 1,000 men in a Russian battalion, 4 battalions constituting a regiment, 2 regiments a brigade and 2 brigades a division.

RUSSIAN FIELD BATTERIES.

The field batteries are composed of 8 guns, the horse batteries of 6. The ordinary army corps is made up of 2 divisions, a howitzer division and one battalion of sappers, and has a fighting strength of approximately 32,000 men. The rifle brigades form separate organizations of 8 battalions with 3 batteries attached. The Cossacks, who hold their lands by military tenure, are liable to service for life, and provide their own equipment and horses. At 19 their training begins; at 21 they enter the active regiment of their district; at 25 they go into what is termed the "second category" regiment, and at 29 the "third category" regiment, followed by 5 years in the reserve. After 25 years of age, their training is 3 weeks yearly. In European Russia the field army consists of the Imperial Guard and Grenadier Corps, 27 line army corps and 20 cavalry divisions; in the Caucasus of 3 army corps and 4 cavalry divisions. The Asiatic army is composed of Russians with a few Turkoman irregular horse, and is mainly stationed in East Siberia. Since the Russian-Japanese war these forces have been increased and re-organized into a strong army which, at the outbreak, was capable of mobilizing, together with auxiliary troops, more than 200,000 men.

The small-arm of the infantry is the "3-line" rifle of the 1901 model. It has a magazine holding five cartridges, a caliber of .299 inches, a muzzle velocity of 2,035 foot seconds, and is sighted to 3,000 yards. The arm of the cavalry and Cossacks has a barrel 2¾ inches shorter, but uses the same ammunition, and is provided with a bayonet which no other mounted troops use. The field piece is a Krupp rapid-fire, shielded gun, of the 1902 model, with a muzzle velocity of 1,950 foot seconds, the shell weighing 13½ pounds.

AUSTRIA-HUNGARIAN ARMY.

There are 472,716 men in the army of Austria-Hungary during times of peace, with a war strength of 1,360,000 soldiers. Military service is universal and compulsory, beginning at the age of 19 years, and ending at the age of 43 years. The term of service in the common or active arm of the service is for two years in the case of the infantry and three years in the cavalry and horse artillery.

There is a Landwehr, or first reserve, in which the term of service is 10 years in the infantry, and seven for the cavalry or horse artillery, which service is followed by that in the Landsturm, or second reserve, in which the soldier serves until his forty-second birthday. Hungary possesses a separate and distinct Landwehr and Landsturm, which constitute the Hungarian National army. There is also a supplementary reserve intended to maintain the units of the common army at full strength.

The Empire is divided into 16 army corps districts, each presumed to furnish a complete army corps of two divisions to the active army. Every infantry division is composed of two brigades of 8 battalions each, 1 artillery brigade and 10 batteries of six guns, a regiment of cavalry, and a rifle battalion. The army corps also contains a regiment of field artillery or howitzers, a pioneer battalion and a pontoon company, and numbers about 34,000 combatants.

There are 6 permanent cavalry divisions, each made up of 2 brigades—24 squadrons, 3 batteries of horse artillery and a machine-gun detachment numbering about 4,000 men. It is estimated that the war strength is, active army, 1,360,000; Austrian Landwehr, 240,000; Hungarian Landwehr, 220,000; Landsturm, 2,000,000 and reserve of 500,000, or a grand total of 4,300,000.

The infantry carries the Mannlicher magazine rifle, .315-caliber and a cavalry carbine of the same make. The field gun is a Krupp which uses a 14½-pound shrapnel and the field howitzer is a 10.5 centimeter piece which fires a 30-pound shell. The Hungarian cavalry is accounted fine, but the main force is not regarded as efficient as the German or French.

THE ITALIAN ARMY.

The army of Italy on a peace footing is only about 250,-860 men, exclusive of the troops in Africa, but the country is able to mobilize a large force, and some of its branches of service are the most efficient in the world. Service is compulsory and general, beginning at the age of 20 years. After two years in the standing army there are six years in the reserve, four years in what is known as the mobile militia and seven years in the territorial militia.

There is compulsory training in both the reserve and the territorial militia, ranging from two weeks to six weeks. In organization each division of the army consists of 2 brigades composed of 2 regiments, comprising 3 battalions, together with a regiment of field artillery, with 5 batteries. The division has a war strength of 14,156 officers and men and 30 guns. The cavalry division comprises 2 brigades of 4 regiments and 2 horse batteries. Each army corps has two divisions in which are included a regiment of field artillery, 3 heavy batteries, a regiment of cavalry and one of light infantry.

There is available for army service the military police, known as the Carabinieri, besides the aeronautical corps, with half a dozen or more companies, 30 aeroplanes and a dozen airships. There are also the frontier troops organized for defense of the mountains, and which troops waged heroic and picturesque warfare in the mountain passes. There are in these troops 8 regiments of Alpine infantry, comprising 26 battalions, and 2 regiments of 36 mountain batteries.

The army strength approximates 2,600,000, made up of

700,000 active army, 400,000 mobile militia, which is the second line of defense, and the territorial militia, about 1,500,000. The infantry is armed with a magazine rifle of 6.5 millimeters caliber known as the Mannlicher Carcano, but up to the beginning of the war the territorials used a different type.

GREAT BRITAIN'S ARMY.

The military establishment of Great Britain consists of the Regular army and the Territorial army, aside from the Indian army and the local forces in the various colonies. These armies are recruited from youth between the ages of 18 and 25 years, who are recruited by voluntary enlistment. The enlistment period is for 12 years, although it can be prolonged under certain circumstances to 21 years.

Three to nine years is the period with the colors, and the remainder of the enlistment is with the Army Reserve. Many men elect to serve seven years with the colors and five with the reserve. Recruits are subjected to five months' training, and each year are called out for six weeks, supplemented by six days' musketry practice for the infantry.

The Home army consists of 9,740 officers and 172,610 men, the Army Reserve of 147,000 and the Special Reserve of 80,120, and the Territorial army of 313,485, a total of 724,955 men. Raised to war strength, these forces would number 29,-330 officers, 772,000 men and 2,072 guns, the batteries being of six guns, except the heavy batteries and those of the Territorial army, which have four. During the Boer War England put more than 1,000,000 men in the field.

The United Kingdom is divided into seven "commands," and the London district, all of which include from two to three territorial divisions, and one to four territorial cavalry brigades, in addition to detachments of varying size from the Regular army. Two nearly full divisions are stationed at Aldershot and in Ireland, one complete division in the Southern and one in the Eastern "command." There are also six aeroplane squadrons, each with 18 aeroplanes.

The Lee-Enfield rifle, caliber .303, is the arm of the infantry and cavalry. In the Regular army the field artillery has an 18-pounder Armstrong gun, the horse artillery a 13-pounder, the field howitzers are 40-pounders, and the heavy batteries are armed with 60-pounders.

The Territorial army was organized along the lines of the American militia, and could scarcely be expected to distinguish itself when pitted against the German regulars.

BELGIAN ARMY PEACE FOOTING.

The Belgian army peace footing is 3542 officers and 44,061 men, with a war strength estimated at from 300,000 to 350,000. The infantry is armed with the Mauser rifle, the artillery with a shielded Krupp quick-fire piece of 7.5-centimeter caliber.

In 1913 the Netherlands had in its standing army 1,543 officers and 21,412 men and 152 guns. On a war footing it could probably be raised to 270,000 men. The small arm is the Mannlicher rifle and carbine, the field gun is the same as that of Belgium.

Servia has 10 divisions, divided into 4 army corps. The peace footing is 160,000, and the war strength about 380,000. The rifle is the Mauser model of 1899, and the field piece a quick-firing gun of the French Schneider-Canet system.

Bulgaria has a peace army of about 3,900 officers and 56,000 men. It is armed with the Mannlicher magazine rifle, the Mannlicher carbine, the Schneider quick-fire gun and a light Krupp for the mountain batteries. On a war footing the country musters 4 army corps and 550,000 men.

Roumania's army is about 5,460 officers and 98,000 men. On a war footing it has 5 army corps and 580,000 men. The infantry uses the Mannlicher magazine rifle and the cavalry the Mannlicher carbine. The field and horse batteries are armed with the Krupp quick-fire gun of the model of 1903.

In 1912 Greece had a peace establishment of 1,952 officers and 23,268 men, but the recent war has caused her to augment them to 3 army corps, and her war footing is not far from 250,000 men. The infantry is armed with the Mannlicher-Schonauer rifle of the 1903 model and the field artillery with Schneider-Canet quick-fire guns.

Japan has a peace strength of 250,000 men, with a reserve of 1,250,000, and a total war strength of 1,500,000 men, out of a total available force capable of fighting of approximately 8,239,372 men.

SPAIN'S STANDING ARMY.

The standing army of Spain is 132,000 men. The reserves are estimated at 1,050,000, and the total war strength at 1,182,-000. The total available unorganized force is 2,889,197 men.

The army of Denmark on a peace footing is 13,725 men, with a reserve of 71,609. The total war strength is a little more than 85,000 men, and the total fighting population is approximately 470,000.

Sweden has a peace strength in excess of 75,000 men, and a reserve of more than 500,000, giving an estimated war strength of 600,000 men. The total available unorganized force is about 500,000.

Norway has a standing army a little larger than that of Denmark—about 18,000 men—with 90,000 reserves, giving a total war strength of about 110,000 men. The unorganized force available is about 360,000 men.

Portugal has a peace strength of 30,000 men, with a reserve of 225,000, making a total war strength of more than one-quarter of a million. The unorganized fighting material is more than 800,000.

Turkey, which reorganized its forces within recent years, has a peace strength of 210,000 men, about 800,000 reserves, giving a war strength of over a million, and has a total available unorganized force to call upon of more than 3,000,000.

The little army of Montenegro is a permanent body of about 35,000 men. There are no trained reserve forces, but there is an available fighting population of 68,000, outside of the army, to call upon.

CHINA'S MILITARY RESOURCES.

Recent events throw some doubt on the figures regarding China's military resources, but the last available figures credited the great Republic of the East with a force of 400,000 men, augmented by 300,000 reserves. With this total war strength of 700,000 soldiers, estimates of the available unorganized fighting material reaches the stupendous figure of 63,000,000.

Brazil has a peace strength of 33,000, with more than 500,000 reserves, with more than 4,000,000 unorganized available material.

As relating to the armed strength of the nations abroad, some reference to the system of fortifications which protect the various countries is interesting at this point. Following years —in fact, centuries—of study, Central Europe has been strongly fortified with a system of embattlements which have reached the limits of human ingenuity.

In the east of France, along the frontier where France, Switzerland and Germany meet, there are the first-class fortresses of Belfort, Epinal, Toul and Verdun in the first line, reinforced by Besancon, Dijon, Langres, Rheims, La Fere and Maubeuge in the second line, with smaller fortifications close to the German frontier at Remirement, Luneville, Nancy and other points. Along the Italian frontier the fortresses are situated at Grenoble, Briancon and Nice, with Lyons in the rear. There are strong forts at all naval harbors, the defense of Paris consisting of 97 bastions, 17 old forts and 38 forts of an advanced type, the whole forming entrenched camps at Versailles and St. Denis.

On that line of the German frontier which faces France there are the fortresses of Neu-Breisach, Strassburg, Metz and Diedenhofen, in the first line, with Rastatt, Bitsch and Saarlouis in the second line, and Germershein in the rear. Situated opposite Luxemburg is Mainz, with Coblentz and Cologne opposite Belgium and Wesel opposite Holland.

All along the northern coast, from Wilhelmshafen to Memmel, the German coast is strongly fortified. Memmel is the pivot point of the northern and eastern frontier, the latter frontier being protected by Konigsberg and Allenstein, of the first line, and Danzig, Dirschau, Graudenz, Thorn and the Vistula Passages, of the second line. South of this point are Posen, Glogau and Breslau, which face Poland, while beginning at Neisse the strong defense against Austria consists of fortifications at Glatz, Ingolstadt and Ulm, the approaches to Berlin being guarded by Magdeburg, Spandau and Kustrin.

POLISH QUADRILATERAL.

Along the line of the Russian frontier which guard that country from attacks by the Germans are the fortresses of Libau, on the Baltic; Kovna, Ossovets and Ust-Dvinsk, in the Vilna district, and in Poland there are situated Novo-Georgievsk, Warsaw and Ivangorod, on the Vistula, and Brest-Litovsk, on the Bug—four strongholds known as the Polish Quadrilateral. Guarding Petrograd are the smaller fortifications of Kronstadt and Viborg, with Sweaborg midway down the Gulf of Finland near Helsingfors. Sebastopol and Kertch, in the Crimea, and Otchokov, near Odessa, are the fortifications which guard the Black Sea.

Along the Austrian frontier are the strong embattlements of Cracow and Przemysl, on the road to Lemberg in Galicia. These forts face Poland. In Hungary there are Gyula-Fehervar and Arad, on the Maros River, and which guard the approach from the angle of Roumania. On her frontier facing Servia there are Alt-Orsova and Peterwardein, on the Danube, and Sarajevo, in Bosnia, with Temesvar and Komorn blocking the approach to Vienna from the southeast. On the Adriatic are Cattaro, on the edge of Montenegro, and the naval arsenals of Pola and Trieste. All the Alpine passes of the Tyrol are fortified, but neither Vienna nor Budapest has any defenses.

The fortifications of Italy, aside from those on her coasts, extend in a line from Venice, through Verona, Mantua and Piacenza to Alessandria and Casale, which face the French frontier.

CHAPTER X.

THE WORLD'S NAVIES.

GERMANY'S SEA STRENGTH—GREAT BRITAIN'S IMMENSE WAR FLEET—IMMENSE FIGHTING CRAFT—THE UNITED STATES' NEW BATTLE CRUISERS—THE FASTEST AND BIGGEST OCEAN FIGHTING SHIPS—THE PICTURESQUE MARINES: THE SOLDIERS OF THE SEA.

JUST as Germany at the outset of the war had the most efficient and, broadly speaking, the greatest army in the world, so England had the greatest navy in the world. As a matter of fact, Great Britain's domination of the seas was very largely responsible for the development of the super-submarine by Germany, and the putting into effect of the submarine warfare which proved so disastrous to the Allies. This for the reason that Germany, having sought for means to offset Great Britain's power and control of the seas, turned to the underseas craft.

Up to the accession of Emperor William II—the Kaiser —Germany's navy was little more than a joke. In 1848 the National Parliament voted six million thalers for the creation of a fleet, and some boats were constructed. But the attempts to weld Germany, then little more than a federation, into a nation having failed, the fleet was put up at auction, and actually sold in 1852. Prussia, a separate state, had started a fleet of her own and purchased the German boats.

This fleet, just before the American Civil War, consisted of four cruisers, carrying 28 cannon, and one cruiser having 17 cannon, besides which there were 21 "cannon boats," carrying two and three cannons each. The Prussian fleet merged into the North German Confederation in 1867, and in turn became part of the fleet of the new German Empire in 1871.

In the war with France the German fleet played no part. There were one or two clashes between French and German small boats, but that was all. Even the successful outcome of

171

the war did not inspire Germany to build up a navy. Plans for the greater navy were first outlined about 1882, but for a period of seven years not a battleship was built, concentration being placed upon the torpedo boat. The idea of developing the torpedo boat fleet belong to the present Grand Admiral von Tirpitz, then a young officer. The fleet became the best in the world, but its usefulness was soon checked by the new inventions, searchlights, gatling guns, etc.

Germany's fleet legislation of 1898 for the first time looked ahead and established rules for future building. The Spanish-American and the Boer wars disquieted Germany, and about 1900 the fleet was doubled by legislation. In 1906 the campaign of submarines, torpedo boats and greater battleships began. Part of the program required that 12 torpedo boats be built each year. Additional legislation for the construction of cruisers and battleships was effected in 1908, and in 1912, until at the beginning of the war, Germany had 38 ships of the line, 14 armored cruisers, 38 protected cruisers, 224 torpedo boats and 30 submarines. There were no torpedo-boat destroyers, the small cruisers taking their places. The naval organization contained 73,000 officers and men. The largest boats are the dreadnoughts, which are divided into several classes. One of the last of these built by Germany was the Derfflinger, which had a displacement of 28,000 tons.

The personnel of the German navy prior to the war was 79,197 officers and men.

THE BRITISH NAVY.

Because of the fact that the territory of Great Britain is scattered over the face of the globe and that it is necessary to use the highways of the sea for reaching her various possessions, the navy of that country is undoubtedly the greatest collection of fighting ships ever gathered together under one flag.

In order to take care of her population of 1,625,000,000 she has gathered together a navy consisting of 60 modern battleships, 9 battle cruisers, 34 armored cruisers, 17 heavy protected cruisers, 70 light cruisers, 232 destroyers, 59 torpedo boats of the latest type, 75 submarines, together with 50 seagoing auxiliaries of the fleet, which are used as mother ships to destroyers, mine-layers, distilling ships, oil ships, repair and hospital ships, with 145,000 officers and men.

The first group, completed between 1895 and 1898, includes six battleships, all of 14,900 tons displacement, 12,000 horsepower and 2,000 tons coal capacity. The speed is 17.5 knots, the armor belt being from 10 to 14 inches at the big guns and with a mean armor belt of 9 inches. The armament consists of 4 12-inch guns, 12 6-inch rapid fire, 16 3-inch rapid fire, 12 3-pounder rapid fire, 2 light rapid fire and 2 machine guns. They have one torpedo tube above water and two under water.

MONSTERS OF THE SEA.

A later group of six was built in 1900 and 1902. These monsters of the sea are of 12,950 tons displacement, 13,500 horsepower and have 2,300 tons coal capacity. They have a speed of 18.25 knots, 6 inches of armor belt and from 8 to 12 inches protection for her big guns. The armament consists of 4 12-inch rapid fire guns, 12 6-inch rapid fire, 10 3-inch rapid fire and 2 light rapid fire and 2 machine guns. There are four torpedo tubes.

Gradually England developed larger and larger vessels from this point, increasing the displacement in each group from 16,350 tons in 1906 to 20,000 in 1911, and finally to 25,700, when the Queen Elizabeth and Warspite were completed in 1915. These boats—England's superdreadnoughts—are of 58,000 horsepower (turbine), 4,000 tons oil capacity. They have a speed of 25 knots, 13.5 inches of armor belt and from 8 to 13.5 inches protection for the big guns. The armament consists of 8 15-inch, 16 6-inch and 12 3-inch rapid fire guns. They have five torpedo tubes. There were 150,609 officers and men in the navy when England entered the war.

THE FRENCH NAVY.

At the beginning of the war the French navy ranked fourth among the navies of the world. She had 18 battleships of the older types, and which ranged in date of launching from 1894 to 1909. There were building at that time eight ships of about 23,095 tons displacement. Although France had no battle cruisers, she had 19 armored cruisers. The heavier of these ships had a designed speed of 23 knots, and carried from 2100 to 2300 tons of coal. Their main batteries consisted of 2 7.6-inch rapid fire and 8 6.4-inch rapid fire guns.

Two protected cruisers, the D'Entrecasteaux and the Guichen, and 10 light cruisers of no fighting importance completed the list of French ships.

France was, however, strong, so far as numbers go, in destroyers, torpedo boats and submarines, there being 84 destroyers, with displacements of 276 to 804 tons and speeds of 28 and 31 knots. She possessed 135 torpedo boats and 78 submarines, but many of these were of small size. One hundred and one of her torpedo boats had displacements of about 95 tons, and 20 of the submarines had displacements of 67 tons.

Of the submarines, there were 33 which had a displacement of 390 tons, 2 of 410 tons, 6 of 550 tons, 2 of 785 tons and 7 of 830 tons. This displacement, which was surface, is usually 70 per cent of the submerged. The larger submarines carry from six to eight torpedo tubes. In the early part of 1916 the French Government had 12 submarines building, these latter having surface displacement of 520 tons and having Diesel motors of 2000 horsepower. The speed of these submarines is 17½ knots on the surface and 8 knots submerged.

Attached to the French fleet are 16 auxiliaries, used as mine-layers, submarine destroyers and aeroplane mother ships, of from 300 to 7,898 tons.

There were 61,240 officers and men in the navy of France when war was declared.

THE RUSSIAN NAVY.

With the ending of the Russo-Japanese war the Russian navy was given an overhauling. There were but three of the old battleships of the Russian navy left after this fateful struggle, these being the Tri Sviatitelia, the Panteleimon and the Czarevitch. The Russian Government labored diligently to build up her navy, and is still doing her utmost to readjust that branch of her service.

With the outbreak of the great war she had six armored cruisers, none of which was in the Black Sea. These averaged in tonnage from 7,900 to 15,170 tons displacement. There were eight cruisers of from 3,100 to 6,700 tons, and of no fighting value whatever.

Russia had but 14 torpedo boats, all small and of little value. She had a fairly good fleet of destroyers and submarines, having 91 of the former and 55 submarines.

There were 36,000 officers and men in the service when hostilities opened.

THE AUSTRIAN NAVY.

When the war was declared Austria, Germany's supporter, had nine battleships ready. These were completed since 1905, as follows: In 1906 and 1907 there were finished three battleships which displaced 10,433 tons, had 14,000 horsepower and 1315 tons coal capacity. They had a speed of 19.25 knots, 6 to 8.25 inches of side armor and 9.5 inches protection for the big guns. The armament consisted of 4 9.4-inch, 12 7.6-inch rapid fire, 14 3-inch rapid fire and 16 smaller guns. They had two torpedo tubes.

In 1910 three other ships were added to the navy. These were slightly larger than those described just above, having a displacement of 14,268 tons, with engines of 20,000 horsepower. They had three torpedo tubes.

Three ships of 20,000 tons displacement were launched in 1912 and 1913. They had a speed of 20 knots and four torpedo tubes. Three other battleships had been built up until 1906, and these, together with 10 light cruisers, were in the Austrian navy at the breaking out of hostilities.

The torpedo boat destroyers, of which there were 18, must not be forgotten. Twelve of these were of 384 tons, capable of making 28½ knots. These carried 4 12-pounders and 2 21-inch torpedo tubes. They were built for oil fuel.

There were six submarines in this navy, these being of moderate size, ranging from 216 to 235 tons displacement on the surface.

THE JAPANESE NAVY.

There were 9 first-class battleships in the Japanese navy at the beginning of the world war. Of battle cruisers there were 5, while of the older battleships 13 were ready for orders. Twelve first-class cruisers were ready for duty, and there were 9 second-class cruisers and 9 third-class cruisers. Of gunboats there were 5, 60 destroyers, 37 torpedo boats and 15 submarines. The personnel of the Japanese navy consisted of 47,000 officers and men.

THE ITALIAN NAVY.

Italy was ready for her part on the seas with 7 first-class battleships, 8 of the older type, 9 first-class cruisers, 5 second-class cruisers, 10 third-class cruisers, 5 gunboats, 46 destroyers, 75 torpedo boats and 20 submarines. There were 36,000 officers and men to handle these ships.

THE TURKISH NAVY.

When hostilities were declared Turkey had a navy consisting of 2 first-class battleships, 3 battleships of an older type, 2 first-class cruisers, 2 second-class cruisers, 4 third-class cruisers, 8 gunboats, 2 monitors, 10 destroyers and 8 torpedo boats. The officers and men in the Turkish navy numbered 30,000.

UNITED STATES NAVY.

The United States navy, which has made an enviable reputation for itself wherever and whenever the boats and men have been engaged, ranked third at the beginning of the war. While not of the heaviest type, the boats were of the most improved models, and maintained on a basis that justified the belief that they would stand up in the face of the severest opposition.

There were 12 modern battleships, 30 of an older type, 10 armored cruisers, 5 first-class cruisers, 4 second-class cruisers, 16 third-class cruisers, 30 gunboats, 9 monitors, 74 destroyers, 19 torpedo boats and 73 submarines, manned by 55,389 officers and men. The California, Idaho, Arizona, Mississippi and Pennsylvania are the latest battleships of the navy, and are of the super-dreadnought type. All of these battleships have a displacement of more than 31,000 tons, and have the most complete equipment that it is possible to command. The batteries consist of 4 13-inch and 14 6-inch guns, 4 6-pounders, together with 4 21-inch torpedo tubes. There is a variation in the batteries, but all have approximately the same kind of armament.

One of these huge vessels is about 625 feet long, and has a speed of from 21 to 23 knots. The Pennsylvania, one of the largest, is of 31,500 horsepower, and cost approximately $7,250,000. In addition to this, Congress had authorized the construction of what is designed to be the supreme type of fighting vessel. The plans for these vessels call for the construction of vessels aproximately 875 feet long and nearly 90 feet wide. Some idea of what enormous vessels these must be may be gained when it is seen that the cruisers are 250 feet longer than the super-dreadnought.

The battle cruisers have six decks, extending from end to end, and are so extensive that they almost constitute a battle-front.

This comparison to a battlefront on land becomes interesting when consideration of it is further pursued. There are even railroads to fetch ammunition to the guns, though they run vertically instead of horizontally. The general headquarters is in the conning tower, to which all lines of "field communication" lead—telegraphs, telephones, etc.

The "observation posts," for directing and correcting the range and aim of artillery, are at the tops of the two wire "bird-cage" masts. This work is helped (as on land) by kite balloons and aeroplanes, which, as part of its fighting equipment, the battle cruiser carries. To blind the enemy ships, under suitable circumstances, the big guns create a "barrage" of water, by directing their fire at the sea in front of the hostile vessels, throwing over them a mass of spray.

AMPLE PROVISION FOR THE WOUNDED.

On board the battle cruiser is a fully equipped field hospital, supplemented by battle dressing stations near the guns, for the emergency treatment of the wounded. To the musicians of the ship's band is assigned the duty of carrying wounded men to the dressing stations and the hospital, the latter being on one of the lower decks, beneath the water level.

The battle cruiser, built long and narrow, has a great speed. The four monster propellers are driven by electricity, which is generated by engines fed with fuel oil. The speed attained is 35 knots an hour, which means the same speed as a train traveling at the rate of 40 miles an hour, since the sea mile, or knot, is longer than the land mile.

In order to obtain this enormous speed it was necessary for the designers of the battle cruisers to sacrifice armor protection. The armor on these ships is but an eight-inch belt. The real object of the battle cruiser is to use its superior speed and overwhelming gun power to overtake and destroy the enemy's ships of the second line, the auxiliaries and scouts.

Each of these vessels has a displacement of 34,800 tons—

meaning, in plain language, that they weigh that much, hence displace that much water when launched. The biggest British battle cruiser, which is the largest battle cruiser afloat, is the British Tiger, which has a displacement of 28,500 tons, and is less in length by 150 feet than these mighty battle cruisers. The Tiger is much less formidably armed, carrying eight 13½-inch guns. The largest German battle cruiser is the Derfflinger, of 26,200 tons, and armed with eight 12-inch rifles.

Our latest commissioned dreadnought, the Arizona, has engines of 31,400 horsepower. The engines of that monster passenger steamship, the ill-fated Lusitania, were of 70,000 horsepower. Those of the Tiger boast 120,000 horsepower. But each of our six battle cruisers has 180,000 horsepower to drive her through the water.

HUGE FIGHTING CRAFT.

These huge fighting craft are the most expensive ships ever built. Each of them cost about $20,000,000, the money outlay being something like $16,500,000, exclusive of armor and guns. And for each battle cruiser must be provided, in the way of personnel, 1,153 enlisted men, 64 marines and 58 officers.

While the American Navy had but 55,389 men when the war opened it was quickly increased, and under the Army bill, which provided for the reorganization and increasing of the land forces, the naval forces were also increased.

The bill increasing the authorized enlisted strength of the navy to 150,000 did not provide for any additional officers above the rank of lieutenant. The increase in the enlisted force amounts to 57,000, the authorized strength at the time of the law's passage being 93,000. Based on the increase, the allowance of officers would be 747 lieutenants and 954 lieutenants junior grade and ensigns.

The increase in the enlisted strength of the Marine Corps from 17,400 to 30,000, or by 12,600, also gives an additional allowance of 504 officers to the corps, which, under the bill, are distributed among the grades of major, captain, first lieutenant and second lieutenant.

The Marine Corps is one of the most picturesque military organizations in the world. There is, probably, no other such body of trained soldiery. While they are under the control of the Navy Department, they can be detached from that branch of the service and assigned for duty with any other branch of the military forces of the country.

POLICEMEN OF THE SEA.

They are the policemen of the sea; they are artillerymen, infantrymen, cavalry, engineers, and soldiers, first, last and all the time. They are the first troops in action, and there is no restriction as to the kind of military duty they are called upon to perform.

The Marines served on shore and on board vessels of the navy throughout the Revolutionary War, two battalions having been authorized by the Continental Congress November 10, 1775. The present organization really dates from July, 1798, when Congress passed an act approving the establishment of an organization to be known as the Marine Corps, consisting of 1 major, 4 captains, 16 first lieutenants, 12 second lieutenants, 48 sergeants, 48 corporals, 32 drums and fifes and 720 privates.

Every one of the 15,000 men who composed the more than a century old Marine Corps when the war broke out was ready and on his toes when the call for action came. There was nothing in the way of scientific preparedness that got by them. In the matter of trench helmets, for instance, when it was time for the American nation to come to the front in the great world war, the Marines had a helmet so much of an improvement on the one used by the Allies that there was no comparison.

Armored motorcars, likewise, of the most improved type, belonged to the Marine Corps when the call for action came.

These cars are capable of making 45 miles an hour, and there were plenty of them for service in the Marine Corps. Some interesting equipment never used before the big war composed part of the quartermasters' stores in the Marine Corps.

It's a marvel what these chaps can do with a big naval gun—one of those big brutes which are bolted down to the deck of a warship. It doesn't look like a thing to be picked up and carted around the country. That's precisely what the heavy artillery companies do, however. It takes them but a few minutes to sling one of these five-inchers over the side of a ship, land it, and take it wherever it is needed. They do this with the aid of a single-spar derrick, some little narrow-gauge trucks and a portable narrow-gauge railroad.

TRANSPORTATION OF BIG GUN.

The method is to lay down the railroad—it can be done very swiftly by men carefully trained in the art of laying tracks over all kinds of ground—put the gun and its mount, with a specially prepared base of extremely heavy timbers, on the tracks, and trundle it to the place where it is needed to pour a rapid fire into the enemy.

Here a pit has been dug, in which is laid down the heavy timber base, riveted together with heavy steel bolts. Then it is well packed with dirt and stone, and the gun carriage made fast ingeniously. The single-stick derrick has been erected alongside, guyed out in four directions with heavy ropes, which are made fast to the ground by means of "dead men," and manipulated by very live gangs of husky marines. A chain block of powerful type is used to pick up the gun carriage and put it in place, and afterwards to swing the gun into its sockets on the carriage.

Later the breech locks and sights are added, and the big five-inch, 40-caliber naval gun is ready to go into action. These big and heavy guns, suitable for long range work with high explosive shells, can be taken a quarter of a mile or so from the ship which carried them, over rough ground, set up and put in operation in a few days' time.

But the heavy artillery base is only one of the Marines' work. They have big howitzers, of the more modern type, most of which are kept at Annapolis, where they can be loaded aboard ship in short order. Men and machines can be mobilized at the strategic points in a very short time.

EVERY MAN'S SERVICE.

The Marine service is unique in many respects. For one thing, it is every man's service. The proportion of officers who have risen from the ranks or who have been commissioned from civilian life is higher in the Marine Corps than in either the Army or the Navy. This, of course, makes for democracy in the corps. An enlisted man, who does not wait until he is too far up in the 20's to enlist, has a very fair chance of earning his commission. Another thing—and this is of prime importance to the ambitious fellow—promotion goes by merit. In the army and navy the young officer is promoted by seniority.

Things are a bit different in the Marine Corps. In this organization a man doesn't absolutely have to wait for his number to come around. If he distinguishes himself above his fellows, he may be promoted without much regard for age or length of service. He goes up as he is able to, by his active ability and his readiness to work hard and effectively for Uncle Sam. There are advocates, of course, of both systems. There are merits which both systems can justly claim. But it goes without saying that this possibility of promotion keeps everybody in the Marine Corps on the jump.

Even the enlisted men who are too old to get commissions have something to work for. Not very long since Congress authorized the appointment of "warrant officers" in the Marine Corps. The Navy had this grade for many years. It is new in the Marine Corps, and is an added incentive to hard work.

Another incentive—and perhaps the strongest one—that

draws young fellows of the up-and-doing sort into the Marine Corps is that of active service. The Marines boast that they are always on the job; that no matter how peaceful the time, the Marines are sure to see "something stirring" right along. It is a saying—and a true one—in the Marine Corps that every marine who has served the ordinary enlistment in the corps since the Spanish-American war has smelt powder. Ever since the fuss with Spain the marines have been covering themselves with glory. In that little war of 1898 the Marines were the first to land in Cuba. They held Guantanamo for three months. In 1890 they saw service in the Philippines; the next year in China. In 1902 the Marines took part in the fighting against Aguinaldo, the wily Filipino leader. In 1903 they put down the rebellion in Panama, captured Colon and opened up the Panama railroad. In 1906 they helped quiet the uprising of that summer in Cuba. They were in Nicaragua in 1909. From 1911 to 1913 they did more duty in Cuba, with a whirl in Nicaragua again in 1912. They helped hold Vera Cruz for three months in 1914. Next year they went to Haiti, where they have been moderately busy from time to time since. Santo Domingo saw them in 1916.

AN UNAPPROACHABLE RECORD.

Neither the army nor the navy can claim anything to beat it—you couldn't tell a marine that the rival branches of the service can claim anything to equal it. And as for the modern implements of warfare—the European armies have no advantage over the marines for testing out new devices. They had armored cars, for instance, as far back as 1906; they began to use motor trucks for military purposes as early as 1909. Every marine expedition is equipped with its quota of armored trucks. They would as soon think of voyaging over the seas to put down an incipient revolution without their armored cars and motor trucks as they would of going to meet the enemy without their rifle.

There used to be an old joke about "Horse Marines." A sailorman on a horse is an incongruous thing—a sight to make you hold your sides. But the marines are not plain sailormen. They are "soldier and sailor, too," and as soldiers they have turned the joke on the old saw about "horse marines." There are "horse marines" these days, and mighty good cavalry they make.

The marine can ride with the best of the cavalrymen. And in the fracas in Domingo there were two cavalry companies of marines organized.

THE MANY-SIDED MARINE.

It takes a bit longer to make an efficient marine than to make an infantryman. This because the marine is a man of many specialties. He is, of course, in season and out of season, an international policeman. That's his job in time of peace. But when he fares abroad to fight his country's battles he may be called upon to do almost any kind of work. He may be an artilleryman; a signalman; an airman. He may be, and usually is, anything that his country needs at that particular time. And he is trained to meet the emergency.

The new recruit, in ordinary times, is sent for his first instruction to Port Royal, down in Georgia. There he has nothing to do but drill, drill, drill, until he can do the infantry evolutions in his sleep. He learns to drill, he learns to keep clean—the Marines are something of a dandy corps—and he learns to take care of himself no matter what happens. He is taught to be a soldier and a man. He learns to walk straight, shoot straight, think straight. And then he goes for a spell to sea—for after all, he needs sea legs as well as land legs.

But these two tricks of duty by no means end the marine's schooling. When he has become an efficient all-around man he may specialize. He may, if he chooses, go into the signal corps and learn the multitude of details connected with this ultra-modern arm of the service. He learns to send messages by every possible means. He learns to operate a radio. And, it might be mentioned in passing, the Marine Corps is equipped with the very finest of radio apparatus. They have big trucks which carry the outfit and supply the power for either sending radio messages or operating huge electric searchlights. Or he may go into aviation.

INTERNATIONAL BOUNDARIES BEFORE THE WAR.

This map shows the boundary lines between nations as they were at the beginning of the war, as also the coast lines of Europe. The latter are brought out in bold relief.

CHAPTER XI.

THE NATIONS AT WAR.

UNEXPECTED DEVELOPMENTS—HOW THE WAR FLAMES SPREAD—A SCORE OF COUNTRIES INVOLVED—THE POINTS OF CONTACT—PICTURESQUE AND RUGGED BULGARIA, ROUMANIA, SERVIA, GREECE, ITALY AND HISTORIC SOUTHEAST EUROPE.

THE real history of the greatest war of all times is the history of the entire world, touching every phase of existence in a manner that has never been approximated by any other conflict. The motives and ramifications are so great that it is almost impossible for the human mind to grasp the significance of many things of importance which, at a glance, seem to be but incidents.

The world looked on expectantly when the war started, because there was a general knowledge of the conditions existing in Europe and the undercurrent was felt by students of international affairs. But that Russia would revolt and the Czar abdicate, as he did in March, 1917, and the iron-ruled country would set up a government of its own—would join the circle of democracies—was not even hinted at. Neither was it intimated that Constantine I, King of Greece, would abdicate in favor of his son, Prince Alexander, as he did in the following June, under pressure, because of his sympathy for Germany.

Neither was there a suspicion that the fire started by the flash of a pistol and the bursting of a bomb in Bosnia would spread until sixteen countries were arrayed against Germany and Austria, supported by the Bulgarians and the Turks. And to these must be added the entrance into the conflict of Canada, Australia, New Zealand, possessions of Great Britain, and smaller possessions of other countries. The flames swept over the face of the earth in this fashion:

Starting with the movement of Austria against Servia, after the assassination of the Archduke Ferdinand, there lined up as a consequence of the alliances formed between the powers, the countries referred to in preceding chapters. The triple alliance was originally an agreement between Germany, Austria-Hungary and Italy, to strengthen their positions, and the Triple Entente consisted of agreements between France, England and Russia.

INVASION OF BELGIUM.

Briefly, the invasion of Belgium by Germany, and her ambitions in the southeast, where Russia had what amounted to protectorate relations, drew first France, England and Russia into the strife, and step by step there became involved nation after nation. The steps, marked by the declarations of war, were as follows: On July 28, 1914, Austria declared war on Servia, and on August 1 Germany made the declaration against Russia. Next Germany turned upon France, on the third day of August, and also on Belgium, whereupon, on the following day, Great Britain declared war on Germany; a day later Austria-Hungary issued the mandate against Russia, and two days later, or on August 8, Montenegro declared war on Austria. Austria accepted the challenge, and then Servia took up the cudgel against Germany. France made formal declaration of war on Austria-Hungary and by the end of August Montenegro had declared against Germany; Great Britain on Austria; Japan on Germany; Austria on Japan; Austria on Belgium. Later, or early in November, Russia declared herself against Turkey, as did France and Great Britain.

For six months the battle raged and the rest of the world regarded the result with grave concern until in May of 1915 Italy, having renounced her alliance with Germany and Austria, declared war first on Austria, then on Turkey. In the fall of 1915 Servia took up arms against Bulgaria, as did Great Britain, France, Italy and Russia. Then Germany declared against Portugal, whose government replied in kind;

Austria followed Germany in the alignment and finally, in August, 1916, there were exchanges of sharp "courtesies"—the complete severance of all diplomatic relations and open warfare—between Roumania and Austria-Hungary; then between Bulgaria and Roumania, with the consequent alignment of the Central Powers. Italy had also made her declaration against Germany specific. So for nine months the war waged with terrible bitterness until on April 6, the United States, by the proclamation of President Wilson, was finally at war with Germany.

IN THE NATURE OF MERE FORMALITIES.

These steps were, in many instances, in the nature of formalities, for the relationships of some of the countries involved placed them in the position of practically being at war before formal announcement was made. The position then, was that Germany, Austria-Hungary and Turkey were supported by Bulgaria, who was anxious to get redress for having been cheated out of what she regarded as her rightful possessions in the settlement of the Balkan war question. Those aligned on the other side were England, France, Russia, Montenegro, Italy, Belgium (which had been making defensive warfare in keeping with her desire to be true to her neutral pledges); Servia, Roumania, Japan, Portugal, the United States, the little principality of Monaco, which is best known as the seat of Monte Carlo, the great gambling center of Europe, and San Marino, a similar "patch" on the map of Europe. Brazil, Guatemala, and the little Republic of Cuba also aligned themselves against Germany in support of the Allies, though there was no actual engagement of their forces. Thus there could be counted as at war against the Central Powers in June, 1917, sixteen countries.

Most interesting of all the countries involved were those belonging to the Balkan group and centering in southeastern Europe. The Balkan nations, Bulgaria, Servia, Montenegro,

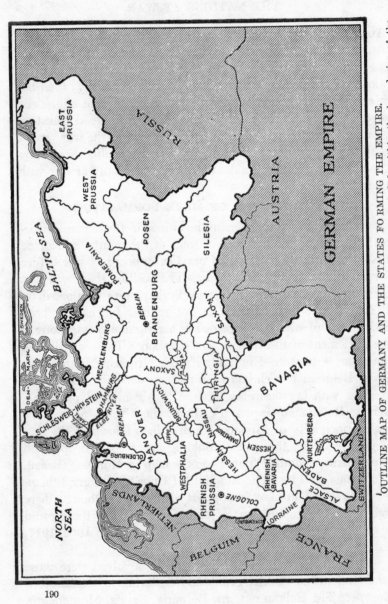

¹OUTLINE MAP OF GERMANY AND THE STATES FORMING THE EMPIRE.

This drawing shows the location of the twenty-five States which were included within the boundaries of the German Empire at the beginning of the war.

with Greece, paved the way for their entrance into the conflict when they formed an alliance, in 1912, for common protection, particularly for the enforcement of one of the provisions of the Berlin Treaty, guaranteeing local government to the Bulgar and Serbian colonies in Macedonia. Montenegro began war on Turkey in October, and Bulgaria, Servia and Greece joined and drove the Turks out of many of their strongholds.

"COMIC OPERA" SOLDIERS.

In a month of fighting the little countries, in the picturesque southeastern section, whose soldiers have been depicted as "comic opera" soldiers, had rent Turkey; Greece had captured the famous Macedonian city of Salonica, once known as Thessalonica, where was located the church in which was addressed St. Paul's Epistle to the Thessalonians; while the Servians had captured Monastir, one of the most important centers in Macedonia, and the Bulgarians had driven the Turks almost to the famed city of Constantinople. The Servian soldiers finally marched to the Adriatic sea, and Albania raised a flag of its own and asked Austria-Hungary and Italy to recognize its independence and grant it protection.

Within little more than two months Turkey had been deprived of the greater portion of her possessions in Europe and a treaty of peace was signed between the allied countries and the Turks. By this agreement Albania became in effect a suzerainty, protected by Austria. But the agreement between Germany, Austria-Hungary and Italy—the Triple Entente—gave those countries a combined power which, when it came to fixing the terms of peace, left the small allied countries of victory at a disadvantage, and while Montenegro and Greece gained some territory, as did Servia, Bulgaria lost what she had gained in the war. Turkey lost 90 per cent of her Empire in Europe, which so aroused the country that the rising of the young Turks followed and the government was reorganized. The enforced terms of settlement, however, set the little countries at each other's throats.

The field of the Balkan battles is the very center of the world's history. Along the Adriatic, Ionian and Agean seas are lands and territories peopled with races that mark their ancestry back to the very darkest ages. The protected country of Albania, with its rocky surface, numbers among its peoples descendants of the Arnauts, whose very origin is a mystery. They were present before the days of Greece and Rome. The Ottoman Turks, the Bulgars from the plains of the Volga and the Ural Mountains, the Serbs, the Roumanians, Russians, Italians, the Slavs, Tartars.

A REGION OF MOUNTAINS.

Albania is a mountainous region along the Adriatic coast, peopled with descendants of the ancients who maintain their characteristics. They are said to be descendants of the Pelasgian races, which inhabited the territory before the Greeks builded their Athens.

The Albanians are wild, daring mountaineers, and though the people have, to all intents and purposes, been under Turkish rule for centuries, they have never recognized the sovereignty of the Sultan. It was originally part of the Turkish Empire in Europe, having been taken by Turkey, in 1467, and is a fertile, but wild country.

The same picturesque people that make up the population of Albania constitute the populace of the little country of Montenegro, which was once part of the Turkish possession. Montenegro contained about 3486 square miles of territory before its acquisitions in the Balkan wars. Aided by Russia, the country obtained its independence from Turkey in 1878, and in 1910 became a kingdom. Its present area is about 5650 square miles and the population 520,000. The capital is Cettinje.

Bulgaria was also once a part of the Turkish possessions,

and under the Treaty of Berlin, in 1878, became a suzerainty. It is a famous pastoral country, inhabited by a people for years held under the Ottoman heel. They are racially Turanians, and kin of the Tartar and Huns, who came into their present fertile country from the vast plains of eastern Russia. They made their way thither more than a thousand years ago, and battling at the very gates of Constantinople, by their fierce crusades, secured the grants from the Byzantine Empire of the territory, which constitutes the Bulgaria of today. The population is nearly 5,000,000, and the country contains about 43,000 square miles.

WHY ITALY ENTERED THE WAR.

Italy's reasons for entering the war, aside from her demands for territory, in exchange for continuance of neutrality, have to do with matters of years gone by, when she began the struggle for her liberation from the Austrian domination. Italy desired, among other things, to acquire Trentino, Goritz, and other adjacent territory controlled by Austria, but Italian in every attribute. Trentino is a rocky region, and strategically valuable to the country possessing it, which was proved by the terrible struggle which the Italians were forced to make in their attacks against the Austrian forces.

The city of Trent is the capital of Trentino, famous in history, and the seat of the long church council in 1545-46. It was in turn controlled by Roman, Goth, Hun, Lombard and Holy Roman Empire. It is the site of many historic buildings, notably the cathedral of Trent, which is a fine example of Lombard architecture, and the church of Santa Maria Maggorie, where the famous Council of the Roman Catholic Church was held. There are old towers, and libraries rich in manuscripts.

Trentino is famous for its mountain passes, over which the Italians have been compelled to drag their heavy artillery and implements of war. The Alpini, the mountaineer soldiers

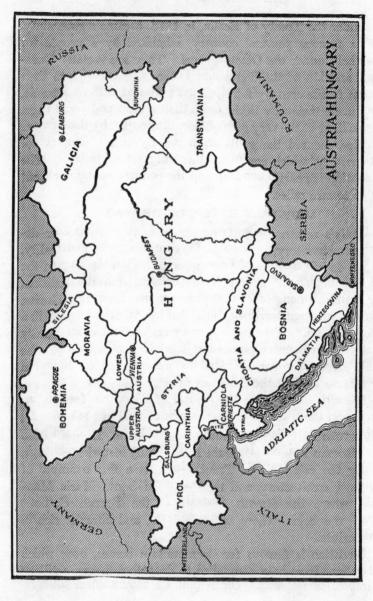

OUTLINE MAP OF THE AUSTRIA-HUNGARY EMPIRE.

Drawn and engraved especially to show the Provinces comprising the Empire, and their locations as they were at the beginning of the war. This is a country of many nationalities and languages.

of Italy, are among the most picturesque in the world. They have scaled the almost perpendicular faces of the Alps, climbing from crag to crag with their bodies roped together, dragging machine guns in pieces strapped to their shoulders. Tolmino, Trieste, Istria, Dalmatia, Avlona, the prime harbor of Albania (seized by Italy in the fall of 1916). These are little spots in the territory logically Italian, which Italy covets.

DIVIDED INTO SIXTEEN DEPARTMENTS,

Italy, since its consolidation into one kingdom in 1870, has been divided into sixteen departments comprising sixty-nine provinces. The country has a total area of 110,623 square miles, and a population of a little more than 35,000,000. The Roman Catholic Church is irrevocably linked to the history of Italy and Rome, its capital, marked the farthest advance of civilization in the ancient days. It possesses four distinct zones, ranging from the almost arctic cold of the mountain belts to an almost tropical heat in the southern lowlands. It is one of the picturesque countries of the world, a center of art, industry and travel.

Servia, which is separated from Austria-Hungary by the Danube, is of precisely the same character as the other rich, mountainous region. The country was subjugated by the Turks, who retained possession of it until 1717. Austria then wrested control from the Turks, and held it until 1791, when Turkey again dominated it. In 1805 the Servians revolted, and secured temporary independence, only to again come under the Ottoman rule. Again it secured freedom in 1815, and by the Treaty of Paris, independent existence was secured for it. Turkey became only a nominal authority. It became a kingdom in 1882, after having become absolutely independent with the Berlin Treaty.

The people are Slavonic, and kin to the Croats of ancient history. They are described as having come from Poland and Galicia, moving down the Danube, into what is the present kingdom. In the fourteenth century the Servian empire comprised the whole Balkan peninsula, from Greece to Poland, and from the Black Sea to the Adriatic. But Servia warred with Turkey, and her troops were defeated in the great battle at Kossovo, and the Ottoman power became supreme. The country has an area of about 34,000 square miles and a population of 4,600,000.

LITTLE BOSNIA'S FUTURE.

Bosnia, where was assassinated the Archduke Francis Ferdinand, of Austria, was a Turkish province, west of Servia, and under the treaty of Berlin was to be administered for an undefined period by the Austrian government. The little section contains about 16,000 square miles and has a population of about 1,750,000, largely of Slavonic origin. They are partly Mohammedans, partly Roman Catholics and Greek Catholics. In the middle ages Bosnia belonged to the Eastern Empire. Later it became a separate kingdom, dependent upon Hungary, only to be conquered by the Turks. It is the mountainous, rugged country of the Julian and Dinaric Alps, but has many fertile valleys, and is well watered by the river Save, and its numerous tributaries.

Greece, the modern kingdom, is one of the countries that for centuries were politically included within the limits of the Turkish Empire. In its present form it represents but a portion of that country, famous in history, as the Greece of the Ancients—that classic land which holds the most conspicuous place in the pages of ancient history—but still it is inclusive of the greatest names belonging to the glorious past. It is the country of Athens, Sparta, Corinth, Thebes and Argos. It is separated from Turkey by a winding boundary, extending from the Gulf of Arta on the west to the Gulf of Salonica on the east.

The earliest settlers were the Pelasgi, who were in course of time replaced by the Hellenes. They, in turn, were succeeded by the Phoenicians, who swayed the country. Athens, Sparta, Thebes and Corinth came into existence and became the centers of political government, of the most progressive advancement in civilization. Civil discords brought on first the Peloponnesian War, about 434 B. C., and made them prey to the Macedonians. Successively invaded by Goths, Vandals and Normans the country came into the possession of the Turks in 1481, though for two centuries the power of the Turk was questioned by the Venitians. Revolt was had from the Ottoman yoke in 1821, and independence was secured by the interference of foreign powers after the defeat of the Turk at the Navarino, in 1827. Through the succeeding years it has been a protected monarchy.

ONE OF THE BALKAN GROUP.

Roumania, the largest of the Balkan group, lying between Russia on the north, and Bulgaria on the south, is the home of the Gacians, descendants of the warlike tribes who for years held their own against Greek and Roman. After the fall of Rome the province became a melting pot, through which the hordes of invaders, passing from Russia to Asia, were in a sense made one people. The Goths, the Huns, the Lombards, the Bulgars and the Magyars traversed the region, leaving many settlers. It became divided into two provinces, Moldavia and Wallachia, known as the Danubian provinces.

Both provinces were conquered by the Turks in the fifteenth and sixteenth centuries, and under Peter the Great the Russians attempted the conquest of the provinces. In 1859 the two provinces were united under a prince whose independence both Turkey and Russia recognized, and in 1881 the country declared itself a kingdom. The province of Wallachia derives its name from the people who early settled there, the Wallachs. The Roumanians claim descent from Vlachi, a colony of Romans, who settled in Thrace, and, in the twelfth century, emigrated to the Danube. The name Roumania is derived from the word Roman, the country having originally been "the Land of the Roumani." Roumania has a population of about 7,600,000 and comprises 64,000 square miles.

Macedonia, famous country of Greece in the time of Philip, father of Alexander the Great, embraced the entire region from the Scardian Mountains to Thessaly, and from the Epirus and Illyria to the river Nestos, taking in what is now part of Salonica. It was reduced by the Persians and subsequently Alexander the Great made it the nucleus of a vast and powerful empire along with Greece. Ultimately it passed under Roman sway, until it was ceded, in 1913, to Greece.

AN OBJECT OF CONTENTION.

Alsace-Lorraine is worthy of note, as comprising one of the territories which for centuries have been the cause of conflict between Germany and France. It is pointed to as the physical evidence of the humiliation of France at the hands of the Germans, in 1870, and has for nearly one-half a century been a German imperial territory. The surrender of Alsace and part of Lorraine was made the principal condition of peace on the settlement of the war of 1870. Bismarck, it is said, might have been content with a language boundary, taking only that portion of the country in which lived those who spoke the German tongue.

For strategic purposes, however, Alsace and Lorraine, with the exception of one district, were taken. The strip or country was to be governed by the power of the German Emperor until the constitution of the German Empire was established. Many of the inhabitants opposed the Prussian domination, and a vote was taken on who would declare themselves Germans and remain in the territory, or French and leave. More than 40,000 left the country and went into France.

The German language was made compulsory in the schools, the courts and the legislative body. The French never forgot their loss, and revenge for that loss has been a subject

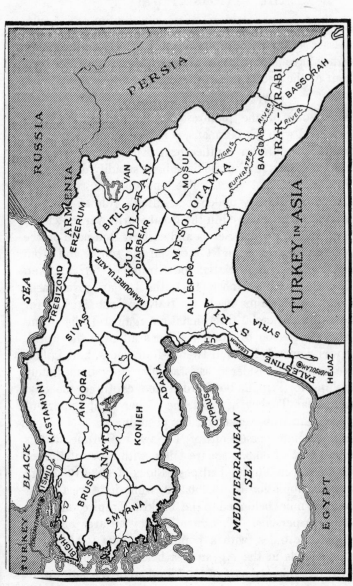

OUTLINE MAP OF TURKEY IN ASIA.

A country where civilization was first born and which is now undergoing a new birth of a new civilization.
The location of the Garden of Eden was between the Tigris and Euphrates rivers. The drawing
shows the country which is mentioned largely in Bible history.

of consideration in their foreign policy ever since the war of
1871. Alsace and Lorraine contain about 5600 square miles,
and together have a population of about two million. About
85 per cent of the people speak German.

PICTURESQUE TURKEY.

Turkey, one of the picturesque and ancient countries
which is aligned with the Germans, is a Mohammedan state of
the Ottoman Empire in southeastern Europe and western
Asia, whose holdings in Europe have been steadily decreasing,
especially during recent years. The immediate possessions of
Turkey, or those directly under the Sultan's rule at the time
this country became involved in the great world war, extended
from Montenegro, Bosnia, Servia and eastern Roumelia on the
north, to the Agean Sea and Greece on the south, and from
the Black Sea to the Adriatic, the Straits of Otranto and
the Ionic Sea. In September, 1911, the Italian government
sent a long list of claims made by Italy against Turkey for
economic and commercial discrimination against Italian commerce, and the person of Italian citizens all over the world.
A reply was demanded within twenty-four hours, and failing
to receive a reply considered satisfactory, Italy immediately
sent warships to Tripoli, bombarded and captured the city.
This meant that Turkey has lost one of her most important
seaports, consequently weakening her position.

The immediate possessions of Turkey in Europe, at this
time, had an area of 65,350 square miles, with a population of
6,200,000. In Asia Turkey had possessions of 693,610 square
miles, with a population of 16,900,000, while in Africa about
398,000 square miles belonged to the Turkish Empire, on which
lived 1,000,000 persons. This gave Turkey an area of about
1,157,860 square miles, with a population of 24,100,000. A
number of islands in the Agean Sea belong to Turkey, and
Egypt is also nominally part of the kingdom of the Sultan.

The population is a motley assortment of races, nationalities and creeds. About 88 per cent being Ottomans or Turks. The Slavic and Rouman races come next in importance, then the Arabs, the remaining population consisting of Moors, Druses, Kurds, Tartars, Albanians, Circassians, Syrians, Armenians, and Greeks, besides Jews and Gypsies.

PHOENIX OF THE GREEK EMPIRE.

The Ottoman Empire arose from the ruins of the old Greek Empire, early in the fifteenth century, Constantinople being made its capital in 1453, after its capture by Mohammed II. At the accession of Mohammed IV, in 1648, the Turkish Empire was at the zenith of its power. Internal corruption caused loss of power, and in 1774, a large slice of territory was ceded to Russia. In 1821 Greece became independent. The Crimean War, in 1854-56, checked Russia for a while, but in 1875 the people of Herzegovina rebelled. A year later the Servians and Montenegrins revolted, and in 1877 Russia began hostile operations in both parts of the Turkish Emipre. At this time Roumania declared her independence. After the fall of Kars and of Plevna, the Turkish resistance completely collapsed, and in 1878 Turkey was compelled to agree to the Treaty of San Stefano.

Within the year the Treaty of Berlin declared Roumania, Servia and Montenegro independent; Roumanian Bessarabia was ceded to Russia, Austria was empowered to occupy Bosnia and Herzegovina; and Bulgaria was made a principality. The main events in the history of the Ottoman Empire since the Treaty of Berlin were the French invasion of Tunis in 1881, the Treaty with Greece, executed under pressure of the Great Powers in 1881, by which Greece obtained Thessaly and a strip of Epirus; the occupation of Egypt by Great Britain in 1882; the revolution of Philippopolis in 1885, by which eastern Roumelia became united with Bulgaria. In 1908 Bulgaria declared its independence and the Young Turk Party extorted a constitution and a parliament from Abdul-Hamud II, who was deposed in 1909 by the unanimous vote of the national assembly. Mohammed V, eldest brother of the deposed Sultan succeeded to the throne.

Russia, "the Great Bear," whose part in the war brought on internal strife and revolution which robbed Czar Nicholas of his throne, traces its history back for more than ten centuries, when the Norse invaded the territory and founded Veliki Novgorod, for many years one of the chief Russian cities. The Norse, to use the modern vernacular, "put Russia on the map" when the Russian army fought its way to the very walls of Constantinople. Much of the early history of the country is legendary, and one of the famous stories is that after Igor, who commanded the great armies, was put to death by rebellious subjects, his widow sought out the territory where her husband had lost his life and pretending to make peace with them, requested every householder to give her a pigeon.

WINGED FIREBRANDS.

When they gladly complied with her request she sent the tame birds back home with flaming firebrands tied to their tails, and they entered their lofts or rests and started fires which destroyed the city of Korosten. The ascendancy of the Romanoff dynasty, which maintained in Russia through the centuries, was established through the atrocities of Ivan the Terrible, who is said to have absolutely destroyed the descendants of the Rurik, the first Norse chieftain. Ivan the Terrible was the first Czar of Russia. He conquered Servia and his domestic infamies and intrigues are among the historical scandals of the country.

Through every reign in Russian history there ran stories of terrible crime, cruelties, infamies, immoralities and degradation. Following the death of Ivan the Terrible came Fedor, one of his sons, who was a weakling in the hands of the Duma of five, one of whom was Boris Godounoff. Fedor reigned but a few years, and Godounoff was elected Czar. He was am-

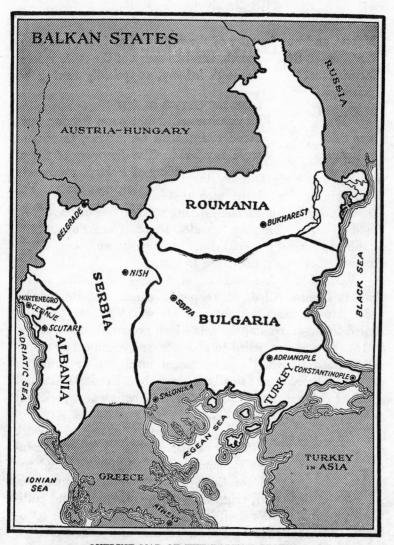

OUTLINE MAP OF THE BALKAN STATES.

This drawing shows the boundary lines as they were at the beginning
of the war. It also shows the location of the principal city of each country.
This part of the world has always been of great importance since the earliest
history of man and nations—a continuous struggle between nations to control this gateway into southwestern Asia.

bitious, and was founder of the system of serfdom, and also of the Russian State Church, and like many of the other rulers of Russia, met death through infamy, supposedly having been poisoned.

BASE IMPOSTER SLAIN.

Boris Godounoff was succeeded by his son Feodor, but he was seized by a pretender, and with his mother, thrown into prison, where they were murdered. The discovery of the plot which was laid at the door of the King of Poland, produced an uprising and Czar Dimitry the Impostor, was slain. Vasili Shouyskie, leader of the mob that slew Dimitry, was proclaimed Czar, but pretenders sprang up, and one of these, who posed as a false Dimitry, invaded Russia from Poland, and established a rival imperial court at Toushin, and some of the Russian cities swore allegiance to him.

Vasili Shouyskie held out at Moscow, and after a time Dimitry's cause failed, whereupon Sigsmund, of Poland, invaded Russia, and put forward his son Vladislav. Vasili, roused to anger, committed acts which provoked Moscow, and in 1610 he was compelled to abdicate, and a council of nobles was formed to run the government until a Czar could be chosen. Vladislav was finally selected, but, Feodor Romanoff sought to prevent his being crowned. There was a period of anarchy, cities were burned, and chaos was complete.

The dignitaries of the church and state finally set to work and supported the candidacy of Mikhial Feodorovitch Romanoff, who was the first Romanoff Czar. He reorganized the empire, and reigned for thirty-three years. His successor, Alexis, the direct heir, reigned for thirty-one years, and cultivated friendly relations with Ukraine and the Cossack country. He was followed by Feodor II, and then came Peter the Great. There were two claimants to the throne, Ivan and Peter, both sons of Alexis by separate wives, and the difficulty was settled by letting the two reign jointly under the regency of Sophia, a sister of Ivan.

When Ivan died Peter assumed the reins, and it was he who gave Russia a frontage on the Black Sea, and on the Baltic, and built St. Petersburg. He did much for the development of Russia, creating a navy and a merchantile marine.

Catherine the First, his widow, followed him in reign, and at her death, Peter II occupied the center of the stage. At his death there was chaos again and counter claims. Anna of Courtland, a daughter of Ivan, brother of Peter the Great, was finally elected sovereign, but she was a mere puppet, vesting her authority in a High Council.

FAMILY'S WRETCHED CAREER.

During her reign her lover, named Biren, held sway and distinguished himself by sending thousands of political exiles to Siberia. At the death of Anna, Ivan IV, her grandnephew, reigned, but was deposed and sent to prison for life, while Elizabeth, youngest daughter of Peter the Great, succeeded him. She permitted the government to be run on comparitively honest lines by favorites, and while they ruled she drank herself to death.

Her nephew, Peter III, succeeded her. He was incompetent and a tool in the Prussian hands. His wife was a German princess, and led a movement which ended in his being deposed, imprisoned and murdered.

Catherine, widow of the murdered Peter, succeeded. She was known as Catherine the Great, and is credited with having been the most infamous of women in all history. Catherine was succeeded by Paul, who was assassinated by his own couriers when he was on the point of joining Napoleon Bonaparte in his conquest of India.

His son was Alexander I, who added Finland and Poland to Russia, and founded the Holy Alliance. He was followed by his son Nicholas, who ruled for 30 years, and crushed the Poles and Hungarians, but died of a broken heart in the Crimean War.

Next came Alexander II, who gained fame as liberator of the serfs, and died the victim of a Nihilist bomb thrower. Alexander III succeeded him, and then came Nicholas II, the last Czar, whose reign lasted 22 years. The beginning of the end was marked by the request of the workingmen in 1905 for an increase in civil rights. They were fired upon, and there was general disorder, until the Czar proclaimed a constitution, and established a Duma, or national parliament, which met for the first time in 1906.

BETRAYAL OF RUSSIA'S MILITARY PLANS.

The outbreak of the war was marked by the personal decree of the Czar to change the name of the capital, St. Petersburg, to Petrograd, but his evident intent to eliminate evidences of German influence did not stop the betrayal of Russia's military plans by German spies within the court circles, and it was charged that supplies were withheld from the Russian army by those within the charmed circle, who were friendly to Germany.

Russia was a party to the Franco-Russian and Anglo-Russian agreement, which constituted the basis of the Triple Entente, but conditions were such that the soldiers refused to fight, and the situation culminated in the uprising which ended with the abdication of the Czar, in behalf of his brother, who, however, declined to accept the throne, unless he should be elected by the votes of the Russian people. The Duma thereupon decided to organize a republican form of government, and so the Russian Republic came into being in March, 1917.

Spain, a fertile country in the southwestern part of Europe, has played a prominent part in the development of the world. She has a coastline extending nearly 1500 miles, and there are about 200,000 square miles included in her territory. The coastlands and the southern section of the country are especially rich in fruits and agriculture. Although watered by many rivers, the land, for the most part, is artificially irrigated.

Up until 1898 Spain held possession of magnificent colonies in Cuba and Porto Rico and the Philippines, but now her colonial possessions are confined to a strip on the west coast of the Sahara, and the island of Fernando Po, with some smaller possessions on the Guinea coast in Africa. Their total area is about 434,000 square miles, the total population being 10,000,000.

SPAIN, PAST AND PRESENT.

Spain formerly composed the ancient provinces of New and Old Castile, Leon, Asturias, Galicia, Estremadura, Andalusia, Aragon, Murcia, Valencia, Catalonia, Navarre and the Basque Provinces. These, since 1834, have been divided into 49 provinces. The capital of Spain is Madrid, and the present constitution dates from 1876. There is a Congress, which is composed of deputies, each one representing 50,000 of the population.

The Roman Catholic faith is the established form of religion, and the priesthood possesses considerable wealth and power, although the dominant influence once possessed has been curtailed of recent years. The peace strength of the army is about 83,000, and what navy she has is practically new, as the Spanish navy was annihilated in the war with the United States in 1898.

During recent years the republican tendencies among the people have found vent in socialism. The Spanish socialist leaders belong mostly to the intellectuals, and here again is the weakness of the movement, whether considered as a means of giving Spain a republic or of liberating her political system under monarchical form. Some of the intellectual leaders among the socialists headed straight for philosophic anarchy, while others expended their energies in building castles in the clouds.

The substantial socialism of the recent period was, however, based on the workingmen's movement. Before the outbreak of the great war the tendency was to affiliate with the groups in other countries of Europe which advocated socialism as an international creed. But when the German socialists placed their country above internationalism, and the French socialists did the same, and the Italian socialists joined in the agitation to force the government into war to get back territory lost to Austria, the international basis of Spanish socialism disappeared.

CHAPTER XII.

MODERN WAR METHODS.

INDIVIDUAL INITIATIVE AS AGAINST MASS MOVEMENTS—TRENCH WARFARE A GAME OF HIDE AND SEEK—RATS AND DISEASE—SURGERY'S TRIUMPHS—CHANGED TACTICS—ITALIAN MOUNTAIN FIGHTING.

WARFARE such as carried on in the Great World War is so different from that of any other of the great wars which the world has seen, that it might be described as a method of fighting distinctively unique. Undoubtedly, more ancient methods, and even ancient weapons, have been employed than were used in any of the wars which have changed, from time to time, the boundary lines of nations. The fighting of mass against mass has been practically obliterated, and modern evolutions where the plan is man to man have developed a mode of fighting where terrible execution has resulted.

Undoubtedly this means of fighting has developed the personal initiative of the soldiers, and the modern fighting machine of the nations is of a high standard, which, together with death-dealing weapons, has resulted in terrible havoc. Massed movements, such as carried on in the War of the Rebellion, have been practically done away with, and although there have been long and costly sieges, they have been carried on by tedious trench fighting, airships, hand grenades, and massive shells fired from guns of great caliber, and with a range which is really marvellous.

Shells are fired, shrapnel in some cases, explosive shells in others, which are timed to the second, so that when fired from guns many miles from the objective point, they explode at a measured distance from the earth. They are exploded within a gauged distance of the target, and the execution is done over a measured area. On the shells are indicators. Within the shrapnel shells are hundreds of small shot. As the shell explodes the shots are scattered over the enemy, and death and destruction are unavoidable.

With bomb shells, fired from guns of the largest caliber, there are also indicators which are timed to the second. The range and time of explosion previously figured out by officers, the shell explodes where it is intended that it shall, and the work of the great explosive is done with resultant damage.

WAR'S MANY DEVELOPMENTS.

The war has developed many of the new methods of fighting and revived many of the old means of warfare. Cavalry has not been as active in the relation in the great war as in any of the wars of comparatively recent date, because of the extensive trench warfare which has formed so much of the fighting plan. Fighting has been a question of trench raids, and barrage fire, followed by the infantry charge through shell holes. The impression brought home to the modern observer is that the older recognized methods of warfare are gone for good.

The thing which war changed in the work of the cavalryman is in the nature of an addition, rather than a subtraction from his duties and the training he must have. The day of cavalry—as cavalry and nothing else—has passed. For today the cavalryman must be familiar not only with the sword, lance and revolver, but with the rifle as well. It has been demonstrated that such long periods of trench warfare may develop that it becomes necessary for him to dismount and make himself valuable in the scheme of military economy by fighting as infantry until such time as the enemy line is broken and he can again take to his horse and the work of harrying the retreating foe.

The war has been full of surprising results as regards cavalry. It was popularly supposed that in facing such terrible modern weapons as the repeating rifle of long range, the machine gun and the automatic field pieces which have become so well known as the French "75s," any body of cavalry which attempted to charge the enemy would be annihilated.

CAVALRY'S SUCCESSFUL CHARGES.

Yet all through the early stages of the war one reads of desperate, and, what is more to the point, successful charges made by British cavalry against batteries of German field pieces. There was one instance in France, just back of the Belgian frontier, where a charge of British lancers against a German battery, which had a commanding position, saved the day for a greatly-outnumbered allied detachment, which was conducting that most difficult of all maneuvers, a rear guard action, covering the retreat of the body of the army. The charge of the lancers took the Germans so by surprise, and was executed with such speed, that despite the heavy fire they poured into the advancing horsemen the latter were at work among them with spear and saber before reinforcements could be brought up. Then the cavalry, dismounting and unslinging their carbines, defended the position with such tenacity that the German advance was delayed several hours, sufficient for the rest of the allied forces to make good its withdrawal and the consolidation of the new lines chosen for defense.

This idea of cavalry serving in the double role of infantry and cavalry is a distinctly American development, a trick which the Federal and Confederate armies taught the world during the Civil War, and of which the British made excellent use in South Africa against the Boers. The fact which this war has established, however, is that the older use of cavalry, in the charge against infantry, artillery and even entrenched positions is still of great value. The idea had developed from the tactics so largely employed in the Civil War of using the cavalry as mounted infantry, that the increased deadliness of modern weapons would make this use of cavalry the sole use.

Now, however, it seems that not even the lance is to be discounted. Given the opportunity to reach his objective, the lance becomes a terrible weapon in the hands of the horseman. In hand-to-hand fighting the man with the rifle and bayonet has some chance against the mounted man with the saber. While fighting upward from a lower level he has a pretty long reach, and the advantage of being completely in control of his own movements, whereas even the most expert horseman cannot control the step and movement of his mount as well as a man can control his own. Barring fire, however, the infantryman has no chance against the lance, with the speed and momentum of the mounted man behind it.

So, for this reason, though they are cumbersome weapons under ordinary circumstances, and make a detachment equipped with them much more likely to be seen, lances were retained by many of the British cavalry regiments, just as the German Uhlans retained them.

CAVALRY'S IMPORTANT SERVICE.

One of the most important services which cavalry fulfills in modern warfare is that of drawing the enemy's fire at the time his positions are being approached. This is done to obtain some idea of his force and the disposition of his guns.

Cavalry detachments are sent scurrying across the front, as though threatening an attack, deliberately furnishing a mark for the enemy gunners that this object of ascertaining his strength may be attained.

The more ordinary work of scouting, advance guard work, and riding wide on the flanks of an advancing force are parts of the cavalryman's work which are more familiar.

In the European conflict with tremendous concentration of troops and continued occupation of the same territory the foraging feature of cavalry work disappeared. It is no longer possible for an army to "live on the country as it goes." Food and supplies must be brought up from depots in the rear through an entirely separate and specialized department of the military organization, which does its work with a celerity certainly undreamed of in former days, even as late as our own war with Spain.

In the modern campaign trenches have been developed to such an extent that it is really marvellous how the soldiers live, and to what an extent the "underground fortresses" have been used for living as well as fighting purposes.

In a letter written by a French soldier who took part in a successful raid upon a German trench, he adequately describes the luxuries enjoyed by the German soldiers in the front line trenches in the Marne. The letter was written by a youth who had been wounded in the fight, and was mailed in April, 1917.

LUXURIOUS DUGOUTS.

"We are now living in German lines and dugouts—a magnificent work we have just now taken—cement and steel are used with profusion, and electricity in every dugout, even in their front lines. Unharmed casements and machine guns in cemented shelters and light railways and immense reserves of food—thousands of bottles of claret.

"But also, at the middle of each staircase, in the wall, a box with about seventy pounds of cheddite—to blow the shelter up in case of retreat. They knew they might have to go back, as they are doing now. America will gain victory, as until the present moment only the bravery of our soldiers can put them back, with much exertion and frequent loss.

"Our men are magnificent in spite of death. We hope your help may be quick and decisive. I think your flying corps especially may be useful, the more as yesterday, with four fellows, I was run through the field, and in a destroyed trench by a German Albatross shooting a machine gun, and flying very low, he missed us quite near. On the other hand, we have just a few days hence seen a sausage balloon destroyed by our men. Anyhow your help may be decisive.

"I believe your joy is great about the Russian revolution.

At home they are happy, too—only let us hope the Russian army may attack this summer—to help us.

"I need not tell you the impression made by your American decision here. We now know victory is sure. Let us hope it may be this year—though you may easily guess such is not my belief—next year.

"I hope my next letter be sent from farther in the German lines—perhaps from a place they have not had time to destroy."

Shorn of all technicalities, the plain method of warfare which has developed as the result of the trench building is that each force establishes lines along miles of front with trenches in rows, one after the other, at measured intervals. The soldiers are thus "entrenched." One force seeks to drive the other from its position.

MANY DEADLY DEVICES.

The force of batteries is directed against the entrenchments, hand grenades, bombs, shells, gases and every device which has fallen to the use of armies is projected at the ditches in which are hidden the enemy soldiers. When, by the concentration of attack the trenches are destroyed or the soldiers driven from their first position, the opposing force has gained if it has succeeded in advancing its own soldiers to occupy and reconstruct the trenches or defences from which the enemy was driven.

The soldiers carry, in addition to the ordinary weapons, a trench spade, and in most cases large knives, which are used to cut away brush or dig in the earth when emergency demands. The close confinement in the trenches tends to develop disease, and the sanitary force of the modern army is a thing that was undreamed of in the olden days. More men died from disease during the Civil War than were killed by bullets or in hand-to-hand encounter.

The percentage of those who die from camp fever has been

reduced to a minimum. Napoleon said that armies travel on
their stomachs, but the European War and the Russian-Japanese War have proven, as did our campaigns in Cuba and
Mexico, that soldiers live by reason of the health which they
are permitted to maintain. Some idea of the conditions which
developed in the trenches may be gained from a study of the
various hospital reports, and investigations which have been
made by physicians.

INFECTED WITH ASIATIC JAUNDICE.

Dr. Hideyo Noguchi, of the Rockefeller Institute for
Medical Research, completed a series of experiments which
showed that apparently healthy wild rats in the European war
zone became infected with Weil's disease, or "infectious jaundice," common in Asia. Weil's disease is characterized by sudden onsets of malaise, often intense muscular pain, high fever
for several days, followed by jaundice, frequently accompanied
by complications. It becomes more virulent as it is successively
transmitted from one victim to another. This is supposed to
explain the much greater mortality, about 38 per cent. in
Japan, as compared with from 2 to 3 per cent. among European soldiers.

The study of the disease was made possible by the successful importation from Japan and Flanders of guinea pigs
and rats which had been inoculated with the causative organism
in those two countries. Experiments previously made showed
that the germ of the disease was carried in the kidneys of a
large percentage of apparently healthy wild rats caught near
the districts where the disease had been epidemic. Experiments in Europe demonstrated the presence of the germ in
rats not only near the infected zones, but also in captured localities some distance from trenches.

For purposes of comparison Dr. Noguchi collected a number of rats in this country and removed their kidneys. His
report states that by inoculating the emulsion made of the kid-

neys of 41 wild rats into 58 guinea pigs during a period of three months, he had been able to produce in three groups of guinea pigs typical cases of infectious jaundice altogether identical with the findings in the guinea pigs which died of the injection of the Japanese and Belgian strains of the disease. The germs taken from wild rats caught near New York produced death in guinea pigs within nine to twelve days.

AMERICA'S GREAT SERVICE IN WAR ZONE.

In studying the conditions and helping to fight the dangers encountered in the battlefields and camps of Europe, no country in the world rendered a greater service than America. Long before the country entered the war hundreds of American nurses, ambulance drivers and surgeons were on the battlefields and in the hospitals of Belgium, France and England. Men who were leaders in the medical and surgical world gave their services to the Allies, and almost every hospital in the United States sent some of its staff.

Through the efforts and study of Dr. Alexis Carrel, of New York, deaths from wounds received in battle were reduced almost 90 per cent. by a system of treatment which he devised. Dr. Carrel began his work in 1914, at Compiegne, in connection with the military hospital, and in collaboration with the Dakin Research Laboratory, under the auspices of the Rockefeller Foundation.

Using a solution of sodium hypochlorite, the plain method of treating wounds which proved such a great boon, was described at the Congress of Surgeons in Philadelphia in 1916, where many of the wonders of war surgery were described. By means of a rubber tube, which is run through or into the wound, the injury is flushed continuously by the solution, for a period of hours or minutes, according to the nature and character of the wound.

The inflammation is reduced, the wound cleaned, and blood poisoning is averted. Under the treatment the soldier's stay in a hospital is reduced weeks and even months, and, as has been stated with authority, where in the old days twenty operations would have been necessary, the modern methods have reduced the percentage to a point where the twenty has become as one.

The story of surgery itself and what it has done in modern warfare would make a wonderful volume. The shattered bones of the legs and arms have been spliced, and laid side by side in open wounds, to knit together and practically form a new limb. Artificial hands, feet, and legs have been made by ingenious mechanics, which are so perfect that those who have been deprived of their natural facilities can use them with a degree of facility never before believed possible.

RESULT OF SCIENTIFIC SURGERY.

Armless men and legless men have worked in the munition factories of both France and of England, and the fact that they are able to do so is due to the genius of surgeons and of scientists. Thoroughness and preparation, coolness in execution and scientific accuracy in all directions is the modern necessity in warfare.

What this means in modern battle, as demonstrated in the last important conflict in the clearing of German East Africa by British forces, was decribed by Reuters' correspondent in an account of the battle of Rufiji River.

This was the last campaign personally commanded by Major General Jan Christian Smuts, the former Boer commander, and resulted in giving the British control of all the coastline and the inhabitable portion of German East Africa.

For two weary months the army lay upon its weapons, consolidating, reorganizing, rebuilding railway lines and piling up great dumps of food and ridding itself of its sick and wounded. Then it moved forward from Morogoro. The object of the advance was the ejection of the enemy from his trenches on the Mgeta River and the seizure of the passages of the Rufiji River.

The battle was directed and controlled from an observation hill at Dathumi, but General Smuts spent little time on the hill. He had made all the dispositions and issued his orders. Nothing remained for him to do and he was back in his camp calmly reading a book.

In the straw hut the brigadier general sat at a table on which was an oriented map showing the strategic and geographical points of the plans which lay before us, at his elbow the telephone and just below the hut the wireless instrument incessantly emitted sparks. Higher up the slope of the hill were the observing stations of the battery commanders.

SIGNALED BEGINNING OF BATTLE.

The burning of huts at Kiruru signaled the beginning of the battle. The brigadier general, a polite little man who has lectured at the staff college for twenty years and who knows the last word in the science of warfare, especially of artillery, called the howitzer battery by telephone.

"Open fire a little to the right of the palm tree," he said. "You have the elevation and direction. The Nigerians will be on the move." Just behind the palm tree and a little to the right a great brown cloud of mud and smoke rose high in the air. From the plain came the boom of heavy guns and all along the river branch rose clouds of smoke, mud and dust.

The staff officer handed in a telegram reading: "The infantry are now about to advance; they ask artillery support."

"Bring the field guns into action," said the general.

It was all so very matter of fact. This little man, who was about to let loose upon the German trenches a hell's broth of fire and disaster, acted as if he were in his own drawing room, deciding how many lumps of sugar he would take with his tea.

Down below on the plain the howitzers were lobbing 60-

pound shells into the German Askaris, the Nigerians were advancing by sharp rushes and the rat-tat of the machine guns and the crackle of musketry broke very faintly. Airplanes sailed above us. A message came from the Nigerians, "We are going to take the enemy's trenches; please lift gunfire." The order was passed along, "All guns lift two degrees."

Little black dots, like tiny ants, are running where the shells are bursting. The Nigerians are rushing the trenches. The forward observing officer reports that the enemy is retiring. The 15-pounders, man-killing guns, shower shrapnel on the German line of retreat.

SUGGESTS A CUP OF TEA.

The infantry report having occupied the German first line trenches, halting for one hour to consolidate. The brigadier-general commented on the difficulty of observation in the humid atmosphere and suggested a cup of tea. It seemed that nothing more would happen until after lunch, so I visited the commander-in-chief. He was occupied for the moment with a volume by George Gisslog and was satisfied with the reports he had received. By dark the whole of the German entrenchments were in our hands.

A volume could be written alone on the changes in tactics which have been developed and practiced by the military geniuses of the contending forces. In the European War the range of artillery and infantry fire was three times what it was in the Franco-Prussian War. The flattening of the trajectory, which means making the bullets go more nearly on a straight line instead of traveling in an arc, has made the fire so effective as to compel the soldiers to "travel on their stomachs." To crawl along the ground like alligators, or advance like moles digging their way into the earth.

The tremendous range of the modern rifle, single arm, or rapidfire gun, and the development of more powerful explosives for ammunition have wrought this change. The bullet will travel a longer distance at a horizontal position than in the old days when ordinary black powder and a smooth-bore gun were used, and so at hundreds of yards distance the soldiers can aim direct to kill, without making elevation allowances.

The machine gun has made it possible for the men to fire from four to five shots for every one that was fired in the Franco-Prussian War and probably ten for every one that was fired in the Civil War. The only time the soldiers exposed themselves on the army frontiers were when they were storming trenches, and this was not attempted until the trench had suffered bombardment so it was made untenable.

DIFFICULT MOUNTAIN FIGHTING

Probably nothing in the warfare of nations has been more colorful and replete with surprises than the campaign waged by the Italian soldiers on the Alpine passes between Italy and the Austrian strongholds, and in the discussion of modern warfare, a brief description of some of the work of these intrepid mountain fighters is interesting.

Much of this fighting has been the most difficult known in the annals of modern warfare, save, perhaps, that done by the famous Younghusband British Expedition to Thibet. And that, by comparison, was a very small matter.

The mere height—altitude—at which the Italian warfare against the Austrians was carried on has been sufficient to entail enormous difficulties and a great additional strain, due actually to difficult breathing in a rarefied atmosphere.

The warfare in the clouds which has characterized the struggle along the Isonzo front has been conducted at an altitude seldom less than 8,000 and often rising to 12,000 feet, which is well within the realm of eternal snow.

Naturally, therefore, most of the fighting was done in bitter cold. To this fact add the other that the Italian soldiers who carried it on were almost exclusively men who had not been accustomed to the cold. They had been drawn from among dwellers in a semitropical climate, and one gets an idea of the immense accomplishments of this army which struggled in the skies.

The average American knows the Italian as immensely industrious, but perhaps is disinclined to credit him with great constructive ability or engineering genius. He would change his estimate of him if he could see him fight and study his battlefield. The Italian warfare of the mountain peak and gorges has been a warfare of construction, even more than it has been a warfare of destruction, and has been rendered possible only by the exercise of engineering genius comparable with that which sent our world-beating American railways through the famous Rocky Mountain passes!

HALTED BY INTIMIDATION.

The fact that Italy's warfare has been invariably against positions stronger than her own is the result of the fact that while, since 1866, Austria continually strengthened her frontier with fortifications, most of them of ferro-concrete, the Italians were not able to fortify at all. Every step in that direction brought forth threats of war. These began at a time when Italy was in no condition to fight, before, as a unified nation, she became a world-power.

Being weak, she was prevented from making any preparations for defense against a foe which continually was obviously getting ready for attack upon her. The mere commencement of preparations might have precipitated war. But Austria continually prepared. Besides, the Italians ever have been a peace-loving nation.

As a natural and inevitable consequence of all these conditions all the dominating positions along the Austro-Italian frontier were strongly fortified by the Austrians. They have long occupied the crest of every mountain in such a way that their guns could rake any Italian approach from below, along a front of 450 miles—about the distance from New York to

Buffalo, and almost the same as that of the whole French-British-Belgian eastern front in this war.

During the winter of 1916, one of the most exceptionally hard winters known in the annals of the Italian Weather Service, the Italians not only have been fighting for their sunny homeland, but have been fighting in a region of eternal snow.

This snow was an obstacle extremely hard to overcome. It may be said never to have been less than six yards deep on the Isonzo front, so the task of the consolidation of positions, enabling troops at once to resist attack and protect themselves from assault from the rear, was highly difficult.

TYPICAL ROAD BUILDERS.

The Italians were ever road-builders, descendants, as they are, of those Romans who built roads for all Europe. While the Austrians were fully supplied with roads of the best and most modern character, there were hundreds of miles on the Italian side where there were not even mule-tracks.

Here was a vast problem.

Literally millions of soldiers were not free to fight, but had been drafted for the road-building work. Carrying picks and shovels, managing steam-shovels, working electric hoists, stringing supporting cables, they were as truly fighting men, however, as any who ever bore rifles or worked machine-guns.

Miles of the roads were rebuilt under Austrian fire, by men who built them well enough, even in the great 8,000-foot heights, that they could bear heavy artillery of vast weights without suffering damage. They built them in such easy gradients that heavy artillery could be moved speedily, the guns and motor-lorries that passed over them frequently weighing as much as fifteen tons.

Nor did the problem end with the construction of these marvel-roads. It was necessary to transport very heavy war material across stretches where the building of any roads whatever was a sheer impossibility. Often it was necessary to take heavy guns as far as might be upon sleighs and then drag them for considerable distances by hand; quite as often it was imperative that across chasms great cables should be rigged on which the guns might be swung, sometimes hundreds or even thousands of feet above the valleys beneath, from one height to another.

The "wireways" by which much of this unique transportation was accomplished are of Italian invention, as were other notable and essential engineering devices of this great war of mountain transportation.

Such contrivances, known as "teleferrica," were introduced for the first time during the winter of 1916, and by summer there were about 200 along the mountainous front. They not only supplied very advanced positions with armament, ammunition and food, but transported men back and forth between them and lower points.

SYSTEM ONE OF TACKLES.

The system was one of tackles (where guns and other heavy freight were to be moved) or cars (like cradles, where men were to be moved), operated by motor-pulleys directly connected up with great electric power. One of the most astonishing and picturesque uses to which these aerial wireways were put was the movement downward of men wounded at the advanced posts with which the teleferrica communicate.

To see wounded men going down these wireways, mere dots, each representing a suspended stretcher upon which a suffering human being is strapped securely, was described as one of the most amazing spectacles of the whole war. The experience, to some wounded men, swinging sickeningly, dizzyingly alone in midair, was probably more terrifying than actual fighting, although there were few, if any, accidents connected with the wireways.

Not infrequently these wireways were within direct range of the enemy fire, and that complicated matters. So far as is known, there has been no instance of a cable cut by gunfire, but in several districts it was necessary that the men, going to their duty and the wounded going backward, having done theirs, must needs be protected in armored baskets, somewhat like those which often are swung beneath observation balloons on the various fronts.

PROBLEMS OF TRANSPORTATION.

The problems of transportation, great as they are, are by no means the only unique difficulties presented to these brave mountain fighters. In this extraordinary warfare mining by means of high explosives was carried on upon a hitherto unequaled scale. Such work with high explosives was not only continually necessary in the construction of roads and fortifications in a region of solid rock, but sometimes proved the only effective means of attack upon the enemy.

The mine was used as an offensive weapon by both sides, and often with very terrible results.

Perhaps the most extraordinary of the campaign was the mine laid by the Italians after infinitely difficult and very extensive tunneling in solid rock at the Cima del Col di Lana.

This immense effort with explosives blew off the whole top of a mountain—and that mountaintop was thickly occupied by Austrians at the time of the explosion of the mine. None on the Italian side knows exactly what the Austrian casualties were, but it is certain that through this one explosion more than an entire company—that is, more than 400—of the enemy's soldiers were destroyed.

An interesting detail of this operation is the fact that while the Italians were tunneling for this great mine they were perfectly aware that the Austrians also were at work upon a similar effort. It amounted to a race with death, and the Italians won it.

Correspondents agree that the thing which most impresses the visitor to the mountain fronts of the Italian army is the immense patience which it has shown in the face of the difficult tasks of this astonishing campaign. Italians usually are regarded as temperamental creatures, but "dogged" has been the word which has meant most in this campaign.

Some of the movements of troops across exposed snow-covered spaces have been marvels of incredible patience. To escape observation the soldiers have been clad in white clothing, but in addition to this it has been necessary for them to lie flat upon their faces in the snow, moving very, very slowly, accomplishing their transfers from point to point literally at snail speed.

With regard to such work, as with regard to the Italian wounded, one thing is remarked by all the officers and those who have been privileged even for a short time to share the hardships of the Italian "common soldier." He never complains. Healthy or hurt, weary or fresh, he takes war with a smile full of flashing teeth and with eyes glittering with interest and good nature.

CHAPTER XIII
WOMAN AND THE WAR.

She has Won "Her Place in the Sun"—Rich and Poor in the Munitions Factories—Nurse and Ambulance Driver—Khaki and Trousers—Organizer and Farmer—Heroes in the Stress of Circumstances—Doing Men's Work for Men—Even a "Bobbie."

IF IT were ever really necessary for woman to "win a place in the sun" she has done so by her activities with relation to the war. We have regarded woman with a high degree of sentimentality, and to her pleas for recognition in world affairs have shrugged our shoulders and intimated that she was fit to bear children, nurse the sick, do household chores and cook, cook, cook; but physically, mentally and by training she was unfit to perform the greater world duties.

But the world war has proved that all the tasks which men claimed women were unfitted to perform can as well be done by what we have been pleased to term the "weaker sex."

The war has proved a truism that old saying, "The hand that rocks the cradle rules the world," and also that the burden of war falls upon women. It is they who give up their sons to their country and send their husbands and boys to the front to serve as fodder for the cannon.

In England the work of women in the war secured for them a degree of recognition in Parliament which all of their agitation and militant tactics failed to produce.

National extremity was woman's opportunity; frank invitation to new lines of work was followed by hearty appreciation on the part of the men; and a proposition to extend suffrage to 6,000,000 English women was based avowedly upon the general gratitude felt for their loyal and effective service in the war. And it is war service, for modern warfare has greatly enlarged the content of that term. In the modern conception

228

those who make munitions or in other ways release others for the front are doing war service as truly as those who bear arms.

Instead of yielding to fame a few isolated Mollie Pitchers, the war brought a largely neglected half of the nation's military strength into practical service. Indeed, though woman dreads war more than man does, if it comes to actual defense of land and home and young, we find, with Kipling, that "the female of the species is more deadly than the male."

THE WORK OF WOMEN.

The work of the women in the munitions factories in England has deservedly attracted large attention, and, doubtless, British historians will for centuries tell how, when England found herself utterly at a loss before her enemies because of a lack of effective ammunition, the women responded "as one man" to meet the need and save the Union Jack from being forced to the shore. It was a repetition, multiplied 10,000 times, of the Presbyterian parson at Springfield, N. J., supplying Washington's army with Watts hymn books when it was retreating to serve as paper wadding for the rifles.

The innovation of the task, the large scale on which it was carried out and the striking success of it make it a major event of the war, even to be compared with the battle of the Marne. And shall not American historians ascribe to the scores of young girls who lost their lives in an explosion at Eddystone, Pa., making munitions, the honor of being the first martyrs of the German-American War?

It was not alone the working girls of England who tired their arms and calloused their hands on the heavy shells. When the work was at its full capacity, a proposition was sent to the women of leisure to undergo three weeks of training in a munitions factory and then take up the work at the week-ends to relieve the regular workers, the women shell machinists, whose strength and skill could best be maintained by saving them from Saturday and Sunday overtime.

There was a strange incongruity in paying them less than the men for the same work. They worked in eight-hour shifts and were required to stand, except during a single half-hour interval. The prospectus of instruction suggested short skirts, thick gloves and boots with low heels, adding that evening dress would not be necessary.

Hotel accommodations were attempted for these "lady" workers, but this proved inadequate, and part of them went to the lodgings with the regular workers. Short skirts were only the first step that promptly led to overalls, and when these English ladies, whom the girls called "Miaows," got well grimed with dust and grease, utterly tired out with handling 12-pound shells and hungry enough to prefer coarse food, they understood the workgirls as never before, and the men, too, and they had a new birth of patriotism. One lady said she found great relief and enthusiasm by thinking of the shells as so many dead Boches or live Tommies.

VARIED OCCUPATIONS OF WOMEN.

Making ammunition and hospital supplies, handling luggage and trunks in baggage rooms, driving motors, conducting trolley cars, carpentry work on wooden houses for the front, are but a few of the occupations in which European women engaged in war service. They have served as lift attendants, ticket sellers, post office sorters, mail carriers, gardeners, dairy lassies, grocery clerks, drivers of delivery wagons and vans, commissionaires. More than a million were added to the industrial workers in England during the first two years of war.

America coming later into the war, its women naturally followed the lead of the English and French along many lines tried and proved to be worth while, but our matrons and maids, famed for their independence and initiative, developed also new lines of patriotic effort. As soon as it was evident that German ambitions included designs upon America, the strong feminine instinct for preservation began to assert itself. Pacifism had no special appeal to the gentler sex at such a time. She got behind the recruiting as if it were her own job, and much of the success of it was due to her efforts.

The Woman's Section of the Navy League may well be described by quoting from its own statement of motive and purpose. "Every mother with sons, every wife with husband, every sister with a brother, feels her heart stand still with the horror of what war may bring to her."

WOMAN'S MANY SERVICES.

These women spread information to arouse interest in the condition of the United States naval forces, aided recruiting for the Naval Reserve, assisted in procuring enrollments for the Naval Coast Reserve, and drawing on their resources provided many needed articles of clothing, equipment and comfort not furnished by the Government. A knitting committee makes sleeveless jackets, helmets, wristlets and mufflers. Comfort kits, games, blankets, underwear, rubber hats, coats and boots are made or bought by the Comfort and Supplies Committee.

The two poles of patriotic service are the production of food and fighting at the front; a world of activity bulges between them. European women are accustomed to farm labor. Millions of peasant women, serfs, all but in name, under the late Russian regime; Balkan women, German and French wives and girls, and, to some extent, the mothers and daughters of the English poor, would have understood Markham's poem better if he had called it, "The Woman With the Hoe."

In the war food crisis the women of America matched the women of the enemy and vied with those of their own allies in persuading mother earth to yield her bounty. In heavy shoes, trousers of jean, rolled-up sleeves and a straw hat, the girls of America here and there turned to the land and took hold of the tasks of the farm.

So far we have mentioned only the work at home that

women took up for the war, but this is only a part; the other pole finds them near. The invaluable service of Red Cross nurses, their zeal and sacrifice and sometimes martyrdom, from Elizabeth Fry and Florence Nightingale to Edith Cavell, have been women's glory for more than half a century. This war multiplied the need many times and veritable regiments of them responded. Their emblem became the symbol universal of mercy, charity and good will.

In addition to the 50 trained nurses for a base hospital, there are 25 hospital aids, who serve without pay. America has 8000 registered Red Cross nurses and scores of thousands are in training for aids.

The effective and helpful work of women in all lines of endeavor, aside from home and family life, has never before been shown so impressively as now. Their energy, willingness, faithfulness and capability in every activity are unsurpassed.

WOMAN BENT ON DOING HER UTMOST.

But woman shares the lot of mankind on earth, and in the issues of life and death, land and home, she fears to do less than her most, and we would fear to have her do less.

The woman for ages has been the war nurse, but the American woman has gone a step further and qualified as the war physician. When the war clouds first hovered over America more than 200 women physicians formally offered their services to the Government. At the graduation exercises of a women's medical college, when America first entered the war, a prominent official made the statement that 3,000 women physicians could find unlimited work of mercy behind the first line of firing in Europe.

The surgeon general of the United States army did not await an actual call to arms to notify a physician that the proffer of the services of women physicians would be accepted when the need came.

"When I spoke to the women," said this physician, "I asked them this question:

" 'Can I tell the Government that it may count upon each and all of you for any work within your power?'

"Their answer was unanimous. It was 'Yes.' "

There is a law prohibiting women from going aboard battleships when they are under way, but such an obstacle has not stood in the way of woman's desire to help where she can when her country calls, and so Miss Loretta Walsh became a member of the United States navy—the first woman enlisted in that branch of the service, with the exception of the nurses' corps. Her title was chief yeoman.

Women announced their readiness to assist in another way —in economizing—one organization having adopted the following resolutions:

RESOLUTION ON ECONOMICS.

"Resolved, That all patriotic women be urged to use their influence on fashions in dress to keep them as economical as possible, and to register their disapproval of such styles as the melon and peg-top skirt, or any other styles that imply extravagant changes in the wardrobe, to the end that the time and money thus saved from clothes may be devoted to the needs of the nation."

How often have we heard: "When war comes, when our homes are threatened, when peril stalks abroad in the land, who shoulders the musket and goes out to fight? The man! The man!"

But woman, knowing better than man the impulses of her own heart, only awaited the opportunity to show what she could do, though, much more than man, she loves peace, detests strife. But she did not await an actual call to arms to show the patriotic spirit with which her soul was fired. Whatever her Government was willing she should do, to that was she prepared to give her best efforts.

Lady Frances Balfour, president of the London Society of National Union of Women Suffragists and president of the Travelers' Aid Society, worked as hard to win the war as any Tommy in the trenches.

A daughter of the eighth Duke of Argyll and the widow of a soldier, she played an important part in Scotch and English public life for many years, and has done much to advance the cause of British women.

An authentic view of the situation as it developed with reference to the reception of women into the everyday work and what American women might do is contained in the following interview with Lady Balfour:

WOMAN AS WAGE EARNER.

"We are doing everything," she said. "We are filling nearly every post. If the House of Lords had not vetoed the bill we would be solicitors, but that must wait for a time. British women are now meeting with success because for the first time they are receiving a proper wage and are able to live in a way to do their best work. The old sweat shop wage has gone, and I hope never to return. Women will never return to the conditions which existed before the war.

"American women start with a great advantage. They have already the entree in the business world and fill many clerical places, whereas our women and girls had to break down the barriers of conservatism existing in a great number of banks. There was the same objection to women workers among the farmers of the South of England, though in Scotland the woman has always done her part on the farm.

"Girls are beginning on the farm at 18 shillings ($4.50) a week; before the war men farm hands worked for 11 shillings ($2.75). Our women are milking cows, running steam plows, digging in the fields and giving complete satisfaction. I dare not venture to predict what will happen in the future, but we can face it with confidence, I am certain. Now we are inspired with the spirit of patriotism; we feel we owe our best to our country; we are ready to suffer hardship just as our brave men are doing in the trenches.

BRITISH WOMEN'S PATRIOTISM.

"The patriotism of British women had stood a hard test; I hope American women have an easier trial. Lloyd George says he hopes America will profit by the mistakes of Britain. For more than a year the government of this country snubbed and discouraged our women. The government does not pay women at the same rate as men; it does not give them the same war bonus. There came a time when the government realized the war could not be won without the women. Then it issued frantic calls for help, and the women responded nobly, just as they would have done months before. I hope your American Government will recognize the value of woman's help from the very start.

"Unfortunately I must judge your women largely by those who come over here for the season in peace days. As I remember they spent a great deal of time and money at the hairdressers, manicures, dressmaking establishments and hotels. But I am certain the great majority of Americans care more for their homes and country and less for display. I feel that they should concentrate on the production of food. We need all we can get and then we shall not have as much as we require. Money, food and ships are the things most needed.

"Your women have been wonderfully generous in giving us money, supporting hospitals and sending us supplies. We can use some of your nurses and women doctors. We have a hospital here in London holding nearly 1000 soldiers and it is run entirely by women. Our Scottish women's hospitals have done grand work in the various theaters of war. Not only the nurses, but the doctors and ambulance drivers are women. We have supplied about 72,000 women for this work alone."

"How have women regarded the discipline of army life?" was asked.

"Wonderfully!" said Lady Frances. "It has been good for them. Just see our women 'bus conductors. They work hard, handle all kinds of people, but I never heard them say they are unable to meet the emergencies which arise. And for the most part they are women who come from very humble surroundings. You hear that women have broken down in health under their work, but it seems to me I have read frequently about American business men suffering from nervous breakdowns and overwork."

SUCCESS BUILT ON RUINS OF FAILURE.

No great victories, either in war or in the ordinary relations of life, are attained without initial blunders. Many a splendid success is built upon the ruins of failure, and this is a fact that the women of Europe learned after the first hysteria occasioned by the marching soldiers, the beat of drums and all the excitement incident to real warfare. American women, when they joined hands with the Allies against Prussianism and all that it meant, builded splendid records of their usefulness upon the mistakes that these women made.

In the summer of 1914 every girl and woman clamored to be a nurse. Women with a great deal of money and no experience opened "hospitals" that were about as fit for the reception and treatment of wounded men as a henroost is capable of housing an eagle. They all wanted to be in the "Red Cross" or "V. A. D." (Voluntary Aid Department) and wear caps and bandage wounds.

Then there were the amateur nurses who didn't know much about nursing, "but would love to try." The daughter of a duke tried to go through a probationary course at St. Bartholomew's Hospital because she thought the uniform "perfectly sweet." But of course this element of "fluffiness" exists on the outside of any great movement. It has to be blown away so that the hard surface of genuine and practical endeavor can be seen and felt. And that is what happened to England. The "fluff" disappeared and women knew where they were, and men realized that women possess a force, a firm and splendid resolve, that gives them the right to step beside men in the march toward victory.

Another craze that amounted to a vice was the furious and ill-considered efforts of totally unskilled women to make shirts and hospital garments for soldiers. If some of the results had not been pathetic one could almost be overcome with the comicality of the whole business. Soldiers' shirts were turned out by a circle of busily sewing ladies that would not fit a dwarf, while probably the next batch of garments dispatched with patriotic fervor to a regimental depot might have been designed for a race of giants.

NATIONAL SERVICE FOR WOMEN.

National service for women as well as for men proved a very substantial portion of Great Britain's strength, but before national service had been generally thought of an organization called the Women's Service Bureau had been formed by a group of influential and intelligent women who were imbued with the idea that only by careful and systematized registration and selection could the matter of feminine war work be successfully arranged.

Lady Frances Balfour was the first president of the Women's Service Bureau, which with the London Society for Suffrage established 62 branches in the city of London and its suburbs.

What the women at the head of this society realized was the necessity for giving the right women the most suitable employment and also to give every applicant for work helpful and practical advice. The need for women's labor in the many trades and professions hitherto closed to them, and for their increased co-operation in those in which they already took part, has been forced home even to unwilling minds.

Here and there on the battlefields of Europe—in Bulgaria, Servia, Roumania, France, Belgium and Russia—have been noted occasionally the presence of a woman warrior, a modern Joan of Arc. It was not expected, however, that in America woman would do more than perform the service work which fell to the lot of the Red Cross nurses and the women practicing conservation and effecting organization in England.

But the women of America were not satisfied with "petticoat preparedness." They rushed to the khaki suits and to the colors with unexpected enthusiasm. One khaki-clad woman walked from San Francisco to New York, making recruiting speeches on the way.

The infantry, the cavalry, the navy, the marines could all point to their girls in khaki.

ALL KINDS OF WOMEN ENLISTED.

As the women enlisted for all kinds of service, so it may be said all kinds of women enlisted—that is, women of all ranks of life—some from society, some from the mills, others from the offices, the shops, the stage, the restaurants and the colleges.

Many years ago the country rang with the name of Tippecanoe, and one of the men who bore arms on the western frontier was William Henry Harrison. The years went by and Benjamin Harrison came to the White House as President.

The Harrison blood showed in the preparedness work, and Old Tippecanoe's great granddaughter helped to make the women of the country fit for the burden of war.

There isn't anything on earth that shows so strongly in the blood as the soldier element, and Elizabeth Harrison, whose great ancestor faced the perils of the frontier warfare, was a leader by force of her inherited ability as a leader. She was elected drill sergeant for the college girls of the New York University.

When the war clouds came she was following inherited bent. All of the Harrison men had been among the country's greatest lawyers and Miss Harrison was studying for the bar.

But just as the warwhoop of the West called Tippecanoe from his books and briefs to bullets and battles, so the daughter of the former President dropped Blackstone and Kent to take up the Drill Regulations and the elementary text books of the army.

She knew that the way to make women fit for their part of war service was to make them strong and healthy and to give them an idea of the things that men-at-arms have to do.

NOTED WOMEN IN THE WORK.

So Miss Harrison was one of the first workers in the movement to teach women the elements of war. Many women of importance in the social and financial world took up the task with a will, and there was a girl for every signal flag, a maid for every wireless station, and an angel for every hospital ward in the making as the men pursued the task of providing guns and the men behind the guns.

Miss Harrison and the girls she drilled at the University wore regulation field service uniform, khaki breeches, coat, heavy shoes and puttees, and a large hat of military cut.

The American Woman's League for Self-Defence and Preparedness was the first woman's military organization in America, according to its president, Mrs. Ida Powell Priest, who is descended from an old Long Island family, Thomas Powell being one of her ancestors.

The first cavalry troop, of which Ethel M. Scheiss was first senior captain, drilled regularly. Their first appearance mounted caused a mild sensation on Broadway. They were most impressively stern soldierettes as they trotted and galloped their horses.

Everywhere the girl in America strove with helpful earnestness to do "her bit." Every strata of society called out its members in a wonderful plan of feminine preparedness. Besides the thousands of women members of the Red Cross

some of the most prominent organizations officered and planned
by women include The National League for Women's Service,
which has branches in every large city in the United States.
They enrolled women as motor car drivers, telegraphers, wireless operators, agriculturists and skilled mechanics.

Miss Anne Morgan, as head of this organization, devoted
an enormous amount of energy to the success of the work.

OTHER SOCIETIES ORGANIZED.

Other societies organized were the National Special Aid
Society, Service of Any Kind, Militia of Mercy, which sends
and provides bandages and other necessities and comforts for
the soldiers; Girl Scouts of America, first aid, signalling and
drills; Daughters of the American Revolution; the Suffrage
Party and the Anti-Suffrage Society; the International Child
Welfare League and the Girls' National Honor Guard. The
Federation of Women's Clubs all over the United States also
organized for any patriotic service that women could perform.

A practical way of doing something to help France and
Servia was offered early in the war by the splendid initiative
of Dr. Elsie Inglis and the Scottish Federation of Women's
Suffrage Societies, who organized hospitals for the wounded,
the staffs of which were all women, and called on other societies
for their support.

The London society responded first by subscriptions from
individual members, then by giving beds, then (in February,
1915) by offering itself as London agent for the hospitals and
undertaking all the practical work, in the sending out of personnel and equipment, which had to be transacted in London.

It is only by carefully systematized organization that great
work of this kind can be carried on. The slapdash, haphazard
of hysterical excitement can have no legitimate place in a movement that provides stepping stones toward the salvation of the
civilized world.

One of the things which will live long in the history of

womankind was the wonderful work done by the magnificently courageous units of Lady Paget's nursing force, which went out to Servia, when that country was laid waste not only by the German beasts, but also by disease.

It was not the fault of those brave women and men that things happened at Uskub and in other Servian towns that do not bear repeating.

It was just the lack of thorough preparedness for a war which was much worse than humanity had thought possible that deepened the tragedy of their situation. In Servia, in fact, the career of the hospitals was quite checkered and the service rendered proportionately more vital.

LONDON-WALES UNIT.

At the time of the Austro-German invasion in the autumn of 1915, the London-Wales Unit was at Valjevo, one of the five Scottish women's hospitals working in the country. It was under the command of Dr. Alice Hutchinson and was very highly organized. Doctor Inglis had herself gone on to Servia to take general charge of the hospitals there in the spring of 1915. From the time that a typhus epidemic was overcome by women doctors early in the year to the time of the invasion all seemed to be going well. Then came three weeks of great pressure of work and of rapid moves from place to place as the enemy advanced into the country. Finally, it became a necessity for the personnel of the different units either to retreat with the Servian army over the mountains into Montenegro or to fall in the hands of the enemy.

The story of the retreat is now very generally known. The journey was one long series of forced marches. Mountains 7000 feet high had to be traversed in blinding snow, almost the whole journey had to be made on foot and it was six weeks before the little band reached the coast. Doctor Inglis meanwhile, with her group of nurses and orderlies, and Doctor Hutchinson, with the London-Wales Unit, had gallantly stayed behind and continued to attend to their Servian wounded and to organize help for them till the work was forcibly stopped by the advancing Austrian army.

UNIT TAKEN PRISONERS.

After being ordered out of Valjevo, Doctor Hutchinson made several attempts to organize hospitals in the line of retreat. She was at Vrnyachka Banja when the Austrians entered the town on November 10, 1915. She and her unit were taken prisoners and interned, first near the Servian frontier and then in Hungary for three weary months. The cheerful courage with which the members of the unit bore hardship and uncertainty and hope deferred has been related by Doctor Hutchinson in a memorable narrative. Their conditions would have been still more intolerable and their release would have been still longer delayed if Doctor Hutchinson herself had not known a great deal more about the Geneva Convention than the Austrian authorities had ever dreamed. She was thus able to assert herself on behalf of those under her in a way which taught her captors something new about British women. At the beginning of February the unit was at last allowed to cross the frontier into Switzerland. It reached England on February 12. It was only the perfection of its organization that carried this brave body of women through amazing hardships.

Abroad women chauffeurs became almost as common in the war as men; the public in Paris and London refused to regard the appearance of a woman on the streets in cap, "knickers" and puttees or heavy boots as unusual, and in need they in many instances not only drove "taxi," but guided ambulances in the hospital service.

The Red Cross in America, in the matter of preparedness, organized a class for women chauffeurs. One of these, started in Philadelphia, had among its instructors Mrs. Thomas Langdon Elwyn and Miss Letitia McKim, both of whom drove ambulances for the Allies in England.

The National League for Woman Service, working in conjuction with the Council of National Defense, canvassed the country through its Bureau of Registration and Information to provide statistics for mobilizing the entire woman-force of the Nation; all of which was done with the approval of the Secretary of Labor.

Perhaps the outstanding incident of industrial employment among women was that of several women in France as locomotive engineers. It is true that they operated only the shunting engines about the yards at the military camps, but it was noted in dispatches in every quarter of the globe that Mesdames Louis Debris and Marie Viard, whose husbands were killed in the war, were piloting the engines which their husbands had formerly driven.

WOMAN'S INGENUITY.

And woman has proved her ingenuity. In the damp trenches of the battlefields abroad the men need protection from the dampness and cold, which ordinary clothing will not provide. It was found that the leather-lined huntsmen's coats, and the sort of garments worn by the chauffeur, the aviator and the mountaineer served the men in the trenches well, and particularly along the Russian frontier and in the cold mountainous regions.

But the price of leather soared, with the demand for millions of pairs of shoes, saddles, harness, headgear, and whatnot, and leather-lined coats were at a premium. The women were not to be denied, and through the Suffrage organizations which turned in to prepare America for the struggle and to render assistance to the Allies, the unique plan was adopted of making linings for the airmen and soldier's coats of old kid gloves.

One group of women in a single section of Philadelphia gathered a thousand pairs of old gloves in a canvass. The seams were ripped and the gloves cut down one side and laid open. The fingers of one glove so treated were dovetailed between the fingers of another glove so cut, and stitched together. Thus one glove was sewed to another until a section of leather was formed sufficient to make a lining for a coat. And many such were devised and incorporated in the garments sent to the front by the various agencies dominated by the women of the land.

WOMEN AS POLICEMEN.

While women to a limited degree were rendering service as "policemen" in certain sections of the United States and on Continental Europe the war was responsible for the development of an organized force in London, which will probably remain a permanent organization to the end of time. Miss Damer Dawson is chief of the London woman "bobbies," and M. S. Allen is chief superintendent.

The force was organized in 1914, shortly after the outbreak of the war and has relieved the men of a large amount of responsibility. The force is uniformed, the women wearing military costumes with visored caps. They operate under the supervision, or with the authority of Sir Edward Henry, Chief Commissioner of the Metropolitan police, and serve for duty at the munition plants where women workers are employed, besides doing regular patrol duty and welfare work.

The service in London is in the nature of a training for special service and the women after sufficient experience are sent to suburbs and small towns to do police duty. They are highly spoken of and declared to be very efficient, rendering service in the barrooms and looking after women in a manner that the regular "bobbies" cannot approximate.

It was declared in England, by way of closing the comment on this phase of the war that no one thing so stimulated the enlistments for service as the execution of Miss Edith Cavell, the English nurse who was shot as a spy by Germany.

That her name will go down in history as a martyr to the cause of liberty and humanity goes without saying.

Miss Cavell had been a nurse in Brussels, and after the occupation of the Belgian capital by the Germans, she remained where she used her private hospital for the nursing of wounded soldiers; not excluding the Germans.   It had been intimated that she had better cross the border, but she insisted on remaining at her post.   Ultimately she was accused of being one of the instigators of a plot to smuggle English, French and Belgian soldiers across the lines, and of serving the enemies of Germany.

To the German mind she was more than a spy; her conduct was reprehensible, because in the capacity of nurse she had won a degree of confidence.   She was therefore held as a spy and traitor.   And though Brand Whitlock, America's Minister to Belgium, and other diplomats sought to save her, she was shot by the ruthless Germans.

CHAPTER XIV
THE TERRIBLE PRICE.

THE human tongue seems almost devoid of power to convey to the human mind what the war has actually cost the world in lives, money, property, ideals and all that is dear to humanity. In all the world there is not a human being who has not contributed something to the awful cost and the loss due to the destruction of property, the stopping of industry, the waste of energy and the curtailment of human endeavor in the interest of civilization, and the effects which the struggle has had upon the world cannot even be approximated in dollars and cents.

We have been taught to regard war as a terrible thing and to realize that thousands must be slain, but in no war in the history of the world has there been as many troops engaged as have been killed in the European war on the battlefields of Belgium and France.

At the beginning of the year 1917 it was estimated that the total casualties of the war were 22,500,000. In a report based on figures compiled in Washington it was stated: The human estimated waste and financial outlay are staggering. The combined casualties of the war, partly estimated because all belligerents do not publish lists, are 22,500,000. The figures included killed, permanently injured, prisoners and wounded returned to the front. Of this number the Central Powers were estimated to have suffered permanent losses in excess of 4,000,000, and the entente perhaps twice that number, Russia being by far the heaviest loser.

The financial outlay, based in part on official reports and

244

statements and in part on estimates, was placed at approximately $80,000,000,000, divided $50,000,000,000 to the entente and $30,000,000,000 to the Central Powers. The entente lost more than 3,500,000 tons of merchant shipping and approximately 800,000 tons of naval vessels. On the other side the loss of naval tonnage was approximately 250,000 tons, and merchant ships aggregating 211,000 tons were reported captured or destroyed.

IMMENSE LOSS TO COMMERCE.

Of the foreign commerce the Central Powers had lost $10,000,000,000 in the two and a half years of war, including imports and exports. The loss of commerce of Great Britain and her allies with the Central Powers probably was in the neighborhood of $7,000,000. This was largely made up at least on the import side by increased trade with the United States and other neutral countries and enlarged trade with the colonies.

Germany lost virtually all her African colonies and all her possessions in the Pacific Ocean, an aggregate of more than 1,000,000 square miles. Turkey also lost a large area of territory held at the outbreak of the war, while Austria lost most of Bukowina and Galicia. To offset the territory losses of the Central Powers, the entente have lost in Europe approximately 300,000 square miles. Of this large area, all of it thickly populated in normal times, 175,000 square miles were wrested from Russia on the eastern battlefield.

The staggering losses in men include the vast number on both sides wounded in such a way as not to permanently cripple them and render them unfit for military service. The figures are based on official reports and estimates by military experts.

Germany's permanent losses were placed at 1,500,000 men, including about 1,000,000 in killed. The permanent losses of Austria-Hungary were placed at about 1,000,000 more than those of Germany, owing to the fact that so much of the hard fighting on the eastern front was in the Austro-Hungarian theater. The losses of the Austro-Hungarians during the drive of General Brusiloff in 1916 were frightful. Large numbers of Austrians were taken prisoner by Brusiloff.

Russia's casualties for the first year of the war were estimated by military experts at more than 3,500,000 men, and these were doubled in the succeeding year, according to estimates by American military experts. Russia returned to the fighting line a smaller percentage of wounded than any of the other great Powers.

GREAT BRITAIN'S CASUALTIES.

Great Britain's casualties were placed in excess of 1,250,-000 despite the limited front of British operations in France in the early stages. The aggregate of Italy's casualties was estimated at 1,500,000, while Belgium's were placed at 200,000, Servia's at 400,000, Montenegro's at 150,000 and Rumania's at more than 300,000.

While the area of the territorial losses of the Central Powers was nearly four times as great as that of the entente group, with the exception of the occupied portions of Bukowina and Galicia, the value of the territory included in them is comparatively small. For example, Germany's African colonies were sparsely settled, largely by natives, with virtually all development in the future. Despite this fact, their loss was a severe blow to Germany.

The territorial losses of the entente covered all but a small corner of Belgium, a highly developed, thickly populated industrial country; a large slice of northern France, virtually all of Servia, all of Montenegro, more than three-fourths of Rumania and 175,000 square miles of Russia, the major part of it in the grain-growing section.

According to military experts on the "war map" of Europe as it stood at that time, the Central Powers had won the war. But when their enormous loss of foreign commerce and territory is considered, their "victory" was shown to have most decided limitations, especially because of their admission that they eventually would have to give up all occupied territory in view of the frightful cost in men and money.

FIGURES POSITIVELY STAGGERING.

Supplementing these statements, as showing the progress of the war, it was stated just before the United States took its memorable step to break off diplomatic relations with Germany, members of the National War Council estimated the total casualties of the war at that time as in excess of the population of the United Kingdom, which in 1911 was more than 45,000,000. This of course included those maimed, injured or so stricken that they were unfit for future service. The number actually killed was estimated at more than 7,000,000.

Staggering as these figures are they are easily conceivable when it is remembered that the German front lines covered more than 500 miles with Allied troops opposing them, and that in a single battle millions of shells were fired by one side or the other. In one battle it was officially reported that 4,000,000 shot and shell were used, and in another the English mined the German trenches for a distance of several miles and blew out the strongholds, using more than 1,000,000 pounds of high explosives.

One of the great 42-centimeter guns of the Germans is said to have used a charge of guncotton involving the use of a full bale of cotton to make the explosive—and a bale of cotton contains 500 pounds. The shrapnel of the heavy field artillery of the United States contains 717 balls or bullets about the size of a common marble, and the shell, so timed that it explodes just before it touches the ground, scatters the bullets or balls over an area estimated at one yard for every bullet, or more than 700 yards. With thousands of such shells being rained over the entrenchments is it any wonder that the list of wounded and killed was great?

Thousands were killed by poisoned gases, and where they were not killed a very large percentage of those affected suffered consequences which rendered them unfit for battle—turned them into invalids. The gas bombs produced hemorrhages of the lungs and bowels in thousands of cases and left those who inhaled the fumes in an anemic and permanently disabled condition. And what of the thousands who succumbed to fevers, and who because of the terrible shock became mental and physical wrecks and were made unfit for further duty on the actual firing lines?

A MATTER OF DOLLARS AND CENTS.

When it comes to the cost in dollars and cents it is possible to tell something of what they mean with reference to war construction and maintenance, although no one can estimate what it represents in destruction. No one has yet devised an accounting system to determine the percentage of "depreciation" through wear and tear on guns and devices that cost thousands of dollars each, but everybody knows that guns wear out and that some of the larger ones have a very decided limit on the number of times they can be fired without being rebored or rifled.

Railroads which have taken years to build and develop have been destroyed, telephone and telegraph lines put out of commission, great castles and temples razed, works of art burned, whole cities devastated, green fields turned into great craters torn up by bombs and shells, factories dismantled, herds of cattle fed into the maw of the armies, and the ruthless Germans even went so far as to wantonly cut down and destroy whole forests and magnificent shade trees which it took generations to grow.

How the indebtedness of the nations grew during the progress of the war is shown in the following statement issued by some of the financial institutions of the country in the Spring of 1917:

"Indebtedness of the seven principal nations engaged in the European war has crossed $75,000,000,000. In the middle of 1914 the indebtedness of these seven nations was $27,000,000,000."

Financing on an extensive scale followed this state of affairs. France issued a second formal war loan, Germany a fifth loan and Russia a sixth loan. Great Britain issued temporary securities in enormous sums.

The war cost $105,000,000 every twenty-four hours, according to the statistics, expenditures of the Entente Allies being fully double those of the Central Allies.

COMPARATIVE WAR EXPENSES.

Without for one moment taking into consideration the billions which were thrown into the war-pot by America the figures are staggering. An interesting comparison is found in the cost of the previous great world wars. The American Civil War, the greatest conflict in prior history cost $8,000,000,000, a sum equalled every three months in the conduct of the European war.

	Approximate cost.
Napoleonic Wars, 1793-1815	$6,250,000,000
American Civil War, 1861-1864	8,000,000,000
Franco-Prussian War, 1870-1871	3,000,000,000
South African War, 1900-1902	1,250,000,000
Russo-Japanese War, 1904-1905	2,500,000,000
European War, 1914-1917 (3 years)	75,000,000,000

It was further estimated that after the year 1917, the payment of $3,800,000,000 a year would be required to pay the interest on the debt, and that the total Government expenditures in Europe for bond interest and support of the various branches of the Governments would require in the neighborhood of 20 per cent of the people's income.

POPULATION AND WEALTH OF COUNTRIES.

Another comparative table that is important to any one desiring to study the costs and their effects is that relating to population and wealth of the principal countries. The latest available figures are:

	Population	Wealth
United States	101,577,000	$187,739,071,090
British Empire	394,930,000	130,000,000,000
Germany	67,810,000	80,000,000,000
France	39,700,000	50,000,000,000
Russia	187,379,000	40,000,000,000
Austria-Hungary	53,000,000	25,000,000,000
Spain	20,000,000	5,400,000,000
Belgium	7,500,000	9,000,000,000
Portugal	5,958,000	2,500,000,000
Italy	37,048,000	20,000,000,000

Taxes have been the main sources for raising money to carry on the war. In Germany taxes on all incomes from the Kaiser to the ordinary business man were kept at the highest rate, the Kaiser paying $500,000 on his fortune of $35,000,000 during the early part of the struggle. This was in addition to his income tax which amounted to $440,000, making a total annual tax of nearly $1,000,000. The Krupps are said to have been assessed at $3,000,000.

When the new military service laws were approved in Paris, which was about the middle of July, 1913, the French Cabinet was at its wit's end to provide the financial end of the tremendous military budget. Investment markets were sluggish, and there were thousands of notes whose values were rapidly depreciating. The French Government was unable to float a loan of $200,000,000 which was necessary for making preparations.

Then in her desperation Paris closed her doors to all

foreign loans. The Viviani Ministry practically duplicated the plan of its predecessor in proposing an issue of $360,000,000 3½ per cent bonds, which were redeemable in 25 years.

One year previously to this financial struggle the Belgian Government had started to raise $62,800,000 in order that the people of this country might prevent its being used as the battleground for the world war which they had seen away off in the future. This money was raised for the purpose of making Antwerp an impregnable fortress.

IMMENSE SUM FOR ARMY AND NAVY.

Russia had taken steps to raise $3,700,000,000 which the Russian Minister of Finance had informed the Budget Committee must be spent in the next five years on the army and navy. During the first year of the war there was $500,000,000 spent by this country in military and naval defence. This does not include the cost of those strategic railroads of which so many were constructed by the Russian Government, and which cost so many hundreds of thousands of dollars.

Previous to the time Great Britain declared war on Germany the House of Commons had voted $525,000,000 for emergency purposes, and within a couple of days of this appropriation an additional $500,000,000 was granted by the British Parliament.

One of the things accomplished by war was to bring out the fact that the resources of individuals are far greater than is ordinarily suspected. In 1870 Bismarck imposed an indemnity of $1,000,000,000 on France, never believing that country could meet the great debt, but with the help of all the inhabitants the debt was lifted within a few months.

When countries are at war the cost of continuing fighting does not stop with those actually engaged. The trade of the world is affected, and this means loss in all quarters of the globe. Of the import trade of the United States more than $500,000,000 was directly with those nations engaged in the

war at the opening of hostilities. This was out of a total of
$1,850,000,000. A great part of this commerce is classed as
among that which yields the greatest import tax, which means
that internal taxes must be imposed on the people to make up
for the money necessary to meet with the yearly loss occasioned
during the continuance of the war.

ANNUAL NATIONAL INCOME.

In the United States there is an annual national income
of $50,000,000,000, the total bank resources being $35,000,-
000,000, the individual deposits being $24,000,000,000, with
cash held by the banks totaling $2,500,000,000, total gold stock
in the country being $3,000,000,000, and available additional
commercial credits on the basis of cash holdings totaling
$6,000,000,000.

The borrowing power of the American Government does
not total less than $40,000,000,000, from domestic sources, and
this does not disturb the ordinary financial and economical
affairs of the nation.

During the first five months in 1917 the Government of
the United States reached a record for expenditures never
before equalled in American history. The total amount
expended was $1,600,000,000.

The chief item of the increase—$607,500,000—was the
purchase of the obligations of foreign Governments in exchange
for loans advanced to the Allies. The sum did not represent by
approximately $140,000,000 the total amount authorized in
loans. An increase of approximately $245,000,000 in the
ordinary disbursements of the Government, chiefly due to
military and naval needs, also was recorded and another item
going to swell the grand total of expenditures was the payment
of $25,000,000 for purchase of the Danish West Indies.

War loans of the six chief European belligerents, early in
1917, aggregated approximately $53,113,000,000.

Loans of the chief Entente nations, Great Britain, France,

Russia and Italy, were placed at about $36,300,000,000; those of Germany and Austria-Hungary, not including the sixth German loan reported to have yielded about $3,000,000,000, at $18,800,000,000.

The amounts of the various loans were placed at:
Great Britain, to March 31, 1917, $18,805,000,000; France, to February 28, $10,500,000,000; Russia, to December 31, 1916, $7,896,000,000; Italy, to December 31, 1916, $2,520,-000,000; Germany, to December, 31, 1916, $11,226,000,000; Austria, to December 31, 1916, $5,880,000,000; Hungary, $1,730,000,000.

The total included the advances made by the United Kingdom and France to the smaller belligerent countries allied with them.

SOME IDEA OF NATIONAL FINANCING.

Some idea of what all this financing means to a country may be judged by the statement of the Chancellor of the Exchequer, who in October, 1916, replying to questions regarding the English loans in the House of Commons, declared that England was paying at that time about $10,000,-000 a day in the United States, for every working day in the year.

When the English mission visited the United States in May, 1917, after the country had entered the war, there was handed to Arthur James Balfour, ex-Premier of England, a check for $200,000,000, said to have been one of the largest single checks ever paid in this country. It was a loan for war purposes. In the month of June it was stated that the total advance made to the Allies was $923,000,000, among the loans made then was one of $75,000,000 to Great Britain, and $3,000,-000 to Servia. The Servian loan, the first made by the United States to that country, was mainly for the improvement of railway lines. A small portion was used for the relief of the distressed population, and Red Cross work.

It was stated that the allied countries would spend in America, in the neighborhood of $200,000,000 a month for the year; which brings attention to the resources which America turned in against Germany when she joined the allied forces. To meet the demands made upon it the Government borrowed at once $3,000,000,000 by popular subscription—a matter of history of which the nation is proud.

From its funds the country loaned Russia $100,000,000, which was the first loan made by the United States to that Government. A credit of $45,000,000 to Belgium was also established by the Secretary of the Treasury. This also was Belgium's first participation in the loan of the Allies.

COUNTRY'S NATURAL RESOURCES.

Aside from the financial resources of the United States, the country is undoubtedly the richest in agricultural, mineral and other natural resources. It annually produces more than 3,500,000,000 bushels of corn, wheat touching the high point of 1,500,000,000 bushels; 1,600,000,000 bushels of oats; 250,000,-000 bushels of barley; 40,000,000 bushels of rye; 22,000,000 bushels of buckwheat; 425,000,000 bushels of potatoes; 77,000,-000 tons of hay; 30,000,000 bushels of flaxseed; 7,000,000,000 pounds of cotton; more than 1,000,000,000 pounds of tobacco; 2,000,000 long tons of sugar and 275,000,000 pounds of wool.

There are nearly 70,000,000 swine, and as many cattle, more than 25,000,000 head of horses and mules, and 62,000,000 sheep. Coal is mined at the rate of more than 500,000,000 tons yearly, and the copper mines yield 1,250,000,000 pounds of metal. Petroleum wells yield 225,500,000 barrels yearly. There are 270,000 manufacturing plants with a yearly output of more than $25,000,000,000. The products of the farm total more than $11,000,000,000 annually.

As to Germany's position, economists all over the world have considered her position as not only lacking soundness, but as crazy—crazy in that no attention whatever has apparently been paid to what are recognized as firmly fixed economic laws. The world has been at a loss to understand Germany's attitude, and it can only be explained by assuming that Germany was perfectly well aware of the entire unsoundness of her commercial and financial position, and was willing, or, in fact, had to risk everything with the hope of acquiring sufficient indemnity, resulting from the war, to bring her financial affairs to a sound basis. Germany's entire structure from the close of the Franco-Prussian war evidently was built upon rotten foundations.

CHAPTER XV
THE WORLD RULERS AT WAR.

WOODROW WILSON, THE CHAMPION OF DEMOCRACY—THE EGOTISTICAL KAISER—
THE GERMAN CROWN PRINCE—BRITAIN'S MONARCH—CONSTANTINE WHO QUIT
RATHER THAN FIGHT GERMANY—PRESIDENT POINCAIRE—AND OTHER NATIONAL
HEADS.

NO matter what the human frailties may be there are always men who rise in the stress of circumstances to unexpected heights. They thrive upon difficulties and in the emergencies become protectors and saviors of men. In the world's greatest melting-pot—the burned and blood-stained battle-fields of Europe—there were tried and tested millions of men of all nationalities and characteristics, and though the experience was one of bitterness, there was found in it the satisfaction that in their own way millions of men proved themselves great.

Out of the hordes that rode over mountains, sailed the seas or picked their way through trenches and across the scarred surface of the earth there looms the figures of some whose names will go down in history for all time. Their names will be written indelibly upon the pages of life and they will be known for ages after the evidences of the great strife have been obliterated and the peace for which the world struggled has been made a permanent thing.

Among those whose names will be forever linked with the terrible war as a leader of men—whose figure stands out against the mass of humanity—is Woodrow Wilson, President of the United States of America. Though he neither faced bullets nor tramped the historic byways of Europe in the terrible struggle, he was to all intents and purposes the commander-in-chief of all the world forces seeking to break the autocratic domination of the Hohenzollerns of Germany and give democracy its place among the nations of the world which its character justifies.

President Wilson, when he was elevated to the highest position in America which the Nation could bestow, was recognized as one of the greatest essayists and students of history, political economy, constitutional law and government in the country. And those who made light of his "book-learning" and referred to him as "the school-master president," came to know that his training and the very character of his life's work fitted him better than probably any other man in America to deal with the great national and international problems which confronted, which culminated with or grew out of America's entrance into the great war.

WILSON'S MANY HONORS.

He was born in Staunton, Va., in 1856, the son of Rev. Joseph Woodrow Wilson, and received his early education at Davidson College, N. C. Subsequently he received a degree at Princeton University and graduated in law at the University of Virginia, later practicing law at Atlanta. After this he received degrees at Johns Hopkins, Rutgers, University of Pennsylvania, Brown, Dartmouth, Harvard and Yale Colleges, and was professor of history and political economy, first at Bryn Mawr College and later at Wesleyan University, and finally professor of jurisprudence and political economy, then jurisprudence and politics and afterward president at Princeton University, from which post he was elected Governor of the State of New Jersey in 1913. He resigned from the Governorship and was elected President of the United States for a term beginning March, 1913, and was re-elected in November, 1916, for a second term beginning March, 1917, both times on the Democratic ticket.

As against the figure of President Wilson there stands that of the Emperor William of Germany, whose policies indirectly precipitated the war and impelled the alignment of nations to defend themselves against his autocratic domination. For years the head of the House of Hohenzollern, descendant of the ancient margraves of Germany who have battled with the old Romans, made it manifest in speech and by action that his ambition was to create a world empire.

GERMANY MUST BE RECKONED WITH.

Once at the launching of one of the great German warships he said: "The ocean teaches us that on its waves and on its most distant shores no great decision can any longer be taken without Germany and without the German Emperor. I do not think that it was in order to allow themselves to be excluded from big foreign affairs that, thirty years ago, our people, led by their princes, conquered and shed their blood. Were the German people to let themselves be treated thus, it would be, and forever, the end of their world-power; and I do not mean that that shall ever cease. To employ, in order to prevent it, the suitable means, if need be extreme means, is my duty and my highest privilege."

In a famous interview in the London "Daily Mail" in 1908, discussing the attitude of Germany toward England, the Kaiser was quoted as follows:

"You English," he said, "are mad, mad, mad as March hares. What has come over you that you are so completely given over to suspicions quite unworthy of a great nation? What more can I do than I have done? I declared with all the emphasis at my command, in my speech at Guildhall, that my heart is set upon peace, and that it is one of my dearest wishes to live on the best of terms with England. Have I ever been false to my word? Falsehood and prevarication are alien to my nature. My actions ought to speak for themselves, but you listen not to them but to those who misinterpret and distort them. That is a personal insult which I feel and resent. To be forever misjudged, to have my repeated offers of friendship weighed and scrutinized with jealous, mistrustful eyes, taxes my patience severely. I have said time after time that I am a friend of England, and your Press—or at least a considerable section of it—bids the people of England refuse my proffered hand, and insinuates that the other holds a dagger. How can I convince a nation against its will?"

And then as if to impress upon the world the belief that he was chosen of God, the Kaiser repeatedly gave voice to such bombastic utterances as when to his son in Brandenburg, he declared: "I look upon the people and nation handed on to me as a responsibility conferred upon me by God, and that it is, as is written in the Bible, my duty to increase this heritage, for which one day I shall be called upon to give an account; those who try to interfere with my task I shall crush."

THE "GOD-APPOINTED" HOHENZOLLERNS.

Again he expressed the same sentiment when he said: "It is a tradition of our House, that we, the Hohenzollerns, regard ourselves as appointed by God to govern and to lead the people, whom it is given us to rule, for their well-being and the advancement of their material and intellectual interests."

And finally in his address to the people in August, 1914, he said at the beginning of war: "A fateful hour has fallen for Germany. Envious peoples everywhere are compelling us to our just defence. The sword has been forced into our hands. I hope that if my efforts at the last hour do not succeed in bringing our opponents to see eye to eye with us and in maintaining the peace, we shall, with God's help, so wield the sword that we shall restore it to its sheath again with honor.

"War would demand of us an enormous sacrifice in property and life, but we should show our enemies what it means to provoke Germany. And now I commend you to God. Go to church and kneel before God, and pray for His help for our gallant army."

This is the picture of "Kaiser Bill" whose egotism gave expression to itself in 1910 when in a speech he said: "Considering myself as the instrument of the Lord, without heeding the views and opinions of the day, I go my way."

EMPEROR WILLIAM'S CHILDREN.

William II, Emperor of Germany and King of Prussia, was born January 27, 1859, succeeding his father, Emperor Frederick the III, in June, 1888. He married the Princess Augusta Victoria, of Schleswig-Holstein-Sonderburg-Augustenburg, and had the following issue: Frederick William, Crown Prince, born May 6, 1882; William Eitel-Frederick, born 1883; Adalbert, born 1884; August, born 1887; Oscar, born 1888; Joachim, born 1890, and Victoria Louise, born 1892.

Crown Prince Frederick William is one of the remarkable figures of the war. A profound admirer of Napoleon he has always made a close study of that great French soldier, and has long been one of the leaders of the war-seeking element in Germany. The Crown Prince, who was born in 1882, is tall, slim and impulsive. The late Queen Victoria, his great grandmother, was his godmother.

After he had completed a military course he attended Bonn University, and on the completion of his college course he set out on extensive travels. After his return he was placed in the offices of the Potsdam provincial government so that he might study local administration. After completing this study he was given a course in the intricate routine through which two-thirds of the German people are governed, by being placed in the Prussian Ministry of the Interior. Naval administration has also been a part of the studies of the Crown Prince, in fact he was deeply engrossed in that study when the war was declared.

The Crown Prince married Duchess Cecilie of Mecklenburg-Schwerin, in 1905.

King George V, of Great Britain, the only surviving son of the late King Edward, was born in 1865. He was the second son of the king, his brother Prince Albert, the heir to the throne, dying suddenly in 1892 and bringing the second son, who had been destined for the navy, into direct succession. In 1893 Princess Mary of Teck, who was to have married Prince Albert, was married to Prince George, and there is one daughter, Princess Mary, and five sons—Edward, Prince of Wales, and Princes Albert, Henry, George and John.

THE DUKE OF CONNAUGHT.

Prince Arthur, the Duke of Connaught, who is now Governor General of Canada, is an uncle of the King. He was married to Princess Louise-Margaret of Prussia, the daughter of Prince Frederick-Charles of Prussia and Princess Marie-Anne of Anhalt. He has three children; Margaret, the oldest, is the Crown Princess of Sweden; Prince Arthur is married to his cousin, Princess Alexandra, Duchess of Fife, and Princess Victoria-Patricia, who is unmarried.

King Edward had three brothers and five sisters, two brothers falling heir in turn to the Duchy of Saxe-Coburg-Gotha.

King George V is uncle by blood to Olaf, Crown Prince of Norway, and by marriage with Queen Mary, to three Princes and three Princesses of Teck. He is brother-in-law to King Haakon VII of Norway and Prince of Denmark, Duke Adolph of Teck, and Prince Alexander of Teck. He is a first cousin on his father's side to Emperor William II of Germany, and his brothers and sisters, among whom, principally, is the Queen of Greece; to Ernst-Louis, Grand Duke of Hesse, and his four sisters, one of whom is the wife of Prince Henry of Prussia, and another is Alice, former Czarina of Russia. The first and second cousins of the King run well up into the hundreds.

The Royal Family of Belgium was founded when, in

1831, the people elected King Leopold I to rule the destinies of that country. The king was married to Princess Louise of Orleans, after which practically all the marriages of the family were with the southern group of royal houses.

There were three children born to the couple, the oldest son succeeding to the throne as King Leopold II. The latter married Archduchess Marie Henriette of Austria. One son, and three daughters were born, the son dying when he was 23 years old. The oldest of the daughters became the wife of Prince Philip of Saxe-Coburg-Gotha, the second wedding Crown Prince Rudolph of Austria-Hungary, who died in youth, and the third becoming the wife of Prince Napoleon Bonaparte. The daughter of Leopold I is the widow of the ill-fated Emperor Maximilian of Mexico, who was executed there in 1867.

SECOND SON OF LEOPOLD I.

The second son of Leopold I was Philip, the Count of Flanders, who was married to Princess Marie of Hohenzollern, sister of the Prince Leopold of Hohenzollern and King Charles of Roumania. The son to this marriage is King Albert of Belgium, who succeeded his uncle, Leopold II, in 1909. The Queen of Belgium is Princess Elizabeth of the Ducal House of Bavaria. Through her King Albert is allied to the Crown Prince of Bavaria, the Grand Duchess of Luxemburg, the Duke of Parma, the late Franz Ferdinand of Austria, and the present heir-apparent, Archduke Charles Francis Joseph. The King and Queen have two sons, Leopold, born in 1902, and Charles Theodore, who is two years younger. There is also a daughter, the Princess Marie-Josephine, born in 1906.

King Nicholas I, ruler of the picturesque little country of Montenegro, which was the scene of much bitter fighting, was born October 7, 1841, and proclaimed Prince of Montenegro, as successor to his uncle Danilo I, in 1860. He became king in 1910. Nicholas I married Milena Petrovna Vucotic.

The children are Princess Militza, who married the Russian Grand Duke Peter Nikolaievitch; Princess Stana, who married George, Duke of Leuchtenberg, but which marriage was dissolved, the Princess subsequently marrying the Russian Grand Duke Nicholas Nikolaievitch. The other children are Prince Danilo Alexander, heir-apparent; Princess Helena, who married Victor Emmanuel, King of Italy; Princess Anna, who married Prince Francis Joseph of Battenberg; Prince Mirko, who married Natalie Constantinovitch; Princess Zenia, Princess Vera and finally Prince Peter, who was born in 1889.

KING OF SERVIA.

Peter I, King of Servia, one of the figures of the war, is the son of Alexander Kara-Georgevitch. He was born in Belgrade in 1844, and was proclaimed King after the murder of King Alexander and Queen Draga. He ascended the throne on June 2, 1903. He was married in 1883 to Princess Zorka, of Montenegro, who died in 1890. He has two sons and a daughter; George, who was born in 1887, and who renounced his right to the throne in 1909; Alexander, born in 1889, and Helen, who was born in 1884. Because of his ill health King Peter, for a long time, delegated authority to his son Alexander for the purpose of government.

Nicholas II, the last Czar of Russia, who abdicated in June, 1917, was born May 18, 1868, and succeeded his father, Emperor Alexander III, on November 1, 1894. He married Princess Alexandra Alice, daughter of Ludwig IV, Grand Duke of Hesse, and has four daughters and one son: Olga, Tatinia, Marie, Anastasia and Alexis.

The family is descended in the female line from Michael Romanof, first elected Czar in 1613, and, in the male line, from Duke Karl Frederick of Holstein-Gottorp. As the result of intermarriages and connections with the royal houses of Germany, they are practically Germans by blood.

It was in fact the German influence, which is said to have been the immediate cause of the revolt in the great country.

The revolution may be said to have had its inception when a small group of men opposed to the German influence at court assassinated the monk Gregory Rasputin, who had a great influence over the Czar.

A REACTIONARY CABINET INSTALLED.

Czar Nicholas in anger dismissed Premier Trepoff and installed a thoroughly reactionary Cabinet. Trepoff had been in office only a short time, having followed M. Sturmer, who had bitterly fought the Duma. It had been commonly reported that the real power in the Russian Government after Sturmer went out was in the hands of the Minister of the Interior, M. Protopopoff. Sturmer had been called to the premiership to succeed M. Goremykin, who was in office when the war began.

The fact that Michael Rodzianko, president of the Duma and one of the leading advocates of liberalization of the Government, was named as the chief figure in the provisional government, showed that the movement is in the hands of the same forces which had demanded the overthrow of the bureaucracy and a more energetic prosecution of the war.

There were many changes in the Russian Government during the war, although the censorship was enforced so rigidly that the significance of the rapid shifts was apparent. Vague reports reached the outside world of high councilors of State who were obstructing instead of assisting the work of carrying on the war, and the strength of German influence at Petrograd. The most conspicuous case of this sort was that of General Soukhomlinoff, former Minister of War, who was dismissed from office and imprisoned as a result of charges of criminal negligence and high treason.

M. Sazonoff, Russia's Foreign Minister at the beginning of the war and an ardent believer in the prosecution of the war, was deposed early in the reactionary regime and sent as envoy to London. It was suggested that the motive for this was not to honor an anti-German, but to get him out of Russia.

MEMBERS OF THE RUSSIAN CABINET.

The members of the Russian Cabinet, as announced for the Provisional Government, were:

. Prince Georges E. Lvoff, well known as president of the Zemstvos' Union, Prime Minister.

Alexander J. Guchkoff, Minister of the Interior.

Paul Milukoff, well known as a Constitutional Democrat leader, Minister of Foreign Affairs.

M. Pokrovski, Minister of Finance.

General Manikovski, chief of the Artillery Department, War Minister.

M. Savitch, Minister of Marine.

M. Maklakoff, Minister of Justice.

M. Kovalevski, Minister of Education.

M. Nekrasoff, Minister of Railways.

M. Konovaloff, Moscow merchant, Minister of Commerce and Industry.

M. Rodischneff, Secretary for Finland.

M. Kerenski, Minister without portfolio.

The executive committee of the Imperial Duma, as the provisional Government styles itself, is composed of twelve members, under M. Rodzianko, including two Socialists, two Conservatives, three Moderates, five Constitutional Democrats and Progressives.

Constantine I, King of Greece, who abdicated in favor of his son, Prince Alexander, on June 11, 1917, under pressure from the Allied countries, was born in 1868. His father, King George, was assassinated at Salonica on March 18, 1913. The abdication of King Constantine in June, 1917, was due to his opposition to the forces in the government which desired to join the Allies in the war against Germany. The influence in favor of the Germans in the royal family of Greece was Queen Sophia, a sister of the Kaiser.

For a time Constantine was a veritable idol in Greece. In 1896 when his country was drifting into war with Turkey, he sounded a warning that the Greek army was unprepared for a campaign. The infantry was armed with condemned French rifles; the cartridges were 15 years old; there was no cavalry; the artillery was obsolete, and the officers few. When the country went to war despite his warning, the result was a disastrous defeat. A similar situation developed when King George tried to oppose the popular clamor for the annexation of Crete. The King knew that Turkey was waiting for another opportunity to crush Greece, and there was a second uprising.

CONSTANTINE BECOMES AN IDOL.

Constantine had been in command of the military forces, and King George was obliged to dismiss him as Generalissimo. In the Balkan war of 1912, however, when he led an army of 10,000 Greeks to the capture of Salonica, causing 30,000 Turks to lay down arms, he became an idol. On ascending the throne, it was said that he aimed to restore the grandeur of the ancient Hellenic Empire, and that he was a firm believer in the old national prophecy that, under the reign of a "Constantine and a Sophia," the Eastern Empire would be rejuvenated and the cross restored on Saint Sophia in Constantinople, supplanting the Crescent of the Turk. In fact, after the Balkan war, when Greece added a section of Turkish territory to her domain, and the islands of Crete were annexed, King Constantine hoisted the ancient Hellenic flag over the fort.

The climax in Grecian affairs was precipitated when Turkey entered the great World War on the side of Germany. The question of intervention on the part of Greece arose, and King Constantine insisted on strict neutrality being observed.

The cabinet, headed by Premier Venizelos, which was for war on the side of the Allies, tendered its resignation. When the operations began against the Dardanelles the Government believed that the time had come for Greece to enter the war. The King refused to countenance the plan, arguing that the sending of forces to the Dardanelles would dangerously weaken the Greek defences on the Bulgarian frontier. Queen Sophia was regarded as bitterly opposed to the country joining the Allies, and was reported to have threatened several times to leave the country.

The criticism directed against Constantine was severe because, under the terms of the treaty made in the Balkan war, Greece was committed to ally herself with Servia if that country were attacked by another power. Austria did invade Servia, but Constantine asserted that the treaty applied only to an attack by another Balkan nation.

ACCUSED OF EVASION.

The occupation by troops of the Entente Powers of a part of Macedonia, and the seizure of Salonica as their base, involved the King of Greece in a long series of clashes with the Entente commanders, and he was accused of evasion and attempting to gain time in the interests of Germany. A temporary understanding was obtained, but meantime the provisional government, headed by Venizelos, had been growing in strength, and obtained the recognition of the Entente Powers.

The Allies laid an embargo on the supplies of Greece, and Constantine was denounced by the people of Crete and other territory, who demanded his dethronement. This was the situation, in a general way, which led to his abdication and his retirement to Berlin, with the Queen, in the summer of 1917.

Alexander, who succeeded his father, was a second son,

born August 1, 1893. He was a captain in the First Regiment, artillery, in the Greek army.

Victor Emmanuel, King of Italy, who threw the weight of his country with the Allies, repudiating the treaty with Germany and Austria-Hungary which established what was known as the Triple Entente, was born in 1869, the only son of King Humbert, second King of United Italy, who was murdered at Monza, in July, 1900. Victor Emmanuel married Princess Elena, daughter of Nicholas, King of Montenegro, and has four children: Princess Yolanda, Princess Mafalda; Prince Humbert, heir-apparent, and Princess Giovanna. The mother of King Emmanuel—Dowager Queen Margherita— is a daughter of the later Prince Ferdinand of Savoy.

TRAGEDY THE PATHWAY TO THRONE.

Charles I, the Emperor of Austria and King of Hungary, was born in 1887 and succeeded his grand uncle, Francis Joseph I, in November, 1916. His way to the throne lay through tragedy, for he came into the crown immediately through the assassination of the Archduke Francis Ferdinand, heir-apparent, and his morganatic wife Countess Sophie Chotek, in Bosnia, and which crime was the signal for the war. Nor would Charles have been entitled to succeed to the throne but for the fact that the Archduke Rudolf, heir-apparent to the throne, committed suicide in 1889.

The right of succession went with his death to the second brother of the then Emperor Francis Joseph, or Archduke Charles Louis, father of the assassinated Archduke Francis Ferdinand. It passed then after the tragedies to Archduke Otto, brother of Francis Ferdinand, Charles I, being the son of the Archduke Otto. The young Emperor married Princess Zita of Bourbon Parma in 1911. She is the daughter of Duke Robert of Parma, and sister of the first wife of Czar Ferdinand of Bulgaria. The Emperor has four children: Francis

Joseph Otto, Adelaide Marie, Robert Charles Ludwig and Felix Frederic August.

Ferdinand of Bulgaria, Czar, is son of the late Prince Augustus of Saxe-Coburg and Gotha and late Princess Clementine of Bourbon-Orleans, daughter of King Louis Philippe. He was born in 1861 and succeeded Prince Alexander, who abdicated. He married Marie Louise, daughter of Robert of Parma, and after her death married Princess Eleanore of Reuss-Kostritz. There are four children by the first marriage: Prince Boris, heir-apparent; Prince Cyril, Princess Eudoxia, Princess Nadejda.

Alfonso XIII, King of Spain, was born May 17, 1886, his father, King Alfonso XII, having died nearly six months previous to his birth. Maria Christina, mother of the heir to the Spanish throne, was an Austrian princess. In 1906 King Alfonso XIII married the English Princess Victoria Eugenie, daughter of the late Henry of Battenberg and Princess Beatrice, a daughter of the late Queen Victoria.

KING ALFONSO'S SONS.

King Alfonso XIII has four sons: Alfonso, Prince of the Asturias, heir to the Spanish throne; Prince Jaime, who is deaf and dumb; Prince Juan, and Prince Gonzalo. There are two daughters, Princess Beatrice, and Princess Maria Christina.

The King's sisters were Maria de las Mercedes, who married Prince Carlos of Bourbon, in February, 1901, and died in 1904, and Infanta Maria Teresa, who died suddenly from the effects of childbirth. She was the wife of Prince Ferdinand, who afterward remarried Dona Maria Luisa Pie de Concha, who was created Duchess of Talavera de la Reina, and given the courtesy title of Highness by Alfonso. Don Carlos, who was born in 1848, and was the pretender to the Spanish throne, was a second cousin to the King. He died in 1909, leaving a son, Prince Jamie, born in 1870, and who is the present pretender, and four daughters.

The Spanish reigning family are the Bourbons, descendants of King Louis XIV of France.

Ferdinand, King of Roumania, was born in 1865, and is a nephew of the late King Carol, who died in 1914. In 1893 he married Princess Marie of Saxe-Coburg and Gotha, and two sons and four daughters were born to the royal couple as follows: Charles, who was born in 1893, and who is heir-apparent; Nicholas, Elizabeth, Marie, Ileana and Mircia, the latter dying when four years old.

POINCAIRE'S VERSATILITY.

President Poincaire, of France, is a bearded, pale-faced, short, and rather stout man, who leaves upon those who come in contact with him, an impression of his mental ability.   He was born in 1860, and is regarded as one of the few strong characters who have held the office of President since the war which brought about the third Republic.   He is an author of widely read books, and has won a place in the French Academy.   As a lawyer he was a leader at the bar, and before being chosen President, in 1913, he served as Minister of Finance, and as Minister of Public Instruction.   While serving as Minister of Finance he is credited with having put on the statutes admirable laws regulating and equalizing the taxations of millions.   President Poincaire is a patron of art, and has been counsel of the Beaux Art, of the National Museum and President of the Society of Friends of the University of Paris.

The Sultan of Turkey, the outstanding nation in the conflict, not Christian, was chosen ruler and took the Osman sword on May 10, 1909, and was designated Mohammed V. His name is Mohammed Reshad Effendi, and he succeeded Abd-ul-Hamid, who was deposed.   The latter became Sultan in 1876, succeeding Abd-ul-Aziz, who was preceded by Abd-ul-Mejid.

The history of the Ottoman Empire is filled with mystery, romance and stories of intrigue, cruelty and barbarities, involving internal wars, uprisings, almost continuous struggles with practically all of the European countries and massacres that aroused the whole world.   Legend assigns Oghuz, son of Kara Khan, father of the Ottoman Turks, whose first appearance in history dates back to 1227 A. D.

The reign of Abd-ul-Aziz in the latter part of the last century was marked by many massacres and the extravagant conduct of affairs by the Sultan, who visited England in 1876 and was honored by Queen Victoria, who bestowed upon him the Order of the Garter.   He was deposed and Abd-ul-Hamid succeeded.   He made feeble attempts to reorganize the Government, but his efforts were fruitless and following wars and uprisings and further internal troubles and the loss of territory he was deposed and the present Sultan was chosen.

CHAPTER XVI.
THE WAR'S WHO'S WHO.

Striking Figures in the Conflict—Joffre, the Hero of Marne—Nivelle, the French Commander—Sir Douglas Haig—The Kaiser's Chancellor—Venizelos—"Black Jack" Pershing.

ONE of the most striking figures among those whose names are irrevocably linked with the history of the world fight for democracy, is that of Joseph Joffre, Marshal of France, former Commander of the French forces and victor of the famous battle of the Marne, who led the French Mission to the United States, after America entered the war.

The Commander-in-Chief of all the French armies, a man of humble birth, saw the light of day at Perpignan, near the Pyrenees, in 1852.

The future General early showed a deep interest in mathematics and obtained the degree of Bachelor of Science at the College of Perpignan at the early age of 16. He was a student at the Polytechnic Institute when the Franco-German War of 1870 broke out. Joffre was placed in charge of a large part of the defense of Paris and drew the plans of the fortifications in the direction of Enghein. At the age of 19 he was promoted to Captaincy in the presence of Marshal MacMahon and his whole staff.

Marshal Joffre traveled much and spent a great many years fighting France's colonial wars. He served in the Formosa campaign of 1885; constructed a chain of forts at Tonkin, Cochin-China; was decorated for distinguished bravery in leading his troops in action there in the eighties; was Chief Engineer of the Engineering Corps at Hanoi, and undertook the building of a railroad from Senegal to the Niger River in 1892.

Joffre fought through the Dahomey Campaign in 1893;

saved the day for the French in a brilliant rear-guard action and entered Timbuctoo as a conqueror.   Later he proceeded to Madagascar, where he constructed fortifications and organized a naval station.

Recalled to France, General Joffre became a Professor in the War College and obtained his stars in 1901.   He later entered the Engineering Department of the War Ministry; then became Military Governor of Lille.   Later he was promoted to be a Division Commander in Paris and then commander of the Second Army Corps at Amiens.   He gained the honor in 1911 of a unanimous vote of the Superior Council of War making him Commander of all the military forces of France.

A FAMOUS WAR RECORD.

His record in the World War is well known.   Every one has read of his masterly conduct of the retreat from the Belgian border; of his work in regrouping the shattered and retiring French forces; of his ringing appeal to the men to strike back at the moment he had determined upon.   At the Marne he saved France and perhaps the world.

Joffre is unsympathetic and grim when at work.   He has no patience for anything but the highest efficiency.   At a single stroke he cashiered a score of Generals who did not measure up to his standards.   He is a master builder, organizer and strategist.   Though rather taciturn he is loved both by the officers and poilus.   Among the latter he became known as "Papa" Joffre.

He showed by his appointments and acts that a new inspiration — an inspiration of patriotism — controlled the Republic.   Joffre's accession to supreme command symbolized that France had experienced a new birth, that the army was well organized and that the man who for three years had been silently performing the regeneration of the land forces had rightly been placed over the forces he had reformed.

Almost unknown to the masses, Joffre was placed at the head of the French troops in the summer of 1914. Among his associates he was known as an authority on aeroplanes, automobiles, telegraphs and the other details of modern warfare. Above everything else he stood for efficiency and preparedness, and lacked the qualities of the French soldier of literature. To be prepared for instant war had been his effort for three years, and when that time came France found herself nearly as well prepared for the conflict as was Germany, which had prepared for twenty-five years.

ADJURATION TO SCHOOL CHUMS.

One of his few published speeches, made to his old school chums, is on this theme. "To be prepared in our days," he said, "has a meaning which those who prepared for and fought the wars of other days would have great difficulty in understanding. It would be a sad mistake to depend upon a sudden burst of popular enthusiasm, even though it should surpass in intensity that of the volunteers of the Revolution, if we do not fortify it by complete preparation.

"To be prepared we must assemble all the resources of the country, all the intelligence of her children, all their moral energy and direct them toward a single aim—victory. We must have organized everything, foreseen everything. Once hostilities have begun no improvisation will be worth while. Whatever lacks then will be lacking for good and all. And the slightest lack of preparation will spell disaster."

What Joffre said to his chums he had done for the French army, and President Poincare, after the Battle of the Marne, summed up his qualities which made it a French victory in this message to Joffre: "In the conduct of our armies you have shown a spirit of organization, order and of method whose beneficent effects have influenced every phase, from strategy to tactics; a wisdom cold and cautious, which has always prepared for the unexpected, a powerful soul which nothing has shaken, a serenity whose salutary example has everywhere inspired confidence and hope."

These words of the President of the French Republic are an epitome of the character and the military record of Joffre. He is representative of the real France, not the France of Paris and scandals. He is of the peasantry, and he and his kind, men of character, brought about the glorious France of the war.

Among those who accompanied Joffre on his visit to the United States was Rene Viviani, ex-Premier of France and Minister of Justice. He was born in Algeria in 1862, his family being Corsican, and originally of Italian blood.

VIVIANI A SOCIALIST LEADER.

M. Viviani became a lawyer in Paris and built up a large practice. In 1893 he entered the Chamber of Deputies as a Socialist. Together with Briand, Jaures and Millerand he was long a leader of the parliamentary delegation of Socialists. On June 1, 1914, one month before the outbreak of the war, M. Viviani became Prime Minister. He showed himself a brilliant leader and tireless worker. His speeches embodying the spirit of fighting France were read and admired the world over. Many persons consider Rene Viviani France's greatest orator. Volumes of his speeches have had a wide sale.

M. Viviani was succeeded in the Premiership by M. Briand, and recently he became Minister of Justice in the Ribot Cabinet. He is a man of great culture. Though an excellent Latin and Greek scholar, he speaks no English. Rene Viviani has had some experience as a newspaper man, as a special writer and as managing editor of the Petite Republique. His younger son, aged 22, was killed in the war. His older son has been wounded but is back at the front.

Another member of the French mission was M. de Hovelacque, the French Inspector General of Public Instruction.

He is well known in the United States because of his marriage to Miss Josephine Higgins, of New York State.

The Right Honorable Arthur Balfour, ex-Premier of England, who came to America to join in the conferences at which the policies for carrying the war were outlined after America became an Ally, is described as one of the most intellectual statesmen in England, and one who, although he won all the honors his country could give him, never realized his own possibilities. At sixty-nine, at the height of his mental development, he occupies a place in the English cabinet, a place which was given him because of his great hold upon the autocracy of England.

BALFOUR'S INTELLECTUAL ABILITY.

As the Premier of England, as Secretary of Ireland and as the leader of the House of Commons Mr. Balfour displayed great intellectual agility, but at no time was credited with having displayed the industry which spurred on such men as Lloyd George to success. He is of the aristocracy and his position in English politics came to him as the nephew of Lord Salisbury.

He was born in 1848 and educated at Eton and Cambridge and entered the House of Commons at the age of 26. Mr. Balfour was known in his early years as a philosophically and religiously inclined young man, and it occasioned some surprise when he followed the traditions of his family by entering politics.

Some years after taking his seat he joined what was known as the Fourth Party, a conservative rebel faction, consisting of three members, Lord Randolph Churchill, Sir Henry Drummond Wolff and Sir John Gorst. This group constituted a sort of mugwump element that voted independently on every party question and that tried to rouse the Conservatives from their party prejudices and narrow leanings.

To Mr. Balfour belonged the distinguished honor of

attending the Berlin Conference of 1878 as private secretary to Lord Salisbury. In 1885 he became President of the Local Government Board. The Conservatives were thrown out of power for a short time at this juncture, but when they were restored in 1886 Balfour became Secretary for Scotland. Shortly after he was promoted to be Chief Secretary for Ireland.

Despite his gentle manners and quiet ways, the new Chief Secretary ruled the then disturbed Ireland with an iron hand. He was known as "Bloody Balfour" by the Irish agitators until he began to show his milder ways upon the restoration of peace. He remained in Ireland until 1891. He had endured abuse and faced threats and had come away triumphant. From Ireland Mr. Balfour went to England as First Lord of the Treasury.

Arthur James Balfour showed his friendship for the United States when, in 1897, as Acting Secretary for Foreign Affairs, he refused to give England's consent to a continental proposal that Spain be permitted to govern Cuba as she chose.

LIBERALS COME INTO POWER.

When Lord Salisbury died in 1902 Mr. Balfour succeeded him as Prime Minister. He remained in that office until 1905, when the Liberals came into power. In the coalition Ministry formed since the outbreak of the European War, he was nominated First Lord of the Admiralty. He showed remarkable ability in this office. Upon the resignation of Mr. Asquith's Cabinet, Mr. Balfour became Secretary for Foreign Affairs. He is an enthusiastic sportsman and has written a book on golf.

The other English envoys who accompanied Mr. Balfour to Washington were Rear Admiral Sir Dudley Rawson Stratford de Chair, and Lord Walter Cunliffe, Governor of the Bank of England.

Rear Admiral de Chair was born August 30, 1864. He entered the Royal Navy at the age of 14, and received his early training aboard His Majesty's Ship Britannia. He served in the Egyptian war and was naval attache at Washington in 1902.

Admiral de Chair commanded the Bacchante, Cochrane and Colossus successively in the years between 1905 and 1912. From 1912 to 1914 he acted as Assistant Controller of the Navy and subsequently he was the Naval Secretary to the First Lord of the Admiralty. At the outbreak of the war he became Admiral of the training services and of the Tenth Cruiser Squadron. Admiral de Chair is a member of the Royal Victorian Order and a Companion of the Bath.

LORD WALTER CUNLIFFE.

Lord Walter Cunliffe, Governor of the Bank of England, is 52 years old. He received his education at Harrow and at Trinity College, Cambridge, from which he graduated with the degree of Master of Arts. He is a Lieutenant of the City of London.

Lord Cunliffe has been active in the banking field for many years and is a member of the firm of Cunliffe Brothers. He is a Director of the North Eastern Railway Company and has been a Director of the Bank of England since 1895. He became Deputy Governor of the bank in 1911 and has been Governor since 1913. Lord Cunliffe is the first Governor of the Bank of England to receive the honor of re-election after serving his term of two years. In 1914 he was created the First Baron of Headley.

Among the dominating characters of the war and upon whose judgment and ability the destinies of France and the Allies depended for a long period is General Robert Nivelle, Commander of the French armies, and who succeeded General Joffre. General Nivelle is a man of silence; he speaks little. General Nivelle is four years younger than Joffre.

As a boy of fourteen he could not take part as did Joffre and Gallieni and Pau and Kitchener also, in the tragical war of 1870.   Joffre studied at the Ecole Polytechnique, in Paris; Gallieni, at Saint Cyr, without the walls; Nivelle studied at both; he may claim to belong to all arms, artillery, infantry— even cavalry.   And, in his youth, he was not only a magnificent all-round athlete, as indeed he still is, but also a headlong rider of steeplechases, in which, had he been fated to break his neck, his neck would infallibly have been broken.   This is a trait he shares with General Brussiloff, and, like the great Russian General, he was famous for the skill with which he tamed and trained cavalry mounts.

SERVES AS JUNIOR OFFICER.

As a junior officer Nivelle saw service in the French General Staff; his part in the expedition to China we have recorded; he also served in Northern Africa.   So that, like Joffre, Gallieni, Lyautey, Roques and so many leaders of French armies, Nivelle gained an invaluable element of his training in the out-of-the-way corners of France's vast colonial empire. which has outposts in every continent and measures nearly five million square miles.

At the outbreak of the World War Nivelle, with the rank of Colonel, commanded the Fifth Regiment of Artillery, which is the artillery element of the Seventh Army Corps, the corps of Besancon and the old Franche-Comite, under the Jura Mountains, at the corner of Switzerland and Alsace.

It was, in fact, in the section of Alsace invaded and re-taken by the French army of General Pau—who lost an arm in Alsace in the war of 1870—that Nivelle struck the first of many hard blows which made him Field Commander of the splendid army of France.   He directed the guns of his Fifth Regiment with such deadly accuracy against a group of German guns that he first scattered their gunners in flight and put them out of action, and then led them off in triumph, twenty-four guns in all, the first great trophy won by the arms of France.

In the battle of the Ourcq, fought with superb tenacity and dash by Manoury and his men, the first decisive blow of the great battle, the first definite victory, was gained; General von Kluck's right wing was smashed in and out-flanked, with the result that the whole German line was dislocated and sent hurtling backward.

In that battle and victory Colonel Nivelle, as he then was, had his part; but it was on the Aisne, a few days later, that a strikingly brilliant act brought him into especial prominence. The Seventh Corps was attacked by exceedingly strong enemy forces and forced backward over the Aisne. Colonel Nivelle, commanding its artillery, saw his opportunity, and, himself leading on horseback, brought his batteries out into the open, right between the retreating Seventh Corps and the strong German forces that were pursuing them, already sure of victory.

VICTORY TURNED TO SLAUGHTER.

With that calm serenity which is his dominant characteristic in action, he let the Germans come close up to his guns in serried masses. Then he opened fire, at short range, with deadly precision, so that the expected victory was turned into a slaughter. The broken German regiments, fleeing to the woods beside the Aisne for safety, ran upon the bayonets of the rallied Seventh Corps, inspired to splendid valor by the magnificent action of their artillery. Of 6000 Germans who made that charge few indeed returned to their trenches.

This was on September 16, 1914. Before the New Year the Artillery Colonel had been made a General of Brigade, and in January, 1915, the new General distinguished himself by stopping the tremendous and unforeseen German drive against Soissons. He was forthwith recommended for further promotion, and on February 18 was gazetted General of Division. Shortly after this be gained new laurels by capturing from the Germans the Quenevieres salient.

This great commander was the son of Colonel Nivelle—
and an English mother, a former Miss Sparrow, whose family
lived at Deal, on the English Channel.   In his married life
General Nivelle has been exceedingly happy.

The dominating figure in the English army when America
entered the fray was Sir Douglas Haig.   He succeeded Sir
John French.

Sir Douglas Haig was born under so favorable a star
that he has long been known as "Lucky" Haig.   Not that he
has depended upon his luck to push him ahead in the army,
for his record as a student and a worker wholly disproves this.
But nevertheless fortune has showered many favors upon him.
Among these favors the first and by no means the least is his
very aristocratic lineage and the consequent high standing he
has had in royal and influential circles.

HAIG'S FAMILY TREE.

Haig's family tree dates back at least six centuries and
he comes of the very flower of Scotch stock.   The virtues of
the "Haigs of Bamersyde" were extolled by the poets of the
thirteenth century.   And to discuss this feature of his career
without giving due credit to the position and influence of his
wife would be ungallant as well as unfair.   She was the Hon.
Dorothy Vivian, daughter of the third Lord Vivian, and maid-
of-honor to Queen Alexandra, and the pair were married in
Buckingham Palace.

He did not enter the army until after his graduation from
Oxford and then he took service in the cavalry, the usual choice
of the English "gentleman."   When twenty-four years old, he
received his commission as a Lieutenant in the Queen's Own
Hussars, one of the ultra-fashionable regiments.   Six years
later he was made a Captain and then decided to take a regular
military course at the Staff College.

In 1898 he took part in Kitchener's campaign up the Nile
and in the Soudan as a cavalry officer.   He was then thirty-

seven years old. He distinguished himself in several engagements, was "mentioned in the dispatches," was awarded the British medal and the Khedive's medal and was promoted to Major.

His career in the Boer war, which followed that in Egypt, was characterized by distinguished services and numerous rapid promotions. It was during this latter war that Haig became attached to the staff of Sir John French, whom he succeeded in France and Flanders. He came out of the war in South Africa a full-fledged Colonel, and with a fresh supply of medals and "mentions." Then he was sent to India as Inspector General of Cavalry.

DIRECTOR OF MILITARY TRAINING.

He remained in the Indian service three years, and then was given a post at the war office in London, with the title of "Director of Military Training." He remained in London three years, when he was sent to India as Chief of the Staff of the Indian Army. Three years later he returned to England and was given what was known as the "Aldershot Command," which, in fact, was the command of the real active British army. He had this post when the war broke. His assignment as Commander of the First Army Corps under Sir John French soon followed.

The man, who next to the Kaiser had more to do with Germany's plans for world domination, is Dr. Theobold von Bethmann-Hollweg, Imperial Chancellor of Germany.

The elevation of Hollweg to the Chancellorship came when Prince Bulow stood in the way of complete domination of Germany's policies by the militarists, headed by the Kaiser. Prince Bulow was dismissed and Bethmann-Hollweg became Chancellor in 1909. From that time on he dedicated his life to the achievement of a single aim—the completion of Germany's plans of aggression.

Bethmann-Hollweg comes from an old Prussian family

ennobled in 1840. He was born about 1855 and was a student with the Kaiser at the University of Bonn. He studied law at Gottingen, Strassburg and Berlin, and for several years followed the law and was appointed a judge at Potsdam.

APPOINTED PRUSSIAN HOME SECRETARY.

In 1905 he was appointed Prussian Home Secretary, and it was then that his name first became familiar to the man in the street in Berlin. Shortly afterward he was appointed Assistant Chancellor of Prince Bulow, who was then Chancellor.

It was during his service as Home Secretary that Bethmann-Hollweg became largely converted to all that the most advanced Prussian militarism stood for. Ultimately be became a far more ardent Pan-German even than Prince Bulow. In a speech at Munich in 1908 he declared that though Germany was then happily free of all immediate anxiety so far as her foreign relations were concerned, her present and future position as a great Power must ultimately rest on her strong arm, and though the strength of her arm was greater than it ever had been it must grow yet stronger.

It was a speech after the Kaiser's own heart—provocative and boasting to a degree. It had, as a matter of fact, it is said, been prepared by the Emperor, and was delivered by the Kaiser's order for the special benefit of Prince Bulow, who had at that time fallen out of favor with the Emperor.

Grand Admiral Von Tirpitz is said to be the man who made the German navy. Having won the recognition of the Kaiser in 1894 he was promoted to Chief of Staff in the German navy, and was placed in command of Kiel. He was made Secretary of State in 1898 and immediately began the building up of the navy. New and modern methods of engineering were developed and finally he made such an impression with the Kaiser that he was ennobled. Von Tirpitz was the principal advocate of Germany's plans during a decade for having the navy powerful enough to equal the combined powers of any three great naval powers.

Sir John Jellicoe, Vice Admiral and Commander-in-Chief of the British Naval Home Fleet had served more than forty years in the navy when the war broke out. He was a Lieutenant at the bombardment of Alexandria and was a member of the Naval Brigade which participated in the battle of Tel-el-Kebir, for activity in which he was presented with the Khedive's Bronze Star for gallant service. He was in command of the naval brigade which went to China in 1898 to help subdue the Boxers and was shot at Teitsang, where he was decorated by the German Emperor, who conferred upon him the Order of the Red Eagle. He was Rear-Admiral of the Atlantic Fleet in 1907-08, and Commander of the Second Home Squadron in 1911-12. To Admiral Jellicoe is given credit for having developed a high degree of efficiency among the gunners in the English navy.

ADMIRAL HUGO POHL.

Admiral Hugo Pohl, of the German navy, was born at Breslau in 1855. He became a Lieutenant in the Imperial German navy when but 21 years of age. He gained rapid promotion, and within a few years was Commodore in charge of the scouting ships. He had charge of setting up the now famous German naval stations from Kiel to Sonderberg in Schleswig in 1908 and was afterwards made Vice Admiral. He wears the medal of the Order of the Crown, bestowed upon him by the Kaiser for admirable service.

One of the men whose names will be forever linked with the war, particularly with relation to the adoption of new methods of warfare, is that of Count Zeppelin, who died on March 8, 1917, and who was the father of the Zeppelin or dirigible balloon. The idea for the big airship did not originate with Count Zeppelin, but with David Schwartz, a young Austrian, who built his first dirigible in 1893. He tried to

arouse interest in his aircraft in Russia, but failed and finally
went to Berlin, where he interested the then Baron Zeppelin.
A balloon was made, but Schwartz fell ill and died. Zeppelin
was later accused of attempting to steal the young Austrian's
patents, and the courts made an award to Schwartz's widow of
$18,000.

Count Zeppelin's first airship came out about 1898. It
was 300 feet long and had an aluminum frame. Short cruises
were made in 1899 and 1900, and the craft maintained a speed
of about sixteen miles an hour. A second airship was completed in 1905, and later a third aircraft was finished. This
dirigible made a cruise of 200 miles at an average speed of
twenty miles. The success led Count Zeppelin to make his
most ambitious attempt and he tried to cross the Alps carrying
sixteen passengers.

IN THE AIR THIRTY-SEVEN HOURS.

He succeeded and passing through hailstorms, crossing
eddies and encountering cross-currents he traveled 270 miles
at an average speed of twenty-two miles an hour. Subsequently he made a flight to England, remaining in the air
thirty-seven hours. Fate played him false, however, in many
of his ventures and he returned home after making remarkable
voyages, only to have his craft destroyed at its very landing
place.

The German Government and the Kaiser joined in giving
him a grant of money to carry on his work, and a plant was
built at Frederichshafen. But while Count Zeppelin's name
will be forever identified with aeronautics the successes which
he attained were not enduring, for the Zeppelins proved not
entirely satisfactory in military warfare in competition with
the aeroplane.

In the counsels of Greece the outstanding figure from the
beginning of the war was Eleutherois Venizelos. He is
credited with being responsible for the national revival in

Greece when the country seemed doomed after the Turkish war of 1897. He was the leader of the country in the movement to join the Allies in the fight against German domination and he swayed the nation and held them as few men have. He was born in the Island of Crete in 1864, and according to tradition, his family descended from the medieval Dukes of Athens. He was educated in Greece and Switzerland and became active in Cretan politics, and won recognition as the strong man of the "Great Greek Island."

TRANSFORMS A NATION.

In less than three years after the distress in which the country found itself in 1909 he transformed the nation into one of solidarity. There had been meaningless squabbles of corrupt politicians and a sordid struggle for preferment. The army was degenerating and the popular fury became so great that there was an uprising of the army, which under the title of the "Military League," ousted the Government and took control of the country. The heads of the League brought forward Venizelos. The League dissolved and reforms were instituted which started the country on a new path, and when the Balkan war broke in 1912 Greece made a record and emerged in many respects the leader of the Balkan states.

Sir John French is one of the English commanders who have rendered yeoman service in the war. He is one of the most striking military figures in England. He has seen service in India, Africa and Canada, and was one of the uniformly successful commanders in the Boer war. At the Siege of Kimberly he was shut up in Ladysmith with the Boer lines drawing closer. He managed to secrete himself under the seat of a train on which women were being carried to safety. Outside the lines he made his way to the Cape, where he was put in charge of cavalry and in a terrific drive he swept through the Free State and reached Ladysmith in time to save the day.

He originally entered the navy, but remained for a short

time. He commanded the 19th Hussars from 1889 to 1903 and then rose steadily in rank until he was made General Inspector of the Forces and finally Field Marshal in 1903.

There should be no discrimination in naming those who have represented America in the country's activities at war, but because they came into the world's line of vision by being sent abroad for service there are some American commanders whose names will ever be remembered.

Vice-Admiral William S. Sims is one of these. He is a Pennsylvanian who was born in Canada. His father was A. W. Sims, of Philadelphia, who married a Canadian and lived at Port Hope, where Admiral Sims first saw the light of day. He went to Annapolis when he was 17 years of age and was graduated in 1880. After this he secured a year's leave of absence and went to France, where he studied French. Subsequently he was assigned to the Tennessee, the flagship of the North Atlantic Squadron and passed through all grades of ships. He received promotion to a Lieutenancy when he was about 30 years of age. For a time he was in charge of the Schoolship Saratoga, and later was located at Charleston Navy Yard, and also with the receiving ship at the League Island Navy Yard, Philadelphia. After this he went to Paris as Naval Attache at the American Embassy. He was similarly Attache at the American Embassy at St. Petersburg.

Admiral Sims was relieved of his European assignment in 1900 and joined the Asiatic fleet, and while abroad studied the methods of British gunnery. When he returned to America later he inaugurated reforms which increased the efficiency of the gunnery in the service 100 per cent. His successful efforts led to his appointment as Naval Aide to President Roosevelt. He made a report on the engagement between the British and German naval fleets at Jutland which was startling, and declared that the British battle cruisers had protected Great Britain from the invasion of the enemy.

When he reached the European waters in command of the United States naval forces, with a destroyer flotilla, and the British officers who greeted him asked when the flotilla would be ready to assist in chasing the submarine and protecting shipping, Admiral Sims created a surprise by tersely replying: "We can start at once." And he did. Admiral Sims married Miss Anne Hitchcock, daughter of Former Secretary of the Interior. The couple have five children.

Major General John J. Pershing, of the United States Army, Commander of the forces in France and Belgium, is one of the most picturesque figures in American military circles. "Black Jack" Pershing is what the officers call him, because he was for a long time commander of the famous Tenth Cavalry of Negroes, which he whipped into shape as Drillmaster, and which saved the Rough Riders from a great deal of difficulty at San Juan Hill in the Spanish-American War. He was also at the battle of El Caney where he was given credit for being one of the most composed men in action that ever graced a battlefield. He served with signal results in the campaign against the little "brown" men in the Philippines; was in charge of the expedition which chased Villa into Mexico.

General Pershing was born in 1864 in Laclede, Missouri, and is tall, wiry and strong. Every inch of his six feet is of fighting material. He is a man of action and has a penchant for utilizing the services of young men rather than staid old officers of experience. Pershing is a real military man, and has been notably absent from such things as banquets and other functions where by talking he might get into the limelight. It is true that he was jumped over the heads of a number of officers by President Roosevelt, but he has carved his way by his own efforts, and no man could have more fittingly been sent to take charge of the American forces abroad than "Jack" Pershing.

CHAPTER XVII.

CHEMISTRY IN THE WAR.

IT IS when men are put to the test that they develop initiative and are inspired to great things. In the stress of circumstances there were created through and in the great war many unusual devices and much that will endure for the benefit of mankind in the future. It is probable that the advancements made in many lines would not have been attained in years but for the necessity which demanded the exertion of men's ingenuity, and in no field was this advancement greater than in that of chemistry.

Any struggle between men is, in the last analysis, a battle of wits, but it remained for those planning and scheming to defeat their fellow men or protect themselves in the world conflict to make for the first time in history the fullest use of the chemist's knowledge. Largely the successes of the war have been due to the studies and activities of the chemists, working in their laboratories far from the actual field of strife.

Not only has their knowledge been turned to the creation of tremendously destructive explosives, the like of which have never before been known in warfare, but the same brains which have been utilized to assist man in his death-dealing crusades have been called upon to thwart the efforts of the warring humans and save the lives of those compelled to face the withering fire of cannon, the flaming grenade and the asphyxiating gas bomb.

In the food crisis which confronted the nations, chemists drew from the very air and the waters of the river and sea, gases and salts to take the place of those which became limited in their supply because of the demands of the belligerents.

The chemist is one of those who fights the battles at home. The resisting steel, the penetrating shell, the poisonous gas, the power-producing oil, the powerful explosive—all these are his contributions to the war's equipment, but he also is the magician who waves the wand and out of the apparently useless weeds and vegetable matter produces edibles. He turns waste products into valuable chemicals or extracts needed chemicals from by-products.

GERMANY'S GREAT PRIVATION.

Germany, deprived of many imports by the sea power of England, first transformed herself into a self-supporting nation through the agency of the chemist. Substitutes had to be provided for food products which the Germans could not get, and it is said that the ability of the Kaiser and his henchmen to withstand the attacks of the Allied forces was due as much to the service rendered by the chemists as by the army and navy.

Not only were artificial foodstuffs manufactured, but natural food products previously neglected were prepared for use. What had been regarded as useless weeds were found to possess food value. A dozen wild-growing plants were found that might be used as a substitute for spinach, while half a dozen others were shown to be good substitutes for salads. Starches were obtained from roots, and cheap grades of oils and fatty wastes of all sorts were turned into edibles.

Up until the advent of the present war cotton formed the base of most of the so-called propellant explosives used in advanced warfare. Such terrible explosives as trinitrotoluene occasionally mentioned in the published war reports, as well as many others, have as the principal agent of destructive force guncotton, which is ordinary raw cotton or cellulose treated with nitric or sulphuric acid, though there are, of course, other chemicals used in compounding the various forms of deadly explosives.

At the same time there are innumerable explosives which are of a distinct class. Lyddite, mentioned occasionally as one of the modern death-dealing explosives, has for a base picric acid. The Lyddite shells referred to occasionally in various articles about the war are shells in which Lyddite is used as the explosive. The largest percentage of explosives used in modern gunnery are those formed of nitrated cellulose —guncotton.

TWO GREAT FACTORS.

Therefore any shortage in the supply of cotton and cellulose is a serious matter in war time, for the country which has the most plentiful supply of ammunition is the one that has the greatest relative advantage. It was, for instance, stated from Washington several times after the war started and the United States commercial and industrial forces were being mobilized, that America could make enough almost unbelievably powerful explosives to blow Germany off the face of the European map, were it possible to transport the dangerous materials. Dozens of new explosive compounds were placed before the Government for consideration and in application for patents. One of the new ones, it was said, was so powerful that little more than a pinch of it exploded beneath such an immense structure as the Woolworth Building, New York, would destroy the entire edifice.

The curtailment of the supply of cotton to Germany when the war started, because of England's blockade, and later when America entered the conflict, threatened disaster to the "Fatherland." The German chemists began working immediately to supply substitutes for cotton, to be used both in the manufacture of explosives and fabrics. They developed the processes of producing cellulose from wood pulp to take the place of cotton for making guncotton, and certain forms of wood fiber and paper were used in the textile trades. Willow bark was one of the substances utilized to a limited degree in making fabrics.

Likewise synthetic—or artificial—camphor to take the place of that secured from nature's own laboratory—the camphor tree—was also produced of necessity, for camphor is an ingredient largely used in making smokeless powder. Before the war most of the camphor was obtained from Japan.

Compounds—alloyed steel, iron and aluminum—have also been used in the industrial world to supplant copper. In America we have been educated to regard copper as the ideal metal for conducting electrical power, but in Europe aluminum was used successfully in a large way, even before the war. After the conflict started in all of the countries where there was a scant supply of copper, substitutes were developed by the metallurgists and chemists.

POTENCY OF MODERN CHEMISTRY.

The acids and salts used in powder making and the creation of explosives were also secured from new places. Nitric acid, which is necessary to the manufacture of guncotton, for many years was made principally with saltpeter and sulphuric acid. Modern chemists, however, made it from nitrogen of the very air we breathe, and in Germany it was made during the war from ammonia and calcium cyanamide, both of which may be obtained from the air.

Many such methods of obtaining acids were known and tested before the war, but the processes had not been perfected to such an extent as to make them commercially profitable. However, the increased prices of chemicals, due to the excessive demands of war, and the absolute necessity for producing them inspired the chemists to get the required results, and Germany by the development of these sources of supply found the acids necessary for her own use in war, whether for explosive making or medical purposes.

Great quantities of sugar are used in making powder and explosives, too, and when the supply became limited the German chemists began producing in larger quantities the chemical substitute—saccharine.   Later even this sweet was denied the population because the chemicals were needed for war uses.   So in every line Germany found use for everything which its chemists and chemical laboratories could produce.

The terrible gas and liquid fire bombs which the Germans were first reported using contained chemical compounds invented for the purpose by the chemists.   Some of the chemicals and the gases produced when the bombs exploded were so powerful that men and animals in the range of the fumes were killed instantly.   The effect was to paralyze them in some cases and it was reported that many of the soldiers were found dead standing upright in the trenches or in the attitudes which they had assumed at the moment they were overcome.

BASIC PRINCIPLE OF BOMBS.

Nitrous-oxide, or chlorine, in some chemical form is supposed to have been the base of the bombs, and concerning the liquid fire it was reported in connection with the dropping of bombs on London from a Zeppelin, that some of the bombs contained what is chemically known as Thermit, which is a mixture of aluminum and iron oxide used in brazing and welding. When ignited the oxygen is freed from the iron and combines with the aluminum with great rapidity.   During the chemical reaction an intense heat is produced—a heat so great that it almost equals that of an electric arc.

So in the world of agriculture and industry the German chemists, recognized leaders of the world, actually made or produced from the air and other unsuspected sources things without which they could not have withstood the siege against them for a single year.   In the absence of concentrated foods for cattle and humans, the chemists produced absolute substitutes.   They took the residue or waste from the breweries and extracting the bitter hops taste from the dried yeast produced a substitute for beef extract.

So also they secured ammonium sulphate by a direct combination of nitrogen and hydrogen in the air. At the same time they utilized other minerals than those usually available for the manufacture of sulphuric acid and placed the country on an independent footing.

But Germany was not alone in its advancement. The United States, which found itself without quantities of dyestuffs and many other chemically produced things when the war came on, took the lesson unto itself and is today nearer self-supporting than it ever was in the history of the nation. The Department of Agriculture has experimented and produced from yeast, vegetable boullion cubes, which taste like beef extract and contain greater nutriment.

DOMESTIC DYE-STUFFS.

America, too, has extracted sulphate of ammonium from the air and the dye-stuffs which we could not get from abroad are being made at home. Two of the things which America found lacking when war developed were potash and acetone, both of which are factors in powder and explosive making. The former is used in the ordinary black gunpowder, but the latter is necessary in the making of the smokeless powder. England wanted Cordite, one form of this powder which the British think is the best propellant in the world. It is made of guncotton and nitroglycerine and acetone is one of the chemicals required in its manufacture. England turned to the United States for quantities of this explosive and also for the acetone, but America did not produce anywhere near enough, and England wanted this country to make something like 20,000,000 pounds of the explosive.

A number of mushroom chemical plants were developed by the powder company to produce the desired acetone—one very much like a vinegar plant near Baltimore, and another at

San Diego, California, where the munitions maker's chemists refined acetone and potash extracted from kelp, or sea weed, and besides supplying the powder and the chemicals which the English needed America developed a permanent industry.

RELIEVED BY AMERICAN INGENUITY.

Carbolic acid, too, was one of the badly needed chemicals of the war, not only for medical purposes, but also for explosive making. Again the ingenuity of America asserted itself and Thomas A. Edison produced the plans for two benzol-absorbing plants which were erected at great steel works and within a few months these plants were turning out benzol and Mr. Edison's carbolic-acid plant was being supplied with the raw material.

And then it was believed that America could not make dyes to take the place of those which came from Germany. All the United States, it was said, would have to wear white stockings. The country just could not produce the dyes necessary, and the product of the American plants was inferior. But America could make the same dyes. She is making them. Right now she is making practically as great a variety as Germany even sent over here.

A few miles outside of Philadelphia, at Marcus Hook, on the busy Delaware river where the ships of the world are being made, the Benzol Products Company turns out large quantities of aniline oil. The aniline oil, the essential basis of aniline dyes, is made into tints as fair and perfect as any the wizards of Germany ever conjured out of their test tubes.

The tale about America's inability was proved to be a fable. The Marcus Hook plant is one of three which sprang up when the war began. Others are the Schoellkopf Aniline and Chemical Works at Buffalo and a third is the Becker Aniline and Chemical Works at Brooklyn. The three are now merged into one great operating company and Germany will have some difficulty in getting back her dye trade when she is ready to again fight for the world markets.

Moreover, the world-famous duPont Company, which has made powder and chemicals for all the nations, turned in and purchased the Harrison Chemical Works in 1917, and besides making "pigments" has entered the coal tar dye industry. The company made an intensive study of the dyeing industries—cotton, calico printing, wool, silk, leather, paper, paints, printing inks, &c., and made plans to meet the requirements of each. The Harrison plant is but one of the immense group operated by the duPont Company and it has been famous for the manufacture of white lead and acids.

A CHEMICAL DISCOVERY.

There is in fact no line in which the chemists of America did not rise to the emergency, and the "romances of the industrial" world are not more entrancing than are those of the medical and other fields. Chemistry, for instance, discovered an anti-toxin for the deadly gangrene, or gas bacillus, poisoning of the battlefields. The discovery was made by research workers in Rockefeller Institute.

It is one of the most important discoveries in medical research as applied to war, having an even greater bearing on the treatment of war wounds than the Dakin-Carrel treatment of sluicing wounds previously referred to. The serum works on the same principle as the anti-tetanus serum used to prevent lockjaw. The gangrene antitoxin is injected to prevent the development of gangrene poisoning.

The serum was developed by Dr. Carrel Bull and Miss Ida W. Pritchett, of the Rockefeller Institute, by immunizing horses by the application of the bacillus germs, then obtaining the resultant serum from the horses. The new serum displaces, in a measure, the Dakin-Carrel method of treating wounds. As soon as a soldier is picked up wounded, the plan is to give him an injection of the serum so that he can be rushed to the rear ambulances with no fear that the deadly gas infection will develop.

The use of the serum means the wiping out of the big death rate from infection, with death resulting merely from wounds that are in themselves fatal. The gas bacillus was discovered by Dr. William H. Welch, of Johns Hopkins University, 25 years ago. The bacillus frequently is present in soil and when carried to an open wound germinates quickly, developing into bubbles of gaseous matter, whence comes the name "gas bacillus." The bubbles multiply rapidly, a few hours often being sufficient to cause death.

A WOUND-FLUSHING SYSTEM.

Possible gangrene poisoning has been offset by the Dakin-Carrel system of constantly flushing the open wounds, but patients are requently too far off to be given the advantage of the flushing method and this is where the serum is chiefly valuable. The ambulance or medical corps "shoots" the serum into the wounded soldier even before they douse his wound with iodine.

The progress that has been made along these lines is indicated by the statement of Lord Northcliffe, who after a visit to the front declared that the annual death rate in the English army was 3 per cent of 1000 and that the average illness, including colds and influenza, was less than in London, despite the discomforts of the trenches.

In the past disease has been as destructive as battles. Biology and pathology, to say nothing of surgery and therapeutics, have made such strides that disease has been virtually eliminated as a factor in warfare. War takes medical science into the field, where the control of large masses of men enables it to develop the highest efficiency.

Even in normal peace conditions biological and pathological science has been accomplishing results not popularly understood. Individual cures by surgery and medicine appeal to personal interests, but these are negligible compared to the prevention of plagues like smallpox, typhus and tuberculosis. If such diseases had not been successfully combated by science three out of four of the present civilized population would not be in existence at all. The organized and intensive application and developments of science, of preventive medicine, constitute the strictly neutral work in this war by which all humanity will profit for all time to come.

In passing it is interesting to note that the great power supplied by Niagara Falls is being utilized to produce some of the chemical marvels. One great industry there is making soda by the electrolytic process. That is, salt brine is pumped from the saline deposits in western New York and piped to the works. This is run into electric cells and through these a current of electricity is led. The salt, which is composed of chlorine and sodium, decomposes under the electric attack. The sodium goes to one pole and combines with water to form caustic soda, whereas the chlorine escapes at the other pole. Let us follow the chlorine, which is a yellowish-green gas, more than twice as heavy as air, and has found a new use as poison gas in the great war—for which all the world should be ashamed.

It is collected and compressed to a liquid form and shipped in containers under pressure for use in chemical works and bleacheries and for the purification of drinking water. It has been found above all things effective in destroying noxious bacilli. A surprisingly small amount of the gas dissolved in the water is enough. In New York city the water has been chlorinated and no single case of typhoid fever has been traced to the supply.

CHAPTER XVIII.

OUR NEIGHBORING ALLY.

CANADA'S RECRUITING—RAISE 33,000 TROOPS IN TWO MONTHS—FIRST EXPEDI-
TIONARY FORCE TO CROSS ATLANTIC—BRAVERY AT YPRES AND LENS—MEETING
DIFFICULT PROBLEMS—QUEBEC AROUSED BY CONSCRIPTION.

THE world has marvelled at the achievement of Canada at Valcartier camp near Quebec and the dispatch across the Atlantic Ocean of a fully equipped expeditionary force of 33,000 men within two months of the outbreak of war between Great Britain and Germany. But the magnitude of that feat cannot be appreciated properly until one considers that on August 4, 1914, Canada had a permanent force of only about 3500 men.

These soldiers, who for the most part were instructors and men on guard duty, provided a nucleus for a training organization. In addition to its "standing army," the Dominion had an active militia numbering approximately 60,000 men. Their training consisted of what has been aptly called "after-supper soldiering." Members of city regiments drilled for one night each week, participated in an annual church parade and spent two weeks every year in summer camp.

The training of the rural regiments consisted almost entirely of the two weeks in summer camp. Yet from these militia units were drawn a large proportion of the men in the first Canadian oversea contingent, while the militia regiments, to a large extent, formed the basis of Canada's recruiting organization after the outbreak of hostilities.

Enlistments during the first two years in the expeditionary force numbered approximately 415,000, while probably 150,000 applicants were rejected as physically unfit.

Immediately upon the declaration of war Major General Sir Sam Hughes, Minister of Militia, telegraphed the officers commanding the militia regiments to commence recruiting for oversea service. After the recruits were signed up and accepted, they lived at home and drilled during the day at the armories throughout the Dominion.

Meanwhile, Valcartier camp was being prepared for the gathering army. The building of this great military center almost overnight was an engineering feat of no mean magnitude. Two weeks after work was started, troops recruited by the militia regiments began to arrive, and before the end of a month Valcartier was a tented city of 25,000 soldiers.

There were some complaints, of course. They were inevitable in an encampment so hastily prepared. But the essentials were there, and when the contingent sailed from Gaspe, on the coast of Quebec, on October 3, it was a well-trained, efficient body of soldiers, besides being the largest army that ever crossed the Atlantic at one time.

AN EFFICIENT COMMANDER.

The contingent was in command of Lieutenant-General Edwin Alfred Hervey Alderson. He was born at Ipswich in 1859 and began his military career with the Militia, going to the regular army in 1878. He joined the Royal West Kent Regiment as Second Lieutenant and rapidly won promotion. He served in the Transvaal, later in Egypt and participated in actions at Kassassin and Tel-el-Kebir, receiving the Khedive's bronze star. Service in South Africa and in India followed, during which General Alderson successively became Captain, Major and Lieutenant Colonel. He became a Colonel in 1903 and was placed in charge of the Second Infantry Brigade, and in 1908 commanded the Sixth Division, Southern Army of India, having meantime been given the rank of Major General.

After the departure of the first contingent recruiting was continued by the militia regiments, and during the winter the men were quartered in exhibition grounds, Y. M. C. As., sheds, etc. In the spring of 1915 existing camps were enlarged and new ones opened.

During this period the recruiting machinery developed from the militia regiments. Through the latter officers were recommended to command new battalions. These O. Cs. selected most of their subordinate officers from their own militia regiments and used the parent organization as a general basis for recruiting operations, headquarters being located at the regimental armories.

The keen competition existing between the militia units was maintained between the new oversea formations, and battalions were raised in a few weeks. For months enlistments all over Canada averaged more than 1000 men daily, and with recruits coming forward at this rate, there was no necessity of protracted delay in bringing battalions up to strength.

DIFFICUTY OF RECRUITING.

There was a disposition, especially in military circles, to attribute the increasing difficulty of the recruiting situation during the winter of 1915-16 and since to a change of system and the introduction of the so-called "political colonels." The change, however, was rather the result of new conditions than the cause of it. Recruiting had slowed down—largely from natural causes.

A new appeal was needed to reach a class of eligible men who had not yet enlisted. The recruiting problem apparently had outgrown the facilities of the militia organizations. Rightly or wrongly, the government commissioned a number of well-known men, without military experience, to raise battalions. Their popularity and local confidence in them were the excuses for their appointment—and the experiment was in the main successful.

Perhaps there was a suggestion of politics about it, although it may be stated emphatically that politics had not been a serious influence in connection with the recruiting, training or leadership of Canada's oversea forces. That such is the case stands to the enduring credit of Major General Hughes.

The attempt to "popularize" recruiting was soon found to entail serious evils. Competition for recruits in an already well-combed field became very keen. The new political colonels realized that their reputations were at stake, and in the effort to fill up their battalions various undignified and regrettable expedients were employed. Cabarets, bean-counting contests, lotteries and callithumpian methods generally marked a period in Canada's recruiting history not pleasant to review, and which brought discredit upon the entire voluntary enlistment system as a permanent method of filling up armies.

TRAINING SERIOUSLY DELAYED.

Besides the moral influence of such schemes to get men in khaki, the recruiting efforts of the political colonels had a serious effect in delaying the training of new men. With their personal reputations as organizers involved, the commanding officers were reluctant to admit inability to fill up the ranks of their units, and repeatedly pleaded for more time.

For months partly recruited battalions made little or no progress with their training, while the officers devised new recruiting "stunts" and while men were being sought in the highways and byways.

The situation was complicated by allowing a number of infantry battalions to recruit in the same area at the same time, with the result that the new men came in driblets, valuable time was lost and much money wasted. In some cases it has taken well over a year from the date when they were authorized before battalions were dispatched oversea—due very largely to ineffective recruiting methods. Battalions were allowed to continue the heart-breaking quest for recruits long after they should have been amalgamated and sent to England. Such amalgamations came ultimately, battalions retaining their identity when leaving Canada only when 600 or more strong.

The high cost of recruits was a direct consequence of competition among battalions recruiting independently in the same territory at the same time. The government allowance was not adequate to maintain the pace and had to be supplemented by private funds.

There was in Toronto a certain group of fifty recruits referred to as the "$10,000 squad," because it is estimated that the cost of recruiting them averaged nearly $200 each, the money coming from private funds of officers and their friends. Perhaps the estimate involves some exaggeration, but many units added to their ranks only at a cost of $50 or more per recruit.

Some idea of the waste of such a system may be secured when it is stated that, with men coming forward freely, the cost of recruiting is considerably less than $10 per man, even after allowing a generous bonus to the recruiting sergeants. More serious than the cost in money was the delay in training men needed at the front.

A POLITICAL IMPOSSIBILITY.

Canada's experience constitutes a severe indictment of the voluntary system of recruiting, although sterner measures at the outset were a political impossibility. The free-will enlistment plan had to be given a thorough test, and its inadequacy demonstrated and repeatedly emphasized before public opinion would support resort to compulsion.

English-speaking Canada at least learned that lesson, and it is extremely doubtful whether the United States would have adopted the selective draft system at the commencement of its participation in the war, if it had not been that the experience of Canada and the United Kingdom established the weakness inherent in the voluntary system.

Besides the camp at Valcartier, a great artillery camp was set up at Petewawa, where the best facilities existed for long range gun practice. Ontario saw two camps at Niagara and

Camp Borden; Manitoba saw one on the plains, Alberta another in the picturesque district near Calgary, while British Columbia had its camp at Vernon.

INADEQUATE RECRUITING.

The volunteer recruiting in Canada, in its incipiency, while resultful, was soon found to be not adequate. Under it, however, there was a widespread response that stirs the blood, for men hurried to the lines from the Yukon and the Peace Rivers; from Hudson's Bay and the farther hinterlands, from prairie and mountain; white men and the red men; cowboys and city chaps, harvesters and hunters, mechanics and mountaineers, backwoodsmen and frontwoodsmen. And also among the enlisters were thousands of Americans who fought side by side with Canadian, Briton and Frenchman.

Canada has large German settlements, including 300,000 German and Austrian settlers in the western provinces. Prompt action was taken on the outbreak of the war to deal with the alien element that might prove dangerous and disloyal. Nearly 10,000 were speedily interned, from Nova Scotia to British Columbia. A large proportion were Austrian laborers who had been railway navvies. These were placed in western camps and used in building trails and roads in national parks, or in clearing the forest for future settlement in Northern Ontario.

Many individuals of known pro-German sympathies were also put out of harm's way, and some famous trials were held which served to give salutary warnings to all others that freedom of speech has its limitations in times of war, and that the rumors that the sinking of the Lusitania was being celebrated behind closed doors was hardly palatable.

Others, again, were caught in attempts to destroy property and it is to the credit of police and military vigilance that few succeeded in their nefarious designs. The internment camp proved a wholesome example, and the pro-German in Canada took the advice of the United States Government to its

German subjects "to keep their mouths shut." It is also a fact that the occupants of the detention camps in the Dominion were well fed and treated, in striking contrast to the disturbing reports that leaked through as to the way Canadian war prisoners in Germany fared.

CANADA'S WAR FINANCIERING.

Next, the story of how Canada is financing her share of the war, for it is a costly business. Three domestic war loans, totaling $450,000,000, were voluntarily subscribed, each in fact being doubly underwritten, and yet the savings of the people in the banks is (1917) the highest on record—over a billion and a quarter. Part of the war revenue is being raised by war taxes on letters, checks, legal documents and some articles of import. Happily the normal revenue of the country was never so large nor the trade of the Dominion so buoyant. All these factors are helping to carry the war burden.

The generosity of the people, under the heavy strain, was most marked. Many millions were given to the various war help funds, chiefly to the Red Cross and the Canadian Patriotic Fund, of 700 branches, which supplements the Government separation allowance to soldiers' dependents by other grants. Canada had, up to that time, by the way, the highest paid soldiery in the world, privates getting $33 a month.

It is interesting to note that there are several branches of the Canadian Patriotic Fund in the United States, which looked after the families and dependents of Americans who enlisted in the Canadian ranks.

Canadian total givings in cash and kind to their own, as well as to the Belgians, French, Servian, Armenian and other funds and Governmental grants of grain and provision, would represent a very much larger figure than that here mentioned.

The orders placed in Canada averaged $1,500,000 worth for every day in the year.

The women of Canada in every way render practical

patriotic service. Hundreds of nurses were placed in overseas and home hospitals. The farmers' wives raised large sums of money as did the school children. Organizations of all kinds came into existence, not alone collecting money, but contributing vast quantities of war material and soldiers' comforts, and sending packages of food and clothing regularly to Canadian prisoners in German camps.

Still another war problem was the care of the returned wounded soldiers, and a serious problem it was. The procession of the disabled was a pathetic one. Military convalescent hospitals were set up in many centres, in addition to the opening of private homes for the same beneficent purpose.

CANADA PART OF AMERICA.

Canada may be an English possession, but to us it is part of America, and certainly no two countries have rested side by side in greater friendship than the "Dominion" and the United States. You can find no great fortifications along the 3000 odd miles of border between Canada and the United States. The countries have lived in peace and harmony and together, or side by side they have battled for peace on the fields of Flanders.

All the world knows what Canada has done on the battlefields abroad, fighting with those troops from Australia, New Zealand, India and lesser English territory, to drive the ruthless Germans back and crush the Empire to which they swear allegiance.

The Canadian troops were taken after landing in France to a point within the country between St. Omer and Ypres, where they served with honor to themselves, their presence having a salutary effect on the British soldiery, who had been facing the German forces. At the battle of Neuve Chapelle the Canadians held part of the line allotted to the first army, and while not engaged in the main attack, rendered valuable help, their artillery being very active, and at the battle of Ypres in April, 1915, they took a notable part.

In the latter part of April, the Canadian division held a line of about 5000 yards, connecting with that of the French troops, and faced the memorable gas attack of the Germans, which was the first noted in the war. The asphyxiating gas was projected into the trenches by means of force pumps and pipes laid under the parapets, the German sappers having carefully placed these conductors. The bulk of the gas was directed against the French, largely made up of Turcos and Zouaves, who were driven back, suffering agonies.

POSITION BRAVELY HELD.

The Canadians suffered to some extent from the poison, and though there were in the commands lawyers, college professors, business men, clerks and workers of all sorts, who had been turned into soldiers within a few months, and without previous military experience, they held their position bravely. The Canadians were, of course, compelled to change their position after the French fell back, and the Allied troops were, to all effects and purposes, routed. But when the Germans, recognizing the weakened position of the Canadians, attempted to force a series of attacks, the Canadian division, as a matter of record, fought through the day and through the night, for forty-eight consecutive hours, and finally, in a counter attack, drove the Germans back and regained a position which had been lost by the British troops in the earlier conflict.

Later, in the face of a devastating fire, in which many officers were killed, battalions of the Canadians carried warfare to the first line of German trenches, and in a desperate hand-to-hand struggle won the trench. This attack, it is said, secured and maintained during the most critical moment of the campaign the integrity of the Allied line.

In connection with the experience of the Canadians with the gas fumes, it is necessary to note that at that time they were unprovided with gas masks, or means of protecting themselves against the fumes, and the best they could do was to stuff wet handkerchiefs in their mouths. The fumes, although extremely poisonous, were not so effective with the Canadians as on the French lines, largely because of the position of the Canadians, and the direction of the wind, but in the several attacks a number of the Canadians were asphyxiated.

HEROES WIN RECOGNITION.

So, all through the Ypres campaign, the Canadians faced the shot, shell and poisonous gases of the Germans, and won recognition for their heroic conduct which will stand to the credit of Canada for all time. At Festubert, Givenchy, and, last but not least, Lens, the Canadians, step by step, kept pace with the Allied advances.

In their general advance on Lens the Canadians occupied the strongest outpost in the defense of that place, and pushing their troops on toward La Coulotte, entered that village. The Germans withdrew in this neighborhood from a line about one and three-quarters miles long.

The task of the Canadians was to capture German outposts southwest of Reservoir Hill. The attack was evidently expected. The Germans scuttled, abandoning ground upon which machine gun fire was immediately turned by Germans located on the hill. This was speedily followed by heavy artillery fire, which continued during the night in the vicinity of the Lens electric station.

The enemy's dugouts were searched, found to be empty, and wrecked.

The German retirement ceased during the night. Patrols sent out opposite Mericourt and to the south found the enemy's front line strongly held. The Germans made huge craters at all cross roads in Avion and leading towards Lens.

Patrols which were sent out reached the summit of Reservoir Hill without opposition and pushed on down the eastern slope and the strong Lens outpost was effectively occupied. Meanwhile, south of the Souchez River the Canadians drove forward on the heels of the retiring Germans. Railway embankments east of Lens electric station were occupied. The advance was then continued toward La Coulotte. As night fell strong parties were sent out to consolidate the positions occupied, while patrols were sent forward to keep in touch with the Germans.

WANTON DESTRUCTION.

Several days previous the Germans were known to be destroying houses in the western part of Lens, with the object of giving a wider area of fire for their guns. It was their intention of clinging to the eastern side of the city and prolonging the struggle by house-to-house fighting.

Under a protecting concentration of artillery fire, Canadian troops successfully stormed and captured the German front line before Avion, a suburb of Lens. By the advance the British line was carried forward to within one mile of the centre of Lens.

The Canadians, heartened by successes gained in a few days at a relatively small cost, decided to attack across the open ground sloping upwards to Avion and the village of Leauvette, near the Souchez River. They met with opposition of a serious character at only one point, where a combination of machine gun fire and uncut wires delayed the advance. The attack was not intended to be pressed home at this particular spot, as the ground specially favored the Germans, so that the delay did no harm. The assaulting troops comprised men from British Columbia, Manitoba, Central Ontario and Nova Scotia.

The attack was made along a two-mile front. On the extreme left, Nova Scotians pushed their way up the Lens-Arras road to the village of Leauvette. Here they took a number of prisoners. At the other end of the line, east of the railway tracks, enemy dugouts were bombed. Their occupants belonged to the crack Prussian Guards Corps, the Fifth Guard Grenadiers, who refused in most cases to come out and surrender.

At daybreak, Canadian airplanes, flying low over Avion, saw few Germans there. Craters which had been made by mine exposions at the crossroads, seriously hindered them in bringing up troops from Lens for counter attacks.

GERMAN AVIATIK DEFEATED.

In an air duel fought at probably the highest altitude at which aviators, up until that time, had met in combat, nearly four miles, a Canadian triplane pursued and defeated a German two-seated Aviatik. The German machine had sought safety by climbing upward and the triplane pursued. At a height of 20,000 feet the pilot of the German craft either fell or jumped from it and disappeared at the moment of the first burst of fire from the gun on the Canadian. The German observer then was seen to climb out upon the tail of the machine, where he lost his hold and plunged headlong. The Aviatik turned its nose down and fell.

It is meet that some note be taken of the fact that while the Canadian soldiers were battling for humanity and the preservation of the British Empire in Flanders there was being celebrated in their native land the fiftieth anniversary of the founding of the Dominion. All Canada took part in the celebration on June 1, 1917, as did large numbers of men from the United States officers' training camp at Niagara, where recruits were preparing to receive Commissions in Uncle Sam's Army.

Up until 1867 Canada had been the scene of bitter strife between the French and British. At that time the provinces were brought quite closely together, and commenced a new era of prosperity. The foundation was then laid for a wonderfully prosperous country, one filled with almost limitless possibilities.

The confederation of Canada had its birth in a meeting of

delegates from all over British North America, which was held in 1864, and these delegates, after deliberating for nearly three weeks, passed a large number of resolutions which formed the basis of what eventually became the Act of Union. In the followig January these resolutions were submitted to the Legislature of Canada and after due debate there was passed in both chambers of Parliament a measure for the purpose of uniting the provinces in accordance with the provisions of the Quebec resolutions. The meeting was in Quebec.

PLAN OF UNION PASSED.

A number of difficulties were encountered, so that it was 1867 before the plan of union was submitted to the Imperial Parliament, where it was warmly received and passed without alteration of any description within a few days. The royal assent was given on March 29, and the act constituting the new Canada went into effect on July 1, which day has since become known as Dominion Day, and is the chief of all Canadian holidays.

The federal Constitution of Canada is contained in an Imperial Act of Parliament, known as the British North America Act, and it is based very largely upon that of the mother country. The ministry of the day holds office at the pleasure of the House of Commons, the members of which are elected by the people. At the head of the affairs is a Governor-General, who is appointed by the crown and paid by the people of Canada. As is the case with the British sovereigns, he acts with and on the advice of the ministers for the time being, and also like the King, he can dissolve the Parliament.

The number of members of the House of Commons is regulated by the following clauses of the act: "On the completion of the census in the year 1871, and of each subsequent decennial census, the representation of the four provinces shall be readjusted by such authority in such a manner, and from such time as the Parliament of Canada from time to time provides.

Previous to the passing of the British North America Act, the great Dominion had consisted of a conglomeration of provinces, some of them of almost fabulous extent, into which the white man from the West had penetrated. Tradition has it that some thousand years ago a Norseman, by name Leif Ericson, coming in his great beaked galley, through the northern seas, from Greenland, was the first white man to stand on Canadian soil.

Another five centuries were, however, to pass before John Cabot, sailing from Bristol, in the days of Henry Bolingbroke, brought the first British ship into a Canadian port. After him the fishermen of Europe came in increasing numbers to the great banks, with the result that little by little, as their tiny vessels touched the American shores, the great continent began to be known to the people of Europe.

DOMINION'S FOUNDATIONS LAID.

It was not really, however, until the year 1534 that the foundations of the Dominion may be said to have been sunk. In that year Jacques Cartier sailed from the port of St. Malo, with two little ships, intending to attempt the northwest passage to Japan. Francis the First was then ruling in Paris, and there was great adventure in the air of France. Cartier did not make the northwest passage, but he did touch the coast of Canada, or, to be more exact, the coasts of Labrador and Newfoundland. It was then the 10th of May, and having sailed around the island, he steered south, and crossing the gulf entered the bay which, by reason of the great heats of midsummer, he named Des Chaleurs. Holding along the coast, he came to the little inlet of Gaspe, and here, at the entrance to the harbor, he erected a huge cross surmounted by the arms and lilies of France. He could find no passage, however, to the northwest, and so he turned his ship, and sailed back to St. Malo.

The Court in Paris heard his story with interest. His cause was taken up by the King; and, as a result, in the succeeding May, he sailed again to the new world with three well found ships. On the day of Saint Lawrence he entered the great bay, to which he at once gave the name of the Saint, and passing on came, in September, to anchor in the Isle of Orleans.

REAL FOUNDER OF CANADA.

The man, however, with whose name the early history of Canada is most fully connected, had not as yet been born. Nor was it until the year 1567 that, at Brouage in Saintonge, Samuel de Champlain came upon the scene. In the year 1603, when Elizabeth was ruling in England, and Henry of Navarre in France, Champlain came to Canada. He had been a soldier of le Bearnais, in the great wars with the League, an officer of marine, and a man with no little knowledge of natural science, as knowledge was then accounted. He came now in command of an expedition, fitted out by the merchants of Rouen, with the idea of forming a Canada company, as England had her Barbary Company, her Eastland Company, her Muscovie Company, or her Turkey Company. And in this way the French came into Canada.

Thus there began those American wars between the two countries, divided at home only by the English Channel, which went on century by century, largely through the employment of the Indian tribes, until that September night when Wolfe's boats drifted in, from the fleet to the shore, and the battle on the Plains of Abraham permanently settled the question of domination in favor of the British.

The British conquest of Canada did not, however, mean the cessation of fighting. There came, presently, the war between Great Britain and the American colonies, one of the most amazing exploits of which was the marvelous march of Arnold and

Montgomery through the forests of Maine to the St. Law-
rence, ending in the wonderful siege, of the year 1775, and the
heroic failure to storm the defenses by scaling the rocks from
the river bed.   Eventually the boundary between the United
States and the British possessions was settled by the Treaty of
Paris, in 1783, just twenty years after an earlier Treaty of
Paris had recorded the surrender of Canada by France to Great
Britain.

CANADA, FROM COLONY TO DOMINION.

For the last century and a half the story of Canada has been
the story first of a British colony and then of a British
Dominion.   A great flood of new colonists had come into the
country after the victory of the States in the War of Independence, when many of the royalists of New England crossed the
border.   As a result, there had grown up the two new provinces
of Upper Canada, now known as Ontario, and New Brunswick.   The relations between all the provinces were, however,
far from harmonious, with the result that what between quar-
rels among themselves and risings against the British authority, the condition of Canada was anything but promising, when,
after the Rebellion of 1837, Lord Durham was sent over to try
to evolve order out of chaos.

He found the "habitant" still unreconciled to the British
rule; he found a condition of many little Pontiacs, all very
much as was that famous village on the summer evening when
Valmond threw the hot pennies to the children, as the auctioneer
and monsieur le cure came down the street; he found another
Canada of British colonists with so little sympathy for the
habitant, that, he declared, the two never met save in the jury
box, and there only to obstruct justice.

It was then that Lord Durham, by a great stroke of statesmanship, brought peace to Canada.   A democratic form of
representative government was bestowed on the people.   The
division of Quebec into two provinces, which the habitant had

desired when they were one, and resented when they were two, was annulled, with the result that the ground was prepared for the union which was to come just thirty years later.

Lord Durham made history and made a nation, for the confederation, when it came, was the inevitable superstructure built upon the foundations of his laying, but he ruined a reputation. His contempt for the conventions of politics, the radicalism of his methods, his failure to make any obeisance to the governmental deities, official or ex-official, combined with his almost superhuman tactlessness, gave his enemies every opportunity they could desire.

He was viciously attacked, and finally throwing up his mission, returned to England and gave up politics.

REPORT NOT TO BE DISPOSED OF.

The good, however, men do lives after them. Lord Durham's report, drafted for him by two master hands, those of Charles Buller and Edward Wakefield, could not be disposed of by perfervid orators or ill-informed editors. It passes into the category of historic and illuminating state papers. And, though Lord Durham fell, when, on the first of July, 1867, the British North America Act became operative, it was the handle of his trowel that struck that great cornerstone of liberty and empire, and declared it well and truly laid: the first of the Dominions, now having a population of approximately 8,000,000.

Thrown upon their own resources, when Great Britain began to draw in its loans of 1911-12, the people of Canada were temporarily at a loss as to how to meet the situation; the hardships which followed, however, prepared them to meet, with resolute determination, the greater problems that crowded upon them in 1915-16. Canada, through all the past, had been a dependent and a debtor nation; the war made it self-reliant, spurred its people on to the development of natural resources, and assured them, not only that the Dominion could stand alone, but that, throughout all the future, it can be a pillar of strength to the Empire and to democracy.

There were times when she was threatened by more than the ordinary difficulties which come to a nation, as when it became necessary in 1917 to pass a Conscription Act, the Province of Quebec threatened to secede. Quebec is a French territory, and it was a matter of world-wide comment that the volunteer enlistments for the Canadian army from the province were insignificant.

While the French Canadians were proud of France and their cousins across the seas, they were opposed to being compelled to fight for England, and the proposal to secede was largely advocated by the French-Canadian clergy.

RECIPIENTS OF UNSTINTED HONORS.

Among the heroic troops that faced the Germans in Flanders none was more honored in all Canada and England than the Princess Patricia's Light Infantry. Out of this battalion, which sailed away from Canada's shores with the first expeditionary force, scarcely one-fourth of the proud number lived through the terrible campaigns of Flanders, in which the Dominion forces participated.

The battalion constituted what was regarded as one of the most efficient military units in Canada, and in August, 1914, had been presented with colors wrought by the hand of Princess Patricia, daughter of the Governor General of Canada, the Duke of Connaught. The Princess, standing beside her mother, the Duchess of Connaught, in Lansdowne Park, Ottawa, presented the colors to the little force, wishing them a safe return, while thousands applauded and the spirit of patriotism ran high.

The "Princess Pats," as they came to be known, had within the organization a large portion of men of military experience who had seen service in South Africa and elsewhere, and consequently when they landed in France they were the first to be sent into the trenches and to action. In the winter and spring of 1914-15 they had some bitter experiences and participated in several desperate attacks and defenses, but it was not until the campaign at Ypres that the organization was almost annihilated, when it faced one of the most terrific bombardments of the war, and fought in a section largely cut off from the main line. Here Lieutenant-Colonel Farquhar, commander of the battalion, lost his life and nearly all of the officers were wounded.

CHAPTER XIX.

THE HEROIC ANZAC.

Forces that Stirred the World in the Gallipoli Campaigns—Famous as Sappers—The Blasting of Messines Ridge—Two Years Tunneling—30,000 Germans Blown to Atoms—1,000,000 Pounds of Explosives Used—Troops that were Transported 11,000 Miles.

WHEN the final history of the war is written, and the years have passed into ages, the story of the Anzac will form a brilliant passage in the book of nations. The Anzac in the campaigns at Gallipoli, the Dardanelles, and in Flanders served England with a loyalty and heroism not excelled by any other force. And what were the Anzacs? They were the soldiers of Australia and New Zealand. Let A represent Australia, N. Z., New Zealand, and A. C., army corps, and you have the basis of the word Anzac.

Generally in the news dispatches, the Anzacs have been referred to as Australians. They are described as fearless, daring and fierce fighters, whose presence added pep to every engagement in which they participated. No more picturesque group has ever been written into the history of armies. Composed of men who were bushrangers, cattlemen, miners and hardy outdoor workers, many of whom served in Egypt, India and wherever the British flag floats, their character is indicated by the fact that they have been at times called the "Ragtime Army."

The description of the landing of these troops at the Dardanelles, where in a rain of artillery fire, they dashed into the Turkish trenches, is one of the most thrilling of the war. With the shells from the ships falling upon the Turkish forces the Anzacs chased the Turks step by step inland, engaging in the most desperate hand-to-hand encounters.

Perhaps the story of that first battle might have been different had not Turkish reinforcements appeared upon the

318

scene. As it was the British men of Anzac were temporarily driven back, retiring with terrible loss. For hours the Australians engaged in solid fighting through a broken and hilly country, digging at night to establish entrenchments, with a renewal of the defense at daybreak, and then repeating the program. This is what the Australians and New Zealanders did, living upon short rations the while.

In all of the campaigns in which the Angacs have participated their work as sappers has been a feature. Sappers, by the way, are those men who, in modern warfare, burrow in the earth, planting mines, digging trenches, dugouts and fortifications. The Australians are fitted for this work for a large percentage of them had civil experience in the mines, and on extensive contract and excavation work.

AUSTRALIAN AND NEW ZEALAND SAPPERS.

Probably one of the most effective attacks of the English against a German stronghold in Belgium was made possible through the work of the Australian and New Zealand sappers. That was the blowing up of the Messines Ridge in June, 1917. In this action the Anzac shone in a manner that can never be forgotten.

On June 7, 1917, the British, with one terrible stroke, tore asunder the strong German position south of Ypres. This stroke was in a little corner of Belgium, where the armies of the Allies had successfully outgeneralled the enemy for two and a half years.

During almost two years of this time several companies of Australian, New Zealand and British sappers were busily but silently engaged in mining the hills of the Messines-Wytschaete Ridge, on which were the guns of the Germans which had been raking the troops of the Allies all this time. Nineteen great mines which contained a total of 1,000,000 pounds of ammonite upon their completion, had been dug into the vitals of these hills. Great charges of this new and powerful explosive had been placed in the mines nearly one year before their completion, yet no one except those actually engaged in the work knew of it. The secret was kept and the troops of Australia and New Zealand worked directly beneath the great German fortifications.

Then came the crucial moment. At exactly 3.10 o'clock in the morning of June 7, the whole series of mines were discharged by electrical contact, and the hilltops were blown high in the air in one terrific burst of flame, which poured forth as from craters of volcanoes. The ground for miles around was rocked as in an earthquake, and the roar emitted was distinctly heard in England by Lloyd George, the Prime Minister, listening for it at his country home 140 miles away.

A PRE-ARRANGED SIGNAL.

The explosion of the mines was a pre-arranged signal for the beginning of a heavy shell fire by the artillery. The whole section affected by the mines was subjected to a most intense shellfire, and following up this death-dealing storm came the troops of General Haig, under Sir Herbert Plumer, who finished the work of the great mines and big guns with a brilliant charge of men, who used rifle and bayonet most effectively. Within a few hours the whole of the Messines Ridge was securely in the hands of the British, and they had captured 7000 prisoners and many guns. The German casualties were estimated at 30,000, those of the British being about 10,000.

Rushing the whole sector south of Ypres, from Observation Ridge to Ploegsteert Wood, north of Armentieres, the British forces succeeded in capturing that position with little loss. Then came the assault of the rear defenses, which were formed by the ridge itself. The natural formation of the land greatly helped the Germans in arranging their defenses, and the fighting was very fierce. The work of British troops, in which were many Australians and New Zealanders, together with English and Irish, all under the command of General Sir

Herbert C. O. Plumer, was given great credit in the reports of the commander to the War Office.

The British War Office summarized the attack as follows in its report of June 8:

"The position captured by us yesterday was one of the enemy's most important strongholds on the western front. Dominating as it did the Ypres salient and giving the enemy complete observation over it, he neglected no precautions to render the position impregnable. These conditions enabled the enemy to overlook all our preparations for attack, and he had moved up reinforcements to meet us. The battle, therefore, became a gauge of the ability of the German troops to stop our advance under conditions as favorable to them as an army can ever hope for, with every advantage of ground and preparation and with the knowledge that an attack was impending.

GERMAN FORWARD DEFENSE.

"The German forward defenses consisted of an elaborate and intricate system of well-wired trenches and strong points forming a defensive belt over a mile in depth. Numerous farms and woods were thoroughly prepared for the defense, and there were large numbers of machine guns in the German garrisons. Guns of all calibers, recently increased in numbers, were placed to bear not only on the front but on the flanks of an attack. Numerous communicating trenches and switch lines, radiating in all directions, were amply provided with strongly constructed concrete dugouts and machine-gun emplacements designed to protect the enemy garrison and machine gunners from the effect of our bombardment. In short, no precaution was omitted that could be provided by the incessant labor of years, guided by the experience gained by the enemy in his previous defeats on the Somme, at Arras, and on Vimy Ridge.

"Despite the difficulties and disadvantages which our troops had to overcome, further details of yesterday's fighting show that our first assault and the subsequent attacks were carried out in almost exact accordance with the timetable previously arranged. * * *

"Following on the great care and thoroughness in preparations made under the orders of General Sir Herbert Plumer, the complete success gained may be ascribed chiefly to the destruction caused by our mines, to the violence and accuracy of our bombardment, to the very fine work of the Royal Flying Corps, and to the incomparable dash and courage of the infantry. The whole force acted in perfect combination. Excellent work was done by the tanks, and every means of offense at our disposal was made use of, so that every arm of the service had a share in the victory."

A good description of the Australian soldier, as he follows up his victory, was given in a story of an American war correspondent, who wrote concerning Flanders:

NEW LAND OF WARFARE.

"After these many months of trench warfare there is keen delight for the Australian soldier in this new land of warfare which the German retirement has opened up. The fighting is in open country now, over gently rolling downs of what looks like grass land. It is really most of it wheat or turnip land which has not been cultivated for a year or two. The country is as open as the Australian central plains.

"It is quite a new sort of battlefield for the Australians. They march down to it through valleys almost exactly like the valleys in the peaceful parts of France. There are whole acres in which one cannot see a single shell hole. Back across the green country or down the open roads come men in twos or threes occasionally, sauntering as one might find them on a country road. They are the wounded helping one another back to the dressing station. The walking wounded have to help each other back in these modern battles. It is no longer looked upon as meritorious for an unwounded combatant to leave the field and help a wounded comrade to the rear.

"Nearest the front the country becomes more feverish. Angry bursts of tawny color are seen in a haphazard sort of way dotting the horizon and the countryside. Here and there are Australians standing behind mounds of earth with their rifles pointed over the top, bayonets always fixed. Frequently, when there is no other shelter there are hastily scooped trenches. A quarter of a mile away another party is lining a roadside, flat on their stomachs in the ditch, bayonets peeping over the top. Shells are whizzing by at the rate of two or three a minute, high explosives bursting on contact behind their backs about as far away as the other side of a cottage parlor.

PRISONER AND ESCORT.

"Frequently one meets a prisoner being escorted to the rear. There is something very impressive about these little processions of two men, prisoner and escort. The prisoner, usually a young German private in neat gray uniform and steel helmet, walks in front. After him, grasping his rifle with both hands across his chest, his weatherbeaten brows puckered as he picks his way over the tumbled stones, comes the living embodiment of the Australian back country. Nine cases out of ten, somehow, the soldier who escorts a prisoner seems to be that bit of pure Australian, either Western Australia or South Australia, the Warrego or the Burdskin.

"He is an earnest man, intent on executing his errand with dispatch and exactitude. 'Can you tell me the way to headquarters?' he asks as he passes. Then he disappears slowly up the street on the heels of his silent companion.

"These Australians are just as good fighters in this new warfare as they were at Gallipoli or in the trenches, perhaps even better. They had their first encounter with German cavalry the other day, but it was only a feint at a flank and lasted but a few minutes."

"Australia is ambitious, some might even say self-centered, and Germany undoubtedly made the mistake of considering that Australia was awaiting a chance to become unfriendly to Great Britain when she started to fight. But no nation ever made a greater mistake. As soon as the House of Hohenzollern placed the mother country in a perilous position Australia was at the command of Great Britain. Notwithstanding the fact that the Australians are primarily peace-loving, most intent on attending to their own affairs, the response to the call was immediate and whole-hearted.

AUSTRALIA'S COMMENDABLE PROMPTNESS.

The Australian centers buzzed with activity, and within two months after war was declared the Australian fleet, which consisted of five unarmored cruisers, three torpedo-boat destroyers, and three light gunboats, which had been built and manned at the expense of the Australians, were in possession of the German Pacific Islands—Samoa, Marshall, Carolines, Pelew, Ladrones, New Guinea, New Britain—had broken the wireless system of the Germans, and had captured eleven of the vessels of Germany. She also forced twenty-five other ships to intern, and prevented the destruction of a British ship in Australian waters.

Then came the scouring of the seas by the German ship Emden, and her trip to Australian waters, with the object of carrying on the work of destruction which had marked her career in South American waters. She lay in wait for Australian transports, with the result that the Australian warship Sydney sent her to the bottom but three months after war had been declared. Shortly after this the Australian fleet drove von Spree's squadron from the Pacific directly into the trap set by Admiral Sturdee at the Falkland Islands.

The fact that all the troops of Australia must be transported to London—a distance via the Suez route of approximately 11,000 miles, and through the Panama Canal of 12,734 miles—did not keep back these brave men from quickly enlisting. The great distance made fighting extremely expensive, but the task was loyally assumed by the military of the far continent. Universal military service was inaugurated for the first time by an English-speaking community, and war loans were offered and quickly accepted. Transports were immediately constructed out of seventy steamers which were requisitioned.

At the declaration of war in November, 1914, the entire Australian army, which consisted of 20,000 men, left Australia for Egypt, and at the end of the first year of the conflict there were 76,000 men in the field. By July, 1916, nearly 300,000 volunteers had been recruited and had crossed the seas. The creation, equipment, and supplying of this army by the people of Australia, a task involving enormous cost and personal sacrifice, constitutes a thrilling chapter in the history of loyalty.

GEOGRAPHICALLY ALIKE.

To those who think that Australia is a little island situated in the Pacific ocean it might be interesting to know that this continent, in size and shape, is almost the exact duplicate of the United States. There are also outlying provinces, that of Papua, a tropical land, offsetting Alaska. Then there is the rich little Lord Howe Island, and Norfolk Island. The surface of Australia is the most level in surface and regular in outline of all the continents, and is the lowest continent, with an average elevation of Ohio.

There are 2,974,581 square miles in Australia, while the land area of the United States is 2,973,890 square miles, a difference of 691 square miles. This, of course, is only the continental United States. Only about one-twentieth of the total area of Australia lies in a latitude farther removed from the Equator than Chattanooga, Tennessee; Clarendon, Texas; and Albuquerque, New Mexico, and there is less than one-third of the area of this unique continent which lies in a cooler latitude than the sugar-cane lands of Louisiana.

The streams of Australia are fewer and carry less water than those of any other continent. The heart of this great island is dry and barren and thinly populated. Most of the inhabitants are found within easy reach of the coastline. The population of this great land, at the census of 1911, was 4,568,-707 persons.

New Zealand is situated a little more than 1200 miles to the east of Sydney, which is in the southeastern section of Australia. It consists of three fairly large islands, together with a number of small adjacent islands. The area is 105,340 square miles, the population being, in 1911, 815,862. The surface of the principal islands is diversified, being mountainous in some parts, and undulating in others. The best harbors are in the northern district.

CHAPTER XX
AMERICA STEPS IN.

PRESIDENT WILSON'S FAMOUS MESSAGE TO CONGRESS—THE WAR RESOLUTION—
APRIL 6, 1917 SEES THE UNITED STATES AT WAR—REVIEW OF THE NEGOTIA-
TIONS BETWEEN GERMANY AND AMERICA—THE U-BOAT RESTRICTED ZONE AN-
NOUNCEMENT OF GERMANY—PREMIER LLOYD GEORGE ON AMERICA IN THE CON-
FLICT.

THE hoisting of the American flag to the top of the staff as the emblem of world-wide Liberty followed the action of Congress in authorizing President Wilson to declare a state of war existed between Germany and the United States. What the conditions were which developed during the months in which Germany to all intents and purposes "laughed up her sleeve" at the United States, ignored our protests against her wanton disregard of human rights on land and sea, can no better be told than in the words of President Wilson himself in his message stating the position which the Government took.

His message to Congress will go down in history, not only as an instrument of world-wide importance, but as a classic in literature. Its effect on the Nations was greater than that of any other message issued by any one country, probably in the history of the world, and while there were critics who regarded some of President Wilson's utterances as too idealistic, time proved that his vision was greater than that of those who criticised him, and within a short time the eyes of the entire world were turned toward Washington, which became the active centre from which the campaign for world-wide democracy was waged.

The hands of Liberty stretched out to Russia, Serbia, Italy, France, Belgium, England, little Montenegro, and they were given help in the most critical periods of their careers. The President's message was presented to Congress on April 3, 1917, as follows:

"I have called the Congress into extraordinary session because there are serious, very serious, choices of policy to be made, and made immediately, which it was neither right nor constitutionally permissible that I should assume the responsibility of making.

"On the third of February last I officially laid before you the extraordinary announcement of the Imperial German Government that on and after the first day of February it was its purpose to put aside all restraints of law or of humanity and use its submarines to sink every vessel that sought to approach either the ports of Great Britain and Ireland or the western coasts of Europe or any of the ports controlled by the enemies of Germany within the Mediterranean.

COMMANDERS UNDER RESTRAINT.

"That had seemed to be the object of the German submarine warfare earlier in the war, but since April of last year the Imperial Government had somewhat restrained the commanders of its undersea craft in conformity with its promise then given to us that passenger boats should not be sunk and that due warning would be given to all other vessels which its submarines might seek to destroy when no resistance was offered or escape attempted, and care taken that their crews were given at least a fair chance to save their lives in their open boats.

"The precautions taken were meager and haphazard enough, as was proved in distressing instance after instance in the progress of the cruel and unmanly business; but a certain degree of restraint was observed.

"The new policy has swept every restriction aside. Vessels of every kind, whatever their flag, their character, their cargo, their destination, their errand, have been ruthlessly sent to the bottom without warning and without thought of help or mercy for those on board, the vessels of friendly neutrals along with those of belligerents.

"Even hospital ships and ships carrying relief to the sorely bereaved and stricken people of Belgium, though the latter were provided with safe-conduct through the prescribed areas by the German Government itself and were distinguished by unmistakable marks of identity, have been sunk with the same reckless lack of compassion or of principle.

"I was for a little while unable to believe that such things would in fact be done by any government that had hitherto subscribed to the humane practices of civilized nations. International law had its origin in the attempt to set up some law which would be respected and observed upon the seas, where no nation had the right of domination and where lay the free highways of the world.

"By painful stage after stage has that law been built up, with meager enough results, indeed, after all was accomplished that could be accomplished, but always with a clear view, at least, of what the heart and conscience of mankind demanded.

SWEEPS RIGHT ASIDE.

"This minimum of right the German Government has swept aside under the plea of retaliation and necessity and because it had no weapons which it could use at sea except those which it is impossible to employ as it is employing them without throwing to the winds all scruples of humanity or of respect for the understandings that were supposed to underlie the intercourse of the world.

"I am not now thinking of the loss of property involved, immense and serious as this is, but only of the wanton and wholesale destruction of the lives of noncombatants, men, women and children, engaged in pursuits which have always, even in the darkest periods of modern history, been deemed innocent and legitimate. Property can be paid for; the lives of peaceful and innocent people cannot be.

"The present German submarine warfare against commerce is a warfare against mankind. It is a war against all nations. American ships have been sunk, American lives taken, in ways which it has stirred us very deeply to learn of, but the ships and people of other neutral and friendly nations have been sunk and overwhelmed in the waters in the same way. There has been no discrimination. The challenge is to all mankind. Each nation must decide for itself how it will meet it.

"The choice we make for ourselves must be made with a moderation of counsel and a temperateness of judgment befitting our character and our motives as a nation. We must put excited feeling away. Our motive will not be revenge or the victorious assertion of the physical might of the nation, but only the vindication of human right, of which we are only a single champion.

ARMED NEUTRALITY IMPRACTICABLE.

"When I addressed the Congress on the twenty-sixth of February last I thought it would suffice to assert our neutral rights with arms, our right to use the seas against unlawful interference, our right to keep our people safe against unlawful violence. But armed neutrality, it now appears, is impracticable.

"Because submarines are in effect outlaws when used as the German submarines have been used against merchant shipping, it is impossible to defend ships against their attacks as the law of nations has assumed that merchantmen would defend themselves against privateers or cruisers, visible craft giving chase upon the open sea. It is common prudence in such circumstances, grim necessity, indeed, to endeavor to destroy them before they have shown their own intention. They must be dealt with upon sight, if dealt with at all.

"The German Government denies the right of neutrals to use arms at all within the areas of the sea which it has proscribed, even in the defense of rights which no modern publicist has ever questioned their right to defend. The intimation is conveyed that the armed guards which we have placed on our merchant ships will be treated as beyond the pale of law and subject to be dealt with as pirates would be.

"Armed neutrality is ineffectual enough at best; in such circumstances and in the face of such pretensions it is worse than ineffectual; it is likely once to produce what it was meant to prevent; it is virtually certain to draw us into the war without either the rights or the effectiveness of belligerents.

"There is one choice we cannot make, we are incapable of making; we will not choose the path of submission and suffer the most sacred rights of our nation and our people to be ignored or violated. The wrongs against which we now array ourselves are not common wrongs; they cut to the very roots of human life.

A CONSTITUTIONAL DUTY.

"With a profound sense of the solemn and even tragical character of the step I am taking and of the grave responsibilities which it involves, but in unhesitating obedience to what I deem my constitutional duty, I advise that the Congress declare the recent course of the Imperial German Government to be in fact nothing less than war against the Government and people of the United States; that it formally accept the status of belligerent which has thus been thrust upon it and that it take immediate steps not only to put the country in a more thorough state of defense, but also to exert all its power and employ all its resources to bring the Government of the German Empire to terms and end the war.

"What this will involve is clear. It will involve the utmost practicable co-operation in counsel and action with the Governments now at war with Germany, and as incident to that, the extension to those Governments of the most liberal financial credits, in order that our resources may, so far as possible, be added to theirs. It will involve the organization and mobilization of all the material resources of the country to supply the material of war and serve the incidental needs of the nation in the most abundant and yet the most economical and efficient way possible.

"It will involve the immediate full equipment of the navy in all respects, but particularly in supplying it with the best means of dealing with the enemy's submarines. It will involve the immediate addition to the armed forces of the United States already provided for by law in case of war at least 500,000 men, who should, in my opinion, be chosen upon the principle of universal liability to service, and also the authorization of subsequent additional increments of equal force so soon as they may be needed and can be handled in training.

WELL-CONCEIVED TAXATION.

"It will involve, also, of course, the granting of adequate credits to the Government, sustained, I hope, so far as they can equitably be sustained by the present generation, by well-conceived taxation. I say sustained so far as may be equitably by taxation because it seems to me that it would be most unwise to base the credits which will now be necessary entirely on money borrowed. It is our duty, I most respectfully urge, to protect our people so far as we may against the very serious hardships and evils which would be likely to arise out of the inflation which would be produced by vast loans.

"In carrying out the measures by which these things are to be accomplished we should keep constantly in mind the wisdom of interfering as little as possible in our own preparation and in the equipment of our own military forces with the duty —for it will be a very practical duty—of supplying the nations already at war with Germany with the materials which they can obtain only from us by our assistance. They are in the field and we should help them in every way to be effective there.

"I shall take the liberty of suggesting, through the several executive departments of the Government, for the consideration of your committees measures for the accomplishment of the several objects I have mentioned. I hope that it will be your pleasure to deal with them as having been framed after very careful thought by the branch of the Government upon which the responsibility of conducting the war and safeguarding the nation will most directly fall.

"While we do these things—these deeply momentous things—let us be very clear, and make very clear to all the world, what our motives and our objects are. My own thought has not been driven from its habitual and normal course by the unhappy events of the last two months, and I do not believe that the thought of the nation has been altered or clouded by them.

FIRM STAND FOR VINDICATION.

"I have exactly the same things in mind now that I had in mind when I addressed the Senate on the twenty-second of January last; the same that I had in mind when I addressed the Congress on the third of February and on the twenty-sixth of February. Our object now, as then, is to vindicate the principles of peace and justice in the life of the world against selfish and autocratic power and to set up among the really free and self-governed peoples of the world such a concert of purpose and action as will henceforth insure the observance of those principles.

"Neutrality is no longer feasible or desirable where the peace of the world is involved and the freedom of its peoples and the menace to that peace and freedom lies in the existence of autocratic governments backed by organized force which is controlled wholly by their will, not by the will of their people. We have seen the last of neutrality in such circumstances.

"We are at the beginning of an age in which it will be insisted that the same standards of conduct and of responsibility for wrongdoing shall be observed among nations and their Governments that are observed among the individual citizens of civilized States.

"We have no quarrel with the German people. We have no feeling toward them but one of sympathy and friendship. It was not upon their impulse that their Government acted in entering this war. It was not with their previous knowledge or approval.

"It was a war determined upon as wars used to be determined upon in the old, unhappy days when peoples were nowhere consulted by their rulers and wars were provoked and waged in the interest of dynasties or of little groups of ambitious men who were accustomed to use their fellow-men as pawns and tools.

"Self-governed nations do not fill their neighbor States with spies, or set the course of intrigue to bring about some critical posture of affairs which will give them an opportunity to strike and make conquest. Such designs can be successfully worked out only under cover and where no one has the right to ask questions.

PRECONCEIVED DECEPTION.

"Cunningly contrived plans of deception or aggression carried it may be from generation to generation, can be worked out and kept from the light only within the privacy of courts or behind the carefully guarded confidences of a narrow, privileged class. They are happily impossible where public opinion commands and insists upon full information concerning all the nation's affairs.

"A steadfast concert for peace can never be maintained except by a partnership of democratic nations. No autocratic Government could be trusted to keep faith within it or observe its covenants. It must be a league of honor, a partnership of opinion. Intrigue would eat its vitals away; the plotting of inner circles who could plan what they would and render account to no one would be a corruption seated at its very heart. Only free peoples can hold their purpose and their honor steady to a common end and prefer the interests of mankind to any narrow interest of their own.

Does not every American feel that assurance has been added to our hope for the future peace of the world by the wonderful and heartening things that have been happening within the last few weeks in Russia? Russia was known by those who know it best to have been always in fact democratic at heart in all the vital habits of her thought, in all the intimate relationships of her people that spoke their natural instinct, their habitual attitude toward life.

POLITICAL AUTOCRACY.

"The autocracy that crowned the summit of her political structure, long as it had stood and terrible as was the reality of its power, was not, in fact, Russian in origin, character or purpose; and now it has been shaken off and the great, generous Russian people have been added in all their native majesty and might to the forces that are fighting for freedom in the world, for justice and for peace. Here is a fit partner for a league of honor.

"One of the things that have served to convince us that the Prussian autocracy was not and could never be our friend, is that from the very outset of the present war it has filled our unsuspecting communities and even our offices of Government with spies and set criminal intrigues everywhere afoot against our national unity and counsel, our peace within and without our industries and our commerce.

"Indeed, it is now evident that its spies were here even before the war began; and it is unhappily not a matter of conjecture, but a fact proved in our courts of justice, that the intrigues which have more than once come perilously near to disturbing the peace and dislocating the industries of the country have been carried on at the instigation, with the support, and even under the personal direction of official agents of the Imperial Government accredited to the Government of the United States.

"Even in checking these things and trying to extirpate them, we have sought to put the most generous interpretation possible upon them because we knew that their source lay, not in any hostile feeling or purpose of the German people toward us (who were, no doubt, as ignorant of them as we ourselves were), but only in the selfish designs of a Government that did what it pleased and told its people nothing. But they have played their part in serving to convince us at last that that Government entertains no real friendship for us and means to act against our peace and security at its convenience. That it means to stir up enemies against us at our very doors the intercepted note to the German Minister at Mexico City is eloquent evidence.

"We are accepting this challenge of hostile purpose because we know that in such a Government, following such methods, we can never have a friend; and that in the presence of its organized power, always lying in wait to accomplish we know not what purpose, there can be no assured security of the democratic Governments of the world.

NATURAL FOE TO LIBERTY.

"We are now about to accept gage of battle with this natural foe to liberty, and shall, if necessary, spend the whole force of the nation to check and nullify its pretensions and its power. We are glad, now that we see the facts with no veil of false pretense about them, to fight thus for the ultimate peace of the world and for the liberation of its peoples, the German peoples included; for the rights of nations great and small and the privilege of men everywhere to choose their way of life and of obedience. The world must be made safe for democracy. Its peace must be planted upon the tested foundations of political liberty.

"We have no selfish ends to serve. We desire no conquest, no dominion. We seek no indemnities for ourselves, no material compensation for the sacrifices we shall freely make. We are but one of the champions of the rights of mankind. We shall be satisfied when those rights have been as secure as the faith and the freedom of the nations can make them.

"Just because we fight without rancour and without selfish object, seeking nothing for ourselves but what we shall wish to share with all free people, we shall, I feel confident, conduct our operations as belligerents without passion and ourselves observe with proud punctilio the principles of right and of fair play we profess to be fighting for.

UNDISGUISED WARFARE.

"I have said nothing of the Governments allied with the Imperial Government of Germany because they have not made war upon us or challenged us to defend our right and our honor. The Austro-Hungarian Government has, indeed, avowed its unqualified indorsement and acceptance of the reckless and lawless submarine warfare adopted now without disguise by the Imperial German Government, and it has, therefore, not been possible for this Government to receive Count Tarnowski, the Ambassador recently accredited to this Government by the Imperial and Royal Government of Austria-Hungary; but that Government has not actually engaged in warfare against citizens of the United States on the seas, and I take the liberty, for the present at least, of postponing a discussion of our relations with the authorities at Vienna. We enter this war only where we are clearly forced into it because there are no other means of defending our rights.

"It will be all the easier for us to conduct ourselves as belligerents in a high spirit of right and fairness because we act without animus, not in enmity toward a people or with the desire to bring any injury or disadvantage upon them, but only in armed opposition to an irresponsible Government which has thrown aside all considerations of humanity and of right and is running amuck.

"We are, let me say again, the sincere friends of the German people, and shall desire nothing so much as the early reestablishment of intimate relations of mutual advantage between us, however hard it may be for them, for the time being, to believe that this is spoken from our hearts.

"We have borne with their present Government through all these bitter months because of that friendship, exercising a patience and forbearance which would otherwise have been impossible. We shall, happily, still have an opportunity to prove that friendship in our daily attitude and actions toward the millions of men and women of German birth and native sympathy who live among us and share our life, and we shall be proud to prove it toward all who are in fact loyal to their neighbors and to the Government in the hour of test.

TRUE AND LOYAL AMERICANS.

"They are, most of them, as true and loyal Americans as if they had never known any other fealty or allegiance. They will be prompt to stand with us in rebuking and restraining the few who may be of a different mind and purpose.

"If there should be disloyalty it will be dealt with with a firm hand of stern repression; but if it lifts its head at all it will lift it only here and there, and without countenance except from a lawless and malignant few.

"It is a distressing and oppressive duty, gentlemen of the Congress, which I have performed in thus addressing you. There are, it may be, many months of fiery trial and sacrifice ahead of us. It is a fearful thing to lead this great, peaceful people into war—into the most terrible and disastrous of all wars, civilization itself seeming to be in the balance.

"But the right is more precious than peace, and we shall fight for the things which we have always carried nearest our hearts—for democracy, for the right of those who submit to authority to have a voice in their own government, for the rights and liberties of small nations, for a universal dominion of right by such a concert of free peoples as shall bring peace and safety to all nations and make the world itself at last free.

"To such a task we can dedicate our lives and our fortunes,

everything that we are and everything that we have, with the pride of those who know that the day has come when America is privileged to spend her blood and her might for the princi- ples that gave her birth and happiness and the peace which she has treasured. God helping her, she can do no other."

While all the world knew that an actual state of war had existed between the two countries for months, the resolution declaring war as adopted by Congress on the plea of Presi- dent Wilson and signed by the President shortly after 1 o'clock on the afternoon of April 6, 1917—Good Friday—was as fol- lows:

"Whereas, The Imperial German Government has com- mitted repeated acts of war against the government and the people of the United States of America; therefore, be it

A WAR RESOLUTION.

"Resolved, By the Senate and House of Representatives of the United States of America, in Congress assembled, that the state of war between the United States and the Imperial German Government which has thus been thrust upon the United States is hereby formally declared; and that the Presi- dent be, and he is hereby authorized and directed to employ the entire naval and military forces of the United States and the resources of the government to carry on war against the Imperial German Government; and to bring the conflict to a successful termination all of the resources of the country are hereby pledged by the Congress of the United States."

Immediately President Wilson issued a proclamation in which he called upon the people of the country to co-operate and give their support, pointing out the necessity for doing things other than putting men upon the firing line. And in his brief proclamation he outlined the entire comprehensive plan which, within a few months, was well under way.

The placing of the navy upon a war footing; the creating

and equipping of an adequate army; the supplying of ships; creating of loans; the financing of the Allies; the conservation of food products; the development of food and material resources; the providing of munitions and supplies for the fighting forces abroad—all of these things were pointed to as necessary in the President's proclamation.

Thus America, which had endeavored to remain neutral during months when Germany was arrogant and insulting, became aligned with the Allies in the struggle which for nearly three years had been waged in Europe.

NEGOTIATIONS CARRIED ON.

The negotiations between this country and Germany over the question of submarine warfare as affecting the lives of non-combatants and the rights of neutrals on the high seas in time of war had been carried on for two years. They had their origin on February 10, 1915, when, following the German announcement of February 4 that "the waters around Great Britain and Ireland, including the whole English Channel, are declared a war zone on and after February 18, 1915," William J. Bryan, then Secretary of State, sent the "strict accountability" note to Berlin.

Through successive stages the exchange of diplomatic papers continued, with growing feeling on both sides, because of the acts of German submarines, until the torpedoing of the cross-Channel steamer Sussex, on March 24, 1916, when the lives of twenty-five American citizens were imperiled and several suffered bodily injuries or shock. This attack resulted in the "Sussex note," or so-called "ultimatum" to Germany.

The Sussex note, signed by Secretary Lansing, and sent to Germany April 19, 1916, concluded with the following declaration:

"Unless the Imperial Government should now immediately declare and effect an abandonment of its present methods of submarine warfare against passenger and freight-carrying vessels, the Government of the United States can have no choice but to sever diplomatic relations with the German Empire altogether."

QUESTIONS GERMANY'S RIGHT.

The first American note to the Imperial Government, of February 10, 1915, disputed the right of Germany to declare such a war zone as it had announced the week before, and contended for the international procedure of "visit and search" before attack on or capture of a neutral vessel. It embodied this phrase:

"If such a deplorable situation should arise (wanton destruction of an American ship) the Imperial German Government can readily appreciate that the Government of the United States would be constrained to hold the Imperial German Government to a strict accountability for such acts of their naval authorities and to take any steps it might be necessary to take to safeguard American lives and property and to secure to Americans the full enjoyment of their acknowledged rights on the high seas."

In reply the German Government sent a note under date of February 16, 1915, setting forth that the war zone proclamation was in reprisal for the "blockade" of Great Britain and that if "at the eleventh hour" the United States should prevail upon Germany's enemies to abandon their methods of maritime warfare, Germany would modify its order. It charged misuse of neutral flags and the arming of merchant ships by Great Britain.

On February 20, in an identic note to Germany and Great Britain, the American Government suggested that both Powers cease their illegal activities. Such an agreement this Government proposed as a "modus vivendi" giving opportunity for further discussion of the points in controversy. Berlin accepted this note as "new evidence of the friendly feelings of the American Government," but reserved a "definite statement" of the position of the Imperial Government until it learned "what obligations the British Government are on their part willing to assume."

Subsequently, on March 28, the British steamship Falaba was sunk, with the loss of 163 lives, including one American. On April 28 the American steamship Cushing was attacked by an aeroplane, and on May 1 the American tanker Gulflight was attacked by a submarine and three United States citizens were lost.

On May 1, also, the German Embassy at Washington caused to be inserted in many of the leading American newspapers the now famous advertisement warning Americans and others from taking passage on the Cunard liner Lusitania, intimating that it would be attacked. This was the day the Lusitania sailed on her ill-fated voyage. A number of the prominent passengers received personal notes when they reached the pier, advising them not to go, but most of them scouted the thought of danger.

SUBMARINE ISSUE AND DIPLOMACY.

After the sinking of the Lusitania, on May 7, off Fastnet, Ireland, with the loss of more than 1100 persons, among them 115 Americans, the submarine issue assumed a large and gravely important place in the realm of diplomacy.

The accumulation of cases affecting Americans was taken up in the first "Lusitania note" to Germany, which was dispatched May 15, 1915. It characterized the attacks on the Falaba, Cushing, Gulflight and Lusitania as "a series of events which the United States has observed with growing concern, distress and amazement." It pointed to Germany's hitherto expressed "humane and enlightened attitude" in matters of international right, and expressed the hope that submarine commanders engaged in torpedoing peaceful ships without warning were in such practice operating without the sanction of their Governmnet. The note closed with these words:

"The Imperial German Government will not expect the Government of the United States to omit any word or act necessary to the performance of its sacred duty of maintaining the rights of the United States and its citizens and of safeguarding their free exercise and enjoyment."

On May 28, 1915, Germany replied with a note which covered a wide range of argument and was in every respect unsatisfactory. It alleged that the Lusitania had masked guns aboard; that she in effect was a British auxiliary cruiser; that she carried munitions of war; that her owning company, aware of the damages she risked in the submarine war zone, was in reality responsible for the loss of American lives, and referred to the fact that the British Admiralty had offered large rewards to ship captains who rammed or destroyed submarines.

PROMISED TO PAY DAMAGES.

The note met none of the contentions of the United States so far as the Lusitania and Falaba incidents were concerned, although a supplementary note did acknowledge that Germany was wrong in the attacks on the Cushing and the Gulflight, expressed regret for these two cases and promised to pay damages. While the American reply to the note was being framed dissension in the Cabinet resulted in the resignation of Secretary Bryan, who contended for a policy of warning Americans off belligerent ships. He resigned because he thought he could not sign the next note to Germany, which he feared would lead the United States into war.

Meanwhile several sensational incidents cropped up in connection with the negotiations, chief of which was the sending of a message to the Berlin Foreign Office by Doctor Dumba, the Austrian Ambassador, afterward recalled at the request of President Wilson, which was represented as stating substantially that Mr. Bryan had intimated to the Ambassador that the vigorous tone of the American notes should not be regarded in Berlin as too warlike.

Secretary Lansing took office as Mr. Bryan's successor, and his reply to the German note took issue with every contention Germany had set up in the Falaba and Lusitania cases, denied flatly the contention that the Lusitania was armed or was to be treated as other than a peaceful merchant ship.

The note averred that the declaration of a submarine war zone could not abbreviate the rights of Americans on lawful journeys, and added: "The Government of the United States therefore very earnestly and solemnly renews the representations of its note transmitted to the Imperial German Government on May 15, and relies in these representations upon the principles of humanity, the universally recognized understandings of international law and the ancient friendship of the German nation."

JAGOW'S EVASIVE ANSWER.

To that note Germany did not reply until July 8, and the German rejoinder was preponderately characterized by American newspapers not as a note, but as an address by Foreign Minister von Jagow to the American people. In official circles it was said to come no nearer to meeting the American contentions than did the former German note.

The nature of the reply was regarded officially as convincing evidence that Germany was holding the submarine warfare negotiations as a club over the United States to force this Government into some action to compel Great Britain to relax the food blockade. President Wilson steadfastly refused to permit the diplomatic negotiations of the United States with one belligerent to become entangled with the relations with another.

To that the United States replied on July 21 that the German note was "very unsatisfactory," because it failed to meet "the real differences between the two Governments." The United States, it declared, was keenly disappointed with Germany's attitude. Submarine attacks without warning, endangering Americans and other neutrals, were characterized as illegal and inhuman and manifestly indefensible. The German retaliation against the British blockade, it maintained, must not interfere with the rights of neutrals, which the note declared were "based upon principles, not expediency, and the principles are immutable." It declared that the United States would continue to contend for the freedom of the seas "from whatever quarter violated, without compromise and at any cost." The American note concluded with these words of warning:

"Friendship itself prompts it (the United States Government) to say to the Imperial Government that repetition by the commanders of German naval vessels of acts in contravention of those rights must be regarded by the Government of the United States, when they affect American citizens, as deliberately unfriendly."

"INFORMAL CONVERSATIONS."

The negotiations at this point seemed to have come to such an impasse that the exchanges of notes between Washington and Berlin were stopped and the controversy was brought into the realm of "informal conversations" between Secretary Lansing and Count von Bernstorff, the German Ambassador. It was thought that much could be accomplished by personal contact which was lost in a cold exchange of documents.

Meanwhile the Arabic was sunk on August 19. Coming close on the unsuccessful Lusitania negotiations and a continuation of submarine attacks in which Americans had suffered, it seemed that the United States and Germany had at last reached the point of a break. Then, on September 1, came the first rift in the threatening situation. Count von Bernstorff presented this written assurance to Secretary Lansing:

"Liners will not be sunk by our submarines without warning and without safety of noncombatants, provided that the liners do not try to escape or offer resistance."

The United States had agreed all along that ships hailed for visit and search by a war vessel took a risk if they attempted to flee, but it contended not for the safety of "liners" alone, but for the immunity of all peaceful merchant vessels. The word "liners" was the perplexing point in Germany's assurances and a complete agreement on what it actually meant never was finally reached.

More hopefulness was added to the situation when, on October 5, the Arabic case was disposed of by Germany disavowing the sinking and giving renewed assurances that submarine commanders had been again instructed to avoid repetition of the acts which provoked American condemnation. Count von Bernstorff delivered to Secretary Lansing this communication:

BERNSTORFF'S COMMUNICATION.

"The orders issued by his Majesty the. Emperor to the commanders of submarines—of which I notified you on a previous occasion—have been made so stringent that the recurrence of incidents similar to the Arabic case is considered out of the question. The Imperial Government regrets and disavows this act and has notified Commander Schneider accordingly."

With that the negotiations reverted to the Lusitania case. Germany already had agreed to pay indemnity for American lives lost, but the negotiations were delayed by a seeming deadlock over the words in which Germany should acknowledge the illegality of the destruction of the liner. Germany, unwilling to use the word "illegal," substituted a declaration that "reprisals must not be directed at others than enemy subjects." A formal communication, including such a declaration and expressing regret for loss of American lives, assuming liability and offering reparation in the form of indemnity, was submitted to Secretary Lansing.

A favorable settlement of the long and threatened con-

troversy seemed to be in sight when all the progress that had
been made was reduced to nothing by Germany's declaration of
a new submarine policy of sinking without warning all armed
merchant ships. That precipitated a new situation so vitally
interwoven with the whole structure of the Lusitania case that
President Wilson declined to close the Lusitania settlement
while the other issue was pending, and there the whole matter
rested while German submarine warfare was contained and new
cases involving loss of American lives piled up.

Finally the accumulation of evidence reached such proportions with the torpedoing of the Sussex that President Wilson,
convinced that assurances given in the Lusitania and Arabic
cases were being violated, dispatched another note to Germany, and went before Congress, reviewed the entire situation
from the beginning, and made this declaration:

PRESIDENT'S DECLARATION.

"I have deemed it my duty to say to the Imperial German
Government that if it is still its purpose to prosecute relentless
and indiscriminate warfare the Government of the United
States is at last forced to the conclusion that there is only one
course it can pursue; and that, unless the Imperial German
Government should now, immediately, declare and effect an
abandonment of its present methods of warfare against passenger and freight-carrying vessels this Government can have
no choice but to sever diplomatic relations altogether."

It will be noted that the President went further than
"liners," and said "passenger and freight-carrying vessels."

In the note sent at this time the President said:

"No limit of any kind has in fact been set to the indiscriminate pursuit and destruction of merchantmen of all kinds
and nationalities within the waters constantly extending in
area where these operations have been carried on, and the roll
of Americans who have lost their lives on ships thus attacked
and destroyed has grown month by month until the ominous

toll has mounted into the hundreds. Again and again the Imperial German Government has given this Government its solemn assurances that at least passenger ships would not be thus dealt with, and yet it has again and again permitted its undersea commanders to disregard those assurances with entire impunity."

OPPOSED TO SUBMARINE WARFARE.

During all the negotiations the Berlin Foreign Office looked to Count von Bernstorff to prevent a break. His attitude was represented as propitiatory from the viewpoint of the United States and opposed to the submarine warfare of Von Tirpitz. On several occasions he is said to have warned his Emperor personally that a continuance of the warfare against which the United States protested would surely lead to a break. Meanwhile the Ambassador's own position was embarrassed by the operations of German sympathizers in the United States plotting against American neutrality. Some of these operations were traced directly to the military and naval attaches of the embassy, who were withdrawn.

Germany's final note in the Sussex case, received in Washington on May 5, said that "the German naval forces have received the following order":

"In accordance with the general principles of visit and search and the destruction of merchant vessels recognized by international law, such vessels, both within and without the area declared a naval war zone, shall not be sunk without warning and without saving human lives, unless the ship attempts to escape or offers resistance."

Contending that the Imperial Government was unwilling to restrict an effective weapon if "the enemy is permitted to apply at will methods of warfare violating the rules of international law," the note expressed the hope that the United States would "demand and insist that the British Government shall observe forthwith the rules of international law." The communication added:

"Should the steps taken by the Government of the United States not attain the object it (the German Government) desires, to have the laws of humanity followed by all belligerent nations, the German Government would then be facing a new situation in which it must reserve to itself complete liberty of decision."

To any such reservations the United States demurred in no uncertain terms.

PRESIDENT WILSON'S REPLY.

"The United States feels it necessary to state," said President Wilson's reply, "that it takes it for granted that the Imperial German Government does not intend to imply that the maintenance of its newly announced policy is any way contingent upon the course or result of diplomatic negotiations between the Government of the United States and any other belligerent Government, notwithstanding the fact that certain passages in the Imperial Government's note might appear to be susceptible of that construction."

In completing the declaration that there must be no misunderstanding that rights of American citizens must not be made subject to the conduct of some other Government, the note concluded by saying: "Responsibility in such matters is single, not joint; absolute, not relative."

The climax came on February 1, 1917, when Count von Bernstorff, German Ambassador at Washington, handed to Secretary Lansing a note from Germany on the U-boat policy, supplemented by the "order" and declaration that the Imperial Government proposed to stop sea traffic in the "zones" which it marked as prohibited, by every means at its command. This is the restricted zone order:

"From February 1, 1917, sea traffic will be stopped with every available weapon and without further notice in the following blockade zones around Great Britain, France, Italy and in the Eastern Mediterranean.

"In the North: The zone is confined by a line at a distance of twenty sea miles along the Dutch coast to Terschelling fireship, the degree of longitude from Terschelling fireship to Udsire (Norway), a line from there across, the point 62 de-

THE BLOCKADE ZONES.

grees north 0 degrees longitude to 62 degrees north 5 degrees west, further to a point three sea miles south of the southern point of the Farve (Faroe?) Islands, from there across a point 62 degrees north 10 degrees west to 61 degrees north 15 degrees west, then 57 degrees north 20 degrees west to 47 degrees north 20 degrees west, further to 43 degrees north, 15 degrees west, then along the degree of latitude 43 degrees north to 20 sea miles from Cape Finisterre and at a distance of 20 sea miles along the north coast of Spain to the French boundary.

"In the south (Mediterranean):

"For neutral ships remains open: The sea west of the line Pt des' Espiquette to 38 degrees 20 minutes north and 6 degrees east, also north and west of a zone 61 sea miles wide along the North African coast, beginning at 2 degrees longitude west. For the connection of this sea zone with Greece there is provided a zone of a width of 20 sea miles north and east of the following line: 38 degrees north and 6 degrees east to 38 degrees north and 10 degrees west to 37 degrees north and 11 degrees 30 minutes east to 34 degrees north and 22 degrees 30 minutes east. From there leads a zone 20 sea miles wide west of 22 degrees 30 minutes eastern longitude into Greek territorial waters.

NEUTRAL SHIPS' RISK.

"Neutral ships navigating these blockade zones do so at their own risk. Although care has been taken that neutral ships which are on their way toward ports of the blockade zones on February 1, 1917, and which have come in the vicinity of the latter, will be spared during a sufficiently long period, it is strongly advised to warn them with all available means in order to cause their return.

"Neutral ships which on February 1 are in ports of the blockade zones can with the same safety leave them.

'The instructions given to the commanders of German submarines provide for a sufficiently long period during which the safety of passengers on unarmed enemy passenger ships is guaranteed.

"Americans en route to the blockade zone on enemy freight steamships are not endangered, as the enemy shipping firms can prevent such ships in time from entering the zone.

"Sailing of regular American passenger steamships may continue undisturbed after February 1, 1917, if

"(a)   The port of destination is Falmouth.

"(b)   Sailing to or coming from that port course is taken via the Scilly Islands and a point 50 degrees north, 20 degrees west.

"(c)   The steamships are marked in the following way, which must not be allowed to other vessels in American ports: On ship's hull and superstructure three vertical stripes one meter wide each to be painted alternately white and red. Each mast should show a large flag checkered white and red and the stern the American national flag. Care should be taken that during dark national flag and painted marks are easily recognizable from a distance, and that the boats are well lighted throughout.

"(d)   One steamship a week sails in each direction, with arrival at Falmouth on Sunday and departure from Falmouth on Wednesday.

"(e)   United States Government guarantees that no contraband (according to German contraband list) is carried by those steamships."

Immediately after the signing of the Congressional resolution declaring America at war, President Wilson ordered the mobilization of the United States Navy, and the Senate voted an emergency war fund of $100,000,000 for the use of the President. The forces of the United States on land and sea and in every country under the sun were notified that a state of war existed.

The entrance of America was regarded throughout the world as one of the most significant moves in the history of nations, and it filled the Allied forces with enthusiasm. Typical of the expressions on the part of the representatives of the Governments at war with Germany was that of Lloyd George, Premier of England, who said:

"America has at one bound become a world power in a sense she never was before. She waited until she found a cause worthy of her traditions. The American people held back until they were fully convinced that the fight was not a sordid scrimmage for power and possessions, but an unselfish struggle to overthrow a sinister conspiracy against human liberty and human rights.

"Once that conviction was reached, the great Republic of the West has leaped into the arena, and she stands now side by side with the European democracies, who, bruised and bleeding after three years of grim conflict, are still fighting the most savage foe that ever menaced the freedom of the world.

"The glowing phrases of the President's noble deliverance illumine the horizon and make clearer than ever the goal we are striving to reach.

DEMOCRACY, FREEDOM AND PEACE.

"There are three phrases which will stand out forever in the story of this crusade. The first is that 'the world must be made safe for democracy,' the next, 'the menace to peace and freedom lies in the existence of autocratic governments backed by organized force, which is controlled wholly by their will and not by the will of their people,' and the crowning phrase is that in which he declares that 'a steadfast concert for peace can never be maintained except by the partnership of democratic nations.'

"These words represent the faith which inspires and sustains our people in the tremendous sacrifices they have made and are still making. They also believe that the unity and peace of mankind can only rest upon democracy, upon the right to have a voice in their own Government; upon respect for the right and liberties of nations both great and small, and upon the universal dominion of public right.

"To all of these the Prussian military autocracy is an implacable foe.

"The Imperial War Cabinet, representative of all the peoples of the British Empire, wish me on their behalf to recognize the chivalry and courage which call the people of the United States to dedicate the whole of their resources to the greatest cause that ever engaged human endeavor."

CHAPTER XXI.
UNCLE SAM TAKES HOLD.

MAKES WORLD'S BIGGEST WAR LOAN—SEIZE GERMAN SHIPS—INTRIGUE EXPOSED—
GENERAL PERSHING AND STAFF IN EUROPE—THE NAVY ON DUTY IN NORTH SEA
—FIRST UNITED STATES TROOPS REACH FRANCE—GERMANY'S ATTEMPTS TO
SINK TROOP SHIPS THWARTED BY NAVY'S GUNS.

SCARCELY had the ink had time to dry on the Nation's command to begin war than Congress voted an appropriation of $7,000,000,000 for war purposes. This, the largest single appropriation ever made by a government in the world, was passed without a dissenting vote. Still later a deficiency bill of $2,827,000,000 for war expenses was passed. Other legislative measures provided for the increase of the army and navy and for "selective conscription," although the latter was passed in the face of considerable opposition on the part of many who believed that in a democracy armies should be raised by volunteer recruiting. Many felt that compulsory service was not in accordance with the ideals of liberty.

The Conscription Act provided for the registration of every male citizen or resident in the United States between the ages of 21 and 31 years, and was enacted on May 19, 1917. Registration of these military available was made on June 5, when 10,000,000 names were entered on the rolls as subject to draft by the Government. The principle of "selective conscription" is that the authorities shall have the right to exempt from military duty among those registered such persons whose employment in civil life is necessary to the maintenance of the industries and business of the country, as well as those who, though physically fit, have others dependent upon them for support.

One of the first acts of the Government after the declaration of war was the seizure of the German merchant vessels interned in United States ports. These vessels had a tonnage of upward of 629,000 tons and were estimated as being worth in the neighborhood of $100,000,000. The seizure was notable in that it was the largest ever made by a country at war.

When the Government went to take charge of the vessels it was found that the German officers had destroyed parts of the machinery in many of them in an attempt to put them out of commission. The condition of the boats was such that all of them had to be put in drydock, and it was several months before some of them could be put in condition for use.

SIXTY RINGLEADERS ARRESTED.

Immediately the ships had been seized an order was issued by Attorney General Gregory for the arrest of sixty alleged ringleaders in German plots, conspiracies and machinations throughout the United States. The Department of Justice, which had long been gathering evidence in connection with the suspects, had complete reports about their activities. They were all German citizens, had participated in German intrigues, and all were regarded as dangerous persons to be at large.

They.were all arrested, bail was refused them, and they were locked up for safekeeping. This was the first step in the general rounding up of the conspirators throughout the country. The men were placed in three groups: Those having previously been arrested charged with violation of American neutrality in furthering German plots of various sorts and who were at liberty under bond awaiting the action of higher courts; those who had been indicted by Federal Grand Juries for similar offenses and were at liberty under bond awaiting the action of the higher courts, and persons who, although they had never been indicted or convicted, had long been under surveillance by the Secret Service, or the investigators of the Department of Justice.

These arrests were the first of alien enemies made in

this country in more than a century, under the direct order of the Attorney General without reference to the courts or obtaining warrants. Under an act of Congress passed in 1798 the President is empowered to adopt this course. The right had not been invoked, however, since the war with Great Britain in 1812.

ARREST OF GERMAN PLOTTERS.

The arrests were only the beginning of the work of the Secret Service Department in a complete investigation of the activities of the thousands of German reservists, stationed in the United States, and suspected of being connected with plots which daily were cropping out. These plots were being exposed constantly. Some were abandoned before being completely worked out, owing to the fact that the Germans suspected they were being shadowed. It was estimated that there were in the United States at the time of the discoveries of conspiracies between 15,000 and 18,000 German reservists in the prime of life, whose energies were undoubtedly being employed in the spreading of the German propaganda. It was upon this army that the Secret Service men kept a close watch, and who were generally found to have within their ranks the men wanted at various times in connection with the advancement of German plans.

Many of the Germans arrested were quasi-officials of the German government. Some of them, it is alleged, were the instrumentalities through which Captain Boy-Ed and Captain von Papen had carried out their activities in this country against the Allies. A number of those arrested were properly classed as spies. Camps were established for the sailors taken from the interned German vessels, and many of them were sent to Fort Oglethorpe, Georgia, where they were held.

The far-reaching influence of the German spy system was at this time laid before the American public, with all of its startling ramifications. For months there had been stories of German intrigue and conspiracies, and the Secret Service had unearthed innumerable plots to destroy ammunition plants and industrial establishments, which would have the effect of making it difficult for America to supply ammunition to the Allies.

The most insidious scheme unearthed by the government was that which had to do with the attempt of Germany to secure the alliance of Mexico and Japan to make war on the United States.

Japan, through Mexican mediation, was to be urged to abandon her allies and join in the attack on the United States.

Mexico, for her reward, was to receive general financial support from Germany, reconquer Texas, New Mexico and Arizona—lost provinces—and share in the victorious peace terms Germany contemplated.

MACHINATIONS OF GERMAN MINISTER.

Details were left to German Minister von Eckhardt in Mexico City, who by instructions signed by German Foreign Minister Zimmerman, at Berlin, January 19, 1917, was directed to propose the alliance with Mexico, to General Carranza, and suggest that Mexico seek to bring Japan into the plot.

These instructions were transmitted to von Eckhardt through Count von Bernstorff, former German Ambassador.

Germany pictured to Mexico, by broad intimation, England and the entente allies defeated, Germany and her allies triumphant and in world domination by the instrument of unrestricted submarine warfare.

A copy of Zimmerman's instructions to von Eckhardt, sent through von Bernstorff, is in possession of the United States government. It is as follows:

"Berlin, January 19, 1917.

"On the first of February we intend to begin submarine

warfare unrestricted. In spite of this, it is our intention to
endeavor to keep neutral the United States of America.

"If this attempt is not successful we propose an alliance
on the following basis with Mexico: That we shall make war
together and together make peace. We shall give general
financial support, and it is understood that Mexico is to reconquer the lost territory in New Mexico, Texas and Arizona. The details are left to you for settlement.

"You are instructed to inform the President of Mexico
of the above, in the greatest confidence, as soon as it is certain that there will be an outbreak of war with the United
States, and suggest that the President of Mexico, on his own
initiative, should communicate with Japan, suggesting adher-
ence at once to this plan; at the same time, offer to mediate
between Germany and Japan.

"Please call to the attention of the President of Mexico
that the employment of ruthless submarine warfare now promises to compel England to make peace in a few months.
                              "ZIMMERMAN."

BETHMANN-HOLLWEG'S FALSE STATEMENT.

This document was in the possession of the government
at the very time Chancellor von Bethmann-Hollweg was declaring that the United States had placed an interpretation
on the submarine declaration "never intended by Germany,"
and that Germany had promoted and honored friendly relations with the United States "as an heirloom from Frederick
the Great."

Of itself, if there were no other, it is considered a sufficient answer to the German Chancellor's plaint that the
United States "brusquely" broke off relations without giving
"authentic" reasons for its action.

The document supplies the missing link to many separate chains of circumstances, which until then had seemed to
lead to no definite point. It shed new light upon the fre-

quently reported but indefinable movements of the Mexican government to couple its situation with the friction between the United States and Japan.

It added another chapter to the celebrated report of Jules Cambon, French Ambassador in Berlin before the war, of Germany's world-wide plans for stirring strife on every continent where they might aid her in the struggle for world domination, which she dreamed was close at hand. It added a climax to the operations of Count von Bernstorff and the German Embassy in this country, which had been colored with passport frauds, charges of dynamite plots and intrigue, the full extent of which never had been published.

And last but not least, it explained in a very large degree the attitude of the Mexican government toward the United States on many points.

UNCLE SAM NOT BOTHERED.

But the efforts of the German enthusiasts, which carried them beyond the bounds of reasonable safety in the United States, did not bother Uncle Sam much in the prosecution of his war plans. Within a short period after the declaration of war the country had written a chapter in national achievement unrivalled in the history of the world.

American destroyers were mobilized, outfitted and sent to the North Sea within a few days after the nation entered the conflict. With them went their own supply vessels and numerous converted craft adapted to naval use. Their number and the exact duty they have assumed never have been revealed, but that they have been recognized as a formidable part of the grand allied fleet was evidenced by the designation of American Vice Admiral Sims to command all the forces in the important zone off Ireland.

The fleet began actual duty in the European waters on May 4, and the presence of the vessels and the American sailors was the subject of official correspondence. The British

Admiralty announced the arrival of the American destroyers as follows:

"The British Admiralty states that a flotilla of United States destroyers recently arrived in this country to co-operate with our naval forces in the prosecution of the war.

"The services which the American vessels are rendering to the allied cause are of the greatest value and are deeply appreciated."

Vice Admiral Sir David Beatty, commander of the British Grand Fleet, sent the following message to Admiral Henry T. Mayo, commander of the United States Atlantic Fleet:

"The Grand Fleet rejoices that the Atlantic Fleet will now share in preserving the liberties of the world and maintaining the chivalry of the sea."

Admiral Mayo replied:

"The United States Atlantic Fleet appreciates the message from the British Fleet and welcomes opportunities for work with the British Fleet for the freedom of the seas."

GENERAL PERSHING IN ENGLAND.

Less than a month later Major General John J. Pershing, with his staff, were safely in England ready to take command of the first expeditionary force that ever set foot on the European shores to make war. General Pershing's personal staff and the members of the General Staff who went to perform the preliminary work for the first fighting force, numbered 57 officers and about 50 enlisted men, together with a civilian clerical force.

The party landed at Liverpool on June 8, after an uneventful trip on the White Star liner Baltic. The party was received with full military honors and immediately entrained for London, where it was welcomed by Lord Derby, the Minister of War; Viscount French, commander of the British home forces, and a large body of American officials.

In London General Pershing was later received at Buckingham Palace by King George.

He was presented to the King by Lord Brooke, commander of the Twelfth Canadian Infantry Brigade. General Pershing was accompanied to the palace by his personal staff of twelve officers. After the audience the officers paid a formal call at the United States embassy.

PERSHING RECEIVES ROYAL GREETING.

After the formal reception the King shook hands with General Pershing and the members of his staff, and expressed pleasure at welcoming the advance guard of the American army. King George chatted for a few moments with each member of General Pershing's staff. In addressing General Pershing the King said:

"It has been the dream of my life to see the two great English-speaking nations more closely united. My dreams have been realized. It is with the utmost pleasure that I welcome you, at the head of the American contingent, to our shores."

Major General Pershing's staff has been characterized as "one of live wires." Most of the officers are West Pointers, but there are among them some who rose from the ranks, including Major James G. Harbord, chief of staff.

General Pershing reached France on June 13, where he was given a tumultuous welcome. He landed at Boulogne in the morning and was met by General Pelletier, representing the French government and General Headquarters of the French army; Commandant Hue, representing the Minister of War; General Lucas, commanding the northern region; Colonel Daru, Governor of Lille; the Prefect of the Somme and other officials.

Among the latter were Rene Besnard, Under Secretary of War, representing the Cabinet; Commandant Thouzellier, representing Marshal Joffre, and Vice-Admiral Ronarch, representing the navy.

The scene in the harbor as General Pershing set foot on French soil was one of striking beauty and animation. The day was bright and sunny. The quays were crowded with townspeople and soldiers from all Entente armies, with French and British troops predominating.

The shipping was gay with flags and bunting, many merchant craft hoisting American flags, while along the crowded quays the American colors were everywhere shown as a token of the French welcome.

PERSHING RECEIVES AN OVATION.

A great wave of enthusiasm came from the crowds as General Pershing stepped upon the quay and as the band played the "Marseillaise" he and the members of his staff stood uncovered. M. Besnard, in greeting the American commander in behalf of the government, said the Americans had come to France to combat with the Allies for the same cause of right and civilization. General Pelletier extended a greeting to the Americans in behalf of the army.

General Dumas, commandant of the region in which Boulogne is located, said:

"Your coming opens a new era in the history of the world. The United States of America is now taking its part with the United States of Europe. Together they are about to found the United States of the World, which will definitely and finally end the war and give a peace which will be enduring and suitable for humanity."

General Pershing stood at parade as the various addresses were delivered and acknowledged each with a salute.

British soldiers and marines lined up along the quays had rendered military honors as the vessel flying the Stars and Stripes, preceded by destroyers and accompanied by hydroplanes and dirigible balloons, steamed up the channel. Military bands played "The Star-Spangled Banner" and the "Marseillaise" as General Pelletier and his party boarded the boat to welcome General Pershing.

After the representatives of the French authorities had been presented to the American officers, the party landed and reviewed the French territorials. The Americans then entered motor cars for a ride around the city. All along the route they were followed by crowds of people who greeted General Pershing with the greatest enthusiasm.

PERSHING IN PARIS.

The General and his staff were taken in a special train to Paris, where General Pershing was received by Marshal Joffre, Ambassador Sharp and Paul Painleve, French Minister of War. In the French capital General Pershing and staff were received by the populace with wild enthusiasm, and for several days they were feted and entertained.

There were, during the short period of entertainment, several incidents which will long be noted in history, as when General Pershing visited the Tomb of Napoleon and when he took from its case the sword of the world conqueror and kissed it, and again when he placed a wreath on the grave of Lafayette.

Within a few days General Pershing had established the army headquarters in the Rue De Constantine and began the work preliminary to the campaign on the firing line.

Second only to the enthusiastic reception tendered General Pershing and his staff was that accorded the first United States Medical Unit, which reached London in June. The vanguard of the American army, composed of 26 surgeons and 60 nurses, in command of Major Harry L. Gilchrist, was received by King George and Queen Mary, the Prince of Wales and Princess Mary, at Buckingham Palace.

The reception to General Pershing and the Medical branch was, however, nothing as compared to the popular demonstration which marked the arrival of the first of the American armed forces on European shores to participate in war. The vanguard of the army reached France on June 27. No official announcement was ever made of the number of men in the first expeditionary force, but it is an incident of modern history that the United States made a record for the transportation of troops across the seas scarcely equalled by that of any other country.

ABSOLUTE SECRECY OBSERVED.

All America knew that troops were being sent to France, but no information had been given as to the time of departure or as to their destination. The world was, therefore, fairly electrified when the announcement was made that in defiance of the German submarines, thousands of seasoned regulars and marines, trained fighting men, with the tan of long service on the Mexican border, in Haiti, or Santo Domingo still on their faces, had arrived in France to fight beside the French, the British, the Belgians, the Russians, the Portuguese and the Italian troops on the Western front.

Despite the enormous difficulties of unpreparedness and the submarine dangers that faced them, the plans of the army and navy were carried through with clock-like precision.

When the order came to prepare immediately an expeditionary force to go to France, virtually all of the men who first crossed the seas were on the Mexican border. General Pershing himself was at his headquarters in San Antonio. There were no army transports available in the Atlantic. The vessels that carried the troops were scattered on their usual routes. Army reserve stores were still depleted from the border mobilization. Regiments were below war strength. That was the condition when President Wilson decided that the plea of the French high commission should be answered and a force of regulars sent at once to France.

At his word the War Department began to move. General Pershing was summoned quietly to Washington. His arrival created some speculation in the press, but at the request of Secretary Baker the newspapers generally refrained from discussion of this point.

There were a thousand other activities afoot in the department at the time. All the business of preparing for the military registration of 10,000,000 men, of providing quarters and instructors for nearly 50,000 prospective officers, for finding arms and equipment for millions of troops yet to be organized, of expanding the regular army to full war strength, of preparing and recruiting the National Guard for war was at hand.

PERSHING SETS UP HEADQUARTERS.

General Pershing dropped quietly into the department and set up the first headquarters of the American expeditionary forces in a little office, hardly large enough to hold himself and his personal staff. There, with the aid of the general staff, of Secretary Baker and of the chiefs of the War Department bureaus, the plans were worked out.

Announcement of the sending of the force under General Pershing was made May 18. The press gave the news to the country and there were daily stories.

There came a day when General Pershing no longer was in the department. Officers of the general staff suddenly were missing from their desks. No word of this was reported. Then came word from England that Pershing and his officers were there. All was carried through without publicity.

Other matters relating to the expedition were carried out without a word of publicity. The regiments that were to go with General Pershing were all selected before he left and moving toward the seacoast from the border. Other regiments also were moving north, east and west to the points where they were to be expanded, and the movements of the troops who were to be first in France were obscured in all this hurrying of troop trains over the land.

Great shipments of war supplies began to assemble at the embarkation ports. Liners suddenly were taken off their regular runs with no announcement. A great armada was made ready, supplied, equipped as transports, loaded with men and guns and sent to sea, and all with virtually no mention from the press.

The navy bore its full share in the achievement. From the time the troop ships left their docks and headed toward sea, responsibility for the lives of their thousands of men rested upon the officers and crews of the fighting ships that moved beside them or swept free the sea lanes before them. As they pushed on through the days and nights toward the danger zone, where German submarines lay in wait, every precaution that trained minds of the navy could devise was taken.

A BRILLIANT CLIMAX.

The brilliant climax to the achievement was made public when it was announced that not only had the last units of the expeditionary force been landed on July 3, but that the American navy had driven off two German submarines, probably sinking one of them, when the transport ships and convoys had been attacked.

The last units of the American expeditionary force, comprising vessels loaded with supplies and horses, reached France amid the screeching of whistles and moaning of sirens. Their arrival, one week after the first troops landed, was greeted almost as warmly as the arrival of the troops themselves.

Many of the American soldiers crowded down to the wharf to greet the last ships of the expedition and the American vessels in the harbor, which had made up previous contingents of the force, joined in the welcome. The late arrival of the supply ships was due not only to later departure from America, but also to the fact that the vessels were slower than those which had come before. The delay caused little anxiety, although it worked temporary inconvenience to the troops, who had been waiting for materials with which to work.

Probably the happiest man in port was Rear Admiral Gleaves, commander of the convoy. From the bridge of his flagship he watched the successful conclusion of his plans with characteristic modesty and insisted upon bestowing the lion's share of credit for the crossing on the navigating officers of his command.

ADVANCE PLANS BRIEFLY SKETCHED.

Sketching briefly the advance plans whereby all units of the contingent had to keep a daily rendezvous with accompanying warships, he said, that, thanks to his navigating officers and despite overcast skies, which made astronomical observations impossible, each rendezvous had been minutely and accurately kept by each unit. The orders he issued at the outset, which comprised scores of details, were observed, the Admiral declared, with such exactness that the contingent units and convoying warships invariably met each other within half an hour of the appointed time.

A big contributing factor in the crossing, according to officers of both branches of the service, was the hearty co-operation between the army and navy. From the time of the departure until the landing there was not the slightest suggestion of friction, and co-ordination played its part distinctively in the success of the expedition.

The startling fact of the entire journey across the sea was that the Navy had won its first victory in driving off attacking submarines. The news of the fight was given out by the Navy Department and the Committee on Public Information, with the announcement of the final landing of the troops and the safe arrival of the supply ships.

The announcement, sponsored by Secretary Daniels, of the Navy, shows beyond the shadow of doubt that the Berlin Admiralty had been "tipped off" that the American expeditionary force was on its way, and had carefully planned to send the transports to the bottom of the Atlantic.

Realizing that an attack might be expected in the war zone, and that every precaution would be taken to ward it off, the Germans moved far out from land, in the hope of catching the American gunners napping. They were fooled. Uncle Sam's jackies were at the guns when the fleet of submarines stuck their periscopes above the waves and trained their torpedo tubes on the lines of transports.

WAVES COVERED WITH SHELLS.

The torpedo boats and other craft opened up and covered the waves with shells. The Germans soon lost at least one submarine and, having had enough of the fight, they disappeared. As the little destroyers dashed straight at the submarines and shot under water explosives in their wake as they submerged, the transports dashed through the night at top speed without having been scratched.

The extreme degree to which the Germans had prepared to destroy the American force is shown by the second part of the official announcement, which tells how another section of the transport fleet was waylaid under cover of darkness, but how the American gunners were too quick for the Germans.

The text of Secretary Daniels' announcement was:

"It is with the joy of a great relief that I announce to the people of the United States the safe arrival in France of every fighting man and every fighting ship. Now that the last vessel has reached port, it is safe to disclose the dangers that were encountered and to tell the complete story of peril and courage.

"The transports bearing our troops were twice attacked by German submarines on the way across. On both occasions the U-boats were beaten off with every appearance of loss. One was certainly sunk, and there is reason to believe that the accurate fire of our gunners sent others to the bottom.

"For purposes of convenience, the expedition was divided into contingents, each contingent including troopships and a naval escort designed to keep off such German raiders as might be met.

"An ocean rendezvous had also been arranged with the American destroyers now operating in European waters in order that the passage of the danger zone might be attended by every possible protection.

"The first attack took place at 10.30 on the night of June 22. What gives it peculiar and disturbing significance is that our ships were set upon at·a point well this side of the rendezvous, and in that part of the Atlantic presumably free from submarines. The attack was made in force, although the night made impossible any exact count of the U-boats gathered for what they deemed a slaughter.

HIGH SEAS CONVOY.

"The high seas convoy, circling with their searchlights, answered with heavy gunfire, and its accuracy stands proved by the fact that the torpedo discharge became increasingly scattered and inaccurate. It is not known how many torpedoes were launched, but five were counted as they sped by bow and stern.

"A second·attack was launched a few days later against another contingent. The point of assault was beyond the rendezvous and our destroyers were sailing as a screen between the transports and all harm. The results of the battle were in favor of American gunnery.

"Not alone did the destroyers hold the U-boats at a safe distance, but their speed also resulted in the sinking of one submarine at least. Grenades were used in firing, a depth charge explosive timed to go off at a certain distance under water. In one instance, oil and wreckage covered the surface of the sea after a shot from a destroyer at a periscope, and the reports make claim of sinking.

"Protected by our high seas convoy, by our destroyers and by French war vessels, the contingent proceeded and joined the others in a French port.

"The whole nation will rejoice that so great a peril is passed for the vanguard of the men who will fight our battles in France. No more thrilling Fourth of July celebration could have been arranged than this glad news that lifts the shadow of dread from the heart of America."

Upon receipt of the announcement, Secretary Baker wrote the following letter to Secretary Daniels, conveying the army's thanks to the navy:

"Word has just come to the War Department that the last ships conveying General Pershing's expeditionary force to France arrived safe today. As you know, the navy assumed the responsibility for the safety of these ships on the sea and through the danger zone. The ships themselves and their convoys were in the hands of the navy, and now that they have arrived, and carried, without the loss of a man, our soldiers who are the first to represent America in the battle for democracy, I beg leave to tender to you, to the Admiral and to the navy, the hearty thanks of the War Department and of the army. This splendid achievement is an auspicious beginning and it has been characterized throughout by the most cordial and effective co-operation between the two military services."

CHAPTER XXII.

A GERMAN CRISIS.

THE active participation of the United States in the war, as distinctly marked by the sending of troops to France, aside from giving needed inspiration to the Allied forces, may be said to have had a decided effect in Germany. While the German subjects are loyal, there has developed in the country, as in every other country, a large element of Socialists and progressives.

Something of a climax was reached in the affairs of the Hohenzollern dynasty just when the United States troops were preparing to take their places on the battle line in France and when the first of the conscripted forces of the country were being summoned to the colors.

With a suddenness that startled the entire world, Dr. von Bethmann-Hollweg, the German Imperial Chancellor, resigned on July 14, thus ending his career as the spokesman of the Kaiser, which he had maintained for a surprisingly long period. At the same time Dr. Alfred Zimmermann, Foreign Minister, who was responsible for the correspondence which revealed the fact that Germany was trying to induce Mexico and Japan to form an alliance against the United States, also quit his post.

The resignation of the Chancellor came quite unexpectedly, for von Hollweg, in the prolonged party discussion and heated debates of the main committee of the Reichstag which had been in progress, seemed to have triumphed over his opponents.

His opponents had been clamoring for his head, but he

372

made concessions, and by the declaration that Germany was fighting defensively for her territorial possessions evolved a formula which for a time seemed satisfactory to both those who clamored for peace by agreement and those who demanded repudiation of the formula, "no annexation and no indemnities." In this position Dr. von Hollweg was backed by the Emperor.

The advent of the Crown Prince upon the scene—summoned by his imperial father to share the deliberations affecting the future of the dynasty—seems to have changed entirely the position with regard to the Imperial Chancellor. The Crown Prince at once took a leading part in the discussions with the party leaders, and his ancient hostility toward Dr. von Bethmann-Hollweg, coupled with his notorious dislike for political reform, undoubtedly precipitated the Chancellor's resignation.

APPOINTMENT OF DR. GEORG MICHAELIS.

The resignation of Dr. von Hollweg was followed by the appointment of Dr. Georg Michaelis, Prussian Under Secretary of Finance and Food Commissioner.

The fall of Theobald von Bethmann-Hollweg removed the last of the statesmen who were in charge of the great Powers of Europe at the beginning of the war, and brought to an end a career which in successful playing of both ends against the middle was almost without parallel in recent history.

Chancellor von Bethmann-Hollweg, an aristocrat and personal friend of the Emperor, stood out strongly against democratic agitation before the war, and at times was sharply outspoken in his defiance of socialism and his rejection of any move toward making the Chancellor and his subordinates, the other Ministers, responsible to the Reichstag. Yet in the early stages of the war he became known as a moderate, and it has been generally accepted that his influence was usually employed against the breaking of relations with America and ruthless submarine warfare.

PRESERVES A JUDICIOUS BALANCE.

When the opposition of the parties favoring the most desperate measures became too strong for him, he conceded a little ground, taking up a middle position in which he balanced himself for a long time against both the Conservative Junkers and the National Liberal trust magnates on the one side and the radical Socialists on the other. Neither side could claim him; neither could interpret his ambiguous utterances as support of its policies, and between the antagonisms of the two he maintained his position until at last he was overthrown by the attack of Erzberger, leader of the more liberal wing of the Catholic party, the traditional holders of the middle ground.

Bethmann-Hollweg's agility was demonstrated by the fact that he survived Asquith and Grey, Viviani, Sazonoff, Berchtold, Salandra, Jagow, and all the rest of the statesmen who were in power in Europe in August, 1914.

In personality the Chancellor was studious, scholarly and pleasant, lacking the brilliance of his predecessor, Von Buelow, but generally regarded as one who was if anything too mild rather than too severe.

Dr. Georg Michaelis, the successor to Hollweg, was the first commoner to be appointed to that high office, without even a "von" before his name.

The son of a Prussian official, he was born on September 8, 1857, in Haynan, Silesia. He received a university education, making the law his profession. In 1879 he became a court referee in Berlin, and in 1884 was attached to the District Attorney's office in that city. Several years later he went as professor of law and political economy to the University of Tokio.

Returning to Germany in 1889, he was chosen District Attorney for Berlin. His services won much praise and he was afterward sent by the government as an official in the provisional government at Trevas, Germany. In 1897 he was transferred to Westphalia, where he was Chief Councilor for the government there.

In 1900 he was made Provisional President of Liebnitz and in 1902 First Privy Councilor in Breslau. His work there won him an appointment as Under Secretary of State in the Department of Finance, which post he held in connection with his work as Food Commissioner.

Doctor Michaelis was selected for the post of Prussian Food Commissioner in February, 1917, after all efforts of Adolph von Batocki's organization—the food regulation board —had failed to lay hands on large supplies of grain, potatoes and other produce which the Prussian landlords were holding for the fattening of cattle and swine instead of making them available for general consumption.

GOVERNMENT ORDERS DISREGARDED.

The orders of Herr Batocki and the Central Government for the surrender of these supplies were disregarded or evaded at least, if not, as charged in Germany, with the actual assistance and support of the reactionary Prussian Minister of Agriculture, Baron von Schorlemer.

Doctor Michaelis was eventually selected as Food Controller as the result of an agreement between von Bethmann-Hollweg and the military authorities as a fearless, determined official, who would execute his mission without fear or favor and produce results if such were possible. The selection was justified.

The conditions in Germany which marked the ascendancy of the Crown Prince in the deliberations of the Imperial Government and brought about the upheaval in the Ministry are the logical result of the system under which the country is ruled.

There is, in the mind of the public generally, a theory that Germany with its Bundesrath and Reichstag has a government akin to that of England and even the United States, but the impression is an erroneous one. It is true that Germany has a dual system of government and independent state sovereignties. There is, however, nothing democratic about the system.

To begin with, the Kaiser is a constitutional monarch in his capacity as German Emperor, but as King of Prussia he is a self-appointed and arrogant ruler—all that he advertises himself to be in the way of a God-chosen ruler.

STATUS OF GERMAN SOVEREIGNTY.

To understand the difference in relationship between the King of Prussia and the German Emperor it is necessary to realize that the German constitution describes the Emperor thus: "The presidency of the Union belongs to the King of Prussia, who bears the title of German Emperor." On the other hand the King of Prussia, who happens to be the Kaiser, has his right to rule by birth. When the first king was crowned, about 1701, he placed the crown upon his own head, and that right has descended to King William. But as German Emperor the duties of the Kaiser are as clearly defined as those of the ruler of a modern democracy.

The difference between the Kingdom and the Empire is that the German Empire is a creation of sovereign states, ruled over by German Grand Dukes, Princes, and whatnot, who trace their lineage back to the days when might was right, and who won their power to rule by defeating their fellow men. At one time there were several hundred of these ruling princes. When Napoleon got through in Germany there were about twenty-two left. The German Empire today consists of these twenty-two states, and three free cities, comprising in all a group of twenty-five communities. It is a bond or association. It consists, in fact, of the twenty-five communities, of which it is composed, and represented by twenty-five kings, dukes, princes, etc., and not by the 65,000,000 population of the communities themselves. The sovereignty rests with the princes of the several states, who have bestowed a fixed power upon the Kaiser. As Emperor his office dates back to 1871.

The legislative machinery which has been devised for the use of these German sovereigns consists of the Bundesrath and the Reichstag. Sometimes the Bundesrath is likened to our Senate, or to the hereditary English House of Lords, while the Reichstag is compared to the House of Representatives or the House of Commons. But comparisons are odious.

THE BUNDESRATH.

The Bundesrath is an assembly in which the German kings, grand dukes, dukes, princes, etc., come together (by proxy) to direct the affairs of the Empire. Each of these sovereigns sends a specified number of delegates, in accordance with the provisions of the constitution. Thus the Kaiser, as the King of Prussia, sends seventeen delegates, while the King of Bavaria sends six. The total number of delegates is fifty-eight, so right in the beginning the Kaiser has a pretty good representation.

The delegations in the Bundesrath vote en masse—that is the "unit rule" prevails. The seventeen delegates from Prussia must vote as instructed by the Kaiser, and if there chanced to be but one member present he still would cast seventeen votes for the delegation. The members of the Bundesrath are referred to quite frequently as ambassadors. There is no need for discussion in the body since the delegations vote, in any event, as a unit.

The power of the German Bundesrath is, however, astonishing. Usually the lower house is supposed to be the one in which originates legislation, such as finance, affecting the people. But in Germany it is the Bundesrath which has the power to tax, and the lower chamber, the Reichstag, merely has the vetoing power.

This makes the taxing power in Germany primarily the privilege of the crown.

The financial program is prepared by the Chancellor, who is the direct representative of the Kaiser, and responsible only to him. In other governments members of the ministry are appointed by the legislative bodies, but the Chancellor is personally named by the Kaiser, and is not even a member of the Reichstag. He has the right, however, to address this body, as the privilege of a member of the Bundesrath of which, as the personal representative of the Kaiser, he is the presiding officer.

Since the Bundesrath, as already shown, practically controls the German Empire, and the King of Prussia, with his seventeen votes in the Bundesrath holds sway in that body, it is easy to see how the Kaiser is the dominating figure in the German Empire.

THE KAISER'S DUAL PREROGATIVE.

A unique provision of the German constitution is that fourteen votes in the Bundesrath can defeat any proposed amendment, and since the Kaiser controls seventeen votes, as King of Prussia, besides several others, he has a voting strength which can block any attempt to change the regime. Also, as King of Prussia, he can instruct his Chancellor to prepare laws to be introduced in the Bundesrath.

It is the power which the Kaiser possesses, as the King of Prussia, which gives him his control as the German Emperor. Prussia is the largest of the German states, and when the Kaiser, as King of Prussia, says that he is master in Prussia, he speaks the truth.

There is a ministry in Prussia, and the head of this body is usually the same person who occupies the position of Imperial Chancellor, and the Kaiser appoints this Minister as well as his associates, whom he can remove without reference to the Ministry as a body. There are two chambers in Prussian Ministry commonly known as the House of Peers, and the House of Representatives.

Just to give the King of Prussia a little more control, he has the right to appoint all the members of the House of Peers, and also to designate the number. The House of Representatives, on the face of it, is a popular body, because the members are supposed to be elected by universal suffrage. The taxpayers vote for representation in this chamber, but they do not vote directly nor on equal terms.

Members of the House of Representatives are chosen by an electoral college, and several hundred of these colleges are selected at each election. Though taxpayers vote for the electors, all the votes do not have the same relative value. The taxpayers whose combined taxes represent one-third of the whole amount of taxes in an electoral district choose one-third of the members from that district to the House. Those who pay the next one-third of the taxes choose another third of the electors, and the remaining body of voters choose the last third.

CHAPTER XXIII
UNCLE SAM AND THE NEUTRALS.

WHEN America first declared its intentions there were in the United States thousands who held to the theory that "America in War" simply meant that we should shut ourselves within our borders, perhaps furnish supplies to the Allied forces, lend money to England, France, Belgium and Russia, use our navy to protect our merchant shipping and go about our business, leaving the fighting to the forces joined in conflict against Germany.

They were disabused when the English and French Commission and the representatives of Belgium and Russia made it apparent that it would be necessary for America to actually raise a fighting army and General Pershing was sent to France. But they learned, too, that mobilizing the forces of the country and waging warfare were not simple matters. The truth was brought home that the whole nation must fight; that it must use its brains, its money, its resources of every sort, its whole power, both in an offensive and in a defensive way.

Not only must its soldiers and sailors face the guns of the Teutons, but the machinery of government must be used to bring the arrogant Hohenzollerns to their knees. Some startling things were discovered, and the brains of the diplomatic force of the government were put to the test. International problems arose which were never before encountered in the history of nations.

England with its blockade against Germany, and Germany with its submarine warfare against British and neutral shipping, developed problems which had to be solved relative to keeping Germany from getting supplies which would enable her to withstand the siege, and also as to the sending of supplies to England, Belgium, France and Russia, and particularly to our own forces fighting with the Allies in France.

A BIG FACTOR IN WAR.

Unfortunate as it may seem, one of the biggest factors in waging successful war is to prevent the enemy from getting food supplies. It is a frequently repeated truism that "an army travels on its stomach," and in the pleas for conservation and efficient management the leaders in every country declared frequently that "the war would be won by the last loaf of bread," or that it was not a question of ammunition, but of wheat.

One of the serious problems which the government was therefore called to face within a very short period after the American troops were first landed in France was that of dealing with the food situation, both at home and abroad. At that time the German U-boats had sunk merchant ships having a total of more than 5,000,000 tonnage, and the food situation was precarious in the Allied countries. Germany, on the other hand, because of long preparation for the struggle, coupled with efficient management and practices, was more largely independent of other countries.

At this time it was learned that Germany was securing large quantities of foodstuffs through the medium of some of the neutral countries. America was, therefore, called upon to take steps to prevent the Germans getting supplies from this country, through the intermediary of Holland and the Scandinavian countries. As a result the government placed an embargo on a long list of articles including fuel, oils, grains, meats and fodder. The embargo, which was made effective by a proclamation of President Wilson, forbade the carrying of such supplies as were mentioned from the United States or its territorial possessions to neutral countries.

The purpose of the embargo was not to prevent the neutral countries from securing foodstuffs from America for their own consumption, but to prevent their reselling such supplies at a profit to Germany. The position of the government was made plain in the statement of President Wilson, who said:

DOMESTIC AND FOREIGN NEEDS.

"It is obviously the duty of the United States in liberating any surplus products over and above our own domestic needs to consider first the necessities of all the nations engaged in war against the central empires. As to neutral nations, however, we also recognize our duty. The government does not wish to hamper them. On the contrary, it wishes and intends, by all fair and equitable means, to co-operate with them in their difficult task of adding from our available surpluses to their own domestic supply and of meeting their pressing necessities or deficits. In considering the deficits of food supplies, the government means only to fulfill its obvious obligation to assure itself that neutrals are husbanding their own resources, and that our supplies will not become available, either directly or indirectly, to feed the enemy."

While the conservation of our resources had a great deal to do with the issuing of the embargo, the action was partly taken as the result of information lodged by England that Holland, Sweden and Norway had been supplying Germany and her allies with food, despite the latter's hostile action in sinking ships owned by the neutrals. The government made an investigation and discovered that the shipment to these neutral countries had become abnormally large. It was reported, particularly, that many Holland business men had become fabulously wealthy by trading in the supplies which came from America, and which they resold to Germany.

The embargo became operative under a method of license procedure, so that all shipments could be watched by the government authorities. The order compelled all persons seeking to export goods to make application for a license to the Secretary of Commerce, or bureaus designated in various parts of the country.

In support of the contentions that the neutral countries were supplying Germany, Great Britain furnished the Government with the following table as representing the minimum of food exports from Scandinavia and Holland to Germany in 1916: Butter, 82,600 metric tons; meat, 115,800 tons; pork products, 68,800 tons; condensed milk, 70,000 tons; fish, 407 tons; cheese, 80,500 tons; eggs, 46,400 tons; potato meal, 179,-500 tons; coffee, 58,500 tons; fruit, 74,000 tons; sugar, 12,000 tons; vegetables, 215,000.

These figures are most impressive, it is asserted, in relation to fats, the scarcest thing in Germany. Fat, it is claimed, is the only food seriously lacking now in the diet of the German people. Imports of this food, the British declare, furnish one-fourth of the daily German fat ration.

NATIONS WHO SUFFER FROM EMBARGO.

There are five neutral countries whose positions were anything but enviable during the war, and it is perhaps worth interpolating a little something about them at this particular point. Norway, Sweden, Holland, Denmark and Switzerland were the neutrals at the time the embargo was placed on foodstuffs.

Switzerland, as all the world knows, is one of the most picturesque countries in Europe, and is a republic in the west central part of the continent, bounded on the north by Baden, Wurtemburg and Bavaria; on the east by the Tyrol, on the south by Italy and on the west by France. There is no national tongue, three languages being spoken within the boundaries of the republic. Where it comes in contact with the French frontier, the French language is largely spoken; while Italian is the language spoken in the southern part, where it is bounded by Italy. In the northern section the German language is spoken. The country has an area of 15,992 square miles.

In the main, Switzerland is mountainous, the chief valley being that of the Rhone, in the southern part. The most level tracts are in the northwestern section, where there are a number of mountain-locked valleys. Mountain slopes comprise about two-fifths of the area of the country, and practically all of the rivers are rapid and unnavigable. The forests are extensive and consist of large trees. Cereals, along with hemp, flax and tobacco, are raised, and the pasture lands are fertile and abundant. Hence, the dairy products, as well as hides and tallow, are produced in profusion. Fruits of the hardier varieties grow well and profitably.

A FEDERAL UNION.

The republic consists of twenty-two States or Cantons which form a Federal Union, although each is virtually independent in matters of politics. The Swiss Constitution, remodelled in 1848, vests the ruling executive and legislative authority in a Diet of two houses—a State Council and a National Council. The former consists of 44 members—two from each Canton—and corresponds in its functional action with the United States Senate. The National Council is the more purely representative body, and is composed of 128 members elected triennially by popular suffrage. Both chambers combine and form what is called the Federal Assembly.

The chief executive power is exercised by the so-called Federal Council, or Bundesgericht, which is elected triennially. Its governing officers are the President and Vice President of the republic. International and inter-cantonal questions are discussed before and adjudicated by the Bundesgericht, which serves as a high court of appeal. The army consists of 142,999 regulars and 91,809 landwehr; total, 231,-808 men of all arms. Every adult citizen is de facto liable to military service, and military drill and discipline are taught in all the schools. The Protestant faith forms the ruling form of religion in 15 of the cantons, Roman Catholicism prevailing in the rest. Education is well diffused by numerous colleges and schools of a high grade; and its upper branches are cared for at the three universities of Berne, Basle and Zurich.

Denmark, whose home possessions comprise 14,789 square miles, is, by the way, barely one-half the size of Scotland. It consists of a peninsular portion called Jutland, and an extensive archipelago lying east of it. It has a number of territorial possessions in the Atlantic ocean, among them the islands of Iceland, Greenland and the Faroe islands in the north.

GERMAN AMBITION FRUSTRATED.

One of its possessions in the West Indies was purchased by the United States almost at the time America entered the war, and created a situation which was not calculated to inspire the friendship of Germany for the little country, since it was intimated that Germany would liked to have had the island for a base. The islands cost the United States about $25,000,-000. Including the colonial possessions, the total area of the Danish possessions is 80,000 square miles, the population being 2,726,000 persons.

Copenhagen is the capital, the other chief cities being Odense, Aarhuus, Aalborg, Randers and Horsens. For administrative purposes Denmark is divided into 18 provinces or districts, besides the capital, nine of these making up Jutland and the other nine comprising the island possessions. On the south Denmark is bounded by Germany and the Baltic, on the west it is washed by the North Sea; while to the north lies Norway, separated by the Skagerrack, and on the east lies Sweden, separated by the Cattegat and the Sound.

The line of seaboard is irregular and broken, and the low, flat nature of the country necessitates the construction of dykes, in many places, in order to prevent the ocean from making inroads. There are few rivers, and these are small and not of value commercially. Timber is not abundant, and minerals are scarce and of little value. The climate is generally moist and cold, fogs are frequent and the winters generally severe. Cereals, potatoes, wool and dairy products are the principal products. Cattle raising is carried on extensively, much of the beef being exported.

The Danes, physically, are sturdy, and represent the truest physical characteristics of Scandinavian types. The people are brave, sober and industrious, and the sailors from this country are among the leading navigators of the world. The government is a constitutional monarchy, with the executive power vested in a king and a ministry, who are held responsible to the Rigsdag, which is the parliament.

LANDSTHING AND FOLKSTHING.

This parliament consists of a Senate, or Landsthing, and a lower house, or Folksthing. The Evangelical Lutheran Church is the State religion, but all other persuasions are fully and freely tolerated. Education is compulsory, and is largely disseminated. The army consists of 60,000 men, while the navy is quite small, having a personnel of about 4000 officers and men.

The authentic history dates from 1385, the year of the accession of Margaret, the "Semiramis of the North," and wearer of the triple Scandinavian crowns. The latest monarch, Frederick VIII, came to the throne in 1906.

Holland, the most picturesque of the neutral countries, aside from Switzerland with its wonderful scenery, is credited with having profited very largely by the war. It rests along the North Sea and adjoins the German Empire on the east and borders Belgium on the South. It contains about 11 provinces, with a total area of 12,582 square miles and a population of about 6,000,000.

Always one thinks of windmills, dykes, fat cattle, butter,

eggs, ducks and green farms when Holland is mentioned, and it is in many respects one of the most highly developed commercial countries in the world. The country manufactures many articles of world-wide distribution, including chocolate, linens, fine damasks, pottery, chemical and pharmaceutical products, and Amsterdam is a center of diamond-cutting.

It has a large mercantile marine and was at one time a termendous maritime power, doing an immense trading business in many waters. It still has rich and extensive colonies, including the Dutch possessions in the East Indies, comprising the Sunda Islands, except a portion of Borneo and Eastern Timor, and New Guinea. Java and Madura are two of the richest of the group and have a population of more than 30,000,000. There are also possessions in the West Indies and in South America.

A SMALL BUT EFFICIENT ARMY.

The Dutch army has approximately 40,000 officers and men and is regarded as one of the most efficient armies in the world of its size. There is also a colonial army in the East Indies with 1300 officers and 35,183 men. Its navy has 4000 officers and men and has about 200 vessels of all sorts, none of them of the modern dreadnought or super-dreadnought type.

The history of the rich little country is one of the most interesting in literature. It was originally part of the Empire of Charlemagne. Subsequently, it became divided into a number of petty principalities, and by heritage became a possession of the Austrian monarchy. In the long struggle against the Spanish power it became one of the Seven United Provinces. The country made rapid progress, and during the 17th century withstood the power of Louis the XIV of France, but later was overrun by the French, and finally in 1806 was made a kingdom by Napoleon, in favor of his brother Louis. Under the Treaty of Paris Belgium and Holland were united to form the Kingdom of the Netherlands, and this arrangement remained until 1830, when Belgium broke away. Holland attempted to reduce the revolting province by force, but the powers intervened and an adjustment was made. The last King was William, III, who died in 1890, leaving his daughter Wilhelmina, then but 10 years old, Queen.

Of the neutral countries none endured more than heroic Norway. With a long coast line practically undefended and with the full force of the German navy anchored but a few hours away, and a none too friendly country on her land border, possessing an army greater than her own, Norway's position was extremely difficult.

Had she flung herself into the war with the Allies when the breach came she would have been of little help to them, for she would have placed them in the position of being called upon to help defend her long coast line. It is probable also that a break with Germany would have let loose the Swedish army on the side of the Teutons.

BETWEEN TWO FIRES.

The little country was between two fires, and she suffered great strain. In the first place, while Norway attempted to maintain her export trade and her shipping, the Allies inspected her import invoices and subjected her to much annoyance, while Germany, without provocation, ruthlessly attacked her merchant ships and sent many of them to the bottom of the ocean.

There were intimations that Germany's real intent was to precipitate a rupture which would justify her attack on the little country, which she would be able to subdue with ease and seize the rugged coast and ports of vantage. But Norway remained neutral, and was not at all pleased with the embargo placed upon shipments by the United States, though it developed that the restrictions would not prevent the country from getting its share of grain and other supplies from America.

Norway is the western portion of the Scandinavian peninsula, and has an area of about 125,000 square miles. Its northern coast is washed by the cold waters of the Arctic Ocean, and against the northeast is Lapland, while Sweden bounds it on the east and the famed North Sea on the south and the broad Atlantic on the west.

The rugged country is separated from Sweden by the Kiolen, or the Great Scandinavian chain of mountains, and in the hills and mountains are found the wonderful Norway spruce and fir trees familiar in commerce. Its fisheries and shipbuilding industry are also of great importance in the world of business.

DEMOCRACY OF NORWAY.

The constitution of Norway is one of the most Democratic in all Europe. Although a monarchy, its executive and legislative power is vested in the parliament, called the Storthing, and the King has merely a nominal command over the army and navy, with power to appoint the governor-general only. The latter has a limited right to veto acts of the parliament. Hereditary nobility was abolished in 1821.

Under the treaty of Vienna in 1814, and following the defeat of Napoleon, it was arranged that Denmark must give up Norway, and the two countries were united under the Swedish Crown. Norway demanded a separate consular service in 1905, and the Storthing declared the union with Sweden at an end. Prince Charles of Denmark then became King, reigning as Haakon VII.

The country has a population of 2,340,000, and her full military force mobilized for war is only 110,000 men.

Sweden, Norway's next-door neighbor on the Scandinavian peninsula, in contradistinction to the latter, is a constitutional monarchy, with extraordinary powers vested in the King, who is assisted in the administration of affairs by a council of ministers. The Diet, or legislature, consists of two chambers, or estates, both elected by the people.

Like Norway, the country is very rugged. Lapland and Finland are at the northeast, and on the east is the Gulf of Bothnia and the Baltic, and on the south the Baltic, the Sound and the Cattegat. It joins Norway on the west. Its area is 172,875 square miles, and its coast line is more than 1400 miles long.

Sweden, while it does not have a first-class navy, possesses a score of armored vessels of small displacement, besides torpedo boats, destroyers, etc., and has an army of 40,000 at peace strength. The country is particularly rich in minerals, and some of the finest iron ore in the world comes from its mines. Nickel, lead, cobalt, alum and sulphur are also produced in large quantities; while it gives to the world, too, immense quantities of lumber and larger quantities of hemp, flax and hops.

The reigning monarch is King Gustavus V, who succeeded his father, Oscar II, who died in 1907. The population of the country is about 5,000,000.

Of these neutrals, both Holland and Switzerland did a great deal for the suffering Belgians when Germany pounded through the country of King Albert, sending money for the relief of the sufferers and offering refugees shelter.

CHAPTER XXIV.

THE ACTIONS OF THE WAR.

FROM BOSNIA TO FLANDERS—MARNE THE TURNING POINT OF THE CONFLICT—THE
CONQUESTS OF SERVIA AND RUMANIA—THE FALL OF BAGDAD—RUSSIA'S
WOMEN SOLDIERS—AMERICA'S CONSCRIPTS.

THE end of August, 1917, found twenty-one nations in a state of war and five in what might be termed a condition of modified neutrality, with nearly 40,000,000 summoned to arms and 5,000,000 killed in bitter warfare.

This was the fiery reflection of the shots which caused the death of the Archduke Francis Ferdinand, of Austria, in the quiet little town of Serajevo, the capital of Bosnia, in June, 1914. And so, with their backs to the wall, Austria-Hungary, Germany, Turkey and Bulgaria faced Servia, Russia, France, Belgium, Great Britain, Montenegro, Japan, Italy, Portugal, Rumania, the United States, Cuba, Brazil, Greece, Siam, China and little Liberia, while Guatemala, Panama, Haiti, Uruguay and Bolivia stood by in a position of neutrality, but for the most part indicating a willingness to help the Allies.

And in those elapsed three years after the Bosnia tragedy an Emperor of Austria had died; a Czar had stepped from his throne, and a King had been compelled to toss aside his crown. Prime Ministers and Ministers of War in all of the principal countries, who held the confidence of their peoples when the war started, were no more.

Cabinets had been dissolved and new ones set up, statesmen brushed aside and commanders of the war forces compelled to step out that others might carry on the battles.

Though it was Austria's ultimatum to Servia which precipitated the world-wide struggle, it was Germany that took the first step and crossed the French frontier with its armed forces. After Servia refused to accede to all of the demands of Austria-Hungary and war had formally been declared by the latter country, Russia began a partial mobilization of her armed forces, since she had given warning that she would extend protection to Servia. Germany retaliated by calling together her warring forces and declaring war on the Czar; France came to Russia's aid. Then when Belgium refused to permit the German army to pass through the country and Germany disregarded international treaties and invaded the territory, Great Britain declared war upon the Kaiser, and Montenegro aligned itself with the Allies.

GERMANY'S DESIGNS ON PARIS.

Germany's action and subsequent events prove that the war lords had planned to capture Paris by a swift attack from the north, before France could gather her forces to resist and before Russia was prepared to assist. Belgium, however, proved a stumbling block. The natives, battling like demons for the protection of their homes and honor, held the Teuton hordes at Liege for several weeks, or until the famous fortifications there were reduced, and then the terrible machine of the Germans swept forward until the soldiers were within fifteen miles of the French capital.

It was here, within a few hours' march of Paris, that the French and Allied troops showed their real metal. General Joffre met the German hordes beside the River Marne and with his troops began the battle which was to guarantee the security of the French capital and result in the routing of the army of Von Kluck, regarded as the pick of the Prussian forces. In the famed battle of the Marne there were fought a number of separate engagements, which have been termed the battles of Meaux, Sezanne, Vitry and Argonne.

The German forces were driven back step by step to the north bank of the Aisne, where the army was able to entrench itself and the Germans and the Allied forces began digging themselves into the ground in a manner that had never before been practised in warfare.

While Germany was striking at France, the Russians had invaded Austria, capturing Tarnapol and Lemberg and investing the great fortress of Prezemsyl. Austria was compelled to call upon Germany for assistance and four German army corps, under Von Hindenburg, were drawn from East Prussia and went to the rescue. Instead of trying to stem the progress of the Russians, he made a counter offensive with Warsaw as the objective. Russia was compelled for a time to abandon its positions and retreat, and Von Hindenburg got within seven miles of Warsaw before the Russians rode down upon his forces with 100,000 horsemen and compelled retreat. Von Hindenburg's strategy had, however, been successful, and his action on the Eastern front at this time marked the first step toward his pre-eminence as a military commander.

BRITISH AND GERMAN FORCES COMPARED.

During 1915 the Allied forces were able to do little more than hold their positions. Lord Kitchener had builded up a British volunteer army in which great hopes were placed, but in the matter of offensive military tactics they could not cope with the formidable German forces, nor had the Allies developed an offensive which would win without terrible sacrifice, and in the encounters the very flower of Great Britain's manhood, as well as thousands of the best fighting men of France, were lost to the world forever. It was in this year, when Germany made use of asphyxiating gas for the first time, that Canada received its most stinging blow. The famous Princess Pats, the finest military body of the Dominion, was practically annihilated, and in the final formidable attack of the year made by the French against the Germans in September, the latter were driven back several miles, but at a cost of more than 100,000 French lives.

In this year, too, the Germans succeeded in capturing much territory and a number of valuable positions which had been taken by the Russians, and the combined forces of Von Hindenburg and Von Mackensen finally conquered Poland. Warsaw was evacuated in July, and in August Prince Leopold led the Bavarian into the Polish capital. On August 19 the great stronghold of Kovno fell, and the conquest was made complete with the surrender of Brest-Litovsk.

CONQUEST OF SERVIA.

The conquest of Servia by the Teutons also marked the year 1915. Among the first shots of the war were those fired by the Austrians when they bombarded Belgrade, the capital of Servia, and made an attempt to invade the country. The Servians and Montenegrins almost annihilated Austrian troops which attempted to cross the Danube into Servia, and the Austrian invasion fell. But the combined Austro-German forces invaded the country later as part of the Prussian program to conquer all the territory from the Baltic to the Bosporus. The Entente Allies made an effort to save the little country by landing troops at Salonica, but it was too late. Just before winter set in, the Austro-German forces and the Bulgarian forces, invading from opposite sides, met, and the conquest of the country was complete.

It was in 1915, too, that what is conceded to have been one of the most disastrous and futile campaigns of the war was attempted by England. Constantinople was to be captured and the Turks crushed, with a view of opening communication with Russia by way of the Black Sea. The British fleet was sent out to bombard the Dardanelles, and the now famous Anzacs—Australian and New Zealand troops—were landed on the peninsula of Gallipoli to strike at the Turkish capital from behind. The campaign was waged through the summer, but with little hope of success, and finally abandoned after the

British had lost more than 100,000 of its most daring, hard-fighting and loyal Colonial soldiers.

After this came "Verdun"—that conflict in which France won immortal glory and the German's attack upon the French fortress town of Verdun was successfully repulsed. The battle raged for four months, beginning in February, 1916. The German troops, with the German Crown Prince in command, captured two forts close to Verdun, but little by little the French troops drove them back, and finally, in command of General Nivelle, with General Petain looking after the defense of Verdun, the French, co-operating with the British, made an attack on the Somme, and the Germans were compelled to abandon the Verdun offensive. In the Verdun campaign the Germans lost more than 500,000 men, while the French lost not half the number.

RUSSIA'S CONQUEST OF ARMENIA.

Russia's conquest of Armenia was one of the features of 1916. The troops under General Brussiloff renewed their endeavors in Galicia and for several months made great progress; then Rumania entered the war and the Russian forces in Galicia slowed down. In Caucasus, however, Russian troops gained Erzerum, one of the Turk fortresses, and captured the seaport of Trebizond, practically gaining Armenia. Like the Germans in retreat from Flanders, the Turks practiced unspeakable horrors. Their cruelties were such as to almost exterminate the race.

The tragedy of the Balkans in 1916 was Rumania. With an army of more than half a million men, she entered the war with the approval of the Entente and entered Transylvania. But the Germans began a counter-attack in Dobrudja, and the Rumanians were compelled to withdraw some of their forces from Transylvania. The German commander then threw his forces across the remaining Rumanians and drove them across the border, after which he swung his own troops through the mountain passes into Rumania. The two German forces invading Rumania met at Bucharest, and the Rumanian capital was occupied.

Another fiasco was that of the British expeditionary force which was sent from India by way of the Persian Gulf and up the Tigris river to Bagdad. General Townsend succeeded in getting within 15 miles of Bagdad, but he was defeated by a superior Turkish force and compelled to fall back to Kut-el-Amara. Here his inadequate force, lacking medical and transport facilities, was fairly starved out before he was relieved. He was finally compelled to surrender the last week in April, 1916.

Little more than a year after the collapse of this expedition, however, the famous old city of Bagdad was captured by the English after a well-directed campaign under General Maude.

ITALY S HELP TO THE ALLIES.

Italy, having begun active warfare with the Allies in 1915, waged war along the Austrian border, compelling the Austro-German forces to concentrate a larger body of troops for duty on the Italian frontier, and to that extent materially assisted the Allies. At the same time the Italians fought their way up over the mountains and won more than 500 square miles of territory and took nearly 90,000 prisoners.

The final alignment of the Greeks with the Allies marked the progress of affairs in the middle of 1917, when Constantine was forced from his throne in favor of his second son, and Venizelos was returned as Premier. But the entrance of the Greeks did not materially alter the situation.

The two most important events of 1917 were the entrance of America into the conflict and the revolt in Russia, which caused the abdication of the Czar and turned the great country into a republic. The ultimate in Russia's history is still to be written, but the change was fraught with disaster. The people let free, and unaccustomed to self-government, could not be controlled, and the army became demoralized.

The element which had been loyal to the Romanoffs refused to fight for liberty, and the Germans, taking advantage of the situation, drove the Russian troops back over the frontiers and gained all that the Russians had once taken in conflict. And out of this grew one of the most picturesque incidents of the entire war. Russian women and girls, filled with ideals and with a deep sense of the responsibilities which rested upon the nation, formed a corps, and, dressed in full military costume, went to the front and attacked the German troops. No soldiers of any nation have shown more heroism, or more capability, for the women faced the bullets, and, while they were being mowed down by the German guns, they urged their men to face the enemy and fight—fight—fight.

BRITISH NAVY AN EFFECTIVE ASSET.

While there have been few of the picturesque battles on the seas, which the world has long regarded as a necessary adjunct to a successful war, the work of the British Navy has proved through the period of the conflict to be one of the most powerful and effective assets of the Allied forces. Through the operation of the British fleet, later augmented by an American war fleet, the German ships have been corked up in their home ports and chased from the seas.

The first naval battle of the war was an engagement between portions of the British squadron in the Pacific and a superior German force. The engagement occurred off the coast of Chili in November, 1915. Two British vessels were lost and a third badly damaged. However, a few months later, the German squadron, in command of Admiral von Spee, was met off the Falkland Islands by a second British squadron, and in the engagement four of the German vessels were sunk and a fifth damaged. This vessel was later sunk.

The most important naval engagement was the battle of

Jutland in May, 1916, when Admiral Beatty met a German fleet in the North Sea. The German boats made a dash from the Kiel canal and engaged the British off the coast of Denmark. Both England and Germany claimed victory, the former declaring that Germany lost eighteen ships, while the German Government claimed that the British lost fifteen vessels. Berlin admitted a loss of 60,720 tons and 3966 men, while England conceded a loss of more than 114,000 tons and 5613 men. But the English fleet which engaged the German fighting ships was but a small portion of the force on guard outside of Helgoland and the Kiel Canal, and the effect was to keep the German navy from venturing forth again.

These are the main events which had punctuated the action of the world's fighting machines at the close of August, 1917, when America was preparing to thwart the German U-boats in their destruction of the world's shipping, and had under actual call to arms more than 1,000,000 men, a minor part of which had been safely landed in France.

WORLD'S AWFUL MARITIME LOSS.

In the three months prior to August the German underseas boats had sunk 464 vessels, or an average of 426,000 tons of shipping a month, while America, working with her fleets in conjunction with the British Navy to foil the submarine in its endeavors, was also building more than 12,000 cargo-carrying craft and submarine chasers with which to flood the traffic lanes of the sea.

Likewise, contracts had been awarded for 10,000 flying machines with which to drive the "eyes of the German army," as the air machines are called, from the heavens. Finally, as the Allies in the closing days of August were driving the German hordes back under avalanches of shells, 629,000 of the youth of America, called to fight under the conscript act, were preparing to move to camps in a dozen different sections of the country to train themselves for invading foreign countries and facing the brutal Teutons. Likewise, some 20,000 picked men were training to officer these civilian forces, and half a million men of the National Guards of the various States, formally mustered into the service of the country, were moving by orders of the Government to points whence they would find their way to the side of the loyal French soldiers and the sturdy English, Scotch, Canadian, Australian and virile Italian fighters.

The records of three years show that the American ambulance drivers; daring thousands of our countrymen who fought with the French and English because they believed the war was a just one, and without compulsion; scores of Red Cross nurses, and aviators who hunted the Teutons in the air, all Americans, have had their names written high in the roster of heroes. Americans have always been pioneers and history makers, and they are making history now.

With the approach of cold weather, and following months of intensive training under the direction of French and English soldiers, the American expeditionary forces began actual participation in the great world war as a unit. Previously their achievements were principally in connection with the French aviation corps and ambulance sections.

SINKING OF FIRST AMERICAN WAR BOAT.

The first untoward incident involving America's forces on land or sea was the sinking of the transport Antilles on October 27, 1917, by a German submarine, when 67 men—officers, seamen and soldiers—were lost. The vessel was returning from a French port after having landed troops and supplies. This was the first loss sustained by the United States, and the event brought home the seriousness of the country's participation in the war as no previous event had done.

Almost immediately following this the world awoke one morning to learn that silently and unheralded the American soldiers had marched from their quarters in a French village to the "front" and in a slough of mud had entered the trenches, and for the first time in history United States troops launched shells against the forces of Germany.

The initial shot was fired bv artillerists at the break of day on October 24, and America was formally made an active agent in the horrors of warfare on "No Man's Land." Ten days later the brave Americans, occupying a position in the trenches for instruction, early on the morning of Saturday, November 3, received their baptism of fire, and in the cause of Democracy 3 soldiers were killed, 5 wounded and 12 captured by the Boche forces.

Cut off from the main line of the Allied forces, the Americans were stormed under the protection of a heavy barrage fire by a German raiding party and engaged in a desperate hand-to-hand encounter. The 20 Americans, with several French instructors, according to official report, were pitted against 210 picked Germans. A rain of shells from Boche guns was laid back of the American section so that there was no retreat. The lieutenant in command made a heroic attempt to reach the main fighting line, but was caught in the barrage fire and rendered unconscious from shell-shock.

Previously American scouts had captured a German prisoner—a mail runner; Lieutenant de Vere H. Harden, of the Signal Corps had been wounded by a bursting German shell, and a German gunner was reported killed by an American sharpshooter, as opening incidents of the skirmish.

And so at the beginning of November, 1917, with the whole United States giving support to the Government in subscribing upwards of five billions of dollars to the second Liberty Loan, and all forces working to conserve food, furnish men, ships, ammunition, clothing and supplies to her own troops and to her Allies, the world found America true to traditions, battling for the right and giving her best that liberty might endure and the burden of Prussianism be lifted from humanity.

CHAPTER XXV.

AMERICAN FORCES BECOME FACTOR.

UNITED STATES SOLDIERS INSPIRED ALLIED TROOPS—RUSSIAN GOVERNMENT COL-
LAPSES—ITALIAN ARMY FAILS—ALLIED WAR COUNCIL FORMED—FOCH COM-
MANDS ALLIED ARMIES—PERSHING OFFERS AMERICAN TROOPS—UNDER FIRE—
U-BOAT BASES RAIDED BY BRITISH.

THE influence exerted by the actual presence of the American troops on the western front was soon apparent. The spirits of the English, French and Canadian troops were raised and the presence of the Americans was heralded to the world as an evidence of complete unity on the part of the Allies that meant ultimate death to Kaiserism.

The advent of Uncle Sam's fighting men on the firing line had, however, one serious effect, viewed from the Allied standpoint. Germany realized that every day she delayed in making attack meant the strengthening of the Allied forces by the arrival of additional United States troops, and it was seen by the English and French leaders that the Kaiser would make an early drive to annihilate, if possible, the stubbornly resisting, though somewhat tired and weakened, lines opposing his brutal soldiery. Not for months, therefore, was it permitted the world to know anything about the numerical strength of the American troops sent into France.

Simultaneously with the action of American troops in entering the resisting line of Allied troops on the western front the Austro-German troops had swept into the Italian plains, capturing 100,000 prisoners and upward of 1,000 guns, taking several towns and compelling the retreat of the Second and Third Italian armies. The Italian forces were opposed by four times their number, but it was also said that the unity of the Italian forces was broken by the spreading of German propaganda.

401

The failure of some of the troops was shown in an official dispatch from Rome, in which it was stated:

"The failure to resist on the part of some units forming our second army, which in cowardice retired without fighting or surrendered to the enemy, allowed the Austro-German forces to break into our left wing on the Julian front. The valiant efforts of other troops did not enable them to prevent the enemy from advancing into the sacred soil of our fatherland. We now are withdrawing our line according to the plan prepared. All stores and depots in the evacuated places were destroyed."

ITALIAN HEADQUARTERS CAPTURED.

These troops were compelled to fall back along a front almost 125 miles long and Undine, the Italian headquarters, was captured. Germany had found the weakest spot in the Italian line and occupied about 1,000 square miles of territory before General Cadorna's forces were able to establish a line of strong defense.

The retirement of the Italian troops was one of the most picturesque in the history of the war, and Germany made her gains at terrible cost.

The retirement was accompanied by shielding operations of the rear guard, which poured a deadly fire into the advancing columns and at the same time destroyed powder depots, arsenals and bridges with the double purpose of giving time for the withdrawal of the Italian heavy guns and of preventing military stores falling into the hands of the enemy.

The Germans encountered stubborn resistance on the Bainsizza plateau, and heaps of enemy dead marked the lines of their advance. Around Globo ridge a bersaglieri brigade, outnumbered five to one, held back the enemy while the main line had an opportunity to get its retreat in motion. In one of the mountain passes a small village commanding the pass was taken and retaken eight times during desperate artillery, infantry and hand-to-hand fighting.

Before the Italians were able to establish a line of resistance they were compelled to fall back to the Piave, and at some points to a much greater distance.   Meantime the Allies rushed assistance to the retiring forces, and while the collapse of Cadorna's line was unfortunate, it had the effect of making it more obvious that there should be more unity of operation between the Allied forces.

Russia's republic, under the leadership of Premier Kerensky, collapsing at the same moment, intensified the seriousness of the Allied situation, and largely at the suggestion of America an Inter-Allied War Council was formed.

REVOLT IN PETROGARD.

Premier Kerensky called upon the United States to help Russia bear the burdens of conflict until the forces could be reorganized by the new government.   Almost immediately there was revolt in Petrograd, and the radicals under the leadership of Leon Trotsky, president of the Executive Committee of the Petrograd Council of Soldiers' and Workmen's Delegates, seized the telegraph wires, the State bank and Marie Palace, where the preliminary parliament had suspended proceedings in view of the situation.

The Workmen's and Soldiers' Delegates assumed control of the City of Petrograd and Kerensky was compelled to flee. The Winter Palace was bombarded.   A General Council of the Soldiers' and Workmen's Delegates announced the taking over of government authority:

"We plan to offer an immediate armistice of three months, during which elected representatives from all nations and not the diplomats are to settle the questions of peace," said Nikolai Lenine, the Maximalist leader, in a speech before the Workmen's and Soldiers' Congress today.

"We offer these terms," M. Lenine added, "but we are

willing to consider any proposals for peace, no matter from which side. We offer a just peace, but will not accept unjust terms."

Meantime General Cadorna was relieved of command of the Italian armies and General Diaz put at the head of the Italian forces, while General Foch, chief of staff of the French War Ministry, and General Wilson, sub-chief of the British Staff, were made members of an Inter-Allied Military Committee serving with General Cadorna to straighten out the Italian situation. This was the first step looking to the unifying of the Allied forces which was brought about shortly thereafter by the formation of the Inter-Allied War Council at Versailles. It was chiefly at the suggestion of President Wilson that the War Council was called, the President issuing a stirring appeal in which he pointed out the necessity of unity of control, if the resources of the United States were to be of the greatest value to the Allied interests.

SUPREME WAR COUNCIL.

The Supreme War Council, which was made a permanent body, was composed of the Prime Minister and a member of the Government of each of the Great Powers whose armies were fighting at the front. Each Power delegated to the Supreme Council a permanent military representative whose function was to act as adviser to the Council. As the result of the deliberations of the War Council, and following the suggestion of General Pershing, General Foch was made Commander-in-Chief of the Allied Armies. General Foch was Commander of the French troops at Verdun and a recognized authority on military strategy.

While the problem of solving the military phases of the situation was being considered by the Allied War Council the Russian forces under Kerensky and those under Trotzky, known as the Bolsheviki, clashed again and again at Petrograd, Moscow and other points, and the hope of the Allies as to any help from Russia sank. Germany entered into a peace compact with Ukrainia, and the hand of the Kaiser was seen in the Russian situation when officers of the German Army were reported in Petrograd in conference with the representatives of the various Russian factions. Russia suggested a separate armistice, or a separate peace, against which both the U. S. and France protested.

The failure of the Russian Government to assume any degree of stability made it possible for the Germans to withdraw many troops and transfer them to the Italian and Western Fronts.

One result of the Allied War Council deliberations was to show the necessity of rapid action on the part of the United States and get troops into France so that they might take over a definite sector. While it was estimated that several hundred thousand Americans were in France, the necessity for a larger force was made apparent by the statement that 90 reserves are required for every 400 fighters on the line.

DROPPED THEIR TOOLS FOR RIFLES.

The first bitter attack in which American troops figured was when a company of United States engineers, caught between crossfires, dropped their tools for rifles and joined the English troops in helping to repulse the Germans near Cambrai.

A notable event in the progress of the war was the declaration of war upon Austria by the U. S. on Dec. 8, 1917, Congress adopting a resolution of war with but one dissenting vote.

Events which brought the seriousness of the war home to America began at this point to occur rapidly. First the Torpedo Boat Destroyer Jacob Jones was sunk in the war zone when nearly 30 men were reported lost. This was followed shortly by a report to the War Department that 17 Americans caught in the crossfire by the Germans at Cambrai were missing or killed. The report of the sinking of the Alcedo, a patrol boat, with the loss of several officers, was also received, as was that of the sinking of the U. S. Destroyer "Chauncey" rammed in a collision, when two officers and eighteen men were lost.

One of the high spots of the war and one of the notable events in the history of the world, was the surrender of the City of Jerusalem to the British on Saturday, December 8, 1917. Gen. Allenby entered the famed city and established his troops on the ancient Jerico Road.

The capture of Jerusalem by the British forces marked the end, with two brief interludes, of more than 1200 years' possession of the seat of the Christian religion by the Mohammedans. For 673 years the Holy City had been in disputed ownership of the Turks, the last Christian ruler of Jerusalem being the German Emperor, Frederick, whose short-lived domination lasted from 1229 to 1244.

THE FALL OF JERUSALEM.

Apart from its connection with the campaign being waged against Turkey by the British in Mesopotamia, the fall of Jerusalem marked the definite collapse of the long-protracted efforts of the Turks to capture the Suez Canal and invade Egypt. Almost the first move made by Turkey after her entrance into the war was a campaign against Egypt across the great desert of the Sinai Peninsula. In November, 1914, a Turkish army, variously estimated at from 75,000 to 250,000 men, marched on the Suez Canal and succeeded in reaching within striking distance of the great artificial waterway at several points. For several months bitter fighting took place, the canal being defended by an Anglo-Egyptian army aided by Australians and New Zealanders and French and British forces.

For the greater part of 1915 conflicting reports of the situation were received from the belligerents, but in December of that year definite information showed that the Turks had been driven back as far as El Arish, about eighty-five miles east of the canal. A lull occurred then which lasted for six months, and in June, 1916, the Turks again advanced as far at Katieh, about fifteen miles east of the canal. Here they were decisively defeated, losing more than 3000 prisoners and a great quantity of equipment.

Another period followed in which the situation was greatly confused through the vagueness and contradictory character of the official statements, but in December, 1916, the British stormed El Arish and a few days later severely defeated the Turks at Maghdabah, about sixty miles to the south on the same front. Two weeks later the invaders had been driven out of Egypt and the British forces crossed the border into Palestine. On March 7 they captured El Khulil, southeast of Gaza.

By November 22 the British had pushed within five miles of Jerusalem, on the northwest, and on December 7 General Allenby announced that he had taken Hebron. Jerusalem thus was virtually cut off on all sides but the east.

HISTORICAL INTEREST TO CHRISTIANS.

In sentimental and romantic aspect the capture of Jerusalem far exceeds even the fall of fable-crowned Bagdad. The modern City of Jerusalem contains about 60,000 inhabitants, and is the home of pestilence, filth and fevers, but in historic interest it natually surpasses, to the Christian world, all other places in the world. Since the days when David wrested it from the hands of the Jebusites to make it the capital of the Jewish race Jerusalem has been the prize and prey of half the races of the world. It has passed successively into the hands of the Assyrians, Babylonians, Greeks, Romans, Persians, Arabs, Turks, the Crusaders, finally to fall before the descendants of that Richard the Lion-hearted who strove in vain for its possession more than 700 years ago.

Early in January, 1918, evidence was forthcoming that Germany was preparing to make a final drive on the Western Front to break through and capture some English and

French channel ports before America could be of any great assistance to the Allied forces. As a result Great Britain determined to call 500,000 more men to hold the Huns, and Premier Lloyd George issued a stirring appeal to Labor affected by the Man-Power Bill, which provided for the increase taken largely from the labor forces.

The German intent to launch an offensive was indicated by the withdrawal of German lines north of Italy when important defensive positions were abandoned, and dummy soldiers were left in trench to conceal movement to the rear. Warnings of a great submarine offensive on American boat-lines to France, to be joined with a big drive on land, were received by Secretary of War Baker, and on February 2, the American troops occupying a sector of the Lorraine front in France faced the first big bombardment in what was preliminary to the most bitter drive Germany had attempted in four years of warfare.

SINKING OF THE TUSCANIA.

True to their promise the German submarines started their portion of the offensive and sunk the U. S. troopship "Tuscania" a few days later off the coast of Ireland. The liner carried 2,179 U. S. troops of various divisions besides a crew of 200. The total number of persons lost was 113. The troops included engineers, members of the aero-squadron, and regulars.

The Tuscania was the first troopship to be sunk en route to France, though the Antilles was sunk in October, 1917. This boat, however, it must be noted, was returning from France. At this time 70 lives were lost. The comparatively small loss of life on the "Tuscania" was accepted as evidence of the efficient training and bravery of American troops under all conditions.

The Tuscania was torpedoed when entering what until that time were considered comparatively safe waters. The ships were within sight of land, which was just distinguish-able in the dusk of evening when the torpedo hit the Tuscania amidships. This was at about 7 o'clock.

When the crash came the khaki-clad young heroes of the American army lined up as though on parade, and sang the "Star Spangled Banner" at the top of their voices as the Tuscania sank by inches under them. Across from them their British cousins of the crew came back with the echo-ing "God Save the King," which too cool-headed exponents of what occurred in a crisis of a sea disaster say accounts for the fact the Germans took only a toll of 113 lives out of the 2,397 souls on board the Cunarder when she met her fate.

AMERICAN COURAGE PRAISED.

If the singing man is a fighting man, he also is hopeful, and in the combination of fight and hope there came the baf-fling of the German attempt to reduce the American war forces by almost a full regiment. Taking stock after the disaster, the officers of both the army and navy praised the courage of the Americans as the chief reason for the saving of more than 90 per cent of the men on board.

No submarine was seen until the torpedo struck the Tus-cania fairly amidships. A moment later another torpedo passed astern of the vessel. There was a terrific explosion, and it is believed most of the casualties were caused by this and by subsequent difficulties in lowering the boats.

The vessel immediately took a heavy list and the men were called to their lifeboat stations, but the list prevented the boats from being properly lowered, some of the upper-deck boats falling to the lower deck. Many of the men jumped into the water, and the difficulty in lowering the boats was re-sponsible for many casualties.

The survivors of the Tuscania landed at points in Ireland were received with great honor in the various communities, and great tribute was paid to the surviving soldiers by the Mayor of Dublin.

The American troops on the Tuscania were part of the forces being hurried to France to hold the Germans in check, and at the time American troops were holding a sector with the French in Lorraine, northwest of Toul, while American artillery were supporting the French in Champagne. The date set for the big German drive was announced as January 28, and the fact that Germany made an open proclamation of the fact that they proposed to wage offensive warfare was somewhat puzzling to the minds of those studying the situation. Making her position more impregnable, Germany halted her armies in Russia upon the acceptance of peace terms by the Russian delegation at Brest-Litovsk, which were concluded on March 1, 1918, and daily the activities of the German forces on the Western Front grew in intensity. On March 6, in anticipation of the drive, it was for the first time publicly stated that 81,000 troops of American soldiers were holding an eight mile line on the Lorraine front, with three full divisions in the trenches. The gathering together of this force and other American troops in France drew Secretary of War Baker to the scene of activities. He was the first American Cabinet officer to cross the ocean after America entered the war.

SEIZURE OF ALL DUTCH VESSELS.

Holland having proved herself unwilling to come to a satisfactory agreement at this time on the British-American demand regarding the use of ships, President Wilson ordered the seizure of all Dutch vessels within the territorial jurisdiction of the United States; the Allies ordered a similar seizure abroad. The President's proclamation authorized the navy to take over the vessels to be equipped and operated by the Navy Department and the Shipping Board. A total of 77 ships were added to the American Merchant Marine.

Holland's failure to act was on the propositions that the United States and the Allies should facilitate the importation into Holland of foodstuffs, and other commodities required to maintain her economic life, and that Holland should restore her Merchant Marine to a normal condition of activity.

On March 21 the greatest German offensive of the war actually began on a front 50 miles long, running west and southwest of Cambrai. The preliminary German bombardment covered a front from the River Serre below St. Quentin, and the River Scarpe east of Arras.

FIERCEST BATTLE IN WORLD'S HISTORY.

Field Marshal Haig's report from British headquarters in France described the German offensive as comprising an intense bombardment by the artillery and a powerful infantry attack on a front of more than fifty miles. Some of the British positions were penetrated, but the German losses were exceptionally heavy.

It was reported at the end of the first day that the fiercest battle of the world's history was in progress, and that 80,000 Germans were lost in battle; while Berlin reported the capture of 16,000 Allied prisoners and 200 guns.

The Associated Press correspondent reported that at least forty divisions of German soldiers were identified as actively participating in the attack. No such concentration of artillery had been seen since the war began. The enemy had 1,000 guns in one small sector—one for every twelve yards. The Germans in many sections attacked in three waves of infantry, followed up by shock troops. As a result they suffered very heavy casualties.

The German massed artillery was badly hammered by the British guns.

In the first stage of their offensive the Germans failed badly in the execution of their program, as was attested by captured documents showing what they planned to do in the early hours of their offensive.

By March 24 the attacks of the Germans had been redoubled, and it was estimated that more than 1,000,000 Huns had been thrown into the struggle against the British forces on which the attack was concentrated.

The most notable feature of the attack from the spectacular viewpoint was the bombardment of Paris by monster German cannon, located in the forest of St. Gobain, west of Laon, and approximately 76 miles away from Paris.

BIG GUN ONE HUNDRED FEET LONG.

Though no official description of the big gun was ever given, it was stated by military authorities that it was approximately 100 feet in length, and that several were in use, and more being built by the Germans. At first the statement that a gun could shoot such a distance was doubted, but when 75 persons were killed in Paris and one of the shells hit a church doubt no longer existed. It also developed that the gun was originally an American invention, and that similar weapons were being built by the United States.

The use of the big gun was in the nature of a "side-issue" to bring terror to the French, and in line with the policy of frightfulness instituted by the German militarists. Its use was continued daily. Meantime the German hordes swept on marching in close formation into the very mouths of the rapid-fire guns and against the strongly fixed British lines.

For ten days the hostilities continued, without cessation, with fighting along a whole front such as had never been known before.

The Germans continued to hurl great forces of infantry into the conflict, depending largely on weight of numbers to overcome the increasing opposition offered by the heroically resisting British.

The battle on the historic ground about Longueval was

perhaps the most spectacular of any along the front. It was a battle of machine gunners and infantry. The Germans were pursuing their tactics of working forward in massed formation, and the British rapid-firers' squads and riflemen reaped a horrid harvest from their positions on the high ground. Notwithstanding their terrible losses, the Germans kept coming on, filling in the places of those who had fallen and pressing their attack. The British artillery in the meantime poured in a perfect rain of shells on the enemy, carrying havoc into their ranks. In this section the Germans operated without the full support of their guns, because of their rapid advance.

ENEMY LOSES HEAVILY.

A fierce engagement was also waged about Le Verguier, which the Germans captured, but not until the British infantry holding the place had fought to the last man and inflicted extremely heavy losses on the enemy. The British again fell back, this time to a line through Hervilly, just east of Roisel and Vermand.

The work of the British airmen during the battle was one of the brightest pages. Bitter battles in the air were fought by scores of aviators and the service proved fully its ability to smother the German airmen at a crucial time.

Within a few days it was stated that at least 130 German airplanes were brought down. This compilation of losses has reference to only one section of the battle front, comprising perhaps two-thirds of the line affected.

An official statement regarding British aerial operations said their airplanes were employed in bombing the enemy's troops and transport massed in the areas behind the battlefront, and in attacking them with machine-gun fire from low heights. Twenty-two tons of bombs were dropped in this work, and more than 100,000 rounds were fired from the machine guns.

By March 28 the German losses were estimated at 400,000.

The forces of the Germans were almost overwhelming, the Kaiser sacrificing the man-power of his nation in a last desperate attack.

In consequence no greater stories of heroism have ever been told than are related of the English, French and American troops. The Germans were set for a drive against the English and French channel points with Amiens as an objective, with the idea of breaking through the British lines where they join the French.

AMERICAN FORCES OFFERED TO FRANCE.

The earnestness of the Americans in the situation was proclaimed to the world by the English and French, and General Pershing placed his name and that of his country and men high on the wall of fame by unselfishly offering to France at the most critical period the use of his entire force, to be disposed of and assigned wherever General Foch and his staff decided to use them. Within a few days thereafter the American troops which had been in training were marched in to relieve the stressed English and French.

Everywhere the raging battle was marked by spectacular features not the least of which were provided by a corps of thirty tanks, which waded into the German hordes near Ephey and other points, recovering positions which had been lost by the British.

Canadian armored motorcars also played an important part in checking the Huns, the cars armed with rapid-fire guns being rushed up to support weakening troops.

The progress of the Germans was halted on April 3, and in the following days the British regained several lost positions and the French made gains. But after a pause, during which several hundred thousand new troops were brought in, the Huns renewed the offensive, delivering an attack against the French near Montdidier on a front about 15 miles long. An attack along a front of similar length was made against the British on the Somme.

The first battalion of American troops answering to the call of the French for support reached the British front-line in France, on April 10, on the very anniversary of the entrance of the United States into the war, and within a few days the Americans began to bear the brunt of battle, holding the Germans like veterans.

The first big attack of the Germans launched directly against an American line occurred on April 30, in the vicinity of Villers-Bretonneaux, below the Somme, where the Huns were repulsed with heavy losses. The German preliminary bombardment lasted two hours and then the infantry rushed forward, only to be driven back, leaving large numbers of dead on the ground in front of the American lines.

AMERICANS BOMBARDED.

The German bombardment opened at 5 o'clock in the afternoon and was directed especially against the Americans, who were supported on the north and south by the French. The fire was intense and at the end of two hours the German commander sent forward three battalions of infantry. There was hand-to-hand fighting all along the line, as a result of which the enemy was thrust back, his dead and wounded lying on the ground in all directions. Five prisoners remained in American hands.

"Tell them back home that we are just beginning," said an American lad who was in the thick of the fight and severely wounded with shrapnel. "It was fine to see our men go at the Huns. All of us, who thought baseball was the great American game, have changed our minds. There is only one game to keep the American flag flying—that is, kill the Huns. I got several before they got me."

Details of the engagement show the Americans stuck to their guns while the Germans were placing liquid fire, gas and almost every other conceivable device of frightfulness on them. One of them, who lay wounded in an American hospital, had kept his machine gun going after the chief gunners had been killed two feet away and he himself had been wounded, thus protecting a turn in the road known as Dead Man's curve, over which some of the American couriers passed in the face of a concentrated enemy fire.

As indicating the violence of the offensive, French ambulance men who went through the famous battle of Verdun declared today that, comparatively speaking, the German artillery fire against the Americans was heavier than in any single engagement on the Verdun front at any time.

The German barrage began just before sunrise. In an attempt to put the American batteries out of action the Germans used an unusually large number of gas shells, but the American artillery replied vigorously, hurling hundreds of shells across the Teuton lines. Though successful in resisting the German attack, the Americans lost 183 men captured by the Huns, according to the British report.

Nothing in the history of naval warfare is more picturesque than the story of the raid made by English ships on the German submarine bases at Ostend and Zeebrugge, on the Belgian coast, on April 22. Obsolete cruisers filled with concrete were run aground and blown up in the harbors. An old submarine filled with explosives was used to blow up the piling beside the Mole at Zeebrugge.

One German destroyer was torpedoed, and the British lost a destroyer, two coastal motorboats and two launches.

A fortnight later the old cruiser Vindictive was taken into the submarine base at Ostend and sent to the bottom, blocking the channel, making the attack thoroughly effective.

CHAPTER XXVI

AMERICANS TURN WAR'S TIDE

Brilliant American Fighting Stops Hun Advance—French and British Inspired —Famous Marines Lead in Picturesque Attack—Halt Germans at Chateau-Thierry—Used Open Style Fighting—Thousands of Germans Slain—United States Troops in Siberia—New Conscription Bill Passed— Allied Successes on All Fronts.

ALL history contains no greater story of bravery and heroism than that which echoed around the world concerning the exploits of the American soldiers in France as the war entered its fifth year.

Casting aside all precedent, ignoring the practices which had been developed by the English, French and German commands during four years of stubborn fighting, a little force of Americans—barely a handful, led by the picturesque Marines —brought the Huns to a standstill in their drive upon Paris and turned the tide of war.

Once again history repeated itself, for the Germans were turned back at the beautiful river Marne, where the brave Americans and heroic French smashed their lines. The spectacular event in which the Americans participated was a mere incident of the great conflict raging across France, but the story must ever be one of the outstanding features of the war because of the effect it produced upon the whole situation.

In the struggle against the Huns the Belgian army had been reduced to its lowest ebb; the manpower of France and England had been sapped by constant call for reserves, and the Allied forces, while resisting and fighting heroically, were without reserves to draw upon to effect a decisive blow when the opportunity presented.

The German hordes had swept forward with hammer-like blows toward Paris in what was a continuation of the giant offensive started in March. The second movement was launched under the personal command of the German Crown Prince on May 27, and was directed against four divisions of the British troops and the Sixth French Army. Concentration was on a front stretching from Soissons to Rheims, a distance of about 30 miles.

The Huns were driving on the entire front, but the Crown Prince with crack troops was to have the honor for which he had long been striving—that of crossing the famous Marne and taking Paris. His troops had reached the river between Dormans and Chateau-Thierry at the very spot where the Third German Army had swept across the stream on August 25, 1914. Paris was less than 50 miles away.

Here and there at other points the Germans had been held by the French and English, but as part of the strategy of the French command the enemy had been permitted to advance at this point through lines which would cost him a terrible toll of lives. The French meantime were concentrating on the enemy's flank with the hope of breaking through and pocketing part of the Crown Prince's advancing forces.

Whatever the intent, the Germans were resisting the efforts to stop them. The question was, where would the advance end? The answer was furnished by America.

The enemy had attempted to broaden his Marne salient and had stretched as far south as Chateau-Thierry. It is supposed his purpose was to compel General Foch to meet shock with shock by throwing in his reserve forces, since the German advance had then almost reached shelling distance of Paris.

But the German command had not taken the Americans into their calculations, for here the Prussians met Uncle Sam's fighting men and their French supports and were smashed and thrown back.

Fighting in their own way, in the open, against superior forces, the Marines and troops of the National American Army fought their way to victory, routing the enemy and wresting from them positions absolutely necessary to their further advance.

Immense forces of Germans had been thrown into the fray when the American division, to which the Marines were attached, was ordered into the breach. The bulk of the forces, called to help halt the Huns, were hours away from the fighting front and were being brought up for the purpose of holding a secondary position where they would take up the fighting when the French fell back.

They had captured Cantigny after elaborate preparations under the direction of the French, but here there were no preparations. The American commanders wanted to attack the advancing enemy. The Allied leaders doubted the ability of the Americans to stop the Boche in open combat.

The American commanders pleaded to make war in their own way. Doubting, yet hopeful, the Allied commanders gave consent. The Americans were moved into position. There was no time for rest and they came forward under forced draft, so to speak. Infantry, machine gun companies and artillery swung into position and faced the enemy which aimed a blow at the line where it was supported by the French on the left.

The Boche hordes swarmed across fields. The American gunners raked them with hell's fire. The reputation of the Americans as sharpshooters and marksmen was sustained. Under the most stressful circumstances and while the French observers stood amazed, the Americans took careful aim and shot as though at rifle practice. Every possible shot was made to tell.

The Germans wavered, then halted under the withering fire of machine guns and rifle. On again they came, only to again be repulsed. The ground was strewn with their dead and wounded. Then they began to break and to crawl back to safer positions.

The enemy had been stopped but not driven. They had

fallen back to strong positions, the names of which must go down in history as scenes of terrific fighting—Bouresches and Bois de Belleau—the latter a wooded, rocky parcel of land on which German machine guns were hidden—hundreds of them —while more than a thousand of the enemy's best men were concealed in the thicket and underbrush and in the rocky fissures.

The Americans drove into the wood and charged the stronghold. Sacrifice! Yes, hundreds of brave young Americans died fighting, but not in vain. American artillery swept the woods; little companies of men charged the enemy machine-gun nests, silencing the guns and killing the operators or taking them prisoners. There was no going forward in mass formation under barrage or protecting curtain of fire, but out in the open the Marines and infantrymen rushed on facing terrific fire.

Bois de Belleau was cleared of the Boche. Bouresches fell to the Americans. The capture of the town was a repetition of the taking of the first position. Machine guns protected the town everywhere. In cellar windows, doorways and on roofs the Germans had set up their weapons. But it was the old story—no hail of shot could stop the Americans. Almost without sleep, unable to bring up supplies, the Americans had fought four days with only canned foodstuffs to sustain them.

Stories of the fights are reminiscent of those in which American troops engaged the Indians on the plains in the frontier days. Indeed American Indians—children of the famous old Sioux and Chippewa tribes of Red Men—acted as scouts for Uncle Sam in many of his troops' activities in France, and the methods of the old Indian fighters proved too much for the Germans.

It is estimated that 7000 were killed or wounded by the Americans in this action, and that their prisoners numbered more than 1000. How privates took command of squads and continued to outbattle the enemy when officers were killed; how lone Americans or small groups of them captured squads of Huns or annihilated them, are common stories of heroism written into the official war records of the American Expeditionary Forces in France, and sealed by medals of honor presented to young Americans or confirmed by official words of commendation.

Let the words of General Pershing in an official order to his troops on August 27, stand as part of the record:

"It fills me with pride to record in General Orders a tribute to the service achievements of the First and Third Corps, comprising the First, Second, Third, Fourth, Twenty-sixth, Twenty-eighth, Thirty-second and Forty-second Divisions of the American Expeditionary Forces.

"You came to the battlefield at a crucial hour for the Allied cause. For almost four years the most formidable army the world has yet seen had pressed its invasion of France and stood threatening its capital. At no time has that army been more powerful and menacing than when, on July 15, it struck again to destroy in one great battle the brave men opposed to it and to enforce its brutal will upon the world and civilization.

"Three days later, in conjunction with our Allies, you counter-attacked. The Allied armies gained a brilliant victory that marks the turning point of the war. You did more than to give the Allies the support to which as a nation our faith was pledged.

"You proved that our altruism, our pacific spirit and our sense of justice have not blunted our virility or our courage.

"You have shown that American initiative and energy are as fit for the tasks of war as for the pursuits of peace. You have justly won unstinted praise from our Allies and the eternal gratitude of our countrymen.

"We have paid for successes with the lives of many of our brave comrades. We shall cherish their memory always and claim for our history and literature their bravery, achievement and sacrifice.

"This order will be read to all organizations at the first assembly formations following its receipt."

Aside from being largely responsible for stopping the Huns once again at the Marne, the exploits of the Americans filled the French and English with confidence, aroused their spirits and gave them renewed hope. Incidentally their efforts and methods made apparent the value of surprise attacks and quick blows in dealing with the stolid Huns.

The Allied commanders, quick to take advantage of the situation, gave the enemy no chance to consolidate their positions. The unified forces of Allies attacked with renewed energy all along the line, and the Huns were forced back with a sweep that astonished the world.

By September 1, the Germans had lost practically all that they had gained in their drive from March 21, and in many places they had been driven back across the famous Hindenburg line, the furthest point of retreat of the Germans in 1914, when they were forced back by General Joffre from the Marne, and dug themselves into pit and trench. Dozens of towns were taken and more than 120,000 prisoners were bagged.

Almost as spectacular in its effect on the minds of the French and English, as was the demonstration of American fighting, was the work accomplished in France in providing for the transportation and care of the incoming troops. Here great docks, storage plants, training camps, aviation schools, motor assembling plants, base hospitals and reclamation establishments and railroads, built in less than a year and still growing, represented an investment of $35,000,000 on the part of the United States Government in August, 1918.

Early in May the number of Americans in France was about 500,000. That this number should have been sent across the ocean within the space of one year after America entered the war was regarded as a distinct achievement, but by September it was officially announced that the number had increased to 1,500,000.

Some of these were sent to the Italian front to help in the drive against the Austrians, and about 15,000 troops from the Philippines were sent by the United States into Siberia to give moral support to the Czecho-Slovaks.

The decision to send troops to Siberia was by agreement with the Japanese, and followed a statement issued by the United States on August 4, in which it was stated that "military action was admissable in Russia only to render such protection and help as possible to the Czecho-Slovaks against armed Austrian and German prisoners who were attacking them, and to steady any efforts at self-government or self-defense in which the Russians themselves may be willing to accept assistance." It was stated that the troops were for guard duty, and under the agreement with Japan, the only other country in a position to act in Siberia, each nation sent a small force to Vladivostok.

The British, French and United States Governments gave recognition to the Czecho-Slovaks as an Allied nation—a geographical, political and military entity—with three armies, one in Siberia, one in Italy and one in France, where they had been fighting with the Allies to crush the Huns. The territory which the Czecho-Slovaks claim as their own to govern independently comprises Bohemia, Moravia, Silesia and Slavonika, which lie between and are part of Austria-Hungary and Germany.

With the facilities for handling the troops abroad thoroughly organized and the obvious necessity for furnishing greater manpower to bring about an early defeat of Germany, the United States decided to increase the scope of its conscription and to raise an army of 3,000,000 for immediate service and adopted a new manpower bill which was passed by Congress the last week in August and signed by President Wilson on August 30.

The measure provided for the registration and drafting of all male citizens between the ages of 18 and 45 years, allowing for deferred classification of those engaged in essential work or having obligations which made it impossible for them to render active military service.

Not only the Allied successes on the western front, but also those on the Italian front and in the Balkans, where the French, Italians and Greeks in Albania, with a million troops, advanced against the Germans, Austrians and Turks, made apparent the necessity for further concentration of manpower.

While losing ground on the western front and rapidly being forced to the wall, Germany gave another spectacular twist to her military program by carrying the war to America's doors. With her submarines she sank nearly two score of ships, schooners, barges, tugs, and even a lightship, within a few miles of New York, Boston, Norfolk, Charleston and the Delaware Capes.

But while the U-boats were harassing, no effective assaults were made against the ships which carried American troops abroad. In this connection it should never be forgotten in the glamour of war that while America performed wonders in getting her soldiers overseas, England provided most of the ships, and that it was England's Navy which kept the German Navy in check while America's war vessels and destroyers convoyed the troopships and protected them from the submarines.

CHAPTER XXVII

VICTORY—PEACE

THE GERMAN EMPIRE COLLAPSES—FOCH'S STRATEGY WINS—AMERICAN INSPIRATION A BIG FACTOR—BULGARIA, TURKEY AND AUSTRIA QUIT WAR—MONARCHS FALL—KAISER ABDICATES AND FLEES GERMANY—ARMISTICE SIGNED—NOVEMBER 11, PEACE.

THEN came the fall of autocracy——
Victory! Peace!

With a crash that echoed around the world the autocratic governmental structure builded by the Kaiser and his forebears gave way and came tumbling to the earth in ruins on Monday, November 11, 1918.

The most momentous event in ages had come to pass and victory was perched upon the banner of democracy.

Out of the sacrifice of millions of lives, the desolation of homes and countries, the expenditure of untold energy and incomprehensible billions of dollars in money, there came everlasting, glorious peace.

The great German Empire lay a wreck, given into the hands of the people for remaking, and the arrogant Emperor William Hohenzollern had fled into Holland.

The end came swiftly and with dramatic action. Beaten back by the Allied forces, which gathered strength and inspiration from the irresistible American troops, the German army weakened all along the line from Holland to the Swiss border. The press of power exerted against the German strongholds on every side was felt within the domains and produced internal strife and dissension which undermined and weakened the military organization. Taking full advantage of this situation, the Allied forces on every side quickened and intensified their blows.

The brilliant strategy of Marshal Foch, generalissimo of the Allied armies, brought defeat to the Germans in less than four months. After bringing to an end the German advance of March 21 to July 18 with the second battle of the Marne, he compelled a hurried retirement to the Hin-

denburg line with the evacuation of practically all the territory conquered by the Huns.

Finally, in what may be termed the last phase of the
war, he absolutely demoralized the German forces. The
thrust in this phase was started by the Anglo-Belgian
forces in Flanders and the Franco-American armies in
Lorraine on September 26.

The British also made a gigantic and brilliant drive
between Cambrai and St. Quentin. The whole colossal
defense system of the Germans was shattered and in less
than three months more than 100,000 German prisoners and
5000 guns were taken and 8000 square miles of French and
Belgian territory liberated.

Not only was there great victory on the west, but in
Syria the British army broke the power of Turkey and
liberated Syria, Mesopotamia and Arabia. In Macedonia,
too, an army made up of soldiers of many nations under a
French command compelled the surrender of Bulgaria and
her withdrawal, and swept the last vestige of German control from the Balkans.

On the Austrian front likewise the Italian army,
strengthened and heartened by the presence of American and Allied forces, swept the Austrians before them in
one of the most picturesque offensives of the war, capturing
more than 300,000 prisoners and great quantities of guns
and supplies.

This in brief is the way the German command was
driven to a point of seeking peace to prevent the invasion
of their territory.

The brilliant assaults of the various units and commands of the Allies at points along the entire 200 miles of
western front will go down in history a wonderful military
achievement.

One of the wonderful attacks was that of the American
First Army under General Pershing, when St. Mihiel
salient was annihilated. This salient for four years resisted
all efforts to penetrate it and stood a guardian to great iron
fields running through the Bassin de Briey to the Belgian-
Luxemburg frontier. It formed a strong outpost to the
fortified city of Metz, with its twenty-eight forts, and made
impossible the invasion of German Lorraine from the west.

The offensive of General Pershing was one of the most carefully planned of the war. More than 1000 tanks were operated to open the way for the infantry and cavalry. A greater force of airplanes than were ever concentrated in a single attack menaced the Germans overhead and in a week the Americans encompassed a territory of 200 square miles and threatened the mining center and the forts of Metz, capturing 20,000 prisoners and hundreds of guns and great quantities of ammunition. Moreover, the Verdun-Nancy railway was released.

Support was brought to the Germans and they stubbornly resisted, but many points were gained and held by the Americans.

Another corps of the First American Army, in command of General Hunter Liggett, also made a brilliant attack between the Meuse and Aisne rivers east of Rheims on a front twenty miles long, where the crack Prussian Guards were routed. Here in one of the most bitterly contested battles of the closing days the Americans made an important advance, capturing half a dozen villages.

As at Chateau-Thierry, the Americans in the face of withering fire and against all the instruments of modern warfare handled by the best soldiers in Germany, fought their way through with a bravery that won for them the praises of the highest commands in the French and British armies, as well as from General Pershing.

At the very close of the struggle the Americans arose to the heights of sublime heroism in crossing the river Meuse, capturing the town of Dun and later the town of Sedan, famous as one of the scenes of bitter fighting in the Franco-Prussian War.

The Americans forced their way across a 160-foot river, a stretch of mud flats and a 60-foot canal in the face of terrible fire. Men who could swim breasted the stream carrying ropes, which were stretched from bank to bank and along which those who could not swim made their way over the river. Some crossed in collapsible boats, others on rafts and finally on pontoon and foot bridges, which were constructed under the enemy fire.

This difficult feat accomplished, the men waded through mud to the canal, fighting as they went, and again plunged into the water, swimming the canal, at the far side of which they were compelled to use grappling hooks and scaling irons to mount the perpendicular banks of the canal, along which were the resisting Germans. And finally, when the German Empire fell, famed Sedan was in the hands of the Americans. With the last forward movement they took possession of Stenay when hostilities ceased.

The part the American soldiers played in winning the war, merely as a matter of increased man power, is indicated by the fact that when the end came there were 2,900,000 men in the forces abroad.

The failure of the German submarine warfare and the ability of the British, French and American naval forces to protect troop ships and permit the landing of as high as 200,000 soldiers in France in a single month, had much to do with discouraging the German command.

The withdrawal of Bulgaria on September 27 and her unconditional surrender to the Allies was a distinct blow to Germany. The abdication of King Ferdinand in favor of Crown Prince Boris was shortly followed by the surrender and withdrawal of Turkey, which further weakened Germany's position, and peace offers were made by both Austria and by Germany.

Austria sought a separate peace, but Germany, seeing the handwriting on the wall, asked for an armistice through Prince Maximilian of Baden, who had succeeded Count Von Hertling as Chancellor. But while agreeing to accept as a basis of peace the points established by President Wilson as necessary to an agreement, Germany's military forces continued their ruthless and barbaric warfare.

President Wilson submitted a set of questions to the German Government to ascertain the sincerity and purpose of the request and finally brought the matter to an issue by declaring that nothing short of a complete surrender would suffice and that further negotiations must be taken up with the Allied command.

Meantime King Boris of Bulgaria abdicated and the Government was taken over by the people. This was followed by the surrender of Austria on November 8 and the abdication of the Emperor Charles.

Austria in her surrender agreed to the immediate suspension of hostilities, the demobilization of the army of Austro-Hungary and the withdrawal of all forces from the North Sea to Switzerland, the evacuation of all territories invaded, the evacuation of all German troops from Austro-Hungarian territory and the Italian and Balkan fronts, as well as the surrender of fifteen submarines and all German submarines in Austro-Hungarian territorial waters, together with thirty-four warships, and also the repatriation of all prisoners of war.

With her forces demoralized and Bulgaria, Turkey and Austria out of the war and her power broken in Russia, Germany was driven to the necessity of accepting terms submitted by the Allies as the basis of peace as outlined by President Wilson, and at midnight, November 10, Paris time, the German High Command signed an armistice and hostilities ceased on the following morning, November 11, 1918, at 11 o'clock, Paris time.

The terms of the armistice accepted by Germany were as follows:

I. MILITARY CLAUSES ON WESTERN FRONT:

One—Cessation of operations by land and in the air six hours after the signature of the armistice.

Two—Immediate evacuation of invaded countries: Belgium, France, Alsace-Lorraine, Luxemburg, so ordered as to be completed within fourteen days from the signature of the armistice. German troops which have not left the above-mentioned territories within the period fixed will become prisoners of war. Occupation by the Allied and United States forces jointly will keep pace with evacuation in these areas. All movements of evacuation and occupation will be regulated in accordance with a note annexed to the stated terms.

Three—Repatriation beginning at once and to be completed within fourteen days of all inhabitants of the countries above mentioned, including hostages and persons under trial or convicted.

Four—Surrender in good condition by the German armies of the following equipment: Five thousand guns (two thousand five hundred heavy, two thousand five hundred field) thirty thousand machine guns. Three thousand minenwerfers. Two thousand airplanes (fighters, bombers—firstly D. Seventy-three's and night bombing machines). The above to be delivered in situ to the Allies and the United States troops in accordance with the detailed conditions laid down in the annexed note.

Five—Evacuation by the German armies of the countries on the left bank of the Rhine. These countries on the left bank of the Rhine shall be administered by the local authorities under the control of the Allied and United States armies of occupation. The occupation of these territories will be determined by Allied and United States garrisons holding the principal crossings of the Rhine, Mayence, Coblenz, Cologne, together with bridgeheads at these points in thirty kilometre radius on the right bank and by garrisons similarly holding the strategic points of the regions.

A neutral zone shall be reserved on the right of the Rhine between the stream and a line drawn parallel to it forty kilometres (twenty-six miles) to the east from the frontier of Holland to the parallel of Gernsheim and as far as practicable a distance of thirty kilometres (twenty miles) from the east of stream from this parallel upon Swiss frontier. Evacuation by the enemy of the Rhine lands shall be so ordered as to be completed within a further period of eleven days, in all nineteen days after the signature of the armistice. All movements of evacuation and occupation will be regulated according to the note annexed.

Six—In all territory evacuated by the enemy there shall be no evacuation of inhabitants; no damage or harm shall be done to the persons or property of the inhabitants. No destruction of any kind to be committed. Military establishments of all kinds shall be delivered intact as well as military stores of food, munitions, equipment not removed during the periods fixed for evacuation. Stores of food of all kinds for the civil population, cattle, etc., shall be left in situ. Industrial establishments shall not be impaired in any way and their personnel shall not be moved. Roads and means of communication of every kind, railroad, waterways, main roads, bridges, telegraphs, telephones, shall be in no manner impaired.

Seven—All civil and military personnel at present employed on them shall remain. Five thousand locomotives, fifty thousand wagons and ten thousand motor lorries in good working order with all necessary spare parts and fittings shall be delivered to the associated powers within the period fixed for the evacuation of Belgium and Luxemburg. The railways of Alsace-Lorraine shall be handed over within the same period, together with all pre-war personnel and material. Further material necessary for the working of railways in the country on the left bank of the Rhine shall be left in situ. All stores of coal and material for the upkeep of permanent ways, signals and repair shops left entire in situ and kept in an efficient state by Germany during the whole period of armistice. All barges taken from the Allies shall be restored to them. A note appended regulates the details of these measures.

Eight—The German command shall be responsible for revealing all mines or other acting fuses disposed on territory evacuated by the German troops and shall assist in their discovery and destruction. The German command shall also reveal all destructive measures that may have been taken (such as poisoning or polluting of springs, wells, etc.) under penalty of reprisals.

Nine—The right of requisition shall be exercised by the Allied and the United States armies in all occupied territory. The upkeep of the troops of occupation in the Rhine land (excluding Alsace-Lorraine), shall be charged to the German Government.

Ten—An immediate repatriation without reciprocity according to detailed conditions which shall be fixed, of all Allied and United States prisoners of war. The Allied powers and the United States shall be able to dispose of these prisoners as they wish.

Eleven—Sick and wounded, who cannot be removed from evacuated territory will be cared for by German personnel who will be left on the spot with the medical material required.

II. Disposition Relative to the Eastern Frontiers of Germany:

Twelve—All German troops at present in any territory which before the war belonged to Russia, Rumania or Turkey shall withdraw within the frontiers of Germany as they existed on August first, 1914.

Thirteen—Evacuation by German troops to begin at once and all German instructors, prisoners and civilian as well as military agents, now on the territory of Russia (as defined before 1914) to be recalled.

Fourteen—German troops to cease at once all requisitions and seizures and any other undertaking with a view to obtaining supplies intended for Germany in Rumania and Russia (as defined on August first, 1914).

Fifteen—Abandonment of the treaties of Bucharest and Brest-Litovsk and of the supplementary treaties.

Sixteen—The Allies shall have free access to the territories evacuated by the Germans on their eastern frontier either through Danzig or by the Vistula in order to convey supplies to the populations of those territories or for any other purpose.

III. Clause Concerning East Africa:

Seventeen—Unconditional capitulation of all German forces operating in East Africa within one month.

IV. General Clauses:

Eighteen—Repatriation, without reciprocity, within maximum period of one month, in accordance with detailed conditions hereafter to be fixed, of all civilians interned or deported who may be citizens of other Allied or associated states than those mentioned in clause three, paragraph nineteen, with the reservation that any future claims and demands of the Allies and the United States of America remain unaffected.

Nineteen—The following financial conditions are required: Reparation for damage done. While such armistice lasts no public securities shall be removed by the enemy which can serve as a pledge to the Allies for the recovery or repatriation for war losses. Immediate restitution of the cash deposit, in the National Bank of Belgium, and in general immediate return of all documents, specie, stocks, shares, paper money, together with plant for the issue thereof, touching public or private interests in the invaded countries. Restitution of the Russian and Rumanian gold yielded to Germany or taken by that power. This gold to be delivered in trust to the Allies until the signature of peace.

V. NAVAL CONDITIONS:

Twenty—Immediate cessation of all hostilities at sea and definite information to be given as to the location and movements of all German ships. Notification to be given to neutrals that freedom of navigation in all territorial waters is given to the naval and mercantile marines of the Allied and associated powers, all questions of neutrality being waived.

Twenty-one—All naval and mercantile marine prisoners of war of the Allied and associated powers in German hands to be returned without reciprocity.

Twenty-two—Surrender to the Allies and the United States of America of one hundred and sixty German submarines (including all submarine cruisers and mine laying submarines) with their complete armament and equipment in ports which will be specified by the Allies and the United States of America. All other submarines to be paid off and completely disarmed and placed under the supervision of the Allied Powers and the United States of America.

Twenty-three—The following German surface warships which shall be designated by the Allies and the United States of America shall forthwith be disarmed and thereafter interned in neutral ports to be designated by the Allies and the United States of America and placed under the surveillance of the Allies and the United States of America, only caretakers being left on board, namely:

Six battle cruisers, ten battleships, eight light cruisers, including two mine layers, fifty destroyers of the most modern type. All other surface warships (including river craft) are to be concentrated in naval bases to be designated by the Allies and the United States of America, and are to be paid off and completely disarmed and placed under the supervision of the Allies and the United States of America. All vessels of the auxiliary fleet (trawlers, motor vessels, etc.), are to be disarmed.

Twenty-four—The Allies and the United States of America shall have the right to sweep all mine fields and obstructions laid by Germany outside German territorial waters, and the positions of these are to be indicated.

Twenty-five—Freedom of access to and from the Baltic to be given to the naval and mercantile marine of the Allied and associated powers. To secure this the Allies and the United States of America shall be empowered to occupy all German forts, fortifications, batteries and defense works of all kinds in all the entrances from the Cattegat into the Baltic, and to sweep up all mines and obstructions within and without German territorial waters without any question of neutrality being raised, and the positions of all such mines and obstructions are to be indicated.

Twenty-six—The existing blockade conditions set up by the Allies and associated powers are to remain unchanged, and all German merchant ships found at sea are to remain liable to capture.

Twenty-seven—All naval aircraft are to be concentrated and immobilized in German bases to be specified by the Allies and the United States of America.

Twenty-eight—In evacuating the Belgian coasts and ports, Germany shall abandon all merchant ships, tugs, lighters, cranes and all other harbor materials, all materials for inland navigation, all aircraft and all materials and stores, all arms and armaments, and all stores and apparatus of all kinds.

Twenty-nine—All Black Sea ports are to be evacuated by Germany, all Russian war vessels of all descriptions seized by Germany in the Black Sea are to be handed over to the Allies and the United States of America; all neutral merchant vessels seized are to be released; all warlike and other materials of all kinds seized in those parts are to be returned and German materials as specified in clause twenty-eight are to be abandoned.

Thirty—All merchant vessels in German hands belonging to the Allied and associated powers are to be restored in ports to be specified by the Allies and the United States of America without reciprocity.

Thirty-one—No destruction of ships or of materials to be permitted before evacuation, surrender or restoration.

Thirty-two—The German Government will notify neutral Governments of the world, and particularly the Governments of Norway, Sweden, Denmark, and Holland, that all restrictions placed on the trading of their vessels with the Allied and associated countries, whether by the German Government or by private German interests, and whether in return for specific concessions such as the export of shipbuilding materials or not, are immediately cancelled.

Thirty-three—No transfers of German merchant shipping of any description to any neutral flag are to take place after signature of the armistice.

VI. Duration of Armistice:

Thirty-four—The duration of the armistice is to be thirty days, with option to extend. During this period, on failure of execution of any of the above clauses, the armistice may be denounced by one of the contracting parties on forty-eight hours' previous notice.

VII. Time Limit for Reply:

Thirty-five—This armistice to be accepted or refused by Germany within seventy-two hours of notification.

A few hours before the signing of the armistice Emperor William Hohenzollern abdicated and fled into Holland, to be followed later by his son, the Crown Prince.

Thus came peace after fifty-two continuous months of fighting, in which it is estimated that nearly 10,000,000 were killed and that there were about 27,000,000 casualties, while $200,000,000,000 were expended by the combined nations.

America's casualties were 236,117, divided as follows: Killed and died of wounds, 36,154; died of disease, 14,811; died from unassigned causes, 2204; wounded, 179,625; missing, 1160, and prisoners, 2163.

England by contrast had 658,665 killed, 2,032,122 wounded and 359,145 missing and prisoners during the four years, while Italy had about 1,600,000 casualties; France, 3,500,000; Belgium, 400,000; Rumania, 200,000, and Russia, 6,000,000. All told, twenty-eight nations, with a total population of approximately 1,600,000,000, or nearly eleven-twelfths of the human race, were involved in the world struggle at the close.

THE NEGRO IN THE WORLD WAR.

BEFORE THE WAR.

Civilization evolves destructive forces of change. War is change in explosive form. World notions, points of view, and general ideas of 1914 have spun the cycle of years with accelerated speed. At that time the public mind gained its concept of the Negro from encyclopaedic information. He was regarded as a "sub-species of mankind, dark of skin, wooly of hair, long of head, with dilated nostrils, thick lips, thicker cranium, flat foot, prehensible great toe and lark heel."

He was described as a creature with "mental constitution very similar to that of the child, on a lower evolutionary plane than the white man, and more closely related to the highest anthropoids." His brain weight, we were told, was 35 ounces as compared with the gorilla's 20 ounces and the Caucasians 45.

In America, conception of the Negro has ever fluctuated in direct ratio to the rise and fall of military domination of the affairs of the republic. Whenever the military agencies of the government have been exalted, the Negro has been benefited by reaction of the public mind. From 1865 to 1870 exaltation of the military element of American life brought along not only emancipation of the black man, but that conception of him which resulted in the conferring of manhood rights and privileges. In this short space of five years, so highly had the Negro come into public estimation that, with the protection of the military arm of the government, there were actively engaged in his interest an Emancipation League, a Freedmen's Pension Society, a

Freedmen and Soldiers' Relief, a Freedmen's Aid Society
of the M. E. Church, a Society of Friends of Great Britain
and Ireland for the Relief of Emancipated Slaves of America, an American Missionary Association, a Freedmen's
Bureau, a Freedmen's Bank, a British and Foreign Anti-
Slavery Society, an American Negro Aid Commission, and
other organizations, too numerous for mention. So important, however, was military organization and predomi-
nance to the success of any one of these organizations, that
Carl Schurz, reporting to Congress the condition of the
South, declared: "If the national government firmly and
unequivocally announces its policy not to give up the control of free labor reform until it is firmly accomplished, the
progress of the reform will be far more rapid and far less
difficult than it will be if the attitude of the government is
such as to permit contrary hopes to be indulged in."

In 1870, as the military power of the United States
weakened its control over the nation, forces of opposition
arose to pull down to the depths the black man, who had
been exalted by the agencies of military government. The
Ku Klux Klan, headed by the Grand Wizard of the Invisible Empire, and the Grand Dragon of the Realm, with
malignant fanaticism worshipped the lost cause. Hatred
of white man for Negro, accentuated and embittered by
hatred for the Yankee carpet-bagger and the southern
scalawag, resulted in the rise of a powerful southern par-
tisanship, stunned only so long as military power held sway.
Peonage took place of colored free labor. Disproportionate appropriation of taxes between blacks and whites lowered the Negro measurably year by year. With the complete removal of military supremacy, the Ku Klux courted
publicity which it had hitherto shunned. A leader, the
statesman of the new era, in the person of the late Benjamin R. Tillman, of South Carolina, appeared. He split the
loose organization of southern aristocracy with the blacks

with lily white wedge, and trampled into dust every agency which favored the black man. He deprived the black of all weapons of offence or defence, disfranchised him, shunted him off into the ghetto, and called the world to mock him in his lowly position. This southern statesman lived to see the Solid South come into national power in 1912. From that time, until the beginning of the world war in 1914, the American negro reached the lowest point of his political and social status.

Compared with Anglo-Saxon, Frenchman, Italian, Austrian, German or Russian, he was of an order and degree reputed farthest down. No celebrity attached to his menial state. No distinction might be his as an award from the courts of nations. Dignity, grandeur and majesty applied to Guelphs, Hapsburgs and Hohenzollerns. Theirs was all arrogation of supereminence. And to them all, the Negro, throughout the world, was, if a man at all, preeminently the mere Man Friday.

From such a status of debasement, existing in an intolerable atmosphere of derogation and disrepute, the humble and humiliated American Negro sought the exaltation of international honor. Denied and disavowed at home, through vicissitude of international war, he hoped for affirmation of a new world dictum in acknowledgment of his human qualities and worth. He did not, like Toussaint, long for the high honors of the continental emperor. He sought democratic equality, and he would as lief think of bringing the Kaiser to his level as exalting himself to the plane of that immortal celebrity.

He wanted to make good in public. He wanted to demonstrate both efficiency and initiative. He desired that popular belief conceive him as a man, not a monkey. He wished the Caucasian world to take into its head that he might function as a valuable and serviceable element of twentieth century civilization. He yearned to reveal his powers in every field of endeavor. And he expected that when the Caucasian had arrived at a fair judgment in his behalf, he would issue to him the warrant certifying that he was four-square with the dominant opinion of mankind, and, therefore, entitled to the honors of superior status.

He aimed to compensate the world by presenting a concept of beauty in place of a general notion of repellent ugliness. Instead of being regarded as a "Hottentot with clicking palate, whom the meanest of the rest look down upon for all his glimmering language and spirituality," he wished the world to find in him fitness for survival, conformity with civilization's ideal, example of the world philosophy of forbearance, human relationships, symmetry and poise in adaptation to the world's tasks, and moderation in respect of the higher laws, whose harmonies order and rectify all creation.

He sought to neutralize the misteachings of Adam Smith, of Darwin and Defoe. Smith's "Wealth of Nations" presumed the material debasement of darker peoples of colonial populations, or, in lieu thereof, such debasement of Slav, Serf or Serbian as would compensate the vanity of the superior people. Indirectly, Darwin taught, that the Negro closely approached the missing link between the savage beast and the human. Defoe delighted the world with a picture of the ideal economic status for the maintenance of white superiority over black man. These ideas the Negro wished to topple over.

He felt it necessary to repudiate the indoctrination of racial hatred proclaimed throughout the world by "The Birth of a Nation." He set over against it the reception by all civilization of the Booker T. Washington life story. He wished to substitute recognition of worth in place of the things that debase and make ashamed.

His great puzzle was the Anglo-Saxon, cold, austere and uncomplaisant. This Caucasian, fair of skin, with smooth and wavy hair, small cheekbones and elevated fore-head, appeared a worshipful master whose station, under God, was of preordained and predestined eminence. Occu-pying Eurasia from the Channel to the Ganges, together with the most favored portions of Africa and America, he was the author and agency for law and order for the world. St. Augustine, first archbishop and lawgiver of Canterbury, himself of African descent, the son of Monica and Patri-cius of Carthage, had left the Anglo-Saxon from semi-barbarism to his position of world renown. Would this Anglo-Saxon ever degrade the sons of women of Africa?

The Negro's next puzzle was the French, urbane, amenable and suave. Negro emotions and French sensibili-ties mingled even without recourse to the vehicle of lan-guage. Imbued with all the finer Latin qualities and char-acteristics, the French ever invited the black man to a social world which the Anglo-Saxon denied him. E. W. Lightner, writing as a war correspondent, says:

"Long previous to the war thousands of blacks from various States of Africa were in France, most especially Paris, at the universities, in business and in the better ranges of service. Everywhere and by all sorts and condi-tions of whites, they were treated as equals. During sev-eral visits to the French capital I, an American, knowing full well the prejudices of whites of this country against the race, was amazed to see the cordial mingling of all phases of the cosmopolitan population of the French capi-tal. Refined white men promenaded the streets with re-fined black women, and the two races mingled cordially in studies, industries and athletic sports. White and black artists had ateliers in common in the Latin quarter. . . ."

Thus, at hob and nob with the civilities and honors and embraces of this social life, the Negro felt an unaccustomed giddiness seize him. This giddiness was not caused by lack of social poise, nor incited by the French, but it arose from the dilemma, or rather peril, in which the French intercourse placed him with relation to the adjustment of darker races to Anglo-Saxon civilization.

Nevertheless in 1914, the approach to this court of honour and equality must be made by the Negro—and made under restraint sufficient to assure Anglo-Saxon approval. This was, indeed, a complex problem. Traducers proclaimed his undeveloped capacities; he answered with a claim of long repressed aptitudes. They spoke of intolerable coalescence; he claimed that the times demanded imperative coexistence. They said he had no soul; he claimed the over-soul. They asserted his lecherous character; he referred to statistics. But when they claimed he was pro-German, he stripped for action. World war, and France, prostrate amid its terrors, offered the Negro the great opportunity of the centuries to refute the broadcast propaganda of his enemies.

Beyond the French appeared the German, ungainly, acrimonious and obdurate. Part Saxon, part Hun, part Vandal and Visigoth, a creature of blood and iron, he utilized every force of nature to exterminate his enemies. The Negro knew how to exploit none of nature's elemental energies. But he did know that he could learn how by seizing and mastering the weapons of the enemy.

Of the energies of earth he lacked both scientific mastery and the weapons which give them offensive power and direction. Of the air he lacked all control. Fire he utilized only for purposes of cooking food, but not for the development of machinery of warfare. He has no vessel upon all the seven seas. To seize and master and utilize these energies appeared a thankless job, albeit a necessary one. He voted a grim "Aye."

In doing so, he accepted the challenge of no mere enigma. Of his own volition, he entered upon the path that led through untrod and dangerous ground. It was his problem to cut the Gordian knot of Anglo-Saxon icy reserve that in the end fair England might assume as a policy of world administration the award of citizenship rights to the darker races in the sphere of influence of the league of civilized nations. It was a part of this problem to enter the equation with such deliberate caution as to upset no part of the nicely calculated adjustments of white to darker peoples. And it was also a part of his problem that he should not relinquish his grasp upon the factors that led to honor, recognition and equality.

Germany was indignant as the Negro sought entry to the war. The South was sensitive. The North was quizzical. The whole world was hesitant. The too ardent favor which the Negro found in France gave offence to both America and England. Indeed, for the Negro to lift himself too rapidly by his own bootstraps would have offended England, whose law prohibited emigration of foreign Negroes to South Africa. And it would also offend America, strangely jealous of any sign of unwanted assertiveness the Negro might display. The Negro accepted the challenge to penetrate this maze and labyrinth, with no surety, save God's good grace, of the fate that lay beyond.

To attain the goal of Recognition, it was necessary for him to demand of the people of England, France and Italy, that he be made subject to every test calculated to reveal his worth or inferiority as an individual, business, political or social equal of the allied peoples. The goal of Honor, he had attained in every war waged by America. He was with Jackson at New Orleans, a pioneer in the Mexican struggle, 200,000 strong in the great civil crisis, the acme of terror to Geronimo in the later Indian wars, the hero of San Juan in the Spanish-American combat, and at Carrizal in the latest Mexican imbroglio. By 1914, however, he had lost all rewards of honor which he had previously won. As for Equality, since the Civil War, he had been guaranteed this goal by three amendments to the Constitution of the United States. These forgotten amendments read in part:

"Neither slavery nor involuntary servitude, except as a punishment for crime, whereof the party shall have been duly convicted, shall exist within the United States, or any place subject to their jurisdiction. . . .

"All persons born or naturalized in the United States, and subject to the jurisdiction thereof, are citizens of the United States and of the State wherein they reside. No State shall make or enforce any law which shall abridge the privileges or immunities of citizens of the United States; nor shall deprive any person of life, liberty, or property, without due process of law, nor deny to any person within its jurisdiction the equal protection of the laws. . . .

"Representatives shall be apportioned among the several States according to their respective numbers, counting the whole number of persons in each State. . . .

"The right of the citizens of the United States to vote shall not be denied or abridged by the United States or any State on account of race, color or previous condition of servitude."

America of 1914 was prone to look upon this part of the Constitution as a mere scrap of paper. From what point of vantage might the Negro hope for Honor, Recognition and Equality at the hands of the allied governments?

Land of the free and home of the brave, America is assumed to be so openhearted, munificent and princely, so liberal and so generous that could she but behold a man, of whatever hue, trampled in the mire, or hear his piteous cry, she would hasten to his aid and deliver him. So much does she admire genuine human worth that a man of heart and spirit and fortitude cannot perish while she is nigh at hand. Such, at least, is the assumption.

From the debasement of industrial serfdom, the black workman wished the American people of 1914 to stop the trend of their strenuous existence and behold him . . .

and test him . . . and proclaim him. He not only wished
to be given a free field and a fair chance to work at the same
job, for the same wage, during the same hours, and under
the same conditions as the white workman, but he was
ready to contend for all of the industrial privileges.

The black man of business not only wished to enter into
business competition with members of the Caucasian race
under the same conditions as customarily pertain to such
arrangements, but he was eagerly hoping to insure adjustment of this situation. The black social outcast wished
"jim-crow" railway accommodations and signs proclaim-
ing inequality of race to disappear. He wished sufficient
education to enable him to develop his own society. He,
too, was willing for a world war, for he had come to the
point where he desired immediate and explosive change.
Looked down upon because of his despised blood, the black
American wished to elevate the status of his womankind,
too long disproved and betrayed, to the level of free and
brave womanhood of all the civilized world. Concerning
this situation he was grim. It required but a spark applied
here to explode with terrific outburst the sinister silence of
the volcano.

But in India, in South Africa, in Nigeria, and in all
countries where English rule held sway, England was committed to the policy of the white overseer or foreman for
the black exponent of industry. Nor could she, save
through war, adopt a policy of employing either Indians or
Africans at the same job and for the same wage as that
received by members of the British Labor Party. On the
other hand, France, whose political life was convulsed from
1894 to 1899 by principles of racial prejudice exhibited in
the Dreyfus case, offered every form of equality to the
darker races under her dominion. However, such equality
offered by France was not equal in the sum total of advantage to the partial equality which the Negro received in

America. The French workman gave more hours of toil for less monetary reward. The Negro wanted to bring the French principle of equality to apply in American industry. But the British in 1914 could not agree to industrial equality for black men. Such agreement would upset the nicely calculated economic adjustments of the English system. America would take no step until forced to do so.

It was the problem of the Negro, alone and singlehanded, to grasp the opportunity afforded by world war to bring America to this point of recognition and democratic equality. The Negro, hitherto regarded as the monkeyman, the baby race, the black brute, trained by such ruthless propaganda to disrespect himself, hesitated.

There was no leadership. No ringleader arrayed the mob. No chief appeared. No captain called the hosts. No generalissimo marshalled the black phalanx. No statesman sought entanglement in the meshes of the negro labyrinth. But the Negro proposition for a test of Negro fitness, like Topsy, "just growed." The young Negro possessed the clear eye to see the situation. College trained, his vision was not blinded by proximity to issues of the Civil War, nor by financial dependence, nor by excessive spirituality. The elder Negro possessed the oratorical and linguistic powers to state the case. Also college trained, of long experience, possessing a widespread oratorical clientele, he spoke with a voice that stirred and played upon the heartstrings of all America. Never was such a proposition advanced where men, old and young, despised and rejected, penniless and without credit, without acclaimed leadership or champion, sought position of honor and recognition and equality beside the best fighting forces of the world to help defeat the greatest military machine that hell had ever invented.

Capital and labor, in previous years, had found the Negro wanting. State governments had utilized him for the purpose of increasing taxes and court fees. The national government always handled him in accordance with political expediency, despite his unswerving loyalty. Capital, labor, State government and national government had brought the Negro so low that he was ready in 1914 for any form of relief.

The Negro was ready for change, for one reason, because he had lost the honor of ministership to Haiti, Henry W. Furniss being succeeded by a white man. He was ready for change because, as the continental war proceeded, it became evident that though America might participate, her black colonel, Charles Denton Young, a graduate of West Point, and a distinguished soldier, might receive recognition as the leader of black forces on foreign soil. He was ready for change because it appeared that there had been agreement that no American Negro should participate in a test of world equality upon the field of world honor and renown.

In the American Navy Department, in 1914, time had destroyed the wake of Negro tradition, and the log had been deleted. The Negro has rendered honorable service in the navy. He was with Perry on Lake Erie. During the Civil War, Robert Smalls, a Negro, single-handed, stole the Union cruiser "Planter" from Charleston harbor and brought her into a Union port. Half the men who accompanied Hobson into Santiago harbor were Negroes. Matt Henson was the only man with Peary at the Pole. John Jordan fired the first shot from Dewey's flagship "Olympia," opening the battle of Manila. The Negro wanted change because in 1914 the naval administration reluctantly offered Negroes positions as messmen and cooks. No seamen, no members of the merchant marine, no petty officers, no lieutenants, might apply.

In the American Treasury Department, an ex-Senator of the United States, a colored man, Blanche K. Bruce of

Mississippi, was honored by having created for him the office of register of the treasury. Subsequently the honor was conferred as a political favor upon Judson W. Lyons, of Georgia; William T. Vernon, of Kansas, and J. C. Napier, of Tennessee. The democratic executive was good enough to offer this position, created as a direct result of the Negro's activities during and after the Civil War, to Adam E. Patterson, of Oklahoma. But so great was the pressure from opposing political forces that the name was withdrawn and another position of honor lost to the race. Ralph W. Tyler, auditor of the navy, resigned his position in 1912. A white man was appointed in his place. Screens were erected in this department, shutting the Negro from the view of his erstwhile fellow-clerk. He was sent down in the cellar to emphasize his degradation as he attended to his physical wants. The Negro cried aloud for change, and in his heart he cared not how soon this change should come, nor what form it should take.

The American Post-office Department, by 1914, had taken over the bulk of the express service of the United States. The Negro was found available as a clerk, but seldom, if ever, as a foreman. The appointment of large numbers of Negroes to mere clerical positions did not mean to the Negro recognition of merit. The Negro postmaster had disappeared.

The American Department of the Interior is engaged with domestic affairs of the nation. The Negro constitutes one-tenth of the population and requires one-tenth of the necessities of American life. In 1914, a definite attempt was made in a bureau of this department to give the Negro recognition, honor and near-equality by the policy of segregating him into a Negro bureau. This policy had previously been worked out in Negro school systems and in the army. But the Negro clerks of the Interior Department, by unanimous vote, rejected the proposition for this sort of change. The kind of recognition, the kind of honor and the kind of equality which they desired had taken definite shape in their minds.

The American Agricultural Department, it would appear, should be made up of a large percentage of Negroes. The Negro was essentially an agriculturist before he came to America. He was brought to Virginia for the specific purpose of engaging in agriculture. His development of agricultural conferences in the South in recent years has been a great source of production. The Negro wanted change because this department employed messengers and clerks, but demonstrators seldom, if ever, of his color. Agricultural strategy in 1914 might well have been exonerated if it had employed Negro chief demonstrators and engaged them in interstate contest for quantity production. In one Southern State the Negro operates the greater agricultural area. In another he will operate the greater portion of such districts at an early date. In still another many of the communities of large Negro population have hardly had a white foot set upon them in two decades. The Negroes of these three states could have furnished surplus food for any nation of the allies, but a Negro might receive honor if put in charge of their development at the proper salary and with full authority to act. In 1914, this honor must not be.

In the American Department of Commerce the masters of barter and exchange are exhibited. America seeks to develop the man who can strike a bargain and outbid his competitors. The Negro wanted change because, since the invention of salesmanship he has been declared out of the scope of this department. His social status prevents him from making the proper sales approach. The Negro of 1914 came to this department only as a depositor of funds, or as a beggar for charity. He was not seriously regarded.

Lastly, in the American Department of Labor, the

Negro wanted change because he was regarded in 1914 as the man requiring a boss of another color. He was not regarded as a master mechanic, manufacturer, artist or journeyman, unless the labor union, to which he was ineligible, so regarded him.

In these many ways, by capital and labor, by state and national government, in every department, had the Negro of 1914 been reduced to the state of man without honor in his own country. If war be change, however explosive in form, in 1914 the Negro wanted the world war to come to America from whatever angle that promised him the greatest advantage.

Equality in citizenship, for which the Negro yearned, meant parity of adjustment to conditions of life. Equality may be considered under three forms, industrial, business and political. As the terms are understood in America, the Negro was unanimous in 1914 in desiring industrial, business and political equality. He eagerly watched the fuse of war if perchance he might foresee from the consequent explosion the termination of Anglo-Saxon prejudice. It is but fair to say that he was not the only victim of discrimination at that time. The sub-dominant nations, including the Jugo-Slavs, the Czecho-Slavs, the Serbs and the Serfs of Russia, were subject to discrimination and deprived of the higher places of honor in the world's society.

But the Negro was not immediately concerned with any one's status save his own. He was not concerned that Mexicans, Chinese, Japanese, Filipinos, Porto Ricans or South Africans did not enjoy the advantage of living on American soil. He was only concerned with the fact that, living in America, performing the full duties of American citizenship, he was denied the advantages and privileges of its possession, while Slavs and Serbs of Europe, with white skins, were accorded the fullest measure of democratic opportunity whenever and wherever they set foot on American soil. The Negro wanted the world war to prove that he, too, was a coalescent element in the civilization of the world.

To summarize the burden of the Negro in 1914 we may include Caucasian arrogance, hatred and prejudice of race, injustice of attitude and treatment, personal fear for life and property, improperly requited toil, unrewarded ambition, unmerited disfavor and debased self-respect. What profound pathos in the love which he bore Old Glory!

THE WAR FOR DEMOCRATIZATION.

Germany of 1914 aimed to throw off the yoke which she claimed England wished to fasten on her world relationships. She aimed to dominate the world with German efficiency. She aimed to demonstrate German superiority and expose what she called Anglo-Saxon hypocrisy and cant. Already possessing the world's supply of potash, she struck directly at the coal and iron region of Belgium and Northern France. And she took them on the initial advance. With potash, coal and iron, this was a Teutonic coup for industrial and commercial supremacy indeed. Now well might she dictate who should boycott English goods. Now well might she point to the political and military dishonor of the easy defeat of Belgium and France. Now well might she proceed to the disintegration of these countries by the weapons of poverty, disease, hunger and bitter cold. Little did Germany dream what moral advantage she gave these overrun lands in the hearts of the millions of Negroes of the world. Germany felt assured that Negroes from all Africa would gloat over the assassination of Belgium. She was positive that American Negroes would rejoice. She expected the blacks of the world would rise up and hail her as the champion of a new day.

In the twinkling of an eye she reduced Belgium to industrial serfdom. She made the Belgian merchant a busi-

ness pariah. She reduced the Belgian citizen to a political
Helot, and imprisoned the burgomaster of Brussels, who
refused to yield his citizenship honors.   She made of Belgium a desert. The Belgian woman she whistled at and
made a bye-word and reproach. And she called her treaty
of Belgian neutrality a mere scrap of paper. Namur fell,
and Charleroi and lovely Louvain. Liege succumbed in
those hot August days, and Malines and Tournai and Antwerp. Poor Belgian refugees, starved and naked, fled westward. In remembrance of barbarities in the Congo under
the international commission which placed Belgium in control, the American Negro quoted the poet: "The sins we
borrow two by two we pay for one by one." But there was
no disposition to gloat. The American Negro, be it said,
came to the Belgian relief with money and goods and pray-
ers and tears, and forgot the sins of the fathers of the suffering little kingdom. The secret of this reaction is revealed in the sympathy which the Negro bore toward another people reduced to his American status, without honor,
recognition or equality.

On, on, precipitate, headlong came Germany with dia-
bolic efficiency, thrusting viciously at the heart of France.
Running amuck through St. Quentin and Arras, Soissons
fell and Laon. Rheims surrounded, astride the Marne,
France awaited her invader. Joffre at the gate! Foch in
charge of the defence! On came the Germans! They
crushed his left! They pulverized his right! He dispatched
his courier to headquarters with the famous message: "I
shall attack with my centre. Send up the Moroccans!"
These black troops, thrown in at the first Marne, with the
British to their left, pushed the German right over the
stream. Continuing their action, the colonials won on the
Ourcq, and the Germans evacuatel Upper Alsace. Before
their terrific attack, with the British steadily pressing beside them, General Von Stein admitted his defeat by the

white and black allies. Paris was saved and Foch discovered to the allied world. How the hearts of black Americans thrilled as slowly the news filtered through to them of what the black colonials had done to hold the field for France! It was then that they took it into their hearts that if the United States were ever called upon to participate in this struggle, they would not be denied a place of glory equal to that which their African brethren had achieved.

But there was no time for resolve. The cataclysm involved in the threatened overthrow of English law and orderly procedure throughout the world caused the American Negro to tremble. Always conservative, if there be anything to conserve, the Negro appreciated that English law, when properly interpreted, meant freedom and life and hope eternal to him. He was unwilling to take any chances with a German substitute. The overthrow of English law he looked upon as the impending crack of doom. On came the Germans toward Calais and the Straits of Dover! On to Zeebrugge! On to Ostend! To Ypres! In her supreme desperation, England looked about the world for a force to stay the invader until she could prepare to meet the full force of the attack. She cared not whether aid be white or black, or brown or yellow. She called for help, or else Ypres should fall. Black men of Africa, brown men of India, white and red men of Canada, and yellow men of the Far East heard her call. And while America lifted not a finger, the American Negro lifted up his heart to God and prayed that Anglo-Saxon justice, rigid and cold, so often denied him, should not perish in triumph of the Hun, who knew no law save his own lust and super-arrogation.

Aboard the "Lusitania" there were no known men of color. But there were Caucasian women and children aboard. At what moral disadvantage did Germany put herself with the black millions of America when she riotously celebrated the horrible death her submarines had meted out to these weak and helpless mortals. The "Belgian Prince," first of the vessels torpedoed without warning after President Wilson's manifesto on the subject, had one lone black survivor to tell the tale of horror. He told it to his black brethren and they chafed under the diplomatic restraint, which relieved itself by polite letter writing.

Germany threatened the Panama Canal by disruption in Mexico and Haiti. The Mole St. Nicholas gave command of the canal to anyone of the great powers who might seize it. German influence was at work in Port au Prince. There occurred a riot involving both French and German Legations. The President of Haiti was assassinated. The United States marines stepped in and took over the situation. The American Negro heart went out to little Haiti. Hoping for the best, he feared the worst.

In the midst of this situation, Pancho Villa attacked Columbus, New Mexico. Overnight Negro regiments of regular army and of national guard received word to go to the border. Black troopers of the 10th Cavalry were reported near Casas Grandes on March 17. The 24th Infantry, colored, set out for Mexico, and another Negro command was sent to Columbus on March 22. Through storm and dust and desert of alkali and cacti, the Negro troopers, led by Colonel Brown, came to Aguascalientes. They had passed through a terrible experience that must have daunted all save those who refuse to accept defeat. Hunger and thirst and mirage and exposure must all be overcome. Because of hardships many cavalrymen deserted on May 1, after three months' service in action. But every Negro trooper with Colonel Brown held on and defeated the Villistas in every skirmish.

On a day in June, 1916, a troop from the 10th Cavalry approached the Mexican town of Carrizal. They were forbidden to enter the town for purposes of refreshment. Captain Boyd resolved to make the entry regardless of any regulations the Mexicans might seek to enforce. He was called upon by General Gomez to advance for a parley. As he advanced with his troopers, Mexicans spread out in a wide circle around them. Gomez, himself, trained the machine gun which opened fire. The parley was a mere sham and decoy. Captain Boyd with Lieutenant Adair and eleven soldiers were killed. The rest of the troopers fell on the Mexicans, seized their gun, turned it upon them, and brought to death scores of their number, including Gomez himself. Seventeen black Americans were interned in Chihuahua, but were released eight days after upon demand by the American government. Captain Morey reported that his men faced death with a song on their lips. The lesson which the Mexicans learned by turning a machine gun on Negro troopers was of such force that no trouble has arisen since in this section of the southern republic. The Negro fell face forward in the scorching sand for his honor's sake, and for the honor of all America. He knew that his real enemy was not the Mexican, but the German who had furnished Mexico the means and the will to create disturbance on this side of the Atlantic.

It was not until April, 1917, that President Wilson proclaimed in Congress a state of war existing between the United States of America and the Imperial German Government. At the call for volunteers, Negro regiments of guard, who had served in Mexico, were found at war strength and ready to double themselves overnight. These guard regiments represented the cosmopolitan Negro populations of New York, Chicago, Washington, Baltimore and the State of Ohio. Everywhere the Negro dropped the mattock, left the ploughshare, poised himself at erect stature, passionately saluted Old Glory answered "Here am I!"— counted fours, and away! Pro-German cried: "White man's war!" Propagandist yelled: "Cannon fodder!" Reactionary declared: "It must not be." The Negro burst the gate and entered the arena of combat in spite of all opposition to his service in honorable capacity under the United States government.

The honesty of his purpose was discredited. The Anglo-Saxon mind could not conceive any more than could the German why a man downtrodden as the Negro should rush to arms, save as a baser means of eking out a livelihood better than his civilian state. The Anglo-Saxon little dreamed that the Negro approached the war not only to uphold his cherished tradition, but also with definite ideas of honor, recognition and equality as its outcome. Or rather the Anglo-Saxon was too busy with his own affairs to ascertain the reason why.

His loyalty impugned by those who did not wish to see him uniformed, his fidelity the subject of bitter sarcasm, his trustworthiness disputed, the Negro for once kept his own counsel. German agents were in his midst. They came to his table. They mingled with him in all social intercourse. They brought forward business propositions to seek to make the interests of Negro and German one. Southerners, noting this unaccustomed intimacy of black and white, announced that the Negro had gone over to the enemy. But the Negro kept his own counsel. He called upon the nation to investigate him. And when his loyalty was found untarnished, he called upon the nation to investigate itself. It was through the influence of Robert R. Moton, of Tuskegee, that, after careful investigation, President Wilson put the stain of pro-Germanism where it properly belonged. Said the President:

My Fellow-Countrymen:

I take the liberty of addressing you upon a subject which so vitally affects the honour of the nation and the very character and integrity of our institutions that I trust you will think me justified in speaking very plainly about it.

I allude to the mob spirit which has recently here and there very frequently shown its head amongst us, not in any single region, but in many and widely separated parts of the country. There have been many lynchings, and every one of them has been a blow at the heart of ordered law and humane justice. No man who loves America, no man who really cares for her fame and honour and character, or who is truly loyal to her institutions, can justify mob actions while the courts of justice are open and the governments of the states and the nation are ready and able to do their duty. We are at this very moment fighting lawless passion. Germany has outlawed herself among the nations because she has disregarded the sacred obligations of law and has made lynchers of her armies. Lynchers emulate her disgraceful example. I, for my part, am anxious to see every community in America rise above that level, with pride and fixed resolution which no man or act of men can afford to despise.

We proudly claim to be the champions of democracy. If we really are, in deed and in truth, let us see to it that we do not discredit our own. I say plainly that every American who takes part in the action of a mob or gives it any sort of countenance is no true son of this great democracy, but its betrayer, and does more to discredit her by that single disloyalty to her standards of law and of right than the words of her statesmen or the sacrifices of her heroic boys in the trenches can do to make suffering peoples believe her to be their saviour. How shall we commend democracy to the acceptance of other peoples, if we disgrace our own by proving that it is, after all, no protection to the weak? Every mob contributes to German lies about the United States what her most gifted liars cannot improve upon by way of calumny. They can at least say that such things cannot happen in Germany, except in times of revolution, when law is swept away.

I, therefore, very earnestly and solemnly beg that the Governors of all the States, the law officers of every community, and, above all, the men and women of every community in the United States, all who revere America and wish to keep her name without stain or reproach, will co-operate—not passively merely, but actively and watchfully,—to make an end of this disgraceful evil. It cannot live where the community does not countenance it.

I have called upon the nation to put its great energy into this war, and it has responded—responded with a spirit and a genius for action that has thrilled the world. I now call upon it, upon its men and women everywhere, to see that its laws are kept inviolate, its fame untarnished. Let us show our utter contempt for the things that have made this war hideous among the wars of history by showing how those who love liberty and right and justice and are willing to lay down their lives for them upon foreign fields, stand ready also to illustrate to all mankind their loyalty to the things at home which they wish to see established everywhere as a blessing and protection to the peoples who have never known the privileges of liberty and self-government. I can never accept any man as a champion of liberty, either for ourselves or for the world, who does not reverence and obey the laws of our own beloved land, whose laws we ourselves have made. He has adopted the standard of the enemies of his country, whom he affects to despise.

WOODROW WILSON.

The Negro braced himself, dismissed the German coldly from his household and forebade the pro-German enter. From afar off the enemy propagandist could resort but to derision and ridicule. What an attempt at laughter he made when Haiti entered the side of the Allies! How he pretended to be choking with the ridiculousness of the thing when Liberia offered her services! He flouted the idea of Negro expertness in handling weapons of modern warfare. He ridiculed the idea of Negro discretion in ideas of likely foreign origin. He questioned the potency of the Negro's native talent to meet the European situation. It was the black man's patriotic fervor, ardent in response to the call of Old Glory, zealous with passionate love of fireside and homeland, poignant with the throbbing and thrilling reaction of public-spirited emotion toward France—which overcame all.

The South asked three questions:

First—Shall Negroes and whites of the South both remain in America while the North conducts the war? Second—Shall Negroes of the South remain at home while the flower of southern chivalry, drafted for service, is far away across the sea, annihilated in battle? Third—Shall white men of the South be left at home while southern Negroes are drafted and go abroad to do distinguished service? These questions were resolved into the conclusion that southern Negroes and southern whites both must be drafted and sent against the German foe. There was no alternative.

It was altogther becoming and proper that a man whose race has suffered as the American Negro suffers today, should point the way to this goal of recognition, honor and equality which the Negro knew but as a tradition of those days following the Civil War when Grant administered the affairs of the triumphant party of freedom.

One of those New Yorkers of Hebraic origin, whose Semitic qualities are of the highest ethical type, made the play for partial equality, for partial recognition, for partial honor for the Negro. Joel Spingarn suggested and propagated the idea of a military training camp for Negroes, where they might receive instruction in all branches of military service, be commissioned up to the grade of captain and receive the recognition, honor and equality due to such military rank as they might qualify for. In addressing Negro America, he said:

"It is of highest importance that the educated colored men of this country should be given opportunities for leadership. You must cease to remain in the background in every field of national activity, and must come forward to assume your right places as leaders of American life. All of you cannot be leaders, but those who have the capacity for leadership must be given the opportunity to test and display it."

Mr. Spingarn never realized what forces he would set in motion by mere presentation of this proposition. He merely pointed out the gate. The young Negro brushed aside the opponents among his own race of this policy of segregation. He disregarded the moral principle which had actuated the older Negroes of the Interior Department in refusing to accept segregation, and seized the opportunity to produce some sort of change and readjustment. He must go up. He could go no lower than the policies of previous generations had brought him.

Directly to the President of all the United States he went. "Give us a lift!" he cried, "We want to fight!" To the Secretary of War he shouted most unceremoniously: "Give us place!" "But," was the indirect reply, "we have not the facilities at present. For instance, we have no bedding for the men whom you might muster." It was a young Negro Harvard graduate, Thomas Montgomery Gregory, of New Jersey, who advanced before Secretary Baker. "No bedding, Mr. Secretary? We will sleep on the floor—on the ground—anywhere—give us a lift!"

The Anglo-Saxon mind is subject to orderly reactions. The Secretary of War was taken aback. He realized that the young Negroes had not approached him to sell their labor. He gleaned that it was not for the purpose of barter and exchange they had come forward. Nor had they come with dreams of political advantage and social eclat, nor with vague glimmerings of spirituality. He was not ready to answer. He dismissed the audience with a little more than the usual ceremony. One of the older Negroes of the group, whose uncanny insight had often appeared beyond the orbit of average intelligence, ventured this suggestion: "He will put it up to Pershing."

And so the word got abroad that it would be left to Pershing as to how the Negro should be disposed of. It would be left to John J. Pershing, who in his earlier days had been instructor in a Negro college under the American Missionary Association. It would be left to the man who in 1892 had been a First Lieutenant in the 10th Cavalry in connection with the Sioux campaign in the Dakotas; who had been with the 10th Cavalry in the Santiago campaign in 1898; who had led Negro troops in the Philippines in 1899 till 1903, commanding operations in Mindanao against the Moros; and who had been in command of the Negro troops sent into Mexico in pursuit of Villa in March, 1916. It would be left to the man whose whole life had been spent in close contact with darker races.

To this day the Negro does not know who was directly responsible for the organization of the camp such as Spingarn proposed. It is probable that the honor belongs as much to Henry Johnson and Needham Roberts as to any one else. These black soldiers of Colonel Hayward's 15th New York Regiment, already in France with other regiments of Negro troopers of the national guard, were thrown across No Man's Land on a cold and foggy night as a lookout, far in advance of the sleeping command of thousands of white and colored American troops. The Hun planned their capture for the purpose of psycho-analytic research. It was Roberts who detected their stealthy approach. He called to Johnson. In the twinkling of an eye, the two were surrounded by German troopers. The Negroes faced certain death, but they had lost all claim to honor, recognition or equality, if they did not take with them to eternity at least one German each. Surrounded they resolved to fight it out with shot and gun. Too, too slow! Around them the Germans swarmed like bees. Bayonets then! Too, too close! Aye, butts! Wounded and winded, with knives, skulls, feet, teeth and nails, prehensile toe and larkheel, Henry Johnson and Needham Roberts defeated ten times their number of Germans and held the field of honor. This was a great self-revelation to the

Negro of his powers of more than rudimentary culture, and a mighty incentive from the guard to the soldiery of the 92nd Division.

It settled forever, in the mind of the Negro, what Pershing would say as to the advisability of training Negroes to deliver their best service for their country. That general's report electrified the entire nation. Said Pershing:

"Reports in hand show a notable instance of bravery and devotion shown by two soldiers of an American colored regiment operating in a French sector. Before daylight on May 15, Private Henry Johnson and Private Roberts, while on sentry duty at some distance from one another, were attacked by a German raiding party, estimated at twenty men, who advanced in two groups, attacking at once flank and rear.

"Both men fought bravely hand-to-hand encounters, one resorting to the use of a bolo knife after his rifle jammed and further fighting with bayonet and butt became impossible. There is evidence that at least one, and probably a second, German was severely cut. A third is known to have been shot.

"Attention is drawn to the fact that the colored sentries were first attacked and continued fighting after receiving wounds, and despite the use of grenades by a superior force. They should be given credit for preventing, by their bravery, the capture of any of our men."

Whether this citation arrived May 19, 1917, by design or by accident, it served the purpose of dissolving completely all opposition to the idea of training Negroes to halt the Hun. Immediately thereafter the War Department created a training camp for educated Negroes at Fort Des Moines, Iowa.

THE CRISIS OF THE WORLD.

Des Moines Camp was organized in June, 1917, to train Negroes to the military point where other military men must recognize them, honor them and receive them on the plane of equality due their rank. The camp was designed to develop Negroid snap and vigor to the maximum of military efficiency. For this purpose, as at all other camps, there was created the background of the mother's urge, and the sister's urge, and the sweetheart's urge, the Y. M. C. A. spirit, the college fraternity spirit, and, in addition, the spirit of the elevation of a Negroid order.

The change which came over the men was indicated by their music. Their first group singing of a Sunday consisted of Negro spirituals in spondaic and trochaic verse, and phrased in many minors. The vigor of blood produced by methodical training soon permitted of vocalization only in iambics. "Over There," "The Long, Long Trail," "Sons of America," were songs they sung of hope and not of sorrow. They connoted the Negro's reaction to the cosmic urge.

Over 1200 men took advantage of the experience of the trip to Fort Des Moines for training. Theirs was the 17th Provisional R. O. T. C., but the first of national proportions. Its quota was drawn from every section of the United States. The immediate destiny of the men selected for commission from this camp would be the training of colored draftees of African descent.

Mr. Baker, the Secretary of War, in late summer, referring to the Des Moines Camp, said:

"The work at Des Moines is progressing remarkably well, and the reports I have from it are very good. The spirit of the men is fine, and apparently this camp is going to do a great deal of good, both to the country and to the men involved."

Colonel C. C. Ballou, of the War College, in charge of the work at Des Moines, said on August 19, in a Sunday interview:

"The colored race constitutes more than ten per cent. of our population, and has, since the Civil War, furnished more than its quota of fighting men of the regular army. At home or on foreign soil the ranks of colored regiments are always full, while the white regiments have with difficulty been maintained at peace strength. To question the valor of the colored soldier is to betray ignorance of history. This is the first opportunity in his history to prove on an adequate scale his fitness or unfitness for command and leadership. At Fort Des Moines, Iowa, on June 16, 1917, there assembled the largest body of educated Negroes ever brought together for a single purpose. The candidates who survive are men of marked intelligence and ability. Let any man who doubts the colored men's patriotism go to Fort Des Moines and see men who have given up professions, business and homes in order to learn to defend their country and merit a more considerate judgment of their race. Let any man who doubts the colored man's fidelity and loyalty come to Fort Des Moines and revise his opinions on what he will there learn of the spirit that has stood unswervingly behind the commanding officer in every decision that he has been called upon to make, even though that decision involved sore disappointment and shattering of hopes. These men have been started out on correct lines and will have no false ideas to unlearn."

Hardly any one in America, black or white, believed that 700 Negroes would be commissioned in the army of the United States to receive positions of honor not only beside her other troops, but on the field of battle with the flower of French and English between veteran soldiery. Everything possible to prevent, somehow or other, seemed to arise. The men were put through the bitterest drill in the hottest sun, under the most scorching orders the English language might devise. They represented every section of the United States. Not once did they break. The acid test came, when, already pricked by the numerous situations which arose to flout them, East St. Louis broke forth in the most savage pogrom Anglo-Saxon culture has ever revealed.

While 1200 Negroes, training for leadership, were undergoing the terrific process of forced attrition, their nerves turned raw by army usage, East St. Louis burst forth. Tidings reached Des Moines that the Illinois militia, called in to break up a race riot at East St. Louis, had joined the rioters and slaughtered the Negro population of the community. White women had joined in these attacks, dragging out of their houses colored women, girls and children, stoning and clubbing them to death. Aged Negro mammies, afraid to come out of their homes, had been burned to death by the mob which set fire to them. Black men had been thrown into Cahokia Creek and stormed with bricks each time they rose to the surface until drowned. A crowd of whites had torn a colored woman's baby from her arms, thrown it into the fire of a blazing dwelling, held the mother from its rescue until she, herself, was shot nigh unto death, and then allowed her to plunge into the fire to rescue her little one. Nor was this all.

But out there in camp, isolated from the usual social life, July 2 and 3 and 4, Independence Day, was indeed a test of nerve, already tried and sore and raw, for the young Negroes in training. Why should men train to fight for a country that permitted such barbarous atrocities against their race with impunity. In savage Memphis charred remains of Negroes burned at the stake before a gala mob of 15,000, were thrown from an automobile in the Negro quarter of that city! And the Negroes at Des Moines held on. It has not been recorded in history that there was here proposed any hostile demonstration, or that vengeance and ruthless retaliation was planned. Wise counsel prevailed, and the Negroes at Des Moines held on.

For three months they held on without audible murmur. Negroes from civilian life, from the national guard, from the regular army, destined for every branch of the military service, defied any propaganda, by whomever invented, to break their morale. For three months they held on. And then word came they would not be graduated. A number, in disgust, left the camp. But the great bulk of them, although at the last moment learning that they could be assigned to no military branch save infantry, remained in camp for another month and were finally commissioned as officers in the national army. It was the eleventh hour of the eleventh day of the eleventh month of 1917 that they received their commissions forwarded from the President of the United States. The hour and day and month a year later became famous not only in their history, but in the history of the civilized world.

They were given a grade neither high nor low. The rank of captain was granted to men who were to serve in France and England. The former country proudly made the Negro a general when he merited promotion; the latter was committed to the policy of white officers for colonial troops. In assigning rank as high as the grade of captain, America took the middle ground. In view of the international situation, she could hardly be expected to do more. She had granted partial recognition, partial honor, partial equality. It was for the Negro to gain the rest.

Seven hundred American Negroes commissioned! A baker's dozen of captains, six hundred odd lieutenants, and five hundred who dropped by the way. German propaganda had taken contrary suggestion and forced the Negro to this point of moral advantage. Plunder, arson, lynching and burning at the stake were employed against him to break his morale or incite him against America. But he held on. Seven hundred of the "sub-species, dark of skin, wooly of hair, long of head, with dilated nostrils, thick lips, thicker cranium, flat feet, prehensile great toe and lark heel" had passed every physical, mental, moral and social test and were commissioned in the American army. Doubt existed in the minds of every American citizen, including the Negro officers themselves, that they would ever see service overseas.

Assigned to various camps, the problem of recognition by white soldiers of colored officers immediately was raised, and promptly settled. In only a few cases did open clashes occur. In far more cases was the Negro received with full merited honors of his status, and in some sections on the basis of complete equality. The Negro of a northern locality, accustomed to all immunities and privileges of his home, experienced great difficulty when first assigned to camps near Baltimore, Washington, Houston or Norfolk. He would have passed through this state of his development well enough, settling his difficulties himself as they arose, had not some evil genius prompted the commanding officer of the division in which he was finally to be assembled to issue Bulletin 35, which follows:

"It should be well known to all colored officers and men that no useful purpose is served by such acts as will cause the 'color question' to be raised. It is not a question of legal rights, but a question of policy, and any policy that tends to bring about a conflict of the races, with its resulting animosities, is prejudicial to the military interest of the colored race.

"To avoid such conflicts the Division Commander has repeatedly urged that all colored members of his command and especially the officers and non-commissioned officers, should refrain from going where their presence will be resented. In spite of this injunction, one of the Sergeants of the Medical Department has recently precipitated the precise trouble that should be avoided, and then called on the Division Commander to take sides in a row that should never have occurred had the Sergeant placed the general good above his personal pleasure and convenience. The

Sergeant entered a theater, as he undoubtedly has a legal right to do, and precipitated trouble by making it possible to allege race discrimination in the seat which he was given. He is strictly within his legal rights in this matter, and the theater manager is legally wrong. Nevertheless, the Sergeant is guilty of the greater wrong in doing ANYTHING, no matter how legally correct, that will provoke race animosity.

"The Division Commander repeats that the success of the Division, with all that success implies, is dependent upon the good will of the public. That public is nine-tenths white. White men made the Division, and they can break it just as easily if it becomes a trouble maker.

"All concerned are again enjoined to place the general interest of the Division above personal pride and gratification. Avoid every situation that can give rise to racial ill-will. Attend quietly and faithfully to your duties, and don't go where your presence is not desired.

"This will be read to all organizations of the 92nd Division.

"By command of Major-General Ballou:
                              "ALLEN J. GREER,
                    "Lieutenant-Colonel, General Staff,
                              "Chief of Staff.
    "Official:
      "EDW. J. TURGEON,
          "Captain, Assistant Adjutant,
            "Acting Adjutant."

It was an altogether modern type of Negro that informed the commanding general quietly, but firmly, that he had seriously impaired his usefulness by the tone of his bulletin; that he had proposed a principle which did not bode good for the future of white people of the world when seven-tenths of the world's population was of darker hue. It is to General Ballou's credit that he admitted the question to debate, listened to reason, and capitulated.

But a certain type of southern statesmanship was not amenable to reason. Despite the wishes of the President of the United States, there were published in the "Congressional Record" articles describing the peril involved in arming and training any black peoples for modern warfare. What measure of offense these articles gave to Morocco, to India, to Latin America, to Japan, to China, to Africa, loyally supporting all the cause of France and England, can only be judged by the rebuke which President Wilson gave when his chance came.

It was in the Spring of 1918 when Germany struck through the British forces in Picardy. Then came the allies' "Hurry up!" call. The enemy opened a tremendous drive against the British front, bombarding, storming and attacking along fifty miles from Croiselles to La Fere. On the first day, 16,000 British prisoners were taken. The shelling might be heard across the Channel in Dover. The German penetrated to the third British line, taking 25,000 more prisoners. William Hohenzollern, himself, directed the drive from his headquarters at Spa. Peronne, Ham and Chauny fell. Vast stores and war material was lost, including tanks. At the Lotos club dinner, Lord Reading gave voice to a message from Lloyd George urging the United States to rush men to fill the gap. Albert fell. The real need of England and France became a question of reserves. John J. Pershing, drawing no color line, offered the whole American army.

Germany separated France from her ally. Apprized of America's preparations, she sought to destroy both France and England before the new enemy might hold place. Acceleration of all fighting forces to overseas service became the imperative duty. Not a moment was to be lost. The American Expeditionary Force must be expeditious. Casting about to find those ready to answer the call, America could not deny the preparedness of her 92nd Division of colored troopers.

On Germany came! On to Montdidier! To Amiens!

To Hazebrouck! To Paris! Montdidier gone! "Hurry! Hurry!" cried Clemenceau. "Hurry! Hurry!" pleaded the aged Premier. He could no longer study the possible effects of any action of his office upon the future. His concern was the very present need. He wanted men, regardless of what adjustments their presence might upset in future world relationships.

So came a day when the Negro troopers could no longer be gainsaid. "Give me these men!" cried Joffre. "I am ready for the 92nd," announced Pershing. "We submit that they are men without honor, and of inferior American status," warned some Americans. "We shall test them," was Foch's laconic reply. "But they are black men with but 35 ounces of brain—a sub-species of mankind," America warned again.

And all France cried: "Send us men—men without fear of mortal danger—men of intrepid heart—men of audacity—men of fortitude—men of resolution—men of unquestioning, unreasoning, undying courage—men of elan—men of morale! Send Jew or Gentile—white men, yellow men, brown men, black men—it matters not! Send us men who can halt the Hun!"

So early in May of 1918 went up to sea, partly under their own officers, 90,000 and more American Negroes, registered as of African descent, and drafted to do battle in France. It was sub-species against super-man, broad head against long head, flat nose against sharp nose, thick cranium against Hun helmet. It was this unprecedented synthetic group of black men sailing the sea of darkness on a mission concerning the vital interests of Englishmen and Americans who had misused them for centuries, and concerning beloved France, which laid the real claim for honor and recognition and equality for the American Negro.

The American Negro, as he bade his black comrades "Good-bye! Good luck! God bless you! Take keer o' yo' self!'' felt in his heart that all America ought to forget her prejudices. He felt that if she did not do so, she was indeed only fit to be characterized as narrow-minded, mean-spirited, illiberal and warped—entirely unfit for the position of leadership in democratization of the world.

So taken up with this idea was the entire Negro race that an editorial appearing in the "Crisis," the leading Negro magazine, from the pen of the Negro scholar, W. E. B. Dubois, came as a dash of cold water from an upper window. This article set the whole race agog. There was nothing in it about America's forgetting her prejudices, the idea which filled the Negro heart and soul and mind. It was entitled "Close Ranks!" and read as follows:

"This is the crisis of the world. For all the long years to come men will point to the year 1918 as the great Day of Decision, the day when the world decided whether it would submit to military despotism and an endless armed peace—if peace it could be called—or whether they would put down the menace of German militarism and inaugurate the United States of the World.

"We of the colored race have no ordinary interest in the outcome. That which the German power represents to-day spells death to the aspirations of Negroes and all darker races for equality, freedom and democracy. Let us not hesitate. Let us, while this war lasts, forget our special grievances and close our ranks shoulder to shoulder with our own white fellow-citizens and the allied nations that are fighting for democracy. We make no ordinary sacrifice, but we make it gladly and willingly with our eyes lifted to the hills." While many questioned his motive, all accepted his advice.

While the grievance was not forgotten, it was not allowed to jeopardize the success of the issue to weaken the black man's allegiance. Every mother's son and father's daughter remained loyal under stress and strain which would have caused the white man to curse and die.

THE FIELD OF ACTION.

Regiments of Negro stevedores, earlier in the year, had been drafted and sent overseas. These men were drawn from a specific locality, and did not represent the entire nation. They were in command of white officers. They had been destined for the Service of Supply, a service which America performed so marvelously well that it is difficult to tell, if not here, where her chief glory lies.

Black stevedores from Alabama, and Louisiana, and Mississippi, Virginia and the Carolinas, numbering far more than the entire black forces of the 92nd Division, packed and unpacked the American Expeditionary Force in a manner never attempted since Noah loaded the Ark. Rear Admiral Wilson and General McClure cited several regiments for exceptionally efficient work. The "Leviathan," formerly the German steamship "Vaterland," was unloaded and coaled, in competition with other white and black stevedore regiments, by Company A, 301st Stevedores, young American Negroes, in fifty-six hours, a world record.

What a cheer went up from the black stevedores of the far South when there landed in their midst a mighty band of black infantry, nearly 100,000 strong who, in a few short months had learned the use of powder and shot, of sword and broadsword, of bayonet and bludgeon, of trench knife and battle-ax. Cold steel or blackjack, smooth bore or sawed-off, machine gun or automatic, were all the same to them. It was a great experience for stevedore and infantryman. And the stevedore's heart leaped to his throat as he saw the black officers of the 92nd Division maneuver and march away the men under their command.

The black stevedore wondered why America had brought him so far under white officers to behold such a sight. He beheld black quartermasters, ranking and outranking captains, furnishing their men with provision and supply. The handling of purveyance and cutlery on a huge scale by black commissioned officers was a revelation to the black stevedore of the far South who had never seen such a sight in all his days.

The stevedore beheld arrive Negro signal men, monitors of their troops and of a million whites behind them, death watch to the German enemy, destined to be sentinels and patrolmen of No Man's Land. He saw pass by black American scouts and spies and lookouts and pioneers headed for the frontiers of France to gain an immortal halo of glory.

The stevedore found in his midst elegantly groomed, but speechless Negroes whom, his friends whispered to him, belonged to the United States Intelligence Department. They had come, so the wide-mouthed stevedore was told, to pitt their 35 ounces of brain against the German's 45 ounces, and to prove that the Hun back brain is surplus overweight and should be reduced to Negro proportions. They had come to furnish General Pershing information, news, tidings and dispatch, embassy and bulletin, report and rumor. And the stevedore wondered if General Pershing would expect these Negro men to report to him information with precision and correctitude.

It was the Negro band, fresh from America, which gave the stevedore his greatest delight. Preceding the black troops everywhere, it produced a potpourri of full and semi-scores, melodies and plantation arias, that came as a refreshing novelty to weary English hearts and to the souls of jaded France.

But there were no Negro "big gun" men. The stevedore wondered if the black boys of the 92nd Division would have to get into the fight with Germany, depending upon the kind of barrage which some of the men whom he knew in America might lay down for him. True, the Negro artilleryman had been left behind in America. At Camp Taylor he was spurned and rejected. But he refused to accept rebuff. He won his way into the heart of commanding officer and subaltern, gained his training, made a superior record, witnessed the outpouring of the entire white soldiery of the camp to present arms and salute him as he went away to service, and arrived in France in breathless haste in time to lay down a perfect barrage for his black comrades as they advanced through the terrific fighting in the Argonne and the Marbache. Long will stevedore tradition recite the story of how these black "big gun men" came by.

The black stevedore represented a section of the United States. That section was thoroughly well represented. There was work done better than it ever had been done before. But, on the other hand, the 92nd Division had been drawn from every possible corner of the United States where a quota might be raised. It was the 92nd Division especially, however great might be the deeds of local regiments of guard, that would decide the great ultimate question. Regiments of Negro guard troops from New York, Chicago, Washington, Baltimore, and the State of Ohio, and Negro pioneers from the mountain regions of the Carolinas, might cover their respective localities with the surpassing glory of their achievements. And every regiment of them did. But the real issue was wrapped up in the great 92nd Division, the Negro national army commanded in large measure by Negro officers, which stepped into the international arena on that fateful day in June, 1918.

They landed when the German had spent his third offensive and was at the gates of Paris. Almost the first news which they received after they had settled on foreign soil was that Paris, the magic city which they had come so far to see, was destined to fall into the hands of the German. Albeit Chateau Thierry, the turning point of the decisive struggle of 1918, was only achieved when, for the war, a total of more than a million black men of four conti-

nents had been annihilated, the 92nd Division was eager
for the fray—was anxious to tread the field of action for the
sake of honor, and recognition and equality. It was at
Chateau Thierry, on a day soon after the arrival of the 92nd
Division in France, that Foch, the eminent generalissimo,
but then an almost unknown quantity, again gave voice to
laconicism: "The offensive shall begin and shall continue.
Bring up the colonials!" America was thrown into battle
holding honored position beside Gouraud's invincible
Africanders. The Hun was halted in his tracks, thrown
back across the second Marne, and hunted like a wolf over
the Hindenburg line and into his native lair.

Soissons, Rheims, Verdun, St. Dizier and Chemin des
Dames, all saw Negro troops of the United States in violent
action. In the Marbache, at Belie Farm, and in the Bois
de Tege d'Or, the Negro guard regiments and the Negro
92nd Division went over and at the Hun.

At Voivrette Farm and in the Bois de Frehaut, other
troops of this same division smote German superman hip
and thigh. In Voivrette Woods and in the Bois de Chemi-
not, at Moulon Brook and Seilie Bridge and Epley the 92nd
Division again victoriously contested the field of honor,
against the best soldiers Prussia might afford. From July
until November, their brothers of the Negro guard regiments, of Negro pioneers and Negro casuals were within
earshot of the murderous rumble of contending artillery.
By November 8 every command in the Negro American division, including the units of guard, had more than once or
twice been at the front or over the top and at them.

Ralph W. Tyler, of Ohio, a Negro on the staff of General Pershing, representing the Bureau of Public Information, says of Hill 304:

"I have learned that Hill 304, which the French so
valiantly held, and which suffered such a fierce bombardment from the Germans that there is not a single foot of it

but what is plowed up by shells, and whose sides, even to-day, are literally covered with the corpses of French sol-diers who still lie where they fell, was later as valiantly held by the colored soldiers from the United States, who fought with all the heroism and endurance the best tradition of the army had chronicled.   The colored soldiers who held that bloody and ever historical Hill 304 had the odds against them, but like Tennyson's immortal 'Six Hundred,' they fought bravely and well, firm in the belief 'it was not theirs to reason why—it was theirs to do and die.'   And like the patriots they were, they did DO, and this war's history will so record.''

The Prussian, at last, sought safety in flight.   Brit-isher, Frenchman, Italian, Portuguese, Canadian, black and white American were at his heels.   Italy created a de-bacle in Austria.   And then, wonderful news came through of what was happening in the Near East.

It had been impossible for the Negroes of America to come to France and preserve the nicely calculated adjust-ments which England had set up through the years.   The East Indian, the Arabian, the Egyptian could not but ob-serve, and observing, fail to understand why American Negroes could be entrusted in command of troops, if they were not given the same recognition and honor and equal-ity.   Quietly England prepared them all.   Under General Allenby and dark-skinned officers of the East, the black Caucasians and the brown Caucasians and the yellow Cau-casians fell upon the Turk, until, regardless of his German master, he cried aloud for terms.   The horde of dark-skinned captors of Turkey, under the British supreme com-mand, threatened and attacked Bulgaria, who quickly suc-cumbed.   So came the Turkish armistice, and the Bulga-rian armistice and the Austrian armistice.

The Prussian fled from the field of battle.   He was not swift enough.   Brought to bay, he cried for mercy.   All of the Negro American force was to be hurled at him in the greatest stronghold of the world, Metz. He pleaded with the American President for armistice, and was referred to Marshal Foch. It was the great war hero, with the Hohenzollern house of cards tumbled about him, who decided that for three days, until November 11, fighting must continue, and that in those last hours the Germans must feel at the hands of all the allies the severest punishment that could be meted within a limited time. Britishers, Frenchmen, men of all allied nations sought the honor. The American Negro could not be denied. Although regiments of Negro guard and of the 92nd Division had but recently been in action for a period of from three to five weeks, they craved the honor of being out in front at the stern and bitter end. It was practically the entire Negro fighting force of America which, under its own officers, went over the top at daybreak on the final morning of the great four years' struggle, side by side with white men of various nationalities, who, like them, were ready and most fit for sacrifice or service. In the last hours, when life seemed sweeter than all creation, there thousands of black men of all regiments overseas fell in search of the coveted honor of being nearest Berlin as the thunderous crash and din ceased, to roll no more. Hours before the order came for the supreme and final sacrifice, Negro signal men had caught from the air the message which indicated what was to be their special honor. There was not a man to desert or seek asylum elsewhere. All went over the top together!

At the eleventh hour of the eleventh day of the eleventh month of 1918, the order came to cease firing. The 92nd Division of Negro troops stood at Thann and before Metz, in advance of the progress of troops of all America. The ground which they trod had not been occupied by other than German troops in 40 years. It was the field of honor, and recognition and equality, and must be theirs of necessity. Nature had ruthlessly perfected this type of black

native-born American for the high duties of a soldier. The
war was over. Allies and Americans said to him:

"As brothers we moved together—as brothers—to the
dawn that advanced—to the stars that fled—rendering
thanks to God in the highest, that He, having hid His face
through one long night behind thick clouds of war, once
again will ascend above us in the vision of perpetual
peace."

The Negro felt that, as the ancient Romans were too
faithful to the ideal of grandeur in themselves not to re-
lent, after a generation or two, before the grandeur of Han-
nibal, so he will not ever be the mere son of a peri.

The Negro knew that he could do one thing as well as
the best of men—a greater thing than Milton or Marlowe
or Charlemagne ever did—he could die grandly the death.
Face forward on the flats of Flanders, in Picardy and Lorraine he died grandly, to make the world safe for democracy. For we of America must remember, in all our getting on and up in the world, that, as a psychological
weapon, the bristling bayonet was incomplete until a stalwart, desperate black Negro American citizen got behind
it to fight, not for his gain, but for the uplift of the masses
of humanity.

The war was over. It was still a small voice within
that told the Negro hosts: "As this hath been no white
man's war, neither shall it be a white man's peace."

THE AFTERMATH.

But yesterday the nation tried to think of the Negro
as a southern problem, the solution of which belonged to
statesmanship of the South. Often we have endeavored to
think of him as a national problem, and have tried to per-
suade the national government to take in hand matters of
widespread national interest wherein he was involved. But
now we must of necessity think of the Negro as an interna-

tional problem, ramifications of which are bound up in the roots of aspiration and kindred feeling and powerful potentiality of Frenchman and Britisher, of Asiatic and Slav, and of the great bodies of darker peoples of all the world.

As the Negro becomes an international problem, no single section of a country can be entrusted with the administration of matters pertaining to him. Such administration may be assigned by international conclave to a particular country as its national problem, but the proper channels of administration of international policy will be up from sectional caucus, through national agency to the international parliament, and down from such parliament or league, through national agencies to the section involved. And, furthermore, sectional caucus, unless it would fail in policies of its advocacy, and suffer modification by the Congress or parliament of its central governmental administration, must henceforth regard the Negro not as an aggregate all in a mass, but as a synthesis, composed of gradations from lowest to superior. This is the new concept which the war of 1918 has forced upon America, in spite of the bias of 1914.

Civilization left the parting of the ways when Woodrow Wilson's rallying cry for world democratization lead America into the war. It decided to seek the path of Peace not along the lines of permitted autocracy, but of firmly and thoroughly well administered democracy. In administering democratic government, Negro regiments, graded from private to superior officer, came first as an academic proposition, and, finally, as an actuality. They came four hundred thousand strong. No group of that number can longer be considered as a mere accumulation of black men. One hundred thousand Negroes of the 92nd Division and regiments of guard have been commanded on the field of action by black headmen, with white headlight. They have taken their objectives with speed and control and the man-

476 THE NEGRO IN THE WORLD WAR

agement of both of these elements of transfused morale has
been in the hands of colored college men or their military
equals.

The hour of decision to make the world safe for democracy was the crisis of civilization. Victory on the fields of
France has been the satisfactory denouement. The question naturally arises: Shall there be a happy ending of the
great drama for the white American and a tragic ending for the Negro? Or, rather, as the American brother-
hood gathers about the charmed circle and smokes the pipe
of peace, shall the Negro report: "I see and am satisfied?"

In other words, shall the 92nd Division of Negro fighters and the greater hosts of black war workers overseas, return to America with honor in theory, but not pursued in
fact to its logical finality? Shall these black bulwarks of
the business of world war find the door of the business
world of peace slammed in their faces? Shall these black
survivors of terrific struggle for world democracy return
home only to be declared unfit to vote an American ballot?
Shall the black soldier hero be allowed to take his croix de
guerre into a jim-crow car? Shall the black Red Cross
nurse, rushing to the aid of benighted humanity regardless
of color, be refused accommodation at places of public pro-
prietorship whither she may seek rest or refreshment?
Tragedy begets tragedy. Seventeen seventy-six begot 1861,
and 1861 begot 1914.

The times demand decisive action. Sociological error,
committed today, will cause malformation of an important
member of the American body politic. It will cause the
ship of state to ride an uneven keel. This ship of state must
be brought to her ancient moorings, the Declaration of Independence, the Gettysburg Address of Lincoln, and the
Farewell of Old John Brown on the scaffold.

The tumult has died. Revelry and shouting fill every
program. Is the Negro to return unheralded to homeland,

and with his eyes to the hills, undergo patting and pitying and be given a place in the corner? Or are the colored boys in khaki to announce their return by a vigorous knocking at the gate? Shall they have cause to cry to America: "A house divided against itself cannot stand!" And shall they knock and knock and knock until America sets herself to wonder what has this army Negro to do that he becomes so unceremonious? Or shall they find the gate wide open and triumphal arches erected in every section of the country in their honor to signify that defeat of German autocracy means democratization of every section of the entire world? An international conscience demands for the Negro hero a happy ending of it all.

The Negro looks to the military agencies of America to produce a genuine peace wherein he may live happy ever after. Regarded in America as the most alien of aliens before the war, he demands recognition today as the most loyal of loyalists. But yesterday Anglo-Saxon prejudice persisted in viewing him as a physical alien, a mental alien, a moral alien and a social alien. The Negro is willing to discuss no further this prejudicial conception of himself forced home by libelous propaganda and by governmental administration for hundreds of years, if the agencies of reconstruction will perfect and put in operation a vigorous Americanization policy in his behalf.

Military life has taught the Negro the advantage derived from the use of pure food and balanced ration. It has taken him from the ghetto into the pure air of the open country, and filled his lungs with deep draughts of the free breezes of France. It has removed him from the temptation to imbibe the beverage that destroys human faculties and has accustomed him in a measure to the beneficial use of purified water. It has undertaken through carefully selected work, exercise and recreation to perfect the habits of digestion, assimilation and elimination. The result has

been indeed marvelous. No America Negro who went to
fight for humanity will return to America as the same
physical being. No American will dare stand before the
returned Negro trooper and say: "Behold a sub-species of
mankind, wooly of hair, long of head, with dilated nostrils,
thick lips, thicker cranium, flat foot, prehensile great toe
and larkheel. Yea, behold him, dark of skin, whose men-
tality is like unto a child, and closely related to the anthro-
poid ape; whose weight of brain is only comparable to that
of the gorilla." Where is the American who will dare
stand before any Negro trooper returned from France and
thus mock and deride him? Military agency has completely destroyed the physical concept which the white
world had of the Negro in 1914, by placing him in the focus
of Caucasian binocular vision, wherein his better attributes
become visible in their synthetic relation.

In addition, military life has sharpened the mental
powers of the Negro in command to meet the highest ex-
actions of modern warfare. Colonel Charles Denton Young,
Negro graduate of West Point, if we may trust the record,
is capable of the same high character of mental processes as
John J. Pershing. Military test has proven before the
world that the Negro is no mental alien, but heir to all the
ages of Anglo-Saxon, Roman, Greek and Egyptian culture.

In France the American Negro has produced no
notorious offenders against civil or military usage. He has
arisen to the moral concept of high responsibility for the
future of his race in the estimation of all mankind. There
is no story of moral degeneracy which has yet come from
abroad concerning him. Pitfall, temptation and opportunity for vice and crime have all been shunned in light of
preparation for the higher service. The Negro has proven
his power of moral restraint while guided by leadership of
his own color. As a social being he has sacrificed his life
for the highest form of social existence, democracy. Who,

then, is there to call him alien? Today he is no longer
Negro, nor Afro-American, nor colored American, nor
American of African descent, but he is American—simply
this, and nothing more.

He has been raised to erect stature and made a man by
the military branch of the United States Government, because of signal service to the American peoples. His
prayer is that this military government long may live as
such to train the great mass which he calls kin into a synthetic whole.

As he evolved from a student in a military training
camp to military leadership, so he desires the great military
organization of America to continue to exist, that through
its agency he may attend the training camps which lead to
industrial, business, political and social success. Universal
military education for me and mine and all other Americans is his slogan, and his aim is to recreate the America of
the early Seventies, which became hardened and callous
through the years by reason of resistance to the German
menace of autocracy, but now removed.

This American has made good in public. He has
demonstrated both efficiency and initiative. He has compelled popular belief to conceive him as a man. The Caucasian world he has caused to perceive that he might function as a valuable and serviceable element of twentieth century civilization. Will the Anglo-Saxon issue to him the
warrant of immunities and privileges certifying that he is
four-square with the dominant opinion of mankind, and,
therefore, entitled to superior status?

To this dark-skinned American are attributed all elements of beauty and racial grandeur. Forever in survival
of the world's most fit, he goes on, blending readily with
civilization's high ideal, philosophically tolerating abuse
offered by the less refined, effecting a racial consciousness
of purity in inter-social relationships, adapting himself

with symmetry and poise to the tasks of the world, and bowing in humble respect before the higher laws whose harmonies order and rectify all creation.

What will the black Rip Van Winkle behold as he walks through the corridors of the American Department of State twenty years hence? Will he behold a great black mass still at the veriest bottom of our governmental organization, or will he be caused to marvel at the synthetic gradations of black American from lowest to superior? As he views progress in all departments of the government, will he see this real American organized synthetically in all branches of the service, or will he behold him still employed as the boy or the mere high private? Time and the great heart of America will tell.

The center of gravity of world interest of 1914 has shifted and come to rest at a spot most significant for darker peoples. Victory to all participants in its glorious achievement must be less disastrous than defeat. In order to satisfy the liberal opinion of the world, some form of autonomy must be devised for the newly organized man in America. Durable peace requires that American prejudice be utterly and forever stamped out; first by the reconstructed organization of the American Expeditionary Force, which beheld its organizations of every race and creed under fire and in action; second, by the American people of every locality, who have forced upon them by world war the new concept of a branch of the species once considered inferior; and, third, by the powers of the world, who must prevent the upgrowths in America from offering malignant germs of unrest to their own systems of national government.

After the Negro has proved his value and worth in all of these trying ways, when after this he asks for a full measure of equal rights, what American will have the heart or the hardihood to say him nay?

THE DISGRACE OF DEMOCRACY

By Kelly Miller

August 4, 1917.

Hon. Woodrow Wilson, President of the United States, The White House, Washington, D. C.

Mr. President:

I am taking the liberty of intruding this letter upon you because I feel that the issues involved are as important as any questions now pressing upon your busy attention. The whole civilized world has been shocked at the recent occurrences in Memphis and East St. Louis. These outbreaks call attention anew to the irritating race problem of which they are but eruptive symptoms which break forth ever and anon with Vesuvian violence. For fully a generation American statesmanship has striven to avoid, ignore or forget the perplexing race problem. But this persistent issue will not down at our bidding, and cannot be shunted from public attention by other questions however momentous or vital they may seem to be.

I know that I am taking unwarranted liberties with the ceremonial proprieties in writing such a letter to the President of the United States at the present time. It may seem to partake of the spirit of heckling after the manner of the suffragists. Nothing is further from my purpose. No right-minded American would wish to add one featherweight to the burden that now so heavily taxes the mind and body of the President of the United States who labors under as heavy a load as human nature is capable of sustaining. Every citizen should strive to lighten rather than to aggravate that burden. It is, nevertheless, true that any suppressed and aggrieved class must run athwart the established code of procedure in order that their case may receive a just hearing. Ceremonial codes were enacted by those who are the beneficiaries of existing order which they wish to perpetuate and make unchangeable. They would estop all social and moral reform. The ardent suffragists find it necessary to ruthlessly violate the traditional and decorous modes of procedure in order to promote the reform which they have at heart. On one occasion you felt forced to terminate an interview with a committee of suffragists because they persisted in cross-examining the President of the United States.

There are 10,000,000 loyal citizens of African descent in the United States. They are rigorously excluded from a voice in the government by which they are controlled. They have no regularly constituted organ through which to present their case to the powers that be. They have no seat nor voice in the council of the nation. The late Doctor Booker T. Washington was the accepted spokesman and mediator of the race, but he has no successor. Under former administrations there was a small appointive official class of Negroes. Though derisively designated as the "Black Cabinet," they were on the inside of the circle of governmental control to which they had ready access in presenting the claims of the race. But under the exaction of partisan exigencies even these have been excluded from official position under your administration. Several weeks ago a delegation of colored men from the State of Maryland sought an interview with you concerning the horrible crime of East St. Louis. You were good enough to write Senator France that you were too busy with other pressing issues to grant the request of an interview. The failure of all other methods is my only excuse for resorting to an open letter as a means of reaching you and, through you, the nation at large, concerning the just grievances of 10,000,000 loyal American citizens.

The Negro feels that he is not regarded as a constituent part of American democracy. This is our fundamental grievance and lies at the basis of all the outrages inflicted upon this helpless race. It is the fundamental creed of democracy that no people are good enough to govern any other people without their consent and participation. The English are not good enough to govern the

Irish. The Russians are not good enough to govern the Finns. The Germans are not good enough to govern the Belgians. The Belgians are not good enough to govern the people of the Congo. Men are not considered good enough to govern women. The white people of this country are not good enough to govern the Negro. As long as the black man is excluded from participation in the government of the nation, just so long will he be the victim of cruelty and outrage on the part of his white fellow citizens who assume lordship over him.

These periodic outbreaks of lawlessness are but the out-growth of the disfavor and despite in which the race is held by public opinion. The evil is so widespread that the remedy lies in the hands of the national government.

Resolutions pending before both houses of Congress look toward investigation of the outrage at East St. Louis. I understand that you are sympathetically disposed toward this investigation by Federal authority. Such investigation is important only to the extent that it implies a tardy recognition of national responsibility for local lawlessness. There is no expectation that any additional comprehensive information will result. You may rest assured that there will be a half dozen similar outbreaks before this investigation is well under way. Indeed, since the East St. Louis atrocity there have already been lynchings in Georgia, Louisiana, Pennsylvania and Montana. Every intelligent American knows as much about the essential cause of this conflict as he will know after long and tedious investigation. The vital issues involved are apt to be obscured by technical wranglings over majority and minority reports. What the nation needs is not investigation of obvious fact, but determination and avowed declaration on the part of the President speaking for the people of the United States to put an end to lawlessness wherever it raises its hideous head.

I know that it has been steadily maintained that the Federal Government has no authority over lynchings and local race conflicts. This is not a political contention. This view was maintained under the administrations of Harrison, Cleveland, McKinley, Roosevelt and Taft. Indeed,

President Cleveland, that great American democrat, came nearer recognizing Federal responsibility in such matters than any President before or since his time. During the administration of President McKinley, an atrocious riot occurred in Wilmington, N. C., the city in which you spent your boyhood as the son of a minister of the Gospel. Scores of innocent Negroes were killed and hundreds were driven from their homes. But it was maintained that the President had no authority to interfere. A horrible lynching took place at Alexandria, Virginia, a few miles from the White House, which the President might possibly have observed through his field glasses. And yet it was looked upon as a purely local affair for which the Federal Government had no responsibility nor concern. You recall the atrocities of the riot in Atlanta, a city in which you spent your young manhood as a practitioner of law. But here again even President Roosevelt could find no ground for interference.

These outbreaks are not limited to the Southern States, although they occur there more frequently than elsewhere because of the relatively larger number of Negroes in the total population. There have been lynchings and burnings in Illinois, Kansas, Delaware, Ohio, Indiana, Colorado and other Northern States. The evil is indeed national in its range and scope, and the nation must provide the remedy. Striking indeed is the analogy between the spread of lawlessness today and the extension of the institution of slavery two generations ago. Like slavery, lawlessness cannot be localized. As the nation could not exist half slave and half free under Abraham Lincoln, so it cannot continue half lawabiding and half lawless under Woodrow Wilson. The evil tendency overcomes the good, just as the darker overlaps the brighter phase in the waning moon. If the Negro is allowed to be lynched in the South with impunity, he will soon be lynched in the North, so easy is the communicability of evil suggestion. The lynchings of Negroes has become fashionable in some parts of the country. When a black man is accused of wrongdoing, "Lynch the Negro!" is the cry that springs spontaneously to the lips of man, woman and child. The fashion is rapidly spreading throughout the whole nation. If slavery could have been isolated and segregated in the South that institution might have existed even down to the present time. And so, if lynching could be localized and limited to the Southern States the nation as a whole would have less pretext for interfering. But this cannot be done. Senator Tombs of Georgia boasted that he would call the roll of his slaves under the shadow of the Bunker Hill monument, an ambition which, doubtless, might have been gratified had not the nation arisen in its moral might and blotted out the iniquitous institution altogether. Unless the aroused conscience of the American people, efficiently asserting itself through Federal authority, shall stamp out the spirit of lawlessness, it is easy to prophesy that the Negro will yet be lynched not only in the shadow of the Bunker Hill monument, but on the campus of your beloved Princeton. Already there have been burnings of human beings in the bleeding State of Old John Brown, and in the city where lie the remains of Abraham Lincoln. During the past thirty years nearly 3,000 Negroes have been lynched in various parts of the country. Scores of these have been burned at the stake. Even the bodies of women have been fed to the flames. Thousands of localities in the majority of the States of the Union have experienced these outrages. Our fair land of liberty is blotted over with these foul spots which cannot be washed out by all of the waters of the ocean. It is not easy to calculate the number of persons who have been involved in these lynchings, either as participants or as acquiescent lookers-on, all of whom were potential murderers. So general and widespread has become the practice that lynching may well be characterized as a national institution, to the eternal disgrace of American democracy.

Lynching cannot be confined to the Negro race. Hundreds of white men have been the victims of lawlessness and violence. While these words are flowing from my pen, news comes over the wire that a labor agitator has been lynched in the State of Montana. Although the Negro is at present the chief victim of lawlessness, like any other evil disease, it cannot be limited by racial lines.

It is but hollow mockery of the Negro, when he is beaten and bruised and burned in all parts of the nation and flees to the national government for asylum, to be denied relief on the ground of doubtful jurisdiction. The black man asks for justice and is given a theory of government. He asks for protection and is confronted with a scheme of governmental checks and balances.

Mr. President, you are commander-in-chief of the Army and Navy. You express the voice of the American people in the great world conflict which involves practically the entire human race. You are the accepted spokesman of the world democracy. You have sounded forth the trumpet of democratization of the nations, which shall never call retreat. But, Mr. President, a chain is no stronger than its weakest link. A doctrine that breaks down at home is not fit to be propagated abroad. One is reminded of the pious slaveholder who became so deeply impressed with the plea for foreign missions that he sold one of his slaves to contribute liberally to the cause. Why democratize the nations of the earth if it leads them to delight in the burning of human beings after the manner of Springfield, Waco, Memphis, and East St. Louis while the nation looks helplessly on? You add nothing to the civilization of the world nor to the culture of the human spirit by the technical changes in forms of government. The old adage still remains true:

> "For forms of government let fools contest—
> What's best administered—is best."

If democracy cannot control lawlessness, then democracy must be pronounced a failure. The nations of the world have a right to demand of us the workings of the institutions at home before they are promulgated abroad. The German press will, doubtless, gloat with ghoulish glee over American atrocities against the Negro. The outrages complained of against the Belgians become merciful performances by gruesome comparison. Our frantic wail against the barbarity of Turk against Armenian, German upon Belgian, Russian upon Jew, are made of no effect. It cannot be said that these outbreaks are but the spontaneous ebullitions of popular feeling, without governmental sanction or approval. These outrages occur all over the nation. The nation must be responsible for what it permits. Sins of permisssion are as reprehensible as sins of commission. A few years ago a Turkish ambassador was handed his passports by you for calling attention to the inconsistency between our national practice and performance. The nation was compelled, with a spirit of humiliation, to accept the reproach which he hurled into our teeth: "Thou hypocrite, first cast out the beam out of thine own eye; and then shalt thou see clearly to cast out the mote out of thy brother's eye." Every high-minded American must be touched with a tinge of shame when he contemplates that his rallying cry for the liberation of humanity is made a delusion and a snare by these racial barbarities.

It is needless to attempt to place the blame on the helpless Negro. In the early stages of these outbreaks there was an attempt to fix an evil and lecherous reputation on the Negro race as lying at the basis of lynching and lawlessness. Statistics most clearly refute this contention. The great majority of the outbreaks cannot even allege rapeful assault in extenuation. It is undoubtedly true that there are imbruited and lawless members of the Negro race, as there are of the white race, capable of committing any outrageous and hideous offense. The Negro possesses the imperfections of his status. His virtues as well as his failures are simply human. It is a fatuous philosophy, however, that would resort to cruel and unusual punishment as a deterrent to crime. Lynching has never made one Negro virtuous nor planted the seed of right doing in the mind of a single American citizen. The Negro should be encouraged in all right directions to develop his best manly and human qualities. Where he deviates from the accepted standard he should be punished by due process of law. But as long as the Negro is held in general despite and suppressed below the level of human privilege, just so long will he produce a disproportionate number of imperfect individuals of evil propensity. To relegate the Negro to a status that encourages the baser instincts of humanity, and then de-

nounce him because he does not stand forth as a model
of human perfection, is of the same order of ironical cruelty
as shown by the barbarous Teutons in Shakespeare, who
cut off the hands and hacked out the tongue of the lovely
Lavinia, and then upbraided her for not calling for per-
fumed water to wash her delicate hands. The Negro is
neither angelic nor diabolical, but merely human, and should
be treated as such.

The vainglorious boast of Anglo-Saxon superiority will
no longer avail to justify these outrages. The contact,
adjustment and attrition of various races of mankind constitute a problem which is cotorminous with the ends of the
earth. The lighter and stronger races are coming into contact with the weaker and darker ones. The stronger breeds
of men are relating themselves to the weaker members of
the human family in all the ends of the earth. How does
it happen that in the United States alone, of all civilized
lands, these atrocious outrages are heaped upon the helpless
Negro? The English nation has the largest colonial experience and success since the days of the Roman empire,
and has come into relationship with the various weaker
breeds of men in all parts of the world. But everywhere
under English jurisdiction law and order prevail. In the
West Indies, where Negroes outnumber the whites 20 to 1,
rape and lynching have scarcely yet found a place in the
local vocabulary. In Brazil, under a Latin dispensation,
where a more complex racial situation exists than in the
United States, racial peace and good-will prevail. Belgium
furnishes the only parallel of civilized nations, in the atrocious treatment of a helpless people placed in their charge.
But even the Belgians were forced to modify the rigors of
their outrageous regime in the Congo, under the bombardment of moral sentiment of the more enlightened nations of
the world. America enjoys the evil distinction among all
civilized nations of the earth of taking delight in murder and
burning of human beings. Nowhere else do men, women and
children dance with ghoulish glee and fight for ghastly sou-
venirs of human flesh and mock the dying groans of the helpless victim which sicken the air, while the flickering flames

of the funereal pyre lighten the midnight sky with their lurid glare.

Mr. President, the American conscience has been touched and quickened by the East St. Louis outbreak as it has never been before. Press and pulpit have tried to forget these outrages. At each fresh outbreak they would lash themselves into a spasm of virtue and exhaust the entire vocabulary of denunciation, but, forthwith, would lapse into sudden silence and acquiescent guilt. By some fatuous delusion they seem to hope that the atrocities of Springfield, Wilmington, Waco, Atlanta, Memphis and a thousand other places of evil report would never be repeated, nor the memory rise up to condemn the nation. But silence and neglect merely result in compounding atrocities. The East St. Louis outbreak convinces the nation, as it has never been before, that the time for action has come. The press is not content with a single editorial ebullition, but by repeated utterances insists that the nation shall deal with its most malignant domestic evil. Reproach is cast upon your contention for the democratization of the world, in face of its lamentable failure at home. Ex-President Roosevelt, who is the greatest living voice now crying aloud for individual and national righteousness, has openly proclaimed, in dramatic declaration, that these outbreaks make our moral propaganda for the liberation of mankind but a delusion and a snare. Mr. President, can this nation hope to live and to grow in favor with God and man on the basis of a lie? A nation with a stultified conscience is a nation with stunted power.

Democracies have frequently shut their eyes to moral inconsistencies. The democracy of Greece conferred privilege upon a mere handful of freeman in the midst of ten times their own number of slaves. The Greek philosophers and statesmen were supremely unconscious of this moral obliquity. The Declaration of Independence which declared for the equality of all men was written by a slaveholder. The statesmen of the period, however, hoped that slavery would be of shortlived duration, and would effect its own solution in the process of time. But Thomas Jefferson was keenly sensitive of the moral inconsistency of this attitude, and declared that he trembled when he considered that God is just, and that His justice would not slumber forever. Abraham Lincoln is perhaps the only great statesman of democracy who was absolutely consistent in his logical attitude and moral sincerity. The nation believed in his moral integrity. He uttered no word of cryptic meaning. The people heard him gladly because the words that fell from his lips were not the coinage of his intellect, but the mintage of his heart. The embattled hosts under his high command marched to victory with the Battle Hymn of the Republic resounding in their souls:

> "As He died to make men holy,
> Let us die to make men free—"

To them this phrase had no remote and deferred meaning, but was immediately applicable to their black brother in chains. It was not a barren ideality, but a living impulse. You have given the rallying cry for the present world crisis. But this shibboleth will be robbed of instant meaning and power unless it applies to the helpless within our own gates. If the sons and grandsons of the heroes who battered down the walls of slavery a half century ago could be made to feel with unreserved certainty a renewal of the moral energy which urged their fathers to that high resolve, they would, with heightened enthusiasm for humanity, demolish the Teutonic bulwarks of oppression across the seas.

Doctrine is more than deeds, if it be sound doctrine. Deeds are the outgrowth of doctrine. Doctrine lives forever with persistent potentiality. Doctrine rules the world or throws it into confusion. The power of words is far greater than the meaning of the author. It makes no difference what lay in the minds or practice of the statesmen of Greece. They planted the seeds of democracy, and all mankind will become the beneficiary of the sowing. The intendment of the signers of the Declaration of Independence boots but little. That document will stand for all time as the gospel of human liberty. When you speak of the democratization of the world and the liberation of mankind, you are setting up a standard to which the whole world must rise in the ages to come, despite its attitude at the present time. It may be far from the purpose of our present-day statesmen to admit the Negro into this democracy on terms of equality with the rest. But in spite of the purpose of this statesmanship, this must be the ultimate goal of human democracy. A democracy of race or class is no democracy at all. It is with projected imagination that the Negro will endure until these high-sounding phrases have borne their full fruition. Any other class of the American people, under the strain of distress to which the Negro has been subjected, would imitate Job's distracted wife, and curse the white God and die. The Negro will neither curse nor die, but grin and live—albeit beneath that grin is a groaning of spirit too deep for utterance. The Negro says to his country, "Though you slay me, yet will I serve you."

The Negro's patriotism is vicarious and altruistic. It seems to be an anomaly of fate that the Negro, the man of all men who is held in despite, should stand out in conspicuous relief at every crisis of our national history. His blood offering is not for himself or for his race, but for his country. This blood flows like a stream through our national history, from Boston Commons to Carrizal. Crispus Attucks was the first American to give his blood as an earnest of American independence. The Negro was with Washington in the dark days of Valley Forge, when the lamp of national liberty flickered almost to extinguishment. The black troops fought valiantly with Jackson behind the fleecy breastworks at New Orleans. Two hundred thousand black boys in blue responded to the call of the immortal Lincoln for the preservation of the Union. The Negro was the positive cause of the Civil War, and the negative cause of the united nation with which we face the world today.

The reckless daring of Negro troops on San Juan Hill marked the turning point in the struggle which drove the last vestige of Spanish power from the Western world. It was but yesterday that we buried with honor at Arlington Cemetery the Negro soldiers who fell face forward while carrying the flag to the farthest point in the heart of Mexico, in quest of the bandit who dared place impious foot on American soil. In complete harmony with this marvelous patriotic record, it so happened that it was an American Negro who proved to be the first victim of ruthless submarine warfare, after you had distinctly announced to Germany that such outrages would be considered tantamount to war. In all of these ways has the Negro shown, purposely or unconsciously, his undeviating devotion to the glory and honor of the nation. Greater love hath no man than this, that he lay down his life for his country.

In the midst of the world war for the democratization of mankind the Negro will do his full share. I have personally always striven to urge the Negro to be patriotic and loyal in every emergency. At the Reserve Officers' Training Camp in Fort Des Moines there are over one hundred young colored men who have come under my instruction. The deviltry of his fellow men cannot devise iniquities horrible enough to drive him from his patriotic devotion. The Negro, Mr. President, in this emergency, will stand by you and the nation. Will you and the nation stand by the Negro?

I believe, Mr. President, that to the victor belong the spoils, especially if these spoils be human liberty. After this war for the liberation of mankind has been won through the Negro's patriotic participation, he will repeat the lines of the old familiar hymn somewhat louder than ever:

"Behold a stranger at the door,
He gently knocks, has knocked before,
Has waited long, is waiting still,
You treat no other friend so ill."

As a student of public questions I have carefully watched your attitude on the race problem. You have preserved a lukewarm aloofness from the tangled issues of this problem. In searching your writings one finds little or no reference to this troubled phase of American life. It seems that you regard it as a regrettable social malady to be treated with cautious and calculated neglect. There is observable, however, a passive solicitude. You have kept the race problem in the back part of your mind. Your letter to Bishop Walters during your first campaign for the Presidency, expressing a generous concern for the welfare of the race, though of a general and passive character, caused many Negroes to give you their political support. Under the stress and strain of other pressing issues and the partisan demands of your political supporters you have not yet translated this passive purpose into positive performance. There is, however, something of consolation in the fact that while during your entire career you have never done anything constructive for the Negro, you have never done anything destructive against him. Your constructive opportunity is now at hand. The time has come to make lawlessness a national issue, as a war measure if not from any higher consideration. As a patriotic and military necessity, I suggest that you ask the Congress of the United States to invest you with the power to prevent lynching and to quell lawlessness and violence in all parts of the country during the continuance of the war. Or at least you might quicken the conscience of the nation by a stirring message to Congress calling attention to this growing evil which is gnawing at the vitals of the nation. It is entirely probable that before the war is over you will have to resort to some such measure to control internal disturbances on other accounts. It is inconceivable that this nation should spend billions of dollars and sacrifice the lives of millions of its citizens without domestic uprising and revulsion. In such a time it becomes necessary for the President to exercise all but dictatorial power. The country is willing to grant you anything you ask which, in your judgment, would promote the welfare of the nation in this crisis. You asked Congress to grant undiscriminated use of the Panama Canal as a means of securing international good-will and friendship, and it was granted. In face of the impending conflict, you demanded that Congress should grant the eight-hour demand of the laboring men, and it was done. The suffragists who guard your going in and coming out of the White House were duly convicted under process of law, but were immediately pardoned by you to avoid embarrassment in this war emergency. You asked for billions of dollars and millions of lives to be placed at your disposal for the purpose of carrying on the great conflict, and it was willingly granted. The people have willingly placed in your hands more power than has ever been exercised by any member of the human race and are willing to trust you in the use of that power. I am sure that they will grant this additional authority during the continuance of the present war in order to secure the unqualified patriotic devotion of all of the citizens and to safeguard the honor of democracy and the good name of the republic.

Mr. President, Negroes all over the nation are aroused as they have never been before. It is not the wild hysteria of the hour, but a determined purpose that this country shall be made a safe place for American citizens to live and work and enjoy the pursuits of happiness. Ten thousand speechless men and women marched in silent array down Fifth Avenue in New York City as a spectral demonstration against the wrongs and cruelties heaped upon the race. Negro women all over the nation have appointed a day of prayer in order that righteousness might be done to this people. The weaker sex of the weaker race are praying that God may use you as the instrument of His will to promote the cause of human freedom at home. I attended one of these 6 o'clock prayer meetings in the city of Washington. Two thousand humble women snatched the early hours of the morning before going to their daily tasks to resort to the house of prayer. They literally performed unto the Lord the burden of their prayer and song, "Steal Away to Jesus." There was not a note of bitterness nor denunciation throughout the season of prayer. They prayed as their mothers prayed in the darker days gone by, that God would deliver the race. Mr. President, you can help God answer their prayer. May it not be that these despised and rejected daughters of a despised and rejected race shall yet lead the world to its knees in acknowledgment of some controlling power outside of the machinations of man? As I sat there and listened in reverent silence to these two thousand voices as they sang,—

"On Christ, the Solid Rock, I stand,
All other ground is sinking sand—"

I could not but think of the godless war which is now convulsing the world—a war in which Christian hands are dyed in Christian blood. It must cause the Prince of Peace to groan as in His dying agony when He gave up the ghost on the cross. The professed followers of the Meek and Lowly One, with heathen heart, are putting their trust in reeking tube and iron shard. God uses the humbler things of life to confound the mighty. It may be that these helpless victims of cruelty and outrage will bring an apostate world back to God.

Mr. President, ten million of your fellow citizens are looking to you and to the God whom you serve to grant them relief in this hour of their deepest distress. All moral reforms grow out of the people who suffer and stand in need of them. The Negro's helpless position may yet bring America to a realizing sense that righteousness exalteth a nation, but sin is a reproach to any people.

Yours truly,

KELLY MILLER.

From the Washington Eagle.

Colonel Charles Denton Young, the Negro West Pointer, retired on the outbreak of the war, rides 547 miles on horse-back, from Wilberforce to Washington, to convince the War Department of his fitness to help win the war.